For [illegible]
and Bridget,
with warmest
affection
– [illegible]

Virtue's Faults

Virtue's Faults

Correspondences in Eighteenth-Century British and French Women's Fiction

April Alliston

Stanford University Press
Stanford, California
1996

Stanford University Press
Stanford, California

Printed in the United States of America

CIP data appear at the end of the book

Stanford University Press publications are distributed exclusively by Stanford University Press within the United States, Canada, Mexico, and Central America; they are distributed exclusively by Cambridge University Press throughout the rest of the world.

This book is dedicated
to the mothers of my family:

Holly Hendrickson-Davis
and
Jane Proctor Hendrickson
and to the memory of Lucy Mae Cartwright Alliston

and also to the remembrance of those few before them
whose names I know:

Madeleine de Brunner Proctor, Belle Ross de Brunner,
Elizabeth Proctor, Anne Burt
Carrie Mabel Sauls Catrett Boan

and to the loss of those before them,
whose names are unremembered

Preface

When I began the research for this book in 1983, there was still very little in print about or by women writers in the eighteenth century. Over a decade later, they have become the subject of an established field of literary study, which has gone through enormous transformation and growth within that time. The collective effort begun in the 1970's to explore women writers' relation to literary tradition came belatedly to the eighteenth century, but an increasing recognition of the period's importance to the understanding of literature by women is apparent not only in a continuing accumulation of criticism devoted to it, but also in the recent launching of several series for the republication of primary texts.

The first large burst of energy in the study of eighteenth-century women's writing, mostly in English, had an encyclopedic tendency (I am thinking of works of the mid to late 1980's by Dale Spender, Jane Spencer, and Janet Todd, for example). And as Joan

Hinde Stewart similarly remarks, "French women novelists have until recently been catalogued but not studied" (p. 19). This was a necessary first step of contextualization that mirrored what had been done in the previous decade for nineteenth-century American women writers by Elaine Showalter and others, an archaeological effort that often announced the literary value of the works it unearthed but was too comprehensive to take the time to begin analyzing any of them in the way that all the texts of the national canons have been read. This book is in part a contribution to that work of reading.

One result of the increased attention to literature by women has been the implicit formation of a new canon of literature in the "women's tradition." The female authors who have emerged as candidates for this belated and dubious form of canonization, however, are mainly the same ones that never did quite disappear from collective academic memory: writers such as Behn, Burney, Edgeworth, Shelley, Riccoboni, Graffigny, Staël, Sand. This remains true in spite of some efforts since the late 1980's to make recently rediscovered texts available for wider reading, such as Spender's short-lived Pandora Press series, "Mothers of the Novel." To this day there is still a very real resistance to publishing either works of literary criticism or primary texts that would help us explore what has truly been forgotten. Nevertheless, one promising development during the years I have been working on this book is the appearance of several new series in the 1990's, launched by presses that are willing to take risks for the sake of making the literature of the eighteenth century more fully available to modern readers. For example, the University Press of Kentucky is currently publishing one of the novels discussed at length here, Sophia Lee's *The Recess*, in a new paperback edition, as part of a series of novels in English by eighteenth-century women previously unavailable to students and general readers.

The meanings and politics of canon-formation must be more thoroughly thought through before the women writers who seem already most recognizable and thus least risky to publishers are simply added to the established national canons or set up in an alternative women's tradition. In the process of trying to reconstruct a lost world of women's writing, recent efforts in both criticism and reprinting have tended overall to produce an unbalanced representation of women's literary production of the past, for a variety of reasons.

In Anglo-American studies, a disproportionate amount of attention has been paid to what I would call the Austenian vein in women's fiction—that is, domestic and (ambivalently) antisentimental fiction. It is telling that Nina Baym claims that the nineteenth-century domestic novels she classifies as "woman's fiction" reject the English tradition of "Richardsonian sentimental fiction" in favor of the best-known Austen predecessors, such as Burney and Edgeworth. When *Woman's Fiction* first appeared in 1978, the work had not been done that would have allowed Baym to acknowledge that there were many English women writing novels of sensibility before and after Richardson, who give sensibility and femininity markedly different valences than Richardson does, and whose writing also informed later writers in English. Even Burney's and Edgeworth's fiction was less single-mindedly dedicated to the domestic realism that predominates in Austen and after her, and the novels discussed in the present work tend to be characterized more by conventions of romance than by those of domestic realism.

The "fiction of women's correspondence" identified here includes elements of both domestic fiction and romance, but there is always more of romance than became the literary norm in the nineteenth century. That is partly why it has been relatively ignored even by the Anglo-American feminist revival of women's works. In the current critical arguments around women's roles in the public and private spheres—whether there really were no separate spheres for women, whether the separation of the domestic sphere preserved for women a certain kind of power, and whether feminist women struggled against their entrapment in it—fiction that *represents* the domestic sphere primarily has become the focal point of the literary debate. This book investigates a strain in fiction that works out the relation between public and private spheres in ways that differ from the strategies of nineteenth-century domestic realism. Publication was obviously a public act, although the work of writing and reading, increasingly, was performed in private. The conventions of romance permitted women greater opportunities to represent that boundary crossing as they enacted it.

The most prominent criticism on French women's fiction,

meanwhile, still creates an impression of "the Lafayette peaks and the Sand sierra," to paraphrase Woolf's famous comment on the canonization of English women writers in the 1920's. While this representation is beginning to change as new work is done, it remains stronger than in English studies in part because prominent feminists in France have rarely been interested in reviving works by women writers of the past, and in part because the best-known American feminist critics in French studies, for reasons internal to their academic field, have emphasized the importance of considering women's writing in relation to the national (and mostly male-authored) canon. Fiction of women's correspondence does not fit well into this focus on the French cultural *patrimoine*, since it implies, as I shall argue, an alternative model of literary relations that is critical to the very notion of "tradition." The blind spots created by remaining with the frameworks of national traditions prompted me to contextualize women's writing in the eighteenth century in a way that allows for a comparative approach to it. Despite the advances that have been made in French and English studies of women's literature, the amount of comparatist work in this field has remained negligible. This book is constantly in dialogue with the foundational work done during the 1980's and since by critics who have devoted their considerable talents to early novels by women in those two national traditions. Without them it could not have been.

It must be acknowledged, for legal reasons, that much different versions of parts of this work appeared as a doctoral dissertation in 1988. So much has it changed since then, however, that it is hard to refer to this book and that dissertation with the same pronoun: "it" now includes four chapters that were no part of the dissertation and has entirely lost two that were, while the remaining three that survive in recognizable form from the earlier avatar have been thoroughly revised and reorganized, expanded and then reduced. These changes reflect as much the explosion of research and writing on women and literature in the eighteenth century over the past decade as they do the evolution of my own thinking.

Over the years that I worked on this book, many people gave me help that was vitally important to its progress. They assisted as advisers and commentators, facilitators, healers, shorers-up of morale, and helpers in preparing the manuscript. Since every person who helped me did so in more ways than one, any attempt to categorize or describe the various forms of assistance I received from each of them would be vain. I must nevertheless make special mention that Ellen Brinks, in addition to all the other help she gave me, is partly responsible for the original translations in this work. Otherwise, I list together the names of those who helped bring it into being in so many ways, hoping that if some essential service received over the years escapes my consciousness at the present moment, I may be reminded but forgiven. My heartfelt thanks for helping me write this book go to Kathryn Aschheim, Claudia Brodsky-Lacour, Peter Brooks, Clarence Brown, Leslie Camhi, Margaret Cohen, Stanley Corngold, Florence and Olivier Curchod, Philippe Cusin, Catherine Cusset, Stephanie Daval, Peter Dreyer, Robert Fagles, Julie Farmer, John Feneron, Margaret Ferguson, Norbert Franiel, Rhonda Garelick, Paola Giuli, Debra Gold, Elizabeth Gregory, Margaret Homans, Virginia Jackson, Judith Lewin, Elissa Marder, David Marshall, Mary Pat Martin, Woodson Merrell, Franco Moretti, Dorothea von Mücke, Héloïse d'Ormesson, Thomas Pavel, Lucia Re, Ulfried Reichardt, Patricia Meyer Spacks, Helen Tartar, Karen Van Dyck, Alberto Vourvoulias-Bush, Dorothea Westphal, Jennifer Wicke, and Froma Zeitlin.

For special permission to use their collections, I am grateful to the Bibliothèque du Château d'Oron, the Bibiothèque nationale (Paris), and the British Library. I was also inconceivably lucky to have at my regular disposal, while a graduate student at Yale, the astounding collection of women's novels of the eighteenth century that resides on the shelves of Sterling Memorial Library, as well as access to the collection of the New York Public Library. The rare book collection at Princeton's Firestone Library was also invaluable to me during the revision phase. And I owe many thanks to the Stiftung Preussische Schlösser und Gärten Berlin-Brandenburg for granting me permission to place on the cover of this book the picture that first caught my eye a decade ago at Schloss Sanssouci, in what was then East Germany.

Finally, I am of course most grateful for money. I received financial support for this work from a number of sources at different stages. The Georges Lurcy Charitable and Educational Trust and Yale University enabled me to complete the dissertation and begin to develop my ideas beyond it, through a graduate fellowship that supported a year's writing and interdisciplinary dialogue at the Whitney Humanities Center. Yale University also gave further encouragement and financial relief by awarding the finished dissertation a Theron Rockwell Field Prize. The Columbia Society of Fellows in the Humanities, the Andrew W. Mellon Foundation, and the William R. Kenan Trust provided a haven for research, teaching, and further interdisciplinary discussion that stimulated my ideas for revision in my first year out of graduate school, by granting me a postdoctoral fellowship at the Heyman Center for the Humanities. Princeton University supported the revision and preparation of the manuscript by providing me with paid released time from teaching, research assistance, and funding for summer travel to the Bibliothèque nationale.

A. A.

Contents

Virtue's Faults

Reading Faults

This book is offered as a frame; my hope in offering it is that it will help open up to modern readers the works of the underread writers it includes, as well as the "secret correspondences," to borrow a phrase from one of them, that link them with those of more canonized early women novelists.[1] By offering serious and sympathetic readings of some neglected women's novels of the later eighteenth century, and recontextualizing them in relation to rereadings of better-known women's novels of the longer eighteenth century, I wish to erode the received and too unreflected assumption, or "prejudice," as the eighteenth century would have named it, that these novels simply constitute the "unreadable" margin of "flawed" attempts that centers, at its historical origin, the recognized tradition of the novel.[2] To read the "faults" that the received critical tradition of nonreading finds in these books, rather than simply indicating them with dismissiveness or ridicule, is not an arbitrary choice, but an act demanded by the works themselves. As these novels elaborate and interpret "faults" of various kinds, to perform the same interpretive gesture upon them is to read the texts as they ask to be read, rather than, as too often, at cross-purposes.[3] The purpose of this book is to engage in the act of reading texts that have long been marked as "unreadable," and thereby to provide a model for understanding them on their own literary terms—a model grounded, as it must be, in interpretations of their textual practice.

"Reading faults" is demanded by novels that themselves render legible, by means of their own manipulations of readable frames and faults, a fictional boundary line that was in the process of being inscribed in something like its present form at that historical era of the novel's "rise," in the late seventeenth through the beginning of the nineteenth centuries. I mean the exclusive boundary line that describes the national literary canon, and its linear transmission as a national patrimony (the cultural legacy the French still call *patrimoine*). As Wendell Harris points out, the first "canon"—the biblical one—"was created for the purpose of forestalling change and exiling competition" (p. 191). But in the process, that line of exclusion traces, even as it effaces, the barely legible line of a culturally feminine response to it.[4] This response becomes more fully readable if one directly interprets its texts in women's contributions to the formation of the novel as an emerging genre.

The purpose of the reframing that this book enacts, then, is to read a line of transmission that has been systematically effaced because it exposes aspects of the construction of the line of transmission of national literary tradition, which, to remain in force, must itself remain implicit and invisible. Through such a frame, it should become easier to describe that strange dual line. The apparently straight line of the patrilineal model of literary tradition could more properly be thought of as drawing a Moebian borderline that can never be transgressed by the other it is drawn to exclude, because the outside place it defines for that other is always also contained inside. Or, in Derridean terms, it is metaphorically an invaginated one: it draws the outside as inside and vice versa, offering, not an escape, but at least a space of resistance for the contained and marginalized. I discuss in Chapter 3 more specifically why my reading of women's fictional correspondences led me to choose and modify the Derridean metaphor of invagination for my description of how these texts resist patriline plots; I intend it to describe, not an essential or biological femininity, but a necessary response of the excluded other to the Moebian confines of patrilineal transmission. Such a boundary line cannot be escaped, since it has no outside, but the texts interpreted in this book resist it by rendering both the line of its own resistance and the construction of patrilineality mutually legible. If, as Shari Benstock interprets Jacques Derrida, "The law forbids the crossing of gender/genre boundaries while ceaselessly, helplessly trespassing on its own interdiction," the texts read here enact that trespass, and thus invite this reading (Benstock, p. 88). The fictions read here literally "deconstruct" the patriline borders of the nation as *patrie* in that they expose the fictional basis of its construction, and its form as a paradoxical, rather than a rational, natural, or legible line. To borrow Judith Butler's words from her discussion of the "culturally established lines of coherence" that define distinct genders and sexualities, these fictions expose "the inherent instability of that construction, and the dual consequentiality of [its] prohibition" (pp. 24, 28). But it is possible to read novels that work to expose the structures of their own contained exclusion as they demand to be read only by doing so through a frame that questions the model of national tradition or any literary tradition conceived of upon a patrimonial analogy. What Claudia Johnson has written of Jane Austen is true for her predecessors as well: "The basic strategies of literary history—with its patrilineal models of influence and succession—are indeed inappropriate when applied to an author marginalized from the outset" (p. xvii).

Having opened the door to one of our contemporary survivals of the Enlightenment "Woman Question" (what is the relation of women's writing to literary tradition?), it is time to explore more specific responses to some primary variants of that question: Why is it important for any twentieth-century audience to give sustained readings to novels like Sophia Lee's *The Recess* (London, 1783–85) or Mme de Boisgiron's *Lettres de Mademoiselle de Boismiran* (Paris and Amsterdam, 1777)? Why is it necessary to read other women novelists whose works have been more readily (if still tentatively) received into the canonical line of the Western literary tradition, like Marie de Lafayette, Germaine de Staël, and Jane Austen, in relation to these forgotten women's novels, rather than primarily in relation to the canonical literary tradition? Why, finally, must all of these novels also be read across, rather than strictly within, the borderlines of national tradition?

Reading the Unreadable (and What the Unreadable Reads)

I open my frame (to unpack it in Chapter 3) upon a coherent subgenre of the epistolary novel occurring in England and France during the second half of the eighteenth century.[5] At the moment when, as many literary historians have documented, European women's presence in the literary marketplace dramatically increased, female authors produced a large number of strictly epistolary novels in which the primary fictional correspondences are exchanged between female characters, and in which the reader is inscribed, typically, as a young woman similar in age and situation to the heroine. More than 100 such novels were written, mostly after Richardson, notwithstanding the widely accepted notion among scholars of eighteenth-century English literature that the epistle, a recognized classical and medieval genre, flourished as a dominant novelistic device during the seventeenth and early eighteenth centuries, but was already somewhat archaic when Richardson revived it and Burney and Smollett turned it to their own rather anomalous purposes.[6] Women writing after Richardson (and also, mostly, after Rousseau) would have been so insistently drawn to the epistolary form in its "confidant" version because it enacted their common theme of textual transmission between women. Their use of the form significantly resists the domestic containment of virtuous heroines performed by Richardson's and Rousseau's epistolary fictions, to a large extent on the level of representation, but even more through the *mises-en-abyme* of reading created by the form of women's correspondence. Repetitive framing structures allow these novels to construct their relation with the implied reader as an epistolary exchange between feminine subjects across, and often altogether beyond, the bounds of domestic space. Thus at the same time that they resist the enshrinement of dead women like Clarissa and Julie in the crypt of the domestic sphere, they also circumvent related problems for the expression of feminine voice and community presented by the amorous epistolary tradition.

In order to resist in narrative what Nancy Armstrong calls "the sexual contract," the eighteenth-century social fiction that women willingly enter lifelong domestic confinement by freely choosing their lords and masters, these writers must also resist the heterosexual love letter. Writing women's correspondences, they avoid the plight for female authors of the continuing popular appeal of abandoned and plaintive *héroïdes*, as described by Joan DeJean (*Sappho*, pp. 96–102), as well as the problem laid out by Elizabeth Heckendorn Cook in her reading of Riccoboni's *Fanni Butlerd*, where the private sphere is the region in which men can abuse women unrestrained by the code of honor that regulates their behavior outside it, and the heroine can only avenge herself by "going public" with a private correspondence.

The shared formal and thematic enactment of women's correspondences is closely linked to a common paradigmatic plot, one that turns upon the transmission of inheritances, both textual and material. By combining the epistolary form with the romance plot of inheritance—a primarily textual inheritance, as Chapter 3 will clarify—these novels represent the transmission of texts between women as simultaneously synchronic and diachronic, constantly formed and reformed in the present through direct and indirect correspondences, and also as taking place at once within and without the narrative frame (simultaneously intradiegetic and extradiegetic, to borrow Gérard Genette's terminology). Thus they not only represent issues of female textual inheritance, but attempt to enact them with their readers. The subgenre thematizes and takes to its formal extreme the subversive potential described by Nicola Watson in her discussion of letters written by eighteenth-century heroines more generally, where she describes them as "instituting an exchange system which functions in accordance with a logic inimical to the patriarchal logic of property," and possessing a "secretive ability to disrupt the smooth and public process of patrilineal history" (pp. 15, 193).

While synchronic transmission occurs intradiegetically in the epistolary exchange between characters, the text of that exchange itself consistently becomes an "inheritance" that is passed diachronically from one generation to the next, as a substitute for the substantive, patrimonial inheritance denied the heroine, who as a woman is defined by the laws of patrimonial transmission (literary and literal) as an improper receiver. The parallelism between the exchange of letters and the transmission of inheritance implies a similarity between the two. Thus the diachronic relation created by the transmission of this feminine textual inheritance is structured on the model of the synchronic epistolary exchange, unlike patrimonial inheritance, which is structured on the model of debt, an essentially "diachronic" model because it implies repayment over time.[7] The feminine literary inheritance these works imagine, then, is one that invites readers to participate in a willing exchange, rather than entailing upon them the indebtedness of a received and exclusive privilege or value.

On the extradiegetic level, the novels repeatedly figure themselves—like the epistolary exchanges they represent—as both epistle and inheritance, at once addressed and bequeathed to a young female reader.[8] This subgenre, then—for the novels are close enough in time, in mutual influence, and in their use of formal, rhetorical, and thematic conventions to be classed meaningfully together as such—specifically addresses the problems of the position of women in relation to an enclosing system of textual transmission that is structured and figured as a patrimonial inheritance.[9] It represents that system as founded upon the exclusion of women from the production and transmission of both literary and economic value, for which a negative form of moral value (feminine virtue) must always be substituted, in order to maintain women in their excluded, yet contained and supporting, position. The value of such novels for twentieth-century readers lies in their figuring forth of some of the elisions and substitutions through which we have received our own notion of literary value, and thus in potentially enabling us to avoid the mechanical reproduction of a received and unreflected sense of value that repeats its effacement of the traces of the system through which it has been produced and transmitted to us as readers.

Gilbert and Gubar described how authorship has been conceptualized patrilineally; Marianne Hirsch has since demonstrated that much of the most influential recent narrative theory repeatedly conceives of narrative itself, not only in linear terms, but in patrilineal ones: "The very continuity of narrative, its potential to make sense, from syntax to plot structure, seems to depend on a relation to paternity, whether that relation be subordinate and obedient or rebellious" (*The Mother/Daughter Plot*, p. 51; see also pp. 53–54). The concept of a literary tradition is itself a rhetorical figure for textual transmission that is modeled upon the epic paradigm of patrimonial inheritance, where the anxieties about patriline descent expressed in Homer are assuaged by the substitution of a more verifiable and permanent literary patrilinearity for that of blood.[10] Vergil "inherits" his laurels from Homer, Dante from Vergil. Henry Fielding, fighting to legitimize a genre that had no high classical lineage and was really a hodge-podge of genres patched together mainly by disenfranchised female "hacks," or, worse still, by "feminine" male writers like Richardson, anxiously repaired the apparent patrilineal lapse of the moderns by establishing the novel's epic lineage.[11] As a result of the "battle of the books" in the late seventeenth and earlier eighteenth century, modern literature was recognized as the legitimate offspring of the ancients, while, as Timothy Reiss has recently argued in *The Meaning of Literature*, men were constructed as the proper writers of "literature," with women as its "consumers, or, at best, second-class producers" (p. 201). "Great works really were thought to be seminal" by the mid eighteenth century, as Janet Todd observes (*Angellica*, pp. 120–21). But throughout this battle and its aftermath, women continued to piece together their illegitimate productions according to alternate designs, and to engage in literary correspondences through their manipulations of generic and plot conventions that criticize and resist the model of literary tradition that was in the process of appropriating the marginal genre that they had been allowed, for a while, to call their own.

Both literary tradition and patrimony are systems for the production and transmission of value, whether cultural value or the economic value of "real" property. Both systems enable themselves to define value, to assign it a local habitation and a name—the paternal name and a place within the nation as fatherland—by means of the systematic exclusion of others.[12] In the terms of the patriline model, the original, definitive other, as the very word *patriline* and its cognates inform us, is woman—specifically, woman as (m)other. But the diachronic lines drawn by the patriline model also describe the synchronic borders of a nation-state defined as "fatherland" (the word *patrie* comes up with great frequency in the French novels of the women's subgenre).[13] In this double, synchronic and diachronic representation of literary tradition as patrimony and patrie, women's writings are both exiled and disinherited; they become everywhere and always improper, lacking the real property that establishes proper place. Faced with the impossibility of existing apart, since there is no place outside the Moebian boundaries of the patrie, they are forced to play a subordinate role in a patrilineal literary history.[14] But it is crucial to remember—as the novels it excludes will themselves remind us—that this literary tradition is itself a carefully contrived fiction. Only by reading the strange lines made readable in the fictions of a women's correspondence that is also a feminine inheritance does it become possible to read the equally strange, although seemingly straight, lines of patriline tradition as a fiction.

Women and Tradition

Any attempt to theorize the intertextuality of fiction that figures itself at once as a women's correspondence and as a women's inheritance must confront the question of whether such an intertextuality does or can constitute a "female literary tradition." In recent years many feminist critics have spoken out, not without reason, against the essentialist implications of attempts to trace such a tradition, often insisting that feminist interpretation needs to focus rather on the interconnectedness of men's and women's writing within the historical framework of national tradition.[15] The perception of a necessary connection between the boundaries of national literary tradition and what Naomi Schor has called "intersextuality" is a profound one, for that link is historically at the crux of the very conception of both tradition and nation. The intersection of these boundaries is already recognized in the women's texts to be read in subsequent chapters. All of them are in some sense strong rewritings of the canonical works of their male contemporaries—Marivaux, Richardson, Rousseau—and can profitably be read as such. Read through a broader contextual frame than that of specific "intersextual" relations, however, all of these women's novels struggle more fundamentally with the problematic relation of plotting women (authors, heroines, and readers) to the double boundary of nation and tradition. (I understand "boundary" here with emphasis on its connotations of plot; "boundaries" are the lines that define both the diachronic plot of the narrative of literary tradition and the synchronic plot of ground whose borderlines define the nation-state.)[16] Moreover, as I argue below, female novelists of the later eighteenth century in England and France worked out their relationship to the boundary of national tradition overtly with respect to one another, making use of the same conventions.[17]

For precisely the same reason that I acknowledge the need for "intersextual" readings of these and other works, therefore, I would not agree to reduce contemporary readings of women's writings to their relationship with specific canonical texts within a national tradition, as defined primarily through the works of its canonized male authors. The reason for my disagreement is that novels of women's correspondence already plot themselves over, against, and about their own complex relationship to the boundaries of nation and tradition. Reading fictions of women's correspondence on their own terms thus renders readable the national traditions' plots of transmission in a different way than would be possible by respecting the demand of the "male line" that not only the texts it includes but those it excludes as well should be read, if at all, always on *its* terms.

Rather than describing a plot, correspondence generates one of a very different kind than that of tradition. It plots a gap as much as a line, a complex of connections among women's texts that leaps, in precise and self-conscious ways, the restrictive boundaries of nation and tradition, of national tradition. These novels represent, through the frames of their fictional epistolary correspondences, something similar to the "feminist reading" that Mary Jacobus advocates, by means of which a daughter, at once addressee and inheritrix of a maternal text, is enabled to read a mother's letter *across* the lines of descent, rather than being compelled to repeat her unhappy narrative, to mirror her inherited figure. The daughter as "feminist reader" thus escapes the repetition of "petrifying resemblance" and is enabled to assert difference: "Crossing the fixed lines of chronological reading, the correspondence puts matrilineal structures in question."[18] Or, to quote a different kind of correspondence (some recent labels on Betsey Johnson clothing): "Like Mother Unlike Daughter." Eighteenth-century novels of women's correspondence do profoundly question matrilineal structures, but it is only possible to read their questioning by reading women's correspondence *as such*; that is, as an exchange among women reading and writing for one another.[19] But a correspondence that questions matrilineal structures necessarily questions patrilineal ones as well, including the notion of national literary tradition, since the problem with matrilineal structures, the reason for their reproduction of "petrifying resemblance" in the first place, is that they themselves are "patrifying resemblances," mirroring the patriline structures that serve in the reproduction of maternal resemblance.[20] And just as women's correspondence distinguishes itself from any rigid structures of lineal descent, patriline or matriline, it must not be confused either with any potentially essentializing notions of *écriture féminine* or with the idea of literary "influence" in any direct sense. This book's purpose is not to provide "literary ancestors" to "document the legitimacy of current women's literary activities" (Ezell, *Writing Women's Literary History*, p. 20), but rather to make the effort to read some women's writings of the past as much as possible within the terms they invite by the acts of reading they inscribe within themselves.

Legibility and Illegitimacy

I propose, then, to construct a model for reading the plots, and reading out of the plots, of women's correspondence. These plots do not construct their reader as a legitimate daughter, a destination defined by patrilineal or matrilineal descent, but rather leave themselves to the reader as inheriting stranger, to plot out, but not simply to retrace, the story of textual transmission, to read her own reception of their literary legacy otherwise than through the deceptively (i.e., fictionally) simple lines of descent. Women's correspondence plots the reader as illegitimate heir; such a text will therefore appear unreadable unless it is read illegitimately. The narratology of its plot cannot be elaborated without a multiplicity of fathers, and even of mothers, in mind. Therefore this reading must inevitably be at fault in its failure to legitimize itself by acknowledging the debt of critical descent in a single paternal name (Freud? Lacan? Marx? Derrida? Foucault?), or even with an apparently matriline identification, such as "feminist," since it would be impossible to identify it as belonging to a single one of the multiple feminisms that father themselves severally on psychoanalytic, historical materialist, deconstructive, or empiricist and literary historical traditions.

It is true that we can neither read nor write without fathers in mind; in Langbauer's words, "we as feminists cannot, in devising our own theories, say no to fathers like Freud but must use their very perspectives in our struggles with them" (p. 9). Nevertheless, to identify a single father or that father's paternal lineage, to name one's reading after him, is to return in a fundamental way to a patriline model for reading and writing. Reading on the model of women's correspondence is reading without a name, reading that rejects the reduplication of name and image as figuration of legitimacy, in order instead to engage in a multiple exchange. As such it is also reading at once with and without a frame: reading out of a multiplicity of theoretical frames, reading through the epistolary frames of women's correspondences, the fragmentariness and faultiness of which refuse to close the reader in the exegetical frame of reference of a set of sacred texts.[21]

Along with legitimacy goes the wholeness and singularity of authority and of authorship. The texts I have chosen to read here all bear signatures that are gendered feminine; that is certainly not to say that they are the same signature, yet it is undeniable that they have always been read, and have read themselves, as having in common the fact, and the necessity of response to the fact, that they bear for their cultures the mark of gender.[22] It is impossible to claim, especially since I am writing here of works written in different periods, in different countries and languages, and by women of different social classes, that the authors of these works formed "a subculture within the framework of a larger society," as Elaine Showalter formulated it in her path-breaking work on nineteenth-century British women novelists. Such a claim would be even more difficult to defend in the present case than the claim that the works read here form a "tradition" in the patrilineal sense in which that concept is generally understood. I quote Showalter's formulation, however, because of her use of the word *framework* to describe the western European patriarchal society within some version of which all of these writers found themselves circumscribed, "framed" *as woman.*

One could also quote Joan DeJean's much more recent version of the same defense, which, somehow, in the 1990's as in the 1970's anyone who writes a book on women writers exclusively is expected to make: "Women authors in the ancien régime wrote from a vantage point inevitably defined in part by the fact that their contemporaries responded to them not only as writers but as women writers" (*Tender Geographies*, p. 15). Janet Todd remarks on an analogous phenomenon in England: "What women created in the mid-eighteenth century was not simply writing but *feminine* writing. Prose and poetry were considered firmly gendered, and sensitive readers could immediately tell the sex of the author (*Angellica*, pp. 125–26). By signing in the feminine, eighteenth-century authors do place their works and themselves as authors in a marked relation to that "larger framework," a relation both the frame and the works inevitably define as female, that is, as not-male. Variable and fluid as that relation can be, potentially subverting the very oppositions that define it, the signature that marks author and work as feminine inevitably places both in the impossible, improper place of "the other" within that framework of the larger society and its received notion of literary tradition. That place is impossible because, as elaborated in subsequent chapters, it lies at once within and without the boundaries of the plot through which the writers write and their readers read.

Framed Again? or, Through the Looking-Glass

The importance of framing and the breaching of frameworks, whether to the transmission of "women's correspondences" or to any possible "female tradition" (a tradition that would have to be constructed in response to the patrilineal model), is one of the primary considerations that led me to open my own frame of reading around epistolary fiction by women that represents correspondence between women, and thereby to make it the frame of reference for my reading of female transmission in fiction. As should be clear by now, I use the phrase "female literary tradition" *sous rature*, but have not discarded it because I wish to distinguish it from, rather than to replace it with, the idea of correspondence. The latter is a model for reading, for the textual transmission through which a reader (including the readers who wrote these novels) may or may not choose to construct a "tradition." I myself prefer to emphasize the metaphor of correspondence to represent the relation among these women's texts, because any attempt to construct it as "tradition" would always involve a contradiction between the patrilineality of the concept of "tradition" and the illegitimacy—in patrilineal terms, which remain the only available terms—of the generic lines being described.

The well-documented historical connections that link literary female friendships, letter-writing, women writers, the epistolary form, and the beginnings of the novel in both England and France are grounded in an ideological connection linking femininity, the novel, and the other popular, nonclassical, and private or "familiar" prose forms, as all lying outside the bounds of generic legitimacy, and hence not possessing boundaries that might definitively distinguish them from one another.[23] This lack of distinct boundaries is marked by the number of attempts to define them, particularly in the late seventeenth and early eighteenth centuries.[24] The novel is thus already itself an illegitimate genre made up out of the crossing of unrecognized generic boundaries, which connects it not only with women writers, but also with female personae (whether pseudonyms or heroines) and a general emphasis on feminine subjectivity. But at the moment when the novel begins to come into its own as a literary genre, from the 1760's to the end of the century, the manipulations of framing structures enacted through the epistolary form, the representations of the transmission between women of textual inheritances framed as letters, within the larger contextual frame of a society ever more anxiously structured in its official discourses along the lines of patrimonial transmission, all converge in the epistolary subgenre of women's correspondences. This historically localizable insistence on a form that emphasizes problems of transmission and framing, as it deemphasizes a central authorial or narrative voice in favor of the illusion of direct narration by women who are *not* "authors," makes the subgenre a useful frame of reference from which to open the web of intertextual correspondences that cross not only the generic boundaries of the epistolary, the sentimental, the Gothic, and all the other transgressions that might be said to constitute the novel itself as a genre, but also cross that more inclusive generic boundary, even into the empire of the lyric.[25]

The persistent recurrence in the fiction I read here of the literalized image of the portrait, of the framing of history as example, and of the epistolary framing of those heritable exemplary histories, all of which have become vehicles of a plot motivated by the problems of the impossible position of women within a patrilineal system of inheritance, is not specific, among early women's novels, to the formally defined epistolary subgenre upon which I concentrate in the central chapters. These formal and thematic preoccupations in fact pervade women's novels of the later seventeenth through the early nineteenth centuries, at least. Many of the elements just mentioned are inherited from a romance tradition upon which male novelists drew as well, but upon which female writers of early novels often drew in specific ways, for reasons discussed during the analyses of the individual works.

Although the image of the framed portrait is by no means inherent or exclusive to formal epistolary or other narrative framing structures, the elements of image, plot, and theme represented by the framed portrait and the inheritance of a patrimony are nevertheless empirically linked closely with the epistolary form. Other epistolary novels written by women in the same period confront the same problems without representing women's correspondence literally in an epistolary exchange open to the reader, while in yet others, not written in the epistolary form, letters and other literalized metaphors of framing nevertheless play a crucial role in the plot.[26]

All of these fictions confront the problems of the position of women in relation to the enclosing "frameworks" of patriarchal and patrilineal structures through the setting up and breaking of fictional frames, and specifically the plotting through them of indirect or broken lines of transmission. It is this common plot, in the broadest sense of the term and resonating with all its connotations (narrative line, bounded territory, covert project for revolutionary action, based on secret communications) that renders all the works to be discussed, whether or not they fall into the formal subgenre I have identified at its crux, recognizable as a set of correspondences that cross generic boundaries in the interest of the plot of female transmission.

Alastair Fowler defines the term *subgenre* thus: "Subgenres have the common features of the kind—external forms and all—and, over and above these, add special substantive features" (p. 112). I am using the term in Fowler's sense when I speak of the novels discussed in Chapters 3, 4, and 5; by relating these texts to the works of Lafayette, Staël, and Austen, however, I am demonstrating the truth of Derrida's argument, as succinctly stated by Benstock: "Epistolarity inscribes an absolutely rigid law: the fiction it promotes can only take place within the letter"; however, "establishing a limit between genres, the law opens the possibility that limits can be exceeded, that the boundary can 'form, by invagination, an internal pocket larger than the whole'" (Benstock, pp. 15, 92). Novels of women's correspondence take up Lafayette regardless of the fact that she was writing in a different historical context, while Staël and Austen, in their very correspondence with the eighteenth-century subgenre, transform and move away from it. I propose that these fictions be read, not as establishing a European "female literary tradition," but as constituting an illegitimate narrative genre recognizable through its consistent crossing of the generic boundary lines of novel and romance, of epistolary and memoir forms, of fiction and history, of private and public history, in ways that reflect a feminine-gendered position in relation to those boundaries.

But how is it possible to construct a model for illegitimate reading using the metaphor of the frame, when it has been persuasively argued that that metaphor already tends toward the fixing, killing repetition of the mirror image? Peter Brooks argues in *The Novel of Worldliness* that in the works of Marie-Madeleine de Lafayette and the eighteenth-century French novelists who followed her, to make a portrait of a person is to capture that person, to *fix* (*fixer*) him or her, whether with the eyebeam of the gaze or in the summing-up of the *portrait moral.*[27] In a very different context, but one equally relevant to the present concern, several theorists of psychoanalytically informed feminism have demonstrated the oculocentrism, and hence the phallogocentrism, the *specularity* of predominant modes of reading.[28] The problem of theorizing reading through the frames of correspondence, when both "frame" and "theory" are fraught with the specular, appears to be haunted by an inner contradiction. There is no doubt that the framed portraits in the novels I read here have a specular force, analyzed in detail later on. This force, inherited from the romance tradition, from the tradition of the humanist exemplar, and from the patrilineal model of tradition itself, is one of the specters that haunt the women's genre, but one upon which that genre also performs an exorcism. The frame becomes a readable frame rather than a specular one, an open, fragmentary, and multiplicitous one rather than a closed or normative one, when it becomes an epistolary frame; that is, when the frame and its repetition enter an economy of exchange rather than of passing on. In subsequent chapters I elaborate on how novels of women's correspondence recuperate the frame as matrix, the fragmentary as plurality, and the speculative trace of writing as correspondence. They use the sentimental convention of sympathy in particular to effect this transformation from patriline relations of specularity and indebtedness—that is, of speculation—to feminine relations of equal exchange.[29]

The concept of "readable framing," then, emerges from novels of women's correspondences. "Readable frames" can break through and break into the specular, historical frames inherited from a patriline literary tradition, and help construct a model of transmission that engages their own readers as self-determined heirs in an exchange, rather than as designated, destined (*destinées*) heirs to the debt of patrimony or of its specular images (such as the matrilineal inheritance and the utopian idea of a literary "mother country").

In reading women's correspondences, the rediscovery of a "mother country" is no more to the purpose than the reconstruction of a female or matrilineal literary tradition. The concept of the "mother country" is modeled as directly upon that of the *patrie* as the model of the unified matrilineal inheritance mirrors that of patrimonial succession. As the eighteenth-century fictions themselves tell us, as long as there is a patrie, the "mother country" remains only a form of exile within its boundaries. What I am plotting here is neither the map of a lost mother country nor the visible line of a tradition, but rather the readable lines of women's correspondence, which invite its readers, strange heirs—strangers and therefore heirs—to break the frames of maternal inheritance. Eighteenth-century women in the two strongest nation-states of Europe, by reading each other in and through their own writing, constructed a correspondence that is simultaneously an inheritance, but an inheritance unlike patrimony, one that must be willed as much by its legatee as by its legatrix, one that is structured as an exchange rather than as a debt to the dead, one that has the form of a letter that engages rather than that of an ancestral portrait that fixes the viewer with its ghostly gaze.

I shall devote the rest of this chapter to supplementing my theoretical argument with a more historical argument for reading women's correspondences across national boundaries in order to demonstrate how they have crossed those boundaries in practice as well as in representation, and in crossing them have also transgressed those of patrilineal national tradition. The main excellence of the work already done in the field of women's writing in the eighteenth century is in the area of historicist research; that is not where I mean to make any important original contribution. Some of the valuable information of that kind that has already been made available, however, can help make it possible to set eighteenth-century women's fiction within the framework of a correspondence that crosses the boundaries of national tradition. That framework contextualizes what occupies the main bulk, as it constitutes the main project, of the present book: to give some of the novels I have uncovered in my own researches the kind of close reading that has generally been denied them—even amid the recent wave of enthusiasm for historical knowledge about them and their authors—in an effort to ground a theory of feminine literary correspondence in the texts constituting it, rather than in a theoretical, philosophical, or literary patrimony. In the readings presented in subsequent chapters, therefore, I am myself forced to rely on the rhetoric of example, as are the novelists I am writing about, to present the larger women's correspondence that this chapter and Chapter 3 characterize in more abstract terms. As Freud said in defense of the case history as a valid presentation of psychiatric models, example is the only proof of which any argument about patterns that cannot be submitted to scientific controlled experiments can admit.[30]

Chapter 2 introduces the broader generic elements, iconic, thematic, formal, and narrative, through which I trace the correspondence I have been discussing, beginning with a rereading or reframing of a well-known novel, Marie-Madeleine de Lafayette's *La Princesse de Clèves*. I concentrate this reading of Lafayette's work on that novel's own use of literalized and literary frames in relation to the possibilities and the problems of maternal inheritance as the basis of relationship among characters and between text and reader. This is followed in Chapter 3, at the core of the book, by a description and analysis of the generic coherence of the later eighteenth-century subgenre of the epistolary novel that I have identified as "novels of women's correspondence" in terms of the same formal and thematic concerns. The general discussion of this subgenre is developed in Chapters 4 and 5 through more detailed readings of one English and one French example of the epistolary subgenre. *Lettres de Mademoiselle de Boismiran* and *The Recess* are selected, not so much as straightforwardly typical of the subgenre, but rather as texts that struggle creatively with the problems that arise from the subgenre's attempt to replace patriline relations with maternal and sympathetic ones. Chapter 6 again moves the study beyond the strict formal confines of the subgenre with a discussion of Germaine de Staël's Romantic transformations of the women's correspondence that preceded her, reading *Corinne* as the hopeful tragedy of a heroine who attempts the impossibility of reinserting herself into patriline relations, and destroys herself in the act of exposing the Gothic ruin of patrilineage. The Epilogue opens the discussion towards the nineteenth century with some remarks on Jane Austen's manipulations and recuperations of eighteenth-century women's correspondence in her turn away from sentimental and Romantic conventions (including the epistolary form itself), and toward the construction of a new relationship to readers that produces the illusion we now recognize as "realism."

Crossing the Channel

It is difficult to find mention of eighteenth-century women novelists in French other than Charrière, Genlis, Graffigny, and Riccoboni; meanwhile a deficiency of most considerations of the contemporary English women's fiction is that it is usually seen as filling in a line leading from Richardson (or sometimes Defoe) to Austen, whereas it is at least as important to acknowledge its correspondences with the *précieuses* and with Staël.[31] That eighteenth-century women novelists in England and France read each other at least as much as they read Richardson and Marivaux and Rousseau is indicated in part by the surprisingly large number of those who supplemented their literary earnings by translating each other's works, or who spent time in exile on the other side of the Channel.[32] More important evidence for the same lies in their borrowings from one another, in the similarity of their plots, themes, and settings, their professions of religious tolerance in an age when the laws against Protestants and "popery," respectively, were still harsh; in their constant references to the country across the channel, with plots set there, and above all in their insistent use, in both countries, of images of women in exile both within and without the boundaries of the nation-as-fatherland, the patrie.[33] I shall rarely bother to argue, however, that any particular one of them read any particular work by another.[34] The lacunae of literary history into which these works have fallen do not often contain enough historical evidence to sustain such arguments, which would miss the point in any case. The "correspondences" these works reveal are not those of "influence" (the unidirectional "flow," presumably, of "seminal" works), but those of genre, a sharing of conventions—formal, narrative, thematic, and iconic—such as make it possible to recognize the generic coherence of subgenres or "modes" like the Gothic, the pastoral, amatory fiction, or the bildungsroman. As Joan Hinde Stewart concludes of the coherence she found among French works by women of the same period: "These novels constitute an ongoing conversation among women in which the secret meanings, the points of antagonism and rupture, the seemly subversions were, through the transparency of the fictional conventions, probably as legible to the participants as they are becoming once again to us" (p. 206).

This book attempts to construct the history of a subgenre and its correspondences with novels that do not fall formally within its bounds, on the understanding that representations are not entirely determined by material or even social conditions, and that in fact they can exert an influence on both. What DeJean writes of her history of gender constructions could be repeated with the substitution of the term *genre*: "We can only recreate with confidence a history of the constructions of [genre], a succession of images whose possible historical validity is far less important than the very fact of their widespread usefulness at a particular period. These constructions tell the story of what women were believed/hoped/feared to be capable of accomplishing" (*Tender Geographies*, 9). The subgenre that I call "fiction of women's correspondence" was so useful to women novelists in the later eighteenth century as to be "widespread" across a period of time and a geographic area that included very different social and material realities (as well as national literary traditions).[35] The history of a form or genre is itself perhaps the most reliable form for the history of gender because both are, like patriarchy and patrilineage, largely fictional constructs that organize and lend cultural meanings to disparate events and experiences. Thus this book constructs a history of representations, without making the unnecessary claim that they are direct "'reflections' of the actual practice of the cultures from which they sprang" (Ezell, *The Patriarch's Wife*, p. 7).

Ruth Perry, Nancy Armstrong, and Michael McKeon, as well as Ian Watt and John Richetti, for example, emphasize the significance to the "rise" of the British novel of the changes in societal roles and, more important, the symbolic position assigned to women during the late seventeenth and early eighteenth centuries by a new middle-class ideology. With such general agreement upon the singular significance to the development of the novel of the position of women in a society in transition from an agrarian and aristocratic form to an urban one dominated by the middle class and its cash, it may seem problematic to name the aristocratic, seventeenth-century French précieuses as precursors upon which English eighteenth-century bourgeoises modeled social and literary practices. Nevertheless, references to French women novelists as the originals or standards for what English women novelists were writing in the early eighteenth century abound.[36] Delariviere Manley, for example, often refers to Madame d'Aulnoy and Madame du Noyer as popular standards against which she hardly dares compare herself.[37] Ros Ballaster, quoting Clara Reeve, correctly points out with Jane Spencer that novels by eighteenth-century Englishwomen were still associated with "French romances" in the late eighteenth century, although the English writers had never adopted the tone or form of Scudéry's romances (Ballaster, pp. 190–92; Spencer, *Rise*, p. 184). Indeed, the English novels are closer to the *nouvelles* of writers like Lafayette, but what Ballaster does not discuss is the fact that later eighteenth-century French women novelists *also* rejected the *roman de longue haleine*. In this shift they were probably influenced by the English writers as well as by their own countrywomen, Lafayette and Villedieu (Marie-Catherine Desjardins).

The acknowledged use of literary models at once feminine and French is also associated very early on, as early as the seventeenth century, with the borrowing of French literary women's social innovations. An anonymous eulogist urged the young Jane Barker in 1688 to persevere in writing the novels that she would in fact publish early in the next century, by making a comparison as bold as that between Manley and Madame d'Aulnoy:

> On then, brave Maid, secure of Fame advance,
> 'Gainst the Scaroons and Scudderies of France.[38]

The above felicitous verses were written by a fellow member of a society to which Barker belonged, which collectively published the *Poetical Recreations* in which they appear. This society was modeled directly on the Society of Friendship made famous by the poet

Katherine Philips, but ultimately on the salon coterie of the identical "Scuddery" against whom Barker is invited to measure her own novelistic prowess. Katherine Philips, in imitating the précieuses' social invention of the literary salon, also brought to England that essential doctrine of *préciosité*, first promulgated by Madeleine de Scudéry, of "platonic love." The model, both literary and lived, of close female friendship made possible by the précieuse idea of platonic love was the ancestor, not only of seventeenth-century circles like those of Katherine Philips and Jane Barker, but also of the late eighteenth-century bluestocking culture of "romantic friendship" between women, and of the epistolary fiction of female friendship written by the bluestockings' contemporaries.

The précieuse model is an earlier and more important ancestor than the fictional friendship through correspondence of Clarissa Harlowe and Anna Howe, which itself takes its force and plausibility from the existence of the earlier, strong tradition of such friendships both in women's literature and in women's lives, going back to the seventeenth century in England and originally imported from précieuse France.[39] Although French society and English society differed considerably at this period, the position of women in the respective countries and centuries had essential aspects in common. Women in both cases were regularly handed over by their families to men with whom they shared no mutual affection, and for whose benefit they were required to engage in the only production of goods allowed them, that of heirs to the paternal name and property. Both cultures also shared a predominant legal conception of women as minors, incapable of instituting any legal transaction independently, an attitude supported by scientific and religious ideologies that made women the weaker or more sinful sex.

As Georges Mongrédien observes, the aristocratic précieuses at least enjoyed the best possible version of this state of affairs, since the feudal duties of their husbands kept them often away from home.[40] This not only allowed but prompted them to develop their relationships with each other, relationships not merely close but often exclusive and carried on largely in letters written in the style of love letters. The middle-class English bluestockings, confined a century later to the homes of their all-too-present husbands, were able in their different social situation to make use of the précieuse precedent and model to do the same thing. They partially escaped the confinement of the home through epistolary friendships with other women. The correspondence in which Madame de Sablé and the comtesse de Maure posted their passion from one room to the adjoining one, their aesthetic of languishment preventing them from undertaking the journey necessary for a visit, is in style and circumstance not far from that in which two famous English bluestockings, Mrs Carter (the translator of Epictetus) and her friend Mrs Vesey, read one another's fond letters, by prior arrangement, by the light of the same "fair autumnal moon."[41]

None of the four individual women I have just mentioned wrote novels themselves, but their contemporaries, in both times and places, were working to transform epistolary conventions of female desire from the aggressively masculine homosocial code inherited from the ancients to one based upon a defensive or protective feminine homosociality. DeJean has demonstrated "that Scudéry initially considered epistolary rather than historical prose fiction the form of the future": her first literary work was an epistolary revision of the Ovidian tradition of héroïdes that worked to break the latter's "indissoluble bond between femininity and the love letter defined as the litany of the complaints of the lover left behind." Although Scudéry herself may have had to accept in the end that "the enterprise of epistolary vandalism that was one of the seventeenth century's great commercial success stories" would not reward her attempt to rewrite its misogynist codes, epistolary prose *was* "the form of the future" in that women a century later would use it to follow Scudéry's lead (DeJean, *Sappho*, pp. 98–100). But what Janet Todd says of the shift from early to mid eighteenth century in England holds for France as well: "The fictional separatist communities tinged with lesbianism and hedonism in Manley's works . . . gave way to gentler communities of victimised women coming together to perform charitable functions," in other words, communities based on the ties of *sympathy*, in the eighteenth-century sense of the term, which will be discussed in depth in Chapter 3 (*Angellica*, p. 115).

The précieuses' particular combination of friendship with literature to form a separate female society and a separate female language within the male-dominated framework of aristocratic feudalism is what does in fact link them with the rise of the bourgeoisie, and makes it less surprising that they should have been so influential with middle-class English literary women. First of all, it must be noted that, although préciosité is often thought of as a purely aristocratic pastime, the opposite was in fact the case; préciosité actually encouraged the mingling of ambitious bourgeoises with the aristocracy as nothing but large sums of cash ever had before it.[42] As Londa Schiebinger observes, "neither strictly aristocratic nor bourgeois, salons celebrated the superiority of acquired nobility over inherited nobility, emphasizing the virtues of talent and refinement over noble birth" (p. 30).[43] Two of préciosité's greatest exponents, Scudéry and Lafayette, had a far greater claim to a place at court in their much-admired wits than in their fathers' names.[44] The prominence of these women among the précieuses, despite their small wealth and relatively thin aristocratic pretensions, especially on Scudéry's part, was far from accidental. It was, in fact, characteristic of préciosité as a social force: "Throughout the seventeenth century the nobility felt increasingly threatened, and with reason. There was a constant pressure from below. By the late 1650's it seemed as if every ambitious housewife who had a little money could launch herself into some sort of genteel society by calling herself a précieuse." Dorothy Backer, in her history of the précieuses, sums up the role of préciosité in furthering the rise of the bourgeoisie—as well as of the novel and of women in literature—so well that it is worth quoting her here again:

> *Préciosité* was a factor in this social evolution towards money and away from land. The worldly conventions were of course utterly reactionary and did not admit this. Everyone knew you had to have heraldic credentials to get into Mme de Rambouillet's blue room. But the reality was something else. . . . When we look beyond Mme de Rambouillet and the Fronde to the final stage of the history of the *précieuses*, in the 1650's, we find such a confused mixture of noble and common women, such a muddling of class barriers, that we can actually speak of a levelling spirit as one of the characteristics of *préciosité*. The means to this levelling was literature, the favorite

> hobby of the *précieuses*. Any woman with the literary sensitivity, talent, queerness, bravery, or reading habits of a *précieuse* belonged to the freemasonry, regardless of her class. (pp. 12, 237)

Like romantic friendship after it, préciosité fostered heightened sensibility, female independence, and a sense of solidarity between women.[45] These elements became especially important for the later précieuses and for the eighteenth-century English bourgeoises alike, since the bourgeois marriage market, no longer as much concerned with class purity, was still more crassly materialistic than anything that had preceded it.[46] Mongrédien writes of the entrance and importance of the bourgeoises into the originally aristocratic précieux salons and culture: "It is easy to conceive that, as soon as *préciosité* spread into the bourgeois milieu, all of these unhappily married women confronted their misfortunes and their disappointments, were encouraged to evoke them in common, and finished by leading a veritable crusade against marriage, which for them was nothing but a perpetual servitude."[47] DeJean makes a similar claim, stating that French women writers of the late seventeenth century "made marriage their central literary preoccupation," and Schiebinger extends it beyond the period of the précieuses: "Fears that the learned lady threatened to disrupt the status quo were justified: it was part of the political program of *salonnières* of the seventeenth and eighteenth century to eschew traditional forms of marriage and motherhood."[48] Noting, with earlier critics, that the salons tended to efface distinctions of rank between the nobility and the bourgeoisie, Elizabeth MacArthur relates the précieuses' resistance to marriage to the rise of the letter form, arguing that epistolary resistance to closure reflects the threat posed to the stability of social order by women's resistance to marriage (*Extravagant Narratives*, pp. 40–44).

This "crusade" against marriage, like the letter form, was later taken up in England by the eighteenth-century bourgeoises who preached and sometimes practiced romantic friendship on the French model, as derived through its earlier English imitators in the seventeenth-century platonic friendship societies.[49] The English adoption of the French précieuses "crusade against marriage" may have been a response to the shift after the Restoration documented by Elaine Hobby, according to whom Englishwomen, having enjoyed some new freedoms during the upheavals of the English Revolution, "were driven back into their newly private homes, where they retreated to an espousal of virtue" (p. 11). By the 1720's, Jane Barker and Eliza Haywood were already exalting in fiction the single life and female friendship for women. In Haywood's *The British Recluse* (1722), Cleomira and Belinda, their hearts broken and their reputations ruined by one and the same rake, decide to abandon the impossible world of men and marriage, and go off to live together in the country. Reading these correspondences, it becomes evident that the story of Cleomira and Belinda is not very far, despite geographical and diegetical leaps, from what we read in the letters of Montpensier and Motteville, who plotted to go off into a retirement together where they could be "maîtresses d'elles-mêmes."[50] Their most crucial connection with the fiction of women's correspondence is the recurrent idea of the resistance to marriage and the establishment of female correspondences, if not of actual communities, to replace marriage as the primary form of relationship for women. This connection explains why novels of women's correspondence are so little domestic compared to contemporary fiction of the mid to late eighteenth century. They resist the domestic sphere as the new site for the enshrinement and reproduction of patronym and patriline kinship relations, imagining and enacting, if not practicable alternatives, at least published resistances to it.

The bluestockings, and much of the fiction of contemporary women who wrote epistolary novels of female friendship, were much more in the spirit of Haywood and Philips, indeed of the précieuses' "veritable crusade against marriage," than in that of Richardson. Clarissa repeatedly records her longings to enjoy the single state in the sole company of her dearest Nancy, but Richardson uses this feminine convention to show his heroine in fact entirely entrapped by the either/or of the marriage choices available to her, from which the only exit is death. Her identity and her all-important virtue are entirely defined within the rigid framework of opposing male wills, represented by Lovelace, Solmes, father, and brother—with the beneficent male "will," her grandfather's testament, only serving to set the others into opposition, never serving actually to provide the heritable real estate, the proper place of retirement in which she might actually enjoy the company of Nancy. Much of the women's fiction influenced by *Clarissa* represents an attempt to rewrite Richardson, not simply because Richardson was so influential, but because Richardson himself was trying to rewrite the disruptive movements that threatened domesticity in the prehistory of women's correspondence. As Margaret Anne Doody has remarked, "It is as if Lovelace . . . had read *The British Recluse* with an ironic perception of 'sour grapes' in the feminist ending, and imagined such a situation of feminine defeat from the ego-satisfying view of the rake in the case" (*A Natural Passion*, pp. 145–46; also quoted in Backscheider's discussion, p. 288).

Laurel Thatcher Ulrich reads Richardson similarly as working to domesticate his heroines out of potentially subversive female communities: "Victory over the sensual advances of Mr. B was achieved only by overcoming the governance of Mrs. Jewkes. . . . Bereft of parents and of guardians, [Pamela] must acquire a new world of values, breaking out of the ancient community of women into the sequestered paradise of an idealized marriage" (p. 105; significantly, both of Richardson's most famous novels make the substitute mother, the figure that takes on a crucial and benevolent role in the later fiction of women's correspondence, monstrous and masculinized instruments of male aristocratic surveillance). John Mullan has argued, rightly, I think, that Richardson constructed femininity as a virtuous but extreme and volatile sensibility that was transparently legible in the female body, and marriage as "a necessary domestication" of that excessive feminine sensibility (pp. 111–13). But the fiction of women's correspondence rewrites this construction, making sympathy a connection through which "women are bound together," to be sure, but not simply as a class of bodily "texts"—rather as a literate community that can transgress the domesticating boundaries of the private sphere that would contain them in heterosexual marriage as the moral guarantors of a heterosocial world. Letters and letter-fiction allowed them to transgress those boundaries through imagination, through the post, and through publication, guaranteeing their extradomestic bonds by the power of sympathy itself.

Later female writers of sensibility in France as well as England tried to shift back to the more "feminist" model of *The British Re-*

cluse, while moving beyond it at the same time. Janet Todd has observed that in Marie-Jeanne Riccoboni's work "a release from the progress to death could come through female friendship, defence and comfort in a hostile male world," while Cook has emphasized the same author's insistence on women's choice and agency in sexual relationships outside marriage, in contrast to Clarissa's virtuous entrapment (*Angellica*, p. 143; Cook, pp. 38–39). The mother of Riccoboni's Miss Jenny, for example, is pressed by her husband-to-be to give herself to him before marriage, to prove that she is doing it of her own free will—as Clarissa is pressed by Lovelace. Jenny's mother does not see her only means of self-assertion as the negative one of resistance, as Clarissa does; she feels she is expressing her own will by engaging in premarital sex. Jenny herself, the result of this self-assertive act, is able to escape from the relentless pursuit of another Lovelace figure, to prefer and actually to achieve "the single life" in retirement.

Miss Jenny is also interesting as a rewriting of Marivaux's *La Vie de Marianne* (not surprisingly, considering that Riccoboni was also the author of the *Suite de Marianne*, which is probably why she was never quite as completely forgotten as her female contemporaries). Jenny's story and the structure of her novel is quite similar to Marianne's, except that Jenny is not the manipulative coquette that Marianne is. Another example of the revision of Richardson is one Emma, who is actually sent to the terrifying moated house used as a bogey to intimidate Clarissa. Once there, however, she finds her keeper is really a sympathetic substitute mother, and prefers to stay in retirement with her, returning only in response to the pleadings of female friends.[51] The bluestockings, as unlike Clarissa as are the heroines of these novels, shocked more conservative women by their conduct and writings, in which, following the précieuses, they condemned marriage as a form of slavery to men.[52] Mrs Carter, for example, characterized the latter as "rarely capable of unmixed tenderness to any fellow-creature except their children," meanwhile extolling more stimulating relationships with female friends.

Elizabeth Mavor thus defines romantic friendship, the late eighteenth-century British expression of platonic love: "Very generally speaking the symptoms of romantic friendship were 'retirement,' good works, cottages, gardening, impecuniosity, the intellectual pursuits of reading aloud and the study of languages, enthusiasm for the Gothick, journals, migraines, sensibility and often, but not always, the single state."[53] This feminine and literary way of life was still, in the late eighteenth century, being blamed by its outraged enemies on some latter-day "Scudderies of France." Hester Thrale ascribed it to the influence of some belated précieuses of the contemporary French court: "The queen of France is at the Head of a Set of Monsters call'd by each other Sapphists, who boast her example; and deserve to be thrown with the He Demons that haunt each other likewise, into Mount Vesuvius."[54] The French she-demons take their name, in Thrale's reading (as emphasized by her further classical reference) from the poet Sappho. It is clear, however, that they also derive from a nearer literary mother figure, that of "Sapho," the romance persona assumed by Madeleine de Scudéry. In DeJean's account of the figure of Sappho in French literary history, Scudéry portrays a Sapho who exhorts a younger poet, Erinne, "to follow her literary example and become a poet. This Sapho writes for her female friends and consciously seeks to found a female literary tradition" (p. 102).[55] The bluestockings who shocked Mrs Thrale, as well as many of the British women novelists both before and after Richardson, link themselves through the leaps in the same crooked line of women's correspondence, place themselves within the same open frames of correspondence, as do the queen of France's set of Sapphists.

Representation in the Early Novel: Mimesis and Imitation

It is one of the defining characteristics of the novel as an emerging genre, from *Don Quixote* to *Northanger Abbey*, that it reflects self-consciously upon the relations between mimesis and imitation; that is, upon the exemplary functions of fictional representation. The early novel's preoccupation with exempla reveals the genre's historical and conceptual linkage with the earlier novella tradition, as well as with that of Renaissance historiography and conduct literature.[56] These earlier traditions, coming together in the figure of the exemplum, had always been about the transmission of virtue, but primarily of virtue as understood in the classical sense of *vir*tus, literally "manliness," including "masculine" and active virtues such as bravery, justice, strength, nobility of soul: virtues considered necessary for the betterment and furtherance of the *res publica*, of the public thing, whether that thing be organized as republic, principality, or nation-state.[57] The developing genre's emphasis shifted to feminine virtue by the mid eighteenth century, when even virtues ascribed to heroes began to be those traditionally marked feminine. This shift occurred at least in part through the same correspondence that links Lafayette with Austen.

In the French seventeenth century, the rhetorical figure of example came to be dominated by what had long been only one of the primary visual metaphors through which example might be represented—that of the portrait.[58] This shift in emphasis and expression was great enough to constitute a change of figure, an alteration in how it was conceptualized and thus in how it signified. And yet the seventeenth-century figure of portraiture still functioned in important ways like the Renaissance exemplum, just as, in Foucault's formulation, the classical structure of knowledge as representation, representing itself insistently as *tableau*, as picture, nevertheless retained at its borders the relation of resemblance or similitude that structured thought in the Renaissance.[59] If, as the work of Louis Marin demonstrates, the portrait of Louis XIV signified his power, represented and embodied it so fully that the king himself became a secondary figure to his representation, in that his actual body was less stable, less fully present and self-identical than his representation as source of royal power, it is still possible to see in this seventeenth-century mode of representation the relation of the example to its receiver. For according to the conception articulated by Marin of the relation between the king and his portrait, the king himself continually had to strive to live up to the ideal of power and self-identity as it existed in representation, in his own portrait.[60] The difference was that the example the prince had to strive to imitate had become the representation of himself, rather than of a figure from classical history; what it had in common, on the other hand, with the Renaissance exemplum was that the portrait still figured forth the idea—the absolute power of the king—that supported the "public thing," the state, more fully than did the king himself.

The figure of the portrait as the public, exemplary representation of a self induced to imitate its own static representation actually preceded Louis XIV's consolidation of power, in the *portraits moraux* of Madeleine de Scudéry's *Le Grand Cyrus*, where it apotheosized not the king but the nobility who fought against him to retain their old aristocratic powers.[61] Scudéry's first literary portraits idealized members of the Blue Room's salon society, especially its female members, in such a way as to place them under an implicit injunction to imitate and become worthy of their own portraits, just as the Blue Room's new social standards of *bienséance* imposed a rigid model for imitation primarily on women, who, thus transformed by the social and literary discourse of préciosité, themselves became exemplary figures as far above mere mortal man as the king would soon become. It may have been impossible for men to imitate these "visible deities," as Antoine Badaud de Somaize mockingly called the précieuses, but the necessity of adoring the exemplary beings, of cultivating their favor and avoiding their ire, functioned still more effectively than an injunction of direct imitation to keep gentlemen in line. "Ladies made gentlemen," to quote Carolyn Lougee, but ladies could only make gentlemen by first making themselves ladies. A social and literary influence over the rules of a still male-dominated society was purchased with an extreme of self-control, with the transformation of the self into an unattainable exemplar of bienséance.[62] By the time the portrait of Louis XIV was painted, the figure of portraiture and the exemplary virtue it enjoined upon its subject had itself already begun to undergo a sex change from the Renaissance exemplum of princely *virtus* to the précieuses' portrait moral.[63]

Women on the Verge; or, Example and Transmission Through Female Lines

One of Jane Austen's early works offers its reader the tableau of a daughter viewing another tableau that has been offered her by her mother:

> Poor Creature! the prospect from her window is not very instructive, for that room overlooks the Lawn you know with the Shrubbery on one side, where she may see her Mother walking for an hour together, in earnest conversation with Reginald. A girl of Frederica's age must be childish indeed, if such things do not strike her.

> Is it not inexcusable to give such an example to a daughter? (*Lady Susan*, p. 233)

The surrounding text tells us that such things do indeed strike Frederica, who has already tried literally to run away from her mother's nefarious example. The mother's example is set for the daughter within the frame of the real estate, the house and garden they are both competing to occupy. For the reader, both "prospect" and frame are in turn set within an epistolary interpretive frame: the normative reading of the letter-writer, who insists upon the pedagogical danger that the mother's example will "strike" her daughter rather than be read by her—and will strike with a dangerously contagious force. The example of Lady Susan, by its framing as a contagious "prospect" for the daughter, becomes for the reader a negative example, a model of how a woman ought not to behave—not merely to preserve her own status, but so as not to pass on such a harmful image of feminine conduct to successive generations of women. The mise-en-abyme of framing just described opens the fictional mother's misconduct as an abyss of moral fault that yawns at the feet, not only of the represented daughter, but also of the reader, who is placed at its dangerous verge, ready to make a fatal interpretive faux pas by being "struck" with an image, rather than reading it through all of its frames.[64]

Austen began her career as a novelist by expressly situating herself within a literary correspondence among French and English women authors that grew through the appropriation of both discursive and social elements of préciosité by late seventeenth- and eighteenth-century English novelists. Across the historical divide that separated her from Lafayette, and through the channel-crossing writings of a whole series of eighteenth-century women novelists, Austen placed her text within a correspondence, well established by the time she began writing, in which women portrayed heroines as readers and potential imitators of a text inherited from a mother, and simultaneously purported to frame the reading heroine as an example for the inscribed female reader. Every step taken in the present volume is balanced on the verge of a corresponding precipice, or precipice in correspondence, reopened by each writer who corresponds, ultimately, with Lafayette.

Chapter 2 . . .

What the Princess Left; or, Exemplary Faults in *La Princesse de Clèves*

She thought that she had hollowed herself an abyss from which she would never escape.
—Marie-Madeleine de Lafayette, 'La Princesse de Clèves'

Marie-Madeleine de Lafayette's princess of Clèves is a perfect fictional example of the précieuse who makes herself exemplary by exerting a violent control over herself, and who in so doing "makes gentlemen," as surely as any Mandane or Sapho might, keeping both husband and lover from crossing that social and psychological line of full "possession" where male power threatens to become absolute. The princess's ultimate transformation of herself into an "inimitable example" is motivated and necessitated by the maternal imperative that she live up to her own portrait moral, the picture of herself as ideal woman, as painted for her by her mother.

The princess has often been considered in relation to her mother: as formed by her mother's peculiar education through negative example, or "painting pictures of love"; as controlled and manipulated by her mother's will; as in various ways her mother's heir.[1] But the problematic relation between the transmission of example and the transmission of inheritance from mother to daughter, which generated the plots of so many eighteenth-century novels in both France and England, remains adequately to be understood. If, in *La Princesse de Clèves*, Lafayette is fusing the novella with romance, she is fusing, around the figure of the princess, one genre that is preoccupied with the transmission of example, with another that is equally preoccupied with the transmission of name and inheritance (and thus with the reproduction of social hierarchies). In so doing, she is setting her narrative frame around the problems inherent in both forms of transmission when women are imagined as the subjects of transmission, both senders and receivers, rather than primarily as objects of transmission among men.

The paradigmatic romance plot is about the loss of inheritance and of identity by a noble orphan who proves him or herself innately worthy of the alienated succession by displaying noble qualities (either virtus or feminine virtue). The plot ends with the reinstatement of the rightful heir—often through marriage to the heiress—and thus with a reaffirmation of social norms and hierarchies; prose romance generally shares this aspect with Renaissance comedy. But as Peggy Kamuf notes, Mlle de Chartres enters her historical context, not as a fictional outcast from it, but as a rightful heiress well fixed in the center of its frame (Kamuf, *Fictions of Feminine Desire*, p. 69). Lafayette has written an inverse or tragic romance, in which the heroine begins her story, rather than ending it, with her establishment in a situation that normally constitutes the concluding stasis of romance. Rather than coming into a lost inheritance, she is immediately identified as heiress to the illustrious house of Chartres: in the miniature portrait that introduces her, the fact that she is one of the greatest heiresses in France is mentioned twice in the space of one page (p. 41).[2] Within a few pages of her introduction as heiress, Mlle de Chartres is appropriately married. The reason the novel can unfold from this happy state is that the emphasis is on the unresolved problem of what it means for a woman to be an heiress within a patrimonial system of inheritance.

Maternal Inheritance: Leaving What Is Left Out

The paradox of female transmission is double, for the problem of the daughter as receiver is matched by that of the mother as transmitter. As a widowed mother, Mme de Chartres usurps the role of the father in patrimonial transmission: that of destining her daughter (*destiner* being the word commonly used in French texts of the period for the parents' designation of a spouse for their child). At the same time, she fulfills the role of a mother by transmitting an education in feminine virtue designed to ensure her daughter's proper functioning as the conduit for the destination of patrimony, while protecting her from experiencing the suffering entailed in the thwarting of a female desire that would threaten patrilineal transmission with miscarriage.[3]

In order to understand the plot of maternal transmission in *La Princesse de Clèves*, it is necessary to follow the trajectory of its literalized emblem: the princess's miniature in its jeweled case. I said at the beginning of this chapter that the maternal education is here a demand that the daughter live up to her own portrait moral as painted for her by her mother. While it is true that "in choosing the portrait, Lafayette distinguishes herself from official historians and joins the ranks of her female contemporaries," in fact the full-length portrait moral is left out of *La Princesse de Clèves*, and replaced by a series of miniature descriptive portraits.[4] The longer passage that according to the conventions of Scudéry's romances should have been a portrait moral of the princess, is in fact a portrait of *her mother's education* of her (pp. 40–41).[5] Lafayette is thus distinguishing herself from earlier women's historical romances as well as from official historians. While the portrait moral is missing, the mother's idealized portrait-as-education becomes literalized in the text as the miniature the princess gives to the prince of Clèves, which she later has retouched and allows to be stolen by the duc de Nemours (p. 92).

The shift from the portrait moral of the précieuses to Lafayette's miniature of an education characterized by what the narrator calls "painting pictures," literalized as it is in the miniature portrait of the princess, emphasizes the particular character of Mlle de Chartres's education as one that is transmitted through a feminized form of example figured as maternal inheritance: the miniature portrait specifically forms part of the jewels, the movable property passed from mother to daughter, while full-length portraits would grace the walls of a patrimonial estate.

Textually the miniature portrait, as opposed to a full-length portrait moral, concretizes the intersection in the novel between the novella genre, with its emphasis on example, and the romance genre, with its emphasis on inheritance. In romance, portraits often function as a heritable double representation: they represent wealth through their own exchange value as movable property, and they also represent legitimacy of descent. The portrait's combined resemblance to and possession by the romance hero or heroine thus stands as both evidence and substance of legitimacy. Here the portrait as inherited wealth and evidence of legitimacy is specifically linked to the heroine's other inherited jewels by its being framed within a jeweled case. Together the jewels form a dowry, which represents, in legal terms, the daughter's renunciation of her claim to her own family's name and real property, and thus the need for a match.[6] For the paternal name it leaves out, the mother's legacy substitutes an education in that virtue whose purpose is to ensure that the daughter will take on and uphold the "proper" name, or rather the designated patronym, which the mother cannot transmit, and which can therefore never be proper either to her or to her daughter.[7] By the mobility that allows it to be sent, the portrait literalizes this problem of the appropriation by the widowed mother of the patriarchal power of destination, and of the nature of a daughter's inheritance when what she receives is always destined to be sent elsewhere.

In both its aspects, then, as wealth and mark of legitimacy, the value of the maternal inheritance is incomplete as received by her daughter: it leaves a lack, a space of reception that demands the fulfilling recognition of a "match." But the missing match is not, fundamentally, anything Mlle de Chartres could receive from a marriage partner, not even a suitable name. It is rather her own recognition of her paternal name, signified by her willingness to match it—and herself—with the name that her mother (as proxy for the dead father) designates. Therefore the required "match" can be found neither at the Italian jeweler's, where the princess meets the prince de Clèves, nor at the ball, where she meets the duc de Nemours. She must rather cut its facets from her self, by "living up" to the example that the designated name represents. This entails enclosing her life history within the frame formed by the name, *setting herself*—just as the matched set of jewels would be enclosed in a setting—as an example.[8]

The process of transmission by example, then, requires a complicity on the daughter's part that exceeds simply passive reception. The retouching of the inherited miniature portrait, as a literalization of the princess's self-improving response to her mother's exemplary education, requires its being taken out of its jeweled case: it requires a certain freedom from the inherited frame, if only the freedom entailed in the act of compliance. This paradox of transmission from mother to daughter originates in what Kamuf calls "something left out of the mother's will," its fault: the absence of name and "real property" in female inheritance within a patrilineal system. Between generations of women nothing "real"—no ground, no legible filiation—can be directly passed on or received. The only transmission that is symbolically recognizable is that of the movable ornaments that will transmute the receiver into a hardened bit of the *éclat* that signifies the proper and legitimizes both the name and the ground a daughter cannot inherit. But the transmission of the movable can only be effected by moving the receiver to accept it, to put it on. The princess's own more perfect image, the second miniature commissioned by the dauphine (herself one of a series of mother-substitutes for the princess), *moves* the princess to continue the endless motion of perfecting the image of herself received from her mother, which she does by literally having it altered to resemble the improved appearance of the new miniature.[9] This motion literally necessitates the freeing of that image from the jeweled frame by an act of complicity that intends only to replace it, more perfect, in the same frame.

If there is something left out of the mother's will, however, there is also something left out of the daughter's. Complicity does not necessarily imply will; the princess cannot be assumed to possess a fully formed desire or will of her own that is repressed by her mother's manipulations. To make that assumption is to overlook the paradoxical nature of both example and inheritance as forms of transmission: in both cases, what is transmitted to the receiver at least partially forms the receiver's self. That complicity with the mother's will is the core of feminine virtue, not only here, but in later novels, and already in this novel virtue establishes individual identity even more than do name and social status.[10] The importance of virtue for identity is especially great for women, in relation to whom titles are more slippery signifiers than they are for men. It is not evident that the princess "wills" to comply, to perform the virtuous self-violence prescribed to her by her mother's ideal miniature portrait moral, when her compliance is already delineated in her mother's will.[11]

Improving the inherited portrait with the intention of sending it back to the dead mother's representatives (the prince de Clèves and the dauphine, as argued below) is the literalized gesture of paying the debt of maternal inheritance. Any legacy to a survivor establishes a debt to the dead, but the fact that maternal inheritance substitutes representation for the real—an exemplary image (or text) for real property—exaggerates the relationship of debt to the point where it becomes primary. Where the core of an inheritance is what it leaves out—that is, the demand for a match that must be fulfilled through the complicitous self-violence of living up to the ideal representation—that inheritance is nothing other than a debt that can never be fully satisfied. If the relation of indebtedness that informs all transmission by inheritance becomes the primary, defining feature of maternal inheritance, it is because that which is transmitted by the contiguity of filiation has been stripped of its materiality and reduced to representation, to resemblance itself. Whereas in romance and epic, resemblance between father and son provided the evidence of legitimacy that justified the transmission of real property, resemblance between mother and daughter here constitutes inheritance itself.[12] What is received, that for which a daughter is indebted, is a self cut off from those material bases of individual agency reserved to patrimony, for which maternal inheritance substitutes a representation that entails a space of reception: the freedom that demands the daughter's complicity in performing the self-violence of living up to the exemplary representation.

As the mother's legacy is reduced to representation, the match it demands can have no substantial existence. Thus neither Clèves nor Nemours can ever be the match, the noble name, or the jewel, as Peggy Kamuf reads it, left out of the maternal inheritance and demanded by it. In themselves, both of the men are flawed matches. Clèves fails the test of éclat, or brilliance, as Kamuf has shown, admiring it in the princess without possessing enough of his own to spark her desire. Nemours, on the other hand, appears to radiate too much and in all directions, so that the princess fears that in the economy of circulating desire, he may turn out to be more than a match for her. The princess's persistence in her refusal to take Nemours's name as a match and her consequent persistence in the name and title destined for her by her mother itself constitutes the match, the jewel left out of the mother's will.[13]

Kamuf's reflections on the name that Mme de Chartres destines for her daughter's match are helpful for understanding the function of that match (and its lack) as maternal inheritance: she hears in the name Clèves the verb *cliver*, to cleave, an intersection of the primal contrary senses of splitting, or severing, on the one hand, and on the other—now lost in French—adhesion, clinging, fidelity (*Fictions of Feminine Desire*, p. 91). Besides having lost in French its contrary sense of adhesion by the time the novel was written, *cliver* had already narrowed still further within the remaining sense of splitting: its usage had become specialized within the vocabulary of mineralogy and gemology. All of the literal senses listed for it by Littré involve the cutting of stones: the cleaving of minerals occurring in layers, like slate and mica; a smooth fissure in a stone; the cutting of gems into facets.[14] The name with which the princess is permanently matched thus bears a special relation to the gemstones for which she is seeking a match at the moment when she first meets the bearer of that name.

Clèves represents the flaw, the fissure that would ruin a gem's brilliance—and also a fault in a mineral layer, the very *précipice* that furnishes the other primary figure, besides the portrait, of Mlle de

Chartres's education. For it is upon the verge of this precipice that her dying mother balances the princess, reminding her that it is only through great efforts and great violence that she can hope to hold herself back and avoid "falling like other women." At the same time the match-name signifies the very act of violence that the mother teaches her daughter, the art of *clivage* that cuts the rough gemstone into a brilliant (p. 68; the figure of the precipice also reappears on pp. 125 and 137).[15] In the language of jewels, then, the specialized French usage *does* express contrary senses: of natural fault on the one hand and of perfection through art on the other. If Clèves is a flawed gem and thus an imperfect match for the princess by comparison with Nemours, he only resembles all the more the incomplete set of stones that constitute her maternal inheritance, making him in fact, according to the mother's will, the perfect match. Through his representation, by resemblance, of the fault into which the princess's mother warns her against falling, the prince will continue Mme de Chartres's maternal education, which can itself be seen as a *plan de clivage*, a plan for cutting a rough diamond of a daughter into a matchless woman. In the process of transmitting maternal inheritance, the mother herself is replaced by a representative who will repeat her ever-incomplete gesture: "painting pictures" of a fault or space of reception that invites the daughter to walk the line of its verge—or else fall into the fault it delineates.

Setting Examples: Maternal Destination

If the prince is the plan de clivage named by the mother to succeed her in the office of directing the princess's destiny, the mark of his legitimacy in that succession is his possession of the jeweled frame out of which the portrait is stolen.[16] The significance of this detail is emphasized and clarified by the prince's own joke on the subject; the theft is interpreted by all others present as a simple loss, an effect of chance (*par hasard*), since it makes no sense to them that anyone would steal the portrait without its case; as they see it, the jeweled frame alone can give the portrait value (p. 93). Chance, however, does not exist in *La Princesse de Clèves*. Although the novel has been defined as the genre of chance, while romance plots are directed by Providential design, this is one of the ways in which Lafayette plays with the generic differences she helped develop: the events of *La Princesse de Clèves* are never the effect of chance, always of destiny. One of the reasons the work has given so many critics, ever since its first publication, the impression of gemlike symmetry and clarity is that nothing is allowed to be interpreted by the reader as random, although the characters continually express their desire to do so. The text makes it clear that if an event or a piece of evidence appears to be an effect of chance, it is only because it is being misinterpreted, viewed through the wrong interpretive frame. That is why the search for the missing portrait is fruitless. The princess's husband understands this, alone of those present at the scene of the crime. A lover must have stolen the portrait, he jests uneasily, for only a lover's desire could substitute for the case in conferring value upon it. The prince can see this because he regards the event from the unique double perspective of a husband who is also a lover, but even more because, as the mother's successor, he is also a husband who doubles as a mother.

If events in *La Princesse de Clèves* are destined rather than effects of chance, they are not destined by the Providence of romance, of God the Father—invoked no more here than is the goddess Fortune—but rather by maternal will. Fate here is modeled on maternal destination rather than on *providence* (which refers in earlier usage to patrimony).[17] If the paths taken by human lives are destined, they are destined to repeat examples, just as the miniature representation of the daughter is destined to be sent back to the mother (or her representative), repeatedly replaced into its "setting" in an effort to "live up" to the debt of maternal inheritance. If it does not arrive at that destination, which is also its origin, it can only have been deliberately diverted from its path.

The series of miniatures that the queen of Scots causes to be painted in order to send them back to her mother (which includes the new miniature of the princess), reflecting as it does the novella as a series of exempla related by a queen to an audience of ladies-in-waiting, frames that narrative relation within a gesture of mother-daughter transmission. The fact that this particular figure of narrative transaction, which I am calling "maternal destination," recurs so persistently in the eighteenth century, in the numerous epistolary novels and fictionalized conduct literature in which a daughter separated from her "maternal home" by a recent marriage writes a series of letters to her mother and receives the mother's narration and advice (exactly the same elements, example and precept, that make up the figure of example), situates *La Princesse de Clèves* as the point of transformation between the novella of Marguerite de Navarre and the eighteenth-century epistolary novels of women's correspondence.

The Historical Setting: The Frame of Interpretation

The dauphine's series of miniatures is painted in order to be sent back, not to the representative of the dead mother (as in the case of the princess's inherited portrait), but to the mother as representative of a proleptically dead daughter, of the daughter's own death. Marie Stuart fears her own resemblance to her mother, anxious that the likeness in appearance will entail upon her an inevitable repetition of her mother's unhappy history: "They say I am like my mother, but I fear that I shall resemble her only [*aussi*] in her ill-fated lot; and whatever good fortune may seem to be on my horizon now, I do not think that I shall ever enjoy such" (Cobb, p. 17; Adam, p. 49). The curious effect of the historical setting Lafayette has wrought around the characters she portrays is that it gives this statement the force of prophetic doom, since the reader knows Mary Stuart's unfortunate destiny in advance. This appearance of fatality, the lack of free play either of chance or of individual will in determining the course of private or public history, is by no means peculiar in this novel to the queen of Scots. It pursues most of the historical characters, great and small, female and male, in innumerable moments where the ultimate fate of a particular personage is related long before her story is over, and even sometimes upon the character's first entrance into the text (e.g., pp. 36, 46, 47, 96, 118). Each of these characters is suddenly transformed, in such moments, into a ghostly apparition, fixed lifeless to the reader's view in a historical frame and glimpsed there, for an uncanny moment, from beyond the grave.

Again, the closure of the proleptically complete (and because complete, exemplary) frame of historical narrative operates not on the eschatological model of divine Providence, but on the model of maternal inheritance—that is, on the speculative principle of resemblance to the mother. Destination is collapsed and reversed as speculation, rather than reached through the detours of plot. By repeating her mother's unfortunate destiny even before the narrative of her own life can properly end, the queen dauphine herself comes to resemble a miscarriage, especially in the old sense of the word: a miscarried letter, a miniature diverted from its destination. The difference between the princess's double return of her two miniatures to the two representatives of her dead mother, on the one hand, and the dauphine's sending of the series back to her mother, on the other, is that the latter sends her mother portraits of the ladies of the court, but not of herself. As a miscarriage, the dauphine is less a portrait than a blank center around which the frame of her serial missive organizes itself. She cannot send her own, improved portrait back to her mother, as the princess does, because she is herself a miscarriage, which is to say that the missing portrait of the dauphine has already been replaced, or rather preempted, by another series of portraits, narrative and painted: the twin examples of her mother's unfortunate destiny and of Elizabeth, the heiress Mary might herself have become had her mother's destiny been more fortunate (i.e., had the prior engagement to Henry VIII been honored, [p. 48]). The miscarriage of the mother's destiny literally opens a space that is filled by Elizabeth, who, as the dauphine herself announces, "has been held up to me as an example all my life" (Cobb, p. 61; Adam, p. 89). The history of the daughter's efforts to imitate that example effaces her from the center of its frame before the reader's very eyes, as the exemplary Elizabeth, whose glorious destiny has been to succeed, though a woman, to patrilineal powers, frames her emulative cousin as a mere usurper.

The dauphine's attempt to follow the example held up for her by her mother does not result in an exact repetition of the mother's unfortunate destiny, because, as in the heroine's case, the example the mother holds up for her daughter is not herself, but her desire. The daughter's imitation magnifies the misfortune of her mother's destiny to the degree that she attempts to improve upon it. Set in her historical frame, the dauphine *more than* resembles her mother in her unhappy destiny, and the excess of her misfortune, the interest she pays on her specular resemblance to her mother in her attempt to imitate the example the mother holds out, is the resemblance of her destiny, not to Elizabeth's, but to that of the mother whom, in Mary's imagination, Elizabeth must resemble: "And if she at all resembles her mother, Anne Boleyn, she must be very charming" (Cobb, p. 61; Adam, p. 89). *That* maternal example is the one the dauphine's history ultimately resembles, and it is the one she, in turn, standing in for the princess's mother, passes on to the heroine. It forms the last in the incomplete set of exempla the princess must not imitate.

The history of Anne Boleyn, like that of Diane de Poitiers, is explicitly framed as maternal example, in all its associations with portraiture, inheritance, and instruction. Introduced by way of the mise-en-abyme of maternal examples and resemblances just delineated, it is closed by an interruption of the narrator's voice, announcing that "all the ladies who were present at this narration of events by Madame la Dauphine thanked her for informing them so well" ("de les avoir si bien *instruites*"), and then, abruptly, that "the queen-dauphine was having made some miniature portraits of all the court beauties to send to the queen her mother" (Cobb, p. 64; Adam, p. 91). The intervention sets this history in the same exemplary frame with those of Diane and Mme de Tournon: like the others, the story of Anne Boleyn is offered as "instruction" by a mother-figure, whose gesture of sending back portraits to her own mother models instructions about how such exemplary instruction should be received. The story itself reproduces the mise-en-abyme structure of maternal example, with its allusion to the novellas of Marguerite de Navarre, who in turn appears as a figure within the history. Marguerite is thus framed in exactly the same relation to Anne Boleyn as the one assumed by the queen dauphine in relation to the princess when she becomes her friend and mentor upon her arrival at court. The dauphine also offers the same reason for telling her story as that given by Mme de Chartres and the prince de Clèves before her: to set the princess straight, to disprove a false impression she had received.

Anne Boleyn's portrait, like that of Diane de Poitiers, depicts an ambitious woman who plots to gain power by controlling a king through his passion. But whereas Diane de Poitiers openly entertains his rivals and still rules Henri II, Anne Boleyn is portrayed as a faithful wife to the English Henry, who is nevertheless beheaded by him on false charges of adultery and incest. Viewed from the princess's perspective—from within the narrative time frame—these two examples seem so far opposed as to become mirror images of each other. This apparent opposition, however, serves to emphasize the disparity between that perspective and the reader's, that of historical time. For just as the reader knows Mary Stuart's fate in advance, she also knows Diane's, whose ultimate fall, like Mary's, perfectly exemplifies the Aristotelian precept that informed the Renaissance conception of example: that no man may be judged happy (i.e., virtuous, in the terms of the *Nicomachaean Ethics*) until he is dead.[18]

The three historical portraits, of Diane de Poitiers, Mary Stuart, and Anne Boleyn, form a well-matched set, a coherent series of examples, not only within the Aristotelian precept, but also within the one famously enunciated by Mme de Chartres: "If you judge by appearances at court, you will always be easily deceived, for appearances seldom lead to the truth" (Cobb, p. 25; Adam, p. 56).[19] These are examples, not simply of the instability of appearances, but more specifically of the power of authoritative readers over the interpretation of those unstable appearances.[20] They show the princess that it is ultimately impossible for women to control the meaning even of their own appearance. Whoever has the greatest social and legal authority among those concerned will determine the meaning of appearances through control over the social frame of interpretation. In a patrilineal frame of reference, the question of truth is a question of legitimacy, and that comes down finally to the question of feminine virtue. Since any authority possessed by women, even (indeed especially) that of aristocratic women, derives from and is less than that of a male relation, the truth of their virtue will always be determined, in the end, by the interpretation of a male relation. The only woman who seems miraculously to have escaped this law is also the only one who has escaped the law of the husband (or father), the *alieni juris* of Roman law by which a wife or daughter is subsumed under the legal person of the male relation: the *widowed* Diane de Poitiers, who retains her widowed status and relates to men only outside the law.[21] While it is true that aristocratic French society of the time to a certain extent condoned transgressions of marital fidelity even by women, it did so only to the extent that the appearance of legitimacy—its *vraisemblance*—was preserved, and the recognition of that legitimacy was controlled by a hierarchy of social and legal authority in which women were always ultimately secondary, no matter what their rank. Thus, after the theft of the portrait, the lover, Nemours, has both the portrait and the princess's love, but her husband still possesses the case—the frame, which alone gives her value and preserves, as long as it proves her virtue, her legitimate place in society. The princess herself controls neither.

While the historical frame turns life histories into examples of the precept that "no man can be judged happy until he is dead," the narrative frame makes them examples of another, correlative precept: that no woman can be judged virtuous except as someone more powerful—ultimately a man, ultimately the king—determines. Even before Diane's fall is narrated in the last pages of the novel, the juxtaposition of her history with Anne Boleyn's within the narrative time frame, as they are presented successively to the princess as reader by her mother and mother-substitute, makes it clear that Diane's apparently unshakable power is just as tenuous as Anne's, because just as dependent upon public recognition, as that is determined according to the organization of power within the feudal hierarchy that culminates in the king. The historical frame, however, is set around the entire social hierarchy, so that even the king's supreme power over the frame of interpretation of history is subordinated to the extrahistorical, or fictional, perspective thus created, that of narrator and reader.

The king passes the judgment of implausibility on the narrative of his own death as foretold to him, and in doing so determines the public view of the matter.[22] The reader alone remains free from that determination, possessing, like the prince de Clèves at the scene of the theft, a unique perspective. From that perspective, the reader sees that the king determines the public interpretation of his life history in vain, or at least only temporarily, until the moment he ceases to be king; in the same instant, the narrator reveals that his destiny, too, is shaped by a debt of inheritance that remains a more powerful force even than the apparently absolute agency, the power over the frames of interpretation, that royal inheritance confers. For his fate is to *resemble his father in destiny*, even though he attempts to use his inherited power to dismiss that very resemblance (a killing resemblance in the most literal sense) as implausible:

> I don't know what will happen to Messieurs de Guise and D'Escars, but it doesn't seem very likely I am going to be killed in a duel. The King of Spain and I have just concluded the peace, and had we not come to any peaceful terms, I doubt very much that we would have resorted to a duel! Or, that I should have challenged him *as my father the king challenged Charles V to a combat of honor*. (Cobb, p. 59; emphasis mine)

Historical truth is implausible because it eludes the social authority that determines the meaning of plausibility. The resemblance of the king's destiny to his father's is, of course, also recognizable in his having the same mistress, and it is this very debt of resemblance, once its plot is complete, that topples her in turn.

The historical setting, then, frames apparently random and contradictory examples so that they form a coherent series *for the reader* that fits the classical maxims of exemplarity. Even in the midst of the narrative present, it continually pushes the reader outside the historical frame with which it circumscribes that present and its completed lives, and thus places her in the apparent position of ultimate judge of the meaning of history (although that judgment, of course, is manipulated through the selection and presentation—through framing—of history). This placement of the reader outside the historical time frame while within the narrative one seems to elevate her authority to judge its meaning even above that of the most powerful reader *within* the historical frame: the king.

The agreement of the assembled court with the king's judgment that astrology predicts the implausible and therefore the false is undermined by the *galanterie* to which Nemours turns his public assent. Turning to the princess, he whispers that it has been predicted that he would be made happy by the person for whom he would have the most violent and respectful passion, concluding with the prophetic remark, "*You may judge*, Madame, if I ought to believe in prophecies" (Cobb, p. 59; Adam, p. 88; my emphasis). The force of this remark, which in effect hands over privately to the princess the same power to determine the truth of narrative that he has just publicly ceded to the king, can be understood only when it is perceived through the novel's third level of framing: what I shall call the "fictional" level, because, like the reader's perspective, it remains outside both the historical setting and the social hierarchy that determines the norms of plausibility for the narrative present.

Beyond Historical Setting: The Fault of Framing Fictions

The examples of Diane de Poitiers and Anne Boleyn present a contrast for the princess from her perspective within the narrative time frame, from which the former appears open-ended and the latter complete; this contrast itself forms a contrast with the reader's perspective on the two lives, from which a resemblance appears through the closed frame of history. The third of the examples presented to the princess by the mother and her substitutes—this time by the prince de Clèves—represents yet a third relation to the double frame of narrative and historical time. In contrast to the prophetic jest with which Nemours offers her the authority to judge the meaning of his fate, the scene of the theft of the portrait, on which the prince has such a unique perspective, is introduced by a long dialogue between him and his wife, in which he paints a picture for her edification of the power of lovers over interpretive frames.

Mme de Tournon, the dead woman whose exemplary virtue the princess had always admired, is framed for her by her new husband as an example that proves that even a woman who has been able to fool everyone with what seemed like incontrovertible evidence of virtue may in reality be a consummate deceiver, no more virtuous than an exemplary harlot. The underlying "moral" (or precept) of the portrait of Mme de Tournon is that even the most plausible, the most consistent appearance of virtue a woman may achieve over the whole course of a completed life is not adequate proof that she is truly virtuous—at least when a husband is telling the story. This is where the distinction of gender becomes operative in exemplary virtue: to judge a man happy or virtuous, we have only to look at the facts recorded in the completed narrative of his public life; but since women's virtue is here already being defined in terms of her private conduct, its epistemology is not so clear. The effect of Mme de Tournon's status as a purely *fictional* character is that, while her life is already complete within the narrative time frame, as is Anne Boleyn's, it is a strictly *private* life that escapes the preemptive judgment of historical kings or "extrahistorical" readers. Yet it does not escape that of lovers and husbands.

The lesson that will ultimately be extracted by the princess from the set of exemplary histories passed down to her by her mother and mother-substitutes is about the crucial importance of interpretive frames, and of who controls them, for the epistemology of any history. Indeed, her own interpretation of that precept is what will allow her to elude becoming fixed in its frame as the match that would complete the symmetry of the set. To a series of examples consisting of, first, a woman's life that is complete in historical time but not in narrative time (Diane), second, one that is complete within both time frames (Anne Boleyn), and thirdly, one that exists outside historical time but is complete within the narrative (Mme de Tournon), the princess might add her own history, which at the moment she has received these narratives exists outside historical time and is not yet complete within the fictional narrative. That narrative's lack of foreclosure in contrast to the others, its fictional open-endedness, is the formal expression of the "space of reception," which opens up the possibility of escaping the deadly resemblance that is the speculative debt of inheritance.

The fictionality of the central character allows for a series of tergiversations in the maternal plot, detours precluded by the effect of history, which, like the unhappy maternal destiny, collapses the end into the beginning. These tergiversations make for the princess's divergence from the mirrorlike doublings that structure the whole novel. They allow for the crucial difference between the gesture of transmission that the narrative constructs internally on the model of maternal inheritance, and the final gesture of transmission by which the princess's own fictional history is conveyed to the reader.

They correspond to the paradoxical openness of maternal speculation itself.

The brief space of freedom from the frame, that momentary break and shift in the direction of will, is enough for the unframed portrait to be diverted from its proper destination. But because agency is attached to the patrimony that is left out of the mother's will, the space of freedom is for the daughter always a space of complicity; the will must come from without. The prince retains possession of the jeweled frame that designates him as the mother's successor, but another man controls a larger frame at court: the curtains framing the portrait's circulation as spectacle (even circulation, which like narrative itself consists of trajectory, exchange, relation, is rendered "visible" in this novel through a gesture of framing). By virtue of his ability to manipulate that larger frame, Nemours is able to manipulate the princess's complicity, turning it to the miscarriage of her portrait and away from the complicitous act of "sending back" demanded by the proper addressee.

Nemours breaks the stasis of repetition represented by the series of miniatures in the act of substituting himself for the legitimate *destinataire*, and thereby redirects the plot of maternal inheritance. He first replaces Clèves as addressee of the retouched miniature, usurping the position of the mother through her legitimate masculine successor. This detour is permanent, in that the princess will never be able to shift her complicity back to her husband. She is no longer capable of complying with the plan de clivage, as is demonstrated when she must finally ask her husband to take her to the country, away from the dangers of temptation and detection. She still has the distrust of self inculcated by her maternal education, but she no longer has the will to inflict its violence on herself. Even the will to complicity must now come from without.

The first slippage of the princess from the jeweled frame that makes her the exemplary woman is what makes possible, in turn, her participation in the next substitution of Nemours for a legitimate destinataire, when he stands in for the legitimate destinataire of the misplaced letter. In the episode of the letter, Nemours is substituted for the vidame de Chartres as the letter's addressee, according to the story whose circulation so injures the princess, and that he and she will afterwards collaborate to make plausible. But what is much more crucial for the princess's plot is that she causes Nemours to be doubly substituted for the letter's legitimate destinataire—in fact as well as in their own fictional account—when she gives the letter to him instead of *sending it back* to the queen dauphine. By deliberately diverting the letter from her dead mother's representative (the queen dauphine) to Nemours, the princess for the first time turns the tables (or frames) on him, placing him in the perspective of the series of substitutions of which he, too, forms but one frame.

The entire interest of the court in the letter is in the attempt to read the illegitimacy of the relation it represents. It is because it represents an illegitimate relation that the letter fails to name its own destinataire, and for the same reason, almost any name might plausibly fill the blank. As the opening pages of the novel have shown, history is really written through "illegitimate" affiliations, such as the one that links Diane to the king. In the very process of its attempt to determine the identity of the addressee—that is, to interpret the letter as evidence of an illicit liaison—the court replaces the particular addressee it wishes to expose with its own series of addressees. Each displaces the last in a manner that reflects the hierarchy of power at court and also bears out the narrator's opening statements about the importance of women and of love to the course of politics. Once the privately designated addressee (the vidame) drops the letter, his place as receiver is first usurped by the queen dauphine. The queen then insists that the queen dauphine deliver it to *her*. Thus the same mother substitute who commissions the princess's new miniature in order to send it back to her own mother *also* commissions the fictional letter from the princess and Nemours, in order to send it back, in turn, to her mother-in-law.[23] The dauphine enforces her demand for the counterfeit letter by a moral justification for her claim that is in fact authorized only by her rank within the court hierarchy. In blaming the princess for allowing the original to go back to its author, the dauphine implies a feudal ethic of destination, in which the most powerful reader displaces both the letter's private addressee and its author as the legitimate destinataire of the letter. This is the morality according to which the princess is found guilty of her only fault. She actively gives the letter to Nemours—this time not merely passively failing to prevent him from taking it, as with the miniature. She freely gives him the letter upon his simple demand, thus entering into a compact with him to deceive the dauphine, to violate the latter's claim to the place of legitimate destinataire by not sending the letter back to her. She does this not merely willingly, but with pleasure: "Mme de Clèves, on the pretext she was acting in her uncle's interest, agreed most willingly [*avec plaisir*] to keep all that Monsieur de Nemours had said a secret" (Cobb, p. 89; Adam, p. 115).

The princess's response to the accusation of fault is instructive. She defends herself by saying, "It's not my fault" and displacing the blame onto her husband (p. 116). Having placed herself thus between her mother's double ghosts—her husband and the queen dauphine—the princess plays one off against the other, defending herself from the fault of not sending back the letter by declining to own the fault, sending the fault back to the legitimate bearer of its name.[24] She ghostwrites the fictional letter with Nemours and enjoys her greatest pleasure together with him under the authorization of atonement for the fault towards the dauphine, but also in order to cover up her lie, the fault towards her husband. The letter is ineffectual either as penance or as deception, however, because in the act of writing it, the princess continues to let her own desire get in the way of her fulfillment of the demand for an exact, mirrorlike reproduction of the text that has become the mother's (i.e., the dauphine's): "Madame de Clèves was not bored either, and she too forgot the interests of her uncle" (Cobb, p. 92; Adam, p. 118; note also that it was originally addressed to the one character who still does bear her mother's name).

The unique fault in the princess is not as minor as it may at first appear, although it appears to have gone unremarked. The episode of the miscarried letter ends with one of those moments in which the narrative future is suddenly set before the reader in the frame of past history. Before the narrative of the princess's present history can continue, the reader's attention is drawn to the ultimate consequences of her carelessness in forgery: both her uncle and her substitutive mother will be ruined, and the queen's hatred will be so inflamed against the dauphine in particular that she will drive her into exile from France (p. 118). This moment of historical prolepsis resonates with the earlier one discussed above, in which the reader was presented with the ultimate consequences for the dauphine of this exile. The *faute* for which the dauphine insists upon blaming the princess alone, then, turns out to be none other than that of causing her own death, and hence metaphorically—that is, by a figure of resemblance and substitution—it is the fault of responsibility for the death of the mother.

The threat of responsibility for the mother's death has not gone unremarked by other critics of *La Princesse de Clèves*; clearly what Marianne Hirsch has called the "death-warrant passed on to the daughter by her mother," which can be located in Mme de Chartres's pronouncement that she would be glad to be dead if her daughter were ever to "fall like other women," also places the princess continually under the threat of the same fault, and her husband's dying words redouble it.[25] It is because she lives haunted by that threat and acts under its law that the princess has to reject Nemours's later legitimate offers; in fact she attempts to preserve herself from the fault of her husband's death by passing off the blame once again, this time onto her lover: "It is only too true you were the cause of his death; suspicions which your indiscreet behavior gave him cost him his life just as much as if you had killed him with your own hands" (Cobb, p. 153; Adam, p. 172). The paradox and the irony of the princess's final refusal of Nemours on these grounds is that, as we have seen in her deliberate lie to the queen dauphine—and parallel passing off of the blame—the princess by then is already in the fault and has already herself caused the substitutive mother's death. Her continued attempts to avoid falling over the precipice of this fault already occur within the fault, and must be read through its framing verge.

The princess's final refusal of Nemours represents the two sides of her paradoxical maternal legacy. On the one hand, she is prevented from expressing or acting on desire by the ghosts of her mother and husband ("'Ah! Madame,' Monsieur de Nemours said impatiently, 'what is this *phantom* of duty [*fantôme de devoir*] that blocks my happiness?" [Cobb, p. 153; Adam, p. 172; emphasis mine]). On the other hand, without committing the fault of enacting desire, she has nevertheless already suffered the threatened double punishment for doing so: both the mother's death and the experience of Nemours's betrayal, which she feels even though he is able to clear himself of the miscarried letter's authorship. The lesson of that fictional experience has been impressed on her mind so that it proleptically transforms the future eventuality that the princess herself judges to be the most plausible one—his infidelity—into an event as immutable and irrevocable as if it belonged to the historical past (pp. 119, 174). She has already suffered Nemours's betrayal metaphorically—through the substitution of one person or event for another—just as she has already metaphorically committed the fault of causing the mother's death. In each case the figurative reality of the fault obviates and prevents its literal realization. In a world where representation is substituted for reality, metaphor—or, to put it another way, fiction—is enough. Through her decision to read her fictional experience of betrayal as historical truth, the princess is able to immobilize Nemours as an effective agent, preventing him from realizing his own will by arrogating to herself through the discourse of vraisemblance the absolute power of the well-placed reader over the text.[26]

In determining for herself the meaning of the miscarried letter—by passing judgment on Nemours's fidelity as something *invraisemblable*—the princess demonstrates that she has at last learned the lesson that the mother and her substitutes have been trying to teach her from the beginning of the novel. She does so by framing all their offered examples with the maternal precept: "If you judge by appearances in this place, you will often be deceived."[27] As we saw in each of the exemplary tales told to the princess, of Diane de Poitiers, of Mme de Tournon, and of Anne Boleyn, judgment is made not *by* appearances but *of* appearances, through an exercise of arbitrary power over interpretive frames available only to the most powerful of the persons concerned. The force of her arrogation of this power is emphasized by the parallelism of her interpretive act with that of the most powerful person concerned with the miscarried letter: the queen. Without being able to prove that the miscarried letter is in fact addressed to the vidame, the queen nevertheless decides to believe that it is, and the fate of all involved is determined in consequence of that decision. Even though Nemours is actually able to prove to the princess that the letter was not addressed to him, she exercises an even more arbitrarily powerful decision than the queen's in judging him guilty, not in actuality, but in plausibility—in vraisemblance—and in determining the rest of their romance plot according to that judgment.

Both John Lyons and Harriet Stone argue that the mother's examples belie her precept—"everything, in short, is much as it seems," and that the implausible real triumphs in the novel over the rule of verisimilitude.[28] I argue below that the princess does invent a new logic of the implausible and therefore true, but she does so successfully because and to the extent that she is able, not to disprove or abandon her mother's precept, but to turn it to her own ends. Once the princess learns that "the real" is what one is able to make others believe and recognize as the truth, she is able to make her mother's precept triumph over the "real" in any more conventional sense. To put it another way, once the daughter learns to enforce by her own fiat the reality of her mother's precept, as she does when she decides that Nemours's fidelity cannot be real, even though to all appearances it is, her act of judging according to the norm of plausibility (which would rule out his fidelity as implausible) becomes itself even more implausible than the implausible fact of Nemours's fidelity.

By the midpoint of the novel, the princess appears to have used her maternal inheritance and the space of reception left her within its structure of transmission to negotiate herself into that most implausible state of womanhood, self-destination, which by definition can be received neither through the love of men nor through the example of women. It is important that the princess's judgment here is in no way dependent upon or learned from the example of the queen's decision; immediately after forging the letter with Nemours, the princess, left alone to reflect, recognizes the implausibility of Nemours's constancy and decides to leave for Coulommiers, without waiting to inform herself of the queen's response to their efforts (p. 119). She goes to Coulommiers to perfect herself, not in imitation of the miniature inherited from her mother, but in her own newfound mastery of the gaze, in the possession of the jeweled and magical frames that had been left out of her maternal inheritance. She leaves because she can only exercise her newfound control over the frames of recognition *in private*; her position in the feudal hierarchy remains such that she cannot directly control anyone's recognition but her own—except *through* the control of her own. Her bid to control the publicly recognized interpretation of the narrative of her own life must therefore be read within the framework of the feudal relations she cannot alter.

Narrative Excess

Although the princess makes her famous avowal because she wants control over a place she can keep to herself—from which she can exclude the interpretive gaze of the court, which will always remain beyond her control—her speech act in fact deliberately reconfirms her feudal subordination to her husband, including her acceptance of the feudal wife's traditional responsibilities and her renunciation of male property rights.[29] It emphasizes the nature of the relation between husband and wife under feudal law, in which the wife is defined as her husband's vassal.[30] The princess is renewing her feudal vow of fealty, which for a wife was a promise of reproductive, rather than military service, and especially of reproductive *fidelity*. It is the guarantee of her function in reproducing the patrilineage. In exchange for labor and fidelity, the wife did not receive a heritable estate (although medieval law did tend to allow much greater possibility for women to own land in their own right than existed by the seventeenth century), but received access to and use of the estate. Although such usufruct might often amount in effect to sole control and management when a husband went off—as does the princess's—to fulfill his own feudal obligations, it is not the same as possession, because it does not include rights of inheritance or transmission.[31] The princess's words emphasize her offer of fidelity, rather than a claim to enter the line of inheritance: "However dangerous the course I am taking may be, I take it with joy in order to preserve myself worthy to be yours."[32]

It is clear from the text, nevertheless, that an avowal like the princess's has never been made, which means that somehow it is at the same time standard and unique—that is, exemplary. The standard wife's *aveu* is one that pledges fidelity through an acceptance of the destination of her desire in accordance with the transmission of property—that is, through a denial of female desire and hence of female self-destination. The princess's version is unique because it pledges and proves the same fidelity by actually confessing the "guilt" of female desire, thus playing on both the new and the old senses of the word *aveu* as identified by DeJean: vow of fealty and confession of guilt. But the princess is also playing on two further meanings of the word *aveu*: "evidence" (in the sense of testimony, witness, confession) and "recognition" (in the sense of acknowledging, "owning").[33] For what she is changing here is not the nature of the relation between husband and wife, but rather the nature of the evidence that will be recognized as proof of wifely fealty. The traditional evidence, which the prince demands, is that of vraisemblance—the *public appearance* of fidelity (through her regular and modest appearance at court functions).[34] She, confessing herself incapable of the appearance, although capable of the fact of reproductive fidelity, demands that the free offer of her *private narration* be acceptable as evidence instead of the constrained control in public over her own gaze and expression, and that it even be preferred by virtue of its very implausibility. Her aveu is standard in that it is a recognition of her own place(lessness) in the feudal hierarchy, but unique in that it offers as evidence of her fidelity to her feudal lord only an open and incomplete narrative, by way of refusing the name and portrait he demands for the completion of a "plausible" narrative.

The stakes in the struggle over the nature of acceptable evidence of female fidelity are even greater than the heritable real property, because the power to determine what evidence proves fidelity is the power to determine *recognition*, which seals the legitimacy of all forms of transmission.[35] As a result of the princess's aveu, the evidence of the wife's sexual fidelity, of the husband's exclusive possession, and hence of the legitimacy and legibility of the patrilineage itself, is no longer going to be located in the possession of the portrait in its jeweled frame, as it was according to the mother's will.

Clèves demands both the "whole truth" (including the name of her lover) and the evidence to prove that truth (an accounting for the missing portrait, "qui m'appartenait si légitimement"). Clèves brings in the illegitimate circulation of the princess's portrait as evidence of the falsity of her narration, as he will bring in later, in a similar way, the illegitimate circulation of the narrative of her aveu. His wife successfully denies him both, demanding his recognition (*aveu*) of her unforced confession (*aveu*) as sufficient evidence (*aveu*) of her fidelity to her vows (*aveux*; Adam, p. 124). In doing so, she establishes that the evidence both of fidelity in narration and of fidelity in the feudal relation between husband and wife—that is, feminine virtue—will no longer be determined by fidelity to the standards of vraisemblance, which is to say, by *resemblance* to a normative model. Rather it will lie in what the princess refers to as *force*: the force to exceed the normative narrative demand that legislates the implausibility of her own act of narration (pp. 122–23).[36] For the only way to get free of such a demand without violating it is to exceed it. The princess is able to do so because of the instability inherent in the notion of verisimilitude, an instability derived from the normative figure that precedes it historically: the example.

As Gérard Genette and Nancy Miller observe, the princess's actions appear implausible because they do not fit the maxims of her sociolect.[37] This remark especially interests me because to speak of "maxims" is to speak of exemplarity: one definitive characteristic of example is that it illustrates a maxim, or precept, which can be said to fit it like a frame. But like the paradoxical figure of example, the princess's feudal pledge is both standard and unique: it *does* fit the maxims of its sociolect as an expression of wifely fidelity, yet is at the same time a unique instance.[38] A second paradox of exemplarity is that an example must be complete, perfect, and without fault, and yet the evidence of that perfection, the exemplary life as a series of acts, can only be given in narrative, whose temporality and detours dangerously admit faults and contradictions. Timothy Hampton argues that the tension between two humanist impulses—to unfold the narrative of the historical exemplar's life, and to close that narrative within the fixed frame of exemplarity, the static completion of which is signified in the name and emblematized in the portrait—led to such anxiety in the late Renaissance that it drove authors either to insist too much upon closure and the flawless stability of the exemplar or to flee the rhetoric of exemplarity altogether.[39] The princess's aveu takes advantage of this flaw or fissure in exemplarity and its corollary, verisimilitude, the stability of which is similarly undermined by the tension between truth (the unique) and plausibility (the standard). She uses that fault to escape the standard altogether, to elude the normative demand of example and verisimilitude, which would require her to resemble the fixed model represented in the name and portrait destined for her by her mother.

What is unique about the aveu is that with it the princess exceeds the demand of excess: she exceeds the plausible and offers the true, exceeds the exemplary to become unexampled and inimitable. She does this by refusing to "pay the interest" on her received name and portrait, that is, to send back what her husband is interested in, her portrait and her lover's name, which he sees as a threat to the legitimacy of his own. Instead, she demands credit: credit for the truth of an *incomplete* narrative that lacks evidence other than its own lack of completion and the openness, sincerity, and freedom with which it is offered. For the princess's private history, unlike any of the publicly historical lives that surround hers, is not yet, at the moment of the aveu, an Aristotelian *bio teleio*; it remains therefore to be seen, according to the logic of exemplarity, whether she can truly be judged virtuous and happy, or whether she will "fall like other women." But it is this very openness, this very fault of her desire and of the lack of completion of her narrative, that allows her to withhold her interest, keep from her husband that which interests him, and claim that it is in his own interest (*intérêt*) to give her the credit she demands (p. 135). She has passed, implausibly, from answering a demand with a silence upon which he can impose whatever interpretation he wishes to answering a demand with a demand, the demand that distinguishes fiction from history, but also the true from the plausible: she asks for a suspension of disbelief (p. 122). This is the turn that allows the princess to own (*avouer*) her desire; before this, silent as her portrait, she cannot be said properly to have her own desire. The turn by which she takes up speech and desire is also that by which she begins to construct her own narrative and her own state—to write her own plot—beyond exemplarity and beyond plausibility: in the fault, in the cleavage that both separates and connects, in the permeable boundary between public and private history.

A Plot of One's Own: The Heart of Glass

In leaving the princess in possession of the house at Coulommiers, the prince "leaves her liberty," he does not leave *her* the house. Both wife and husband speak of his "leaving her liberty" using the verb *laisser*, which suggests an inheritance, but what is heritable here is not the estate. The *liberté* he leaves her is that of retirement, the freedom to *se retirer*, as the princess puts it, or as the prince stresses, the liberty to set herself even narrower boundaries than he could ever prescribe for her (pp. 122, 128). The "inheritance" that is sued for and granted, then, is nothing other than the maternal inheritance of which the prince has become the bearer: the space of reception, the liberty to set herself within the house as another in the series of heritable frames that remain, like the jeweled miniature case, in his possession. The difference the princess seeks to achieve through her aveu is only the liberty to withdraw from the public setting so that she will not remain exposed ("demeure exposée au milieu de la cour" [Adam, p. 122; Cobb, p. 97]).

Coulommiers is not in fact "the estate that her husband inherited from his ancestors," but rather a new house, still under construction on the order of both spouses together ("une belle maison . . . qu'ils faisaient bâtir avec soin" [Adam, p. 120; Cobb, p. 95]).[40] Despite the princess's success in winning temporary sole use of this new construction, it soon becomes clear that the real estate as frame has its openings, as did the miniature's jeweled case. The princess's attempt to control the frame of the real estate fails because the division between public and private spheres upon which that attempt relies is itself a "new construction." Joan DeJean and Faith Beasley have recently argued correctly that Lafayette's fiction, as a version of "particular history" (as Beasley terms it), emphasizes the permeability of the division between those spheres (Beasley, p. 29, e.g.). Nevertheless, I argue below that the princess's strategy for establishing control over her own narrative by controlling the frames of is interpretation relies upon the text's investing her with a claim to sovereign authority analogous to that of the king within the state, and that this claim relies in turn upon *increasing* the separation of the private from the public sphere.

The fact that the division between public and private spheres remains so permeable brings us back to the earlier feudal reality, described in the opening pages of the novel, where the blurring of boundaries between private and public history is stressed. The first inconclusive skirmish in the princess's private battle to reinforce those boundaries leaves the hierarchies of the gaze intact and in force at Coulommiers just as much as at court. The same rules still apply in both places, despite her first effort to replace the frames of public recognition with a new kind of private evidence—narrative evidence—not subject to the external, public judgment made available by the metaphor of the gaze.[41] But the private estate, and even her own heart (*coeur*), turns out to be as much an open architectural space as is the court (*cour*).

The frame metaphor expresses the permeability of the boundaries it establishes; any frame, even a locket that encloses a miniature, can always be opened to expose the portrait it contains. Hence the private space where the princess wants to set herself apart is not so safely bounded off from the public exposure of the court as she believes. The princess is never seen inhabiting the château itself, but only the garden pavilion, *le pavillon de la forêt*, a jewellike miniature of the château with walls of glass that stands at the border of the property, framed by the edge of the woods (pp. 121–22, 153). This pavilion, then, is nothing other than a literalized *demeure exposée*, or exposed dwelling, the glass house from which the princess sought to escape by suing for the liberty to leave the court. At the same time, it is a literalized pun on "example," the original meaning of which is a clearing in the woods.[42] As discussed above, it is the aveu she makes in this chasm of exemplarity by which the princess first exceeds exemplarity. Just as she replaces the name and portrait demanded by her husband with an open-ended narration of her own desire, she replaces the singularity demanded by the maternal injunction to exemplarity with a singularity that exceeds exemplarity in its lack of a prior example: "The *singularity* [*singularité*] of such a confession—the like of which she had never heard [*dont elle ne trouvait point d'*exemple]—made her realize all the more its dangers" (Cobb, p. 101; Adam, p. 125; emphasis mine). What this "singularity" wins her, though, is not the house but the pavilion, and the pavilion is nothing other than the architecture of her own heart of glass.

"What path did he find to reach your heart?" the prince demands in desperation during the scene of the aveu ("Quel chemin a-t-il trouvé pour aller à votre coeur?" [Adam, p. 123]).[43] That path has in fact been traced for the reader quite legibly: only a few pages previously, we saw Nemours lost in the forest, searching for the way back to the nearby house of his sister. The path he finds seems at first to be the path of chance:

> At the mention of the word Coulommiers, without any reflection and with no plans [*dessein*], he galloped off at full speed in the direction that was indicated to him. He found himself deep in the forest, *wandering about haphazardly* [et se laissa conduire au hasard] on well-kept paths that he judged led to the château. At the end of one of these paths, he came upon a pavilion. (Cobb, pp. 95–96; Adam, p. 120)

Although he "allows himself to be led by chance," his choice to do so (and it is clearly a choice, albeit an unreflected one) is guided by his recognition of the name of the estate, and by his judgment that the paths are not random, but carefully cut to lead where he wishes to go. The wording of the last sentence quoted furthermore implies that *all* the paths he encounters in the forest lead to Coulommiers, so that there is no room for chance in his selection among them. The road of desire, guided by "ce mot de Coulommiers," male desire directed by the proper name of the real property, leads Nemours to his destination: a heart that turns out to be constructed like a glass house set in a clearing. Nemours's plot is directed here neither by chance nor by Providence, nor even by maternal destination, but by his own desire. Instead of following the "proper" path that would lead back to the *mère-coeur*—to his sister, Mme de

Mercoeur—Nemours follows the path determined by his own desire, but that path inevitably leads to the princess's heart *framed as example*, set in the clearing, in the space of reception left by the mother's will.

The path that leads the princess to the pavilion is a mirror image of the one followed by Nemours. Exactly like her lover, she sees herself as guided by chance, having no intentional plot or design (*dessein*): "She asked herself why she had taken such a chance [*hasard*], and found that she had entered into it [s'y était engagée] almost without any intention [*dessein*]."[44] The verb *s'engager*, while it can mean to enter into a contract, to engage for a debt (as she does with her husband), can also mean to enter upon a particular path, like the one that leads Nemours to the heart of glass.[45] And she soon realizes, like him, that this path is not random, but follows a certain necessity in its course and in its destination: "But when she came to realize that this remedy, violent though it might be, was the only one that could defend her against M. de Nemours, she found that she had no reason for regret, that she had not taken too great a risk at all" ("qu'elle n'avait point trop *hasardé*" [Adam, p. 125; emphasis mine]).[46] This last statement can only be true because of the strong will to self-destination of the princess's desire, against which physical separation is the only defense.[47] The hazard of *hasard* (chance) is really the danger of desire. Whereas the plot of Nemours's desire led him to the dead end of a glass heart, the plot of maternal destination leads the princess to the same place, the only one where she can possess the plot of her own desire. The princess's unique innovation on her mother's precept is to negotiate the maternal space of reception into a private plot in which she can possess her own desire. She does make the violent cut demanded by her mother's will, but in making it she is following the plot of her own desire rather than that of the plan de clivage.

Cutting an "example" or clearing out of the forest is an act of violence that results in the creation of an abyss. The heroine has reformed that abyss into a space of self-destination. She will retreat deeper and deeper into it during the remainder of her history, never again to emerge. What she has "removed" with her cut is not so much the heart or respect of her husband as his *plan*, the *mère-*

coeur; she has killed him as her mother's successor, since by reason of her having cut her own clearing, he no longer has a claim to possess the frame that will render her exemplary. With one stroke she has made herself a widow and carved herself a fault, in the depths of which she will now permanently dwell, having completed the double murder of both of the mother's substitutes, Clèves and the queen dauphine.

Yet Nemours, following the path plotted by his own desire, is able, not only to find his way to the walls of the princess's heart of glass, but actually to infiltrate it. The fact that desire names another as its destination is at the heart of the permeability between public and private space. Through that permeability, combined again with his greater title to agency in the public hierarchy of power, he is able once again to take advantage of her very liberty in order to steal the "portrait" enclosed in her narrative of desire. This time the equivalent of the portrait is his own name, information that the prince claims as legitimately his. He "steals" this information by eavesdropping, just as he once took advantage of the princess's space of reception to steal the portrait of her that belonged *si légitimement* to her husband. As in the earlier scene, Nemours purloins the *evidence* (this time the name of her lover instead of her portrait) that Clèves demands for the establishment of his legitimate possession. Whereas he stole the portrait when it was temporarily out of the jeweled case that would render the princess exemplary, Nemours now steals the name from the very heart of her newly constructed glass house. He dares to circulate the narrative, unlike the portrait; for in the portrait both the prince's legitimate possession and its violation would have been publicly legible, whereas in the narrative, the princess's would not. For the legitimacy of her new construction is recognized by no one but herself.[48]

The scene of the aveu was only the first battle over the determination of the evidence of fidelity; this is clear from the fact that Clèves questions his wife's veracity again after Nemours starts circulating the story, just as he had after the theft of the portrait. He continues to judge her by the standards of vraisemblance ("It is more plausible that the secret has leaked out through you than through me" [Cobb, p. 114; Adam, p. 136]). Indeed, the princess herself continues to judge both husband and lover by that same standard. Just as she determines the meaning of the misplaced letter on the basis of the *plausibility* of Nemours's infidelity, she becomes convinced on the same basis that her husband has betrayed her story, despite his own word to the contrary: "This likelihood [*vraisemblance*] forced her to conclude [la déterminait à croire] that her husband had abused the trust she had placed in him" (Cobb, p. 115; Adam, p. 137). For all of the characters, including the princess, in their efforts to judge of the truth of others' evidence, there is only a choice between the random and the plausible. The third type of explanation, the implausible and *therefore* true—the exemplary—does not occur even to the princess in reference to others. She has reserved it in effect as her own private property, a form of truth and proof that she knows to be unique, exemplary, and therefore all her own. "There could not be another story like mine. . . . No other person but me could have invented it" ("Le hasard ne peut l'avoir fait inventer; on ne l'a jamais imaginée et cette pensée n'est jamais tombée dans un autre esprit que le mien" [Adam, p. 136; Cobb, p. 113]).

The princess continues to invoke verisimilitude in reference to others' actions as well as to the circulation at court of her own story because the essential thing is to control the recognition of those others, all of whom, on their own "ground," which is to say within the court hierarchy, are by definition more powerful than she. What she must do to protect herself at court is to manipulate the recognition, ultimately, of the sovereign. For recognition, rather than walls or physical boundaries, is what defines the domain she creates for herself, just as it is in fact what determines the boundaries of the state. What the princess is fighting for is not an estate, but a state (a pun that works equally well in French), a state that, unlike an estate, lacks fixed or impermeable physical boundaries, but one whose sovereignty she can nevertheless force others to recognize.[49]

"Mistress of the State"

The first episode at Coulommiers was read as a battle between the princess and her husband over the nature of the evidence necessary to prove female fidelity and legitimize her position within the terms of their feudal relationship. Her victory was limited and complicated by the gaze of Nemours. The second episode set there is the inverse of the first: it is a battle between the princess and Nemours, another victory for her, this time limited and complicated by the gaze of her husband (through his representative, the spying manservant). By the time her husband's feudal obligations force him to leave her sole mistress of Coulommiers a second time, the process of its construction has advanced enough for her to have staked a claim to some actual territory. But like the territory of a state, its boundaries consist less in physical defenses than in the power to force others to recognize the claim.[50] The fact that the boundaries for which the princess is fighting are equivalent to the boundaries of a state, both in their nature and in their level of significance, is represented by the portrait at which Nemours finds the princess gazing when he gazes at her through the frame of the window.

Both Nemours and most recent critics focus on the fact that the princess is enraptured by his image, although Faith Beasley has emphasized the importance of the historical painting within which his portrait is miniaturized (p. 155).[51] The thought of the period placed history in a much higher position than portraiture in the hierarchy of painting, much as the legitimacy of the state was of greater significance than that of the individual or the estate. The painting of the siege of Metz has a double resonance, by which it brings together the register of the public, the masculine, the political, and the boundaries of the French nation-state with that of the private, the feminine, the amorous, and the domestic space created through use of the heritable estate. It renegotiates the relation between the two so as to create more sovereignty for the feminine position *within the private domain* than had existed in the aftermath of the princess's first battle. The painting does not simply recall public history as a general idea; it calls up specific intertextual references that underscore both the precariousness of female power in the public sphere and the sovereignty the princess enacts in her private domain at Coulommiers.[52]

The painting refers first to what was said about the siege of Metz at the beginning of the novel. It was an important victory for the

French king: "The emperor Charles V had seen his good fortune come to an end at the city of Metz, which he had besieged to no avail with all the forces of the Empire and of Spain."[53] The unsuccessful siege establishes the boundaries of the French nation against the threatened domination of an empire, and the sovereignty of the French king against that of an aggressor who has far greater "forces" at his disposal. But the importance of this particular moment of official history-making lies in the parallel set up between it and the "picture of love" that the princess is in the act of painting. For what Nemours "sees" when he tries to enter the window at Coulommiers is the end of the "good fortune" he had hoped for from his own aggressive "siege."

While the painting mimetically represents the siege of Metz, it also imitates another picture. The original is one of a series made on the order of Mme de Valentinois (Diane de Poitiers), representing "all the wonderful deeds of the king's reign" (Adam, p. 152).[54] Mme de Valentinois's act of ordering pictures painted reflects in turn the portraits ordered by the queen dauphine, which include the princess's miniature, just as these include a miniaturized portrait of Nemours; they reflect as well the "pictures of love" painted for the princess by her own mother, which include, first and foremost, the portrait of Mme de Valentinois herself (pp. 41, 91). But a crucial difference between Mme de Valentinois's pictures and the others is their destination. Instead of having them painted to send back to her mother or to educate her daughter, Mme de Valentinois destines these pictures to embellish a house she has built for herself at Anet—built on her sole authority, and not, like Coulommiers, together with a husband. As a widow whose sexual relationships remain outside the law, Mme de Valentinois is in a unique feminine position that allows her to construct and own her house entirely in her own right. By copying these pictures, the princess has found a mode of imitation neither prescribed nor proscribed by her mother's will. She thereby substitutes a radically different strategy of laying claim to an inheritance for the one transmitted by her mother or the earlier substitutes either designated by her mother (the prince) or related to her by a deadly resemblance (the dauphine).

Instead of trying to live up to the dauphine's miniature by imitating it, the princess now herself orders that paintings be copied. They remain imitations, but this new act of imitation circumvents the precept that framed her mother's pictures of love, the principle of her maternal education. While holding up to her daughter the narrative portrait of Mme de Valentinois, Mme de Chartres warned her not to imitate that picture. But whereas Mme de Chartres "painted pictures of love" (framing "particular" history as negative or monitory example), Mme de Valentinois paints pictures of war (appropriating the royal act of framing public history as example).[55] By copying the latter only, the princess *imitates Mme de Valentinois's mimetic action without imitating the negatively exemplary portrait of her* as painted by Mme de Chartres. What she imitates, therefore, is not the life of Mme de Valentinois but her historiographical act.[56] Through this act of purely representational imitation, the princess sets herself in a new relation of heirship to the most powerful woman at court, a woman to whom she is related neither by filiation, nor by marriage, nor by resemblance, nor by instruction. By thus setting herself outside recognized patrilineal kinship relations, she stands to gain a third kind of inheritance, distinct from either patrimony or its imitation, maternal inheritance. The plot of this self-destined inheritance is also a new construction and a new state of being, a third state whose sovereignty the princess is fighting to establish.

The princess establishes her new sovereign state in part, then, by establishing herself as heir, through an entirely nonpatriline mode of filiation, to the woman who has been called "mistress of the State," as well as of the king's person ("Elle le gouvernait avec un empire si absolu que l'on peut dire qu'elle était maîtresse de sa personne et de l'Etat" [Adam, p. 38; Cobb, p. 4]). By her act of imitation, the princess does not succeed her model as "mistress of the State," but *exceeds* her by becoming mistress of her own state. Her imitation of the historical paintings creates a mise-en-abyme that likens the princess's state to the French state, besieged but victorious and sovereign—while purifying the term *mistress* of its dependent sense through her resistance to Nemours's campaign to make her also "mistress" of his "person." Diane exerts a precarious and temporary (even though uniquely long-lasting) political power by governing a king, but the princess lays claim, by renouncing such personal political power, to an (e)state of her own. By giving up the kind of political influence historically available to aristocratic women in seventeenth-century France, the princess comes to resemble most—within the private domain she constructs—the only woman mentioned in the novel who rules literally and absolutely in her own right.[57] That woman, Queen Elizabeth of England, also doubles the princess as Nemours's other potential match. The implication is that the independent authority of this great historical queen, too, is preserved by the fact that her proposed marriage to Nemours never takes place.

That the princess imitates, not Diane's personal or political actions, but her artistic mimesis of public history—the fact that she is in effect quoting a quotation out of context and recontextualizing (reframing) it—is what protects her from the resemblance of direct imitation, and from that of direct inheritance. To quote Nancy Miller quoting Luce Irigaray, the princess may be engaging in a form of "'mimeticism,'" or "'play with mimesis,'" by which women are "'not simply reabsorbed in the [mimetic] function . . . [, but] *also remain elsewhere*'" (emphasis emphasized).[58] The princess's "'mimeticist'" act does not enable her to succeed Mme de Valentinois literally, in the represented world, as "mistress of the State." It allows her instead to escape the killing repetition of feminine example and become mistress of the new state in which she establishes herself as absolute sovereign by creating, not her own original mimetic ekphrases of public history, but "'playful imitations'" of the mimetic act by which Diane appropriates public history.

To have imitated the model of Diane de Poitiers directly would have meant imitating the life of a woman who in turn models herself, as the paintings copied from Anet indicate, upon the classical example of Dido. Dido was sole ruler of her own country—until she adorned the walls of her palace with ekphrases of the heroic masculine exploits that secured her realm, only to lose realm and life together with the loss of the depicted hero. Diane thus allusively and proleptically inscribes her own loss, doubly destined by the history of Henri II's death and by the traditional epic discourse about women and empire, upon the very monument to her apparent triumph. Much more ambitiously, the princess's mimeticist strategy allows her to "remain elsewhere," to appropriate the symbolic functions of public history in establishing the recognition of sovereignty while removing herself from that public sphere in which she might exert a precarious influence, but can never adequately control the frames of interpretation.

While the fictional décor of Anet recalls the literary model of Dido's palace, that of Coulommiers recalls its historical model in the château of that name, but with a difference. The real Coulommiers, as Faith Beasley notes (following Micheline Cuénin), was filled by Henriette de Clèves with "busts and statues of illustrious women from history and mythology" (Beasley, p. 226). In replacing such representations of *femmes illustres* with a pictorial history that also recalls the series of tapestries ordered by Louis XIV to "immortalize a succession of [his own] military victories," the fictional princess of Clèves marks her *avoidance* of female exemplars like Dido and Diane even as she imitates their acts of mimetic representation. Only as historian, never as heroine, can the princess effectively imitate Dido or Diane as "mistress of the State." She can exercise the sovereignty of the historian over the representation of events only by appropriating the publicly historical gesture of representing "acts of sovereignty" within the private confines of her own estate.[59]

The open boundaries of the state the princess seeks to establish are enforced by the same means as is the court hierarchy: control over the collective interpretive gaze—that is, over public recognition. Although Nemours's entry into the pavilion is physically impeded for a moment when his sash of office (*écharpe*) catches in the French sash, this does nothing more than sound the alert to the princess. She actually prevents him from entering by calling her reinforcements, the maidservants whose witnessing power is at her command. Here she is on her own ground, the gaze of its *monde* under her control, where for once she can use it to deny Nemours the independent space of privacy.

The novel provides a pre-text for the moment in which Nemours's sash, the sign of his rank, catches him in the window frame and thus threatens to expose him and his desire to the public view. For the incident repeats the faux pas that furnishes the pretext for the princess's return to Coulommiers in defiance of her husband's order that she fulfill her spousal and feudal obligations to him by attending the court ceremonies: "As a great many people crowded the room, she twisted her ankle in her dress and stumbled [elle *s'embarrassa* dans sa robe et fit un faux pas]. She used this as an excuse to leave the place in which she did not have the strength to stay [où elle n'avait pas la *force* de *demeurer*]" (Cobb, pp. 112–13, Adam, 135; emphasis mine). The repetition of the verb *s'embarrasser* in the two passages where Nemours and princess trip makes the faux pas of each the equivalent of the other. The dress that trips her up is the sign of her status at court, just as the sash is for Nemours, and it is the complement of the wearable wealth in jewels that is the substance of her maternal inheritance. The words *force* and *demeurer* in the earlier passage, which became charged with meanings specific to the princess's struggle for her own state just prior to it in the first episode at Coulommiers, underline the contrast between her state or status at court and that which she now occupies at the country estate. "Force" was the free offer of narrative in excess of patriarchal demand that the princess tendered instead of a vraisemblance that could only be maintained by remaining exposed (*demeure exposée*) at court. The estate at Coulommiers, where she can escape continual public exposure and instead direct the gaze of a *monde* composed entirely of the women in her service, is thus defined as the state in which the princess has the force to dwell.

Her husband fulfills his feudal obligations by witnessing a double royal wedding that "mixes affairs of love with affairs of state." It cements the peace signed between the king and the emperor after the siege of Metz; meanwhile, the princess returns to her new state to survey the image of that military victory. The princess's usurpation of the position of the king in her battle for her own private sovereign state is thus associated with the power available to aristocratic women under feudalism in the management of estates and in political influence. But the princess's "new construction" is a private domain, under construction in and by this text. Rather than depicting its sixteenth-century setting, it frames for the reader a proleptic glimpse of the death of feudalism, which had already begun in Lafayette's time. In consolidating the feudal powers under its own control, the centralized state for the first time guaranteed both the sovereignty of the individual and the absolute fidelity of women *within* the private domain.[60] If the princess wishes to claim a new form of private sovereignty, she can do so only by exerting a new extreme of control over the recognition of her absolute sexual fidelity, and she can do that effectively only in a private context.

Although the princess may force a recognition of her own sovereign state, that state still remains a gap caught within the emperor's domain, the pressures of empire always threatening on both sides. Just as Nemours lurked inside the lines during her victory over her husband and exposed her exemplary narrative to circulation at court, in the second Coulommiers episode, her husband's spy hides behind the fence to carry back to his master his eyewitness testimony of her encounter with Nemours. Although that evidence is inconclusive, the prince of course performs upon it another arbitrary act of authoritative reading, looking at it through the normative frame of his own version of verisimilitude: he decides that this evidence proves his wife's infidelity, and that she has at last fallen like other women (Adam, p. 160). For the master, who is still a master in the larger empire that surrounds her state, the man's witness remains "harder" evidence than that of his wife's women, and his own judgment of that evidence more legitimate proof than her words. The force that she has won within the new state in which she will now permanently dwell cannot comprehend the public power that organizes the court. She has neither the ability to fix Nemours permanently in a frame of her own possession nor the power to prevent her husband and feudal lord from recognizing his own version of the truth in her narrative. Moreover, that empire of hostile reading is continually pressing upon her borders. Her force lies rather in "remaining elsewhere" in a state of permanent tergiversation that allows her to turn her back, *tergum versare*, and dis-appear.

Tergiversation is an endless delay in response to the unanswerable demand for a return to the court, to the mother, to marriage—to the patrilineal system all these reinforce. The only reading audience over whose interpretive gaze the princess can have any control is a domestic public—that is, a public of domestics, a private public. Her state is established less in a blurring of boundaries between the two domains than in a symbolic conflation of private with public that is effected precisely through the separation of private from public space. While benefiting from the ways in which that boundary is blurred under the old feudal system, she works towards the construction of a new relation between public and private in which new powers are available to women. Lafayette's novel thus represents the effects of those literary achievements of French women under Louis XIV that Faith Beasley and Joan DeJean have argued were made uniquely possible by upper-class women's relation and response to his absolutist state. Beasley characterizes that achievement as the elaboration of "particular history" as a narrative mode that insists on the intersections of public and private spheres, while DeJean states that such writing was viewed in its time as "claim[ing] . . . new territory for the [novel] by describing with increased precision the life of the heart" (Beasley, *Revising Memory*, p. 29; DeJean, *Tender Geographies*, p. 10). Lafayette's princess literally lays claim to this "territory of the heart" in the glass pavilion, but she establishes her sovereignty over it as a symbolic "state" by *increasing and emphasizing its separation* from the public sphere.[61]

The new "state" established by the princess of Clèves is a feminine space of retirement in which women have the power to determine the meaning of their own plots within the terms of a private exchange of personal narratives that are recognizable as true because freely offered, not subject to a prior demand that would predetermine their meaning in patrilineal terms. This "freedom" and "power" have a high price, however, and it resembles that paid by the précieuses for the power of imposing on a patriarchal and military court the feminine example of bienséance. The end of the war waged by the princess against the double adversaries of husband and lover is an ironic mirroring of the end of the war between the king and the emperor. Like the monarchs after the siege of Metz, the three lovers end up finding themselves "insensiblement disposés à la paix," where "insensibility" shades back to its literal meaning of loss of feeling, grimly coloring the connotations of "peace" in a range of shades from death for Clèves to indifference for Nemours, with the princess's own end comprehending the whole spectrum (Adam, p. 39). Whereas the public peace that establishes the borders of France is sealed by a double wedding, the boundaries of the princess's private peace can be guaranteed only by the truce of retirement, a double refusal of marriage, a double separation from husband and lover.[62]

No Relation: The Reader in Narrative Transmission

By freely exceeding the terms of the patriline demand for which her maternal inheritance has destined her, and thereby becoming implausible—that is, becoming fictional—the princess creates a separate and paradoxical model for the transmission of her narrative: the *relation* of a fictional woman's inimitable example to a reader who is unrelated to her, either by descent or by marriage. Being one of the few completely fictional characters in the book, she would in a very literal sense have been one of the few characters completely unrelated to any of her original aristocratic readers. The play here with the relation of kinship between the contemporary audience and the characters harks back to and undoes the ancient epic tradition in which the aristocratic audience confirmed the authority of its rule on the basis of descent from eponymous heroes.[63] It similarly removes itself from the more contemporary practice by Scudéry in the roman à clef, whose protagonists were understood to represent members of its own courtly audience. Here, the thread of that original authorizing fiction of literary tradition, the fiction of the patrilineal kinship between reader and hero, is cut as neatly as if by the scissors of the Fates.

La Princesse de Clèves is, finally, the relation of an anonymous woman (the author) to a courtly public whose skepticism, or unwillingness to suspend its disbelief in the feminine invraisemblable is well documented and much discussed.[64] Yet for such a public it paints pictures of the implausible, closing its narrative frame as it does around the final tableau of what the princess left, of the princess leaving, disappearing from the historical portrait of her own life: "The short life left to her afforded inimitable examples of virtue [Et sa vie, qui fut assez courte, laissa des exemples de vertu inimitables]" (Adam, p. 180; Cobb, p. 162). The princess does not actually *appear* in her final, implausible portrait; it is rather *sa vie*, the "particular history" of her life, that is, the "rather short" novel that bears her title (not her name), that leaves these examples of inimitable virtue—but to whom? No daughter is invoked, no complicity demanded, no lineage confirmed.

In "leaving," in passing on a "life," or *narrative* of inimitable virtue, rather than its image or example, the novel is structuring its own transmission upon a model that escapes the legitimate relations of inheritance and marriage that invented that virtue and demand the narrative of "living up." The princess, in leaving her inimitable examples, does not live up—she lives beyond, she becomes ghostly. The inimitability of her example transforms the patrilineal model of relation and transmission into a purely narrative relation, a relation that cannot appear, cannot be represented, legitimized, or reproduced through resemblance, cannot be evidenced in the emblem of exemplary portraiture. As the princess leaves, she snips the thread of patrilineal reading and cuts with it the cord of a maternal inheritance that would otherwise have enjoined upon its receiver the reproduction of exemplary feminine virtue, and with it women's prescribed place within patrilineage.[65] The princess's examples are inimitable because they move beyond, with the narrative motion of tergiversation, the frame of any precept that could instruct readers how to interpret them.[66]

Lafayette's intimate relation of the inimitable example from heroine to reader through the frame of public narration is the precursor of the fictional private correspondences, in which one woman addresses histories and examples of feminine virtue to another, that were published in large numbers in later eighteenth-century France and England. Lafayette left to female readers and writers of the subsequent century a way out of the double bind of tradition, in which the model of patrilineal transmission sets around each daughter her inherited debt to maternal death on the one hand and her vassalage to inherited male property and agency on the other, fixing in its frame her resemblance, her vraisemblance, her faithful likeness to a picture of legitimacy she cannot possess. Correspondence, the free and therefore implausible relation of one woman's life history to another, to an unrelated reader who has no legitimate demands upon it, and yet who freely takes an interest, is the connection that leads out—there being no around or outside—right through the looking glass of resemblance. Their works will invest that interest, read and rewrite and pass on again to later readers the uninheritable legacy that the princess left.

Communicable Faults; or, Repetition and Transmission in Fictions of Women's Correspondence

Drawing Interest

Well, she said, since you are taking an interest in me, I shall give you some lines that I had written, not to recount my life—for, in my opinion, all women's stories resemble one another—but to account to myself for the motives that determined me in the course I have chosen: it is not finished, because one never finishes what one writes for oneself, but there is enough to satisfy your curiosity and to prove my sincerity.[1]

I have framed these lines from Germaine de Staël within the opening space of the page so that they may be read as a miniature *portrait moral* of French and English women's epistolary fiction in the later eighteenth century. In a few strokes, they delineate the essential features, not so much of a particular work, as of a generic correspondence. What I mean to lay open here is that correspondence itself: its paradigms and purposes, in short, its plot.[2]

Let me begin to open the portrait in proper précieux style, by taking its features, one by one in narrative sequence, out of the frame in which I have just placed them:

> Since you are taking an interest in me, I shall give you some lines that I had written . . .

The transaction described by this phrase is the master-model of narrative transmission for the entire subgenre in question. It is the assumption with which these novels begin and the gesture with which they end. *Interest* had a very specialized meaning in the eighteenth century. It was an important word in the vocabulary of sympathy; to be "interested" in someone meant at once to pity and to identify oneself with the "interesting" person. The French reflexive form of the verb, *vous vous intéressez*, better expresses the association of the self with the other involved in the idea of sympathy.[3] In both French and English, however, the crucial ambiguity that expresses interest in the other as self-interest, ultimately, puts the term through a curious inversion, whereby to be "interested" in the sympathetic sense comes to mean the opposite of to be "interested" in another equally current, but more strictly self-directed sense: the sense in which one might act from "interested" motives. To be sympathetically "interested," then, is also to be "disinterested."[4]

In response to the disinterested (sympathetic) demand for narrative represented by the verb "to be interested" / *s'intéresser*, a written history is produced—not in the sense that it is created in response to the receiver's demand, but rather, having been written previously and privately, *pour soi*, it is produced in the sense of being offered, "broke open," at the moment of the expression of interest and not before.[5] Neither the interest nor the interesting narrative is offered with the expectation of a return—that is, there is no demand for repayment with a usurious narrative "interest"; the freedom, the simultaneity, the open-ended imperfection, and the reciprocity of the exchange preclude such narrative indebtedness. That these are epistolary novels means that the reader's, as well as the heroine's, interest in the female history is represented within the text: "puisque vous vous intéressez à moi" mirrors and invokes the reader's disinterested demand for a female predecessor's written history, a demand that opens and makes possible both the epistolary exchange within the novel and the act of reading the novel itself. The reader's demand for the heroine's history doubles the heroine's demand for the maternal history. The maternal history is always produced in the absence of the mother (as the novel is produced in the absence of its reader, and offered in the absence of its author)—sometimes written by the mother, but always offered by a substitute—and always written down, to be read apart from its writer or its heroine. (Here the history is offered by Mme de Ternan, one in the series of the heroine's substitute mothers.) The history thus becomes a maternal inheritance, in the sense of being something passed on in absence by a predecessor, but it is one in which the will as testament and the legacy it transmits are one and the same; in which the one who testifies—but does not will—is not the mother; and of which, therefore, the debt of inheritance enforces moral relations rather than kinship relations.

> Not to recount my life—for, in my opinion, all women's stories resemble one another [l'histoire de toutes les femmes se ressemble] . . .

The interest of the maternal history does not lie in the unusual exploits of its heroine, nor, as in the history of the princess of Clèves, in her exceptional status, but precisely in the sameness of all *histoires de femme*. It is this sameness that produces the reader's sympathetic interest, which in turn produces the narrative transaction; it is this sameness that points to a significance behind its own insistence. The purpose of this fiction is not to "recount my life"; not to represent the realities of women's lived experience, but rather to offer women an accounting to themselves for the symbolic resemblances among those lives, separately lived, and then to count on their separateness to resist the repetition of resemblance.

> But to account to myself for the motives that determined me in the course I have chosen . . .

Instead of representing lived experience, the novels transact their offer of an accounting for the motifs that recur in the repeated *histoire de femme*, and for the motivations that lead women to repeat that story—to live it again and to write it again—to pass it on. The effects of the epistolary form, and of the "sympathy" characteristic of literature of sensibility, together make this "accounting to oneself" the only form of recounting offered to a reader.[6]

> It is not finished, because one never finishes what one writes for oneself . . .

The "histoire de toutes les femmes" is neither finished nor perfected. To close such an account would be to deprive it of its value, for its value exists only in the process of its transmission, from the writer to herself or to the reader who puts herself, however uneasily, in her place. To close such a history would be to defeat its purpose, which is not to conclude, but to repeat with a difference, and thus to survive.

> But there is enough to satisfy your curiosity and to prove my sincerity [*confiance*].

Unfinished and imperfect, yet always the same, the effectiveness of this history (*histoire*) lies in the enactment of its transmission, in the opening of a transaction between its writer and its reader. That transaction, as described above, involves a simultaneous and equal exchange of readerly interest and written narration. The model for this exchange is that of the aveu established by the princess of Clèves. The private history is freely offered as evidence (*pour vous prouver*), but not as evidence of truth as defined by the norm of verisimilitude. In place of the opposition between extraordinary virtue and the ordinary fall over the precipice set up by the unsympathetic (ultimately patriarchal) demand for the narrative of virtue these narratives substitute the terms of *confiance*, of the unforced sincerity that places the narration it offers beyond that demand, in excess of it.

The portrait moral I have just unpacked is not a depiction of the "histoire de toutes les femmes" itself, but rather an accounting for the motivations of its writing, of the exchange by which it is passed on. What is left obscure in this preliminary summation of its features, it is the purpose of the following chapters to delineate more clearly. But before returning to the rules of its transmission, let me outline the history of resemblance, the paradigmatic plot to which

Mme de Ternan refers when she says, "l'histoire de toutes les femmes se ressemble."[7] The discussion to follow elaborates in more detail the brief generalizations already given in Chapter 1 about form, plot, and theme in epistolary novels written by English and French women in the later eighteenth century.[8]

At the start of any analysis of a paradigmatic plot, it must be remembered that the paradigm is an abstraction and a construct; every individual text is a "variant" rather than a "pure" example of it.[9] In the language of exemplarity, every instance is both standard and unique. I shall mention numerous examples of the subgenre in the text of and notes to this chapter; more are included in the bibliography.[10] These novels consistently repeat a plot inherited, ultimately, from Greek romance, but recount it within such conventions of realistic fiction as common names, real places, and above all monetary accuracy; the exact financial arrangements and sums that sustain (or, usually, ought to have sustained) their characters' existences are often expounded at length, down to minute details about jointures, dowries, and *rentes viagères*.[11] By combining the conventions of romance with those of an emerging realism, these female novelists authorize themselves to write about women's social and economic oppression, as their experience of it is inscribed in both the literary and the legal conventions of their cultures. The conventional elements of romance structure the subjective experience of that oppression and fantasies of escape from it—as writers from Charlotte Lennox (*The Female Quixote*) to Jane Austen (*Northanger Abbey*) were well aware—while also providing a cover for writing about that experience, albeit indirectly, at a time when all women wrote under the threat of their own fall over the precipice of public opinion (a fall taken by more overtly "feminist" writers like Mary Wollstonecraft).

Their unique combination of romance and realistic conventions partially explains why works in this subgenre have been so easily dismissed without being given a fair reading; their "literary value" has often been judged entirely by the criteria of late realist fiction—that is, by criteria that apply neither to their methods nor to their purposes.[12] As Joan Hinde Stewart remarks of French works of the period, "novels translated historical and psychic realities into the ordered codes of fiction, and the self-conscious and ironic use of the conventions of society and of writing sometimes accounts for a subtle play between conformism and contestation" (p. 7). The paradigmatic plot described below must not be understood as directly reflecting the lived reality of every (or possibly any) individual woman in England and France in the late eighteenth century, nor dismissed as failing to reflect it accurately. Its significance is that women writing fiction for the first time in large numbers almost universally adopted it at some point in their literary production as a mode of writing about and for women, so much so that it saturated more than one national audience for over half a century.

"The Story of Every Woman"

The story begins when the heroine arrives at the "interesting age" of seventeen or so, that age when she is permitted to enter "the world" and fulfill her destiny by marrying appropriately. The interest of that age is that it is the moment at which she becomes, potentially, the vehicle through which the two most important things in her world must be transmitted: patronym and patrimony. She arrives at this moment only to find, suddenly, that things are not as they have seemed; she had indeed become the necessary vehicle of the tenor of society, but at the same time, paradoxically, she has by definition no active part in the system of its transmission. The system explicitly forbids her properly to send or to receive either name or property.[13] She cannot catch the husband who seemed to be coming to her—the man of her choice—because her desires have nothing to do with her capacity as a conduit for the transfer of her father's property, or with her incapacity to transfer his name. She has become (interestingly) the point of intersection of her father's and her suitor's desires to conjoin their own names and fortunes, thus ensuring their transmission to future generations of men.[14]

The transmission of the name is always the primary concern of fathers in these books. Paternal money and property follow where the name goes, as a material reinforcement giving real power to those who bear the sign of power, and weight to the authority of him whose ultimate power lies in the ability to bestow property precisely where he wills. The heroine's orphaned status represents the premise of her exile from that system; it is one of the conventions these early novels borrow from the romance tradition but use to represent the legal (and often actual) situation of women in patrilineal societies.[15] They represent the father as absent for his daughter, her patrimony nothing but her own mysterious lack of origins, with her consequent lack of a place designated as proper within patrilineal society.[16] When the father does appear, the difficulties that prevent the heroine again and again from receiving his inheritance are those that follow from the fact that she cannot pass on his name. The father marries the mother for money or out of sexual desire, but he will not besmirch his name by producing or recognizing any offspring with the mother, whose father's name he considers less illustrious than his own. Or he wants to concentrate all of his affection and property on the son who receives his name, and will waste nothing on a daughter. Or again, the father truly loves the mother and their daughter, but the couple's fathers have objections to the quality of one another's names and disinherit them both. In other books the father has no male heir and insists that his daughter marry either a relative who already bears his name or else someone noble but poor enough to be prepared to give up his own name and take on the father's in exchange for the money that accompanies it.[17] This is the temporal plot of transmission of names that finds its spatial expression in the conceptualization of nation as patrie.

Thus exiled from the transmission of patrimony, the heroine is also consistently a "motherless woman," very much in the sense used by Adrienne Rich to describe Jane Eyre, a heroine clearly descended from those who populate these eighteenth-century novels (Rich, pp. 89–106). *Both* her parents are dead or missing, and she has been brought up by a substitute mother.[18] The mother's substitute has provided the heroine with the one thing that she is allowed to possess in her own right: virtue, a moral value that she is to hold as a substitute for the missing patrimony. Left without the social and material protections of patrimony and patronym, the heroine undergoes a series of adventures (she generally undergoes more than she acts): elopements, kidnappings, incarcerations, deceptions of all kinds, desperate journeys made in flight or pursuit and in general against her will. Through it all, however, she is sustained by the invaluable female inheritance of virtue that enables her to survive.[19]

The maternal inheritance is at once what these novels represent and what they constitute and transact. Mother figures cannot pass on names, but they pass on verbs instead: "I did this [example], you should do that [precept, or *leçon*]." These *leçons et exemples*, as Madame de Boisgiron puts it, or precepts and examples, constitute a specifically feminine legacy within the structure of novels that consistently construct it as a substitute for any inheritance legitimated by the system of the transmission of the patronymics that come to denote value by the accretion to them of money or authority.

The mutually contradictory maternal precepts and examples are supposed to be "good for" the same thing as the patrimony: survival, the extension of life (of narrative, of correspondence). But because the all-encompassing system of names at once excludes and entraps women, survival itself becomes an ambiguous state, involving both compromise and escape. Sometimes the maternal inheritance enables the heroine to survive only to the end of the story (which is, after all, often more than her mother has done), at which point she finds that the only escape is death. Sometimes it is the means by which she recovers her patrimony and reinserts herself into the patrilineage. And sometimes it is that which alone renders her capable, not only of surviving the hazards to which she is exposed as a waif without inheritance, an exile from the system, but of outliving them indefinitely in that other state that is not the patrie, in the isolated female world of "retirement."

As Lafayette had done before them, eighteenth-century women novelists confronted the problem of female transmission within a patrilineal culture; this explains their shared preoccupation with symbolic structures and dynamics of intergenerational transmission. Their heroines' position in relation to the patrilineal transmission of name, property, and status resembles that of women's writing in relation to the patriarchal tradition of literary transmission described in Chapter 1. It is similarly a paradoxical form of exile *from within* the system of exclusionary boundaries. This fiction's preoccupation with feminine exile accounts for the astonishing extent to which the grammar of plot construction and transmission that I am describing in broad terms here functioned as a lingua franca across national boundaries. Despite great differences in the civil and religious laws and customs that shaped the historical practice of patriline transmission in England and in France, the fictional representation of the patrilineal system in novels written in the two countries concentrates on the similarly excluded position of women within that system and tends to literalize the position of female protagonists as one of exile from one to the other of the two countries, as to an apparent outside that is still inside the larger system that comprehends both.

Virtue's Faults

Virtue is the international currency of eighteenth-century heroines, the only thing of value they are allowed to possess in their own right. But virtue is hardly a mere possession, or even an attribute of a heroine, but rather the signifier of her status and worth as heroine. It is what entitles her to claim the interest of her readers. For her publicly recognized function is to serve as a proper example, capable of passing on virtue to real people—that is, to readers:

> I thought that the picture of a heroine whose unfailing virtue is put to every test without ever proving false was always a good example for young ladies. . . . It is through virtue alone that love is pardonable and interesting; without virtue, it is nothing but the most vile and contemptible of weaknesses.[20]

In a gesture typical of the logic of writing in exile—writing from without that nevertheless remains subject to the constraints of that which excludes it—Mme Beccary here gives her reader notice that she may safely offer her interest to the heroine and receive the narrative here passed on because it is the picture of the trial of virtue.[21] It is framed, that is, as an example of exactly the patriarchal narrative that is obviated and subverted by the transaction of sympathetic exchange. Before the reader fairly cracks the book, she must be advised that she can step forward without fearing a fall over the precipice of reading from the dangerous verge of a bad example.

The virtue of eighteenth-century heroines has, like the interest they draw, a specialized meaning. As was already true in *La Princesse de Clèves*, it does not consist, like manly virtue, in the performance of good deeds or serviceable actions, but rather in the avoidance of fault. Now, the avoidance of fault entails the avoidance of anything resembling a deed, since actions necessarily involve consequences and the responsibility for them. Hence the classical virtus of agency comes to be replaced by a feminine virtue of suffering, both in the current sense and in the earlier one of passivity, or "suffering" the action of others. That suffering in turn not only justifies but demands the reader's sympathetic interest. Thus heroines are interesting when they are victims. Thus they are always interesting, since they are always victims of situations that are presumably of close concern to the reader herself, such as the difficulty of preserving virtue and finding the right husband, of arriving at the right destiny or destination. *Virtue cannot act in its own interest*: that is the condition upon which it exacts the reader's proper interest. It is important to the establishment of a publicly recognizable contract for the transmission of virtue between author and reader that the heroine's suffering and her virtue be represented as a tableau, as in Mme Beccary's preface, because the predominant logic of sympathy in the eighteenth century was very much a function of the logic of picture and spectacle, a voyeuristic logic that placed the viewer at a distance and in a position of superiority to the suffering and the virtue with which he sympathized.[22] Later on in this chapter, however, I argue that the mise-en-abyme created by these novelists' use of the epistolary form tends to structure the reader's sympathizing relation to the text in terms of narrative exchange rather than in the culturally predominant terms of spectator and tableau to which Beccary pays lip service.

In keeping with the logic of the tableau, virtue is passed on to a heroine by means of an educative example—that of the substitute mother.[23] Virtue becomes the heroine's only inheritance, often literally named as such in the texts, and comes to substitute for the lacking patrimony. When Marie-Jeanne Riccoboni's heroine, Sophie de Valliere, pauses momentarily in the midst of the troubles ensuing from the loss of her expected patrimony, she reflects upon the virtue of virtue as inheritance:

> The pupil of a respectable woman will always retain at least *the precious inheritance* [*précieux heritage*] that cannot be taken from her: an inviolable attachment to duty, and the consoling certitude of being able to say to herself at all times, "my misfortune is an effect of chance, and not at all that of my own imprudence." (emphasis mine)[24]

By clinging to this "unravishable" form of inheritance, the heroine is able to make it through the phantasmagoria of *hasards*/hazards to the end of her story. That end may be the recovery of her patrimony and reinsertion into the system of its transmission through marriage to the man of her choice (who by one of those miracles of romance has become the proper man by inheriting it himself). It may be her death, or it may be her final retreat into exile, whether an exile in the usual sense, outside the borders of what is aptly called the *patrie*, or one of several forms of exile within the patrie: a convent, for example, or a secular retirement. Or, in the variation that shows the heroine married at the outset, she may or may not find a way to manipulate her inevitably manipulative or tyrannical husband sufficiently to make life tolerable.[25]

Mise-en-abyme; or, Epistolarity and the Senses of Endings

Such manifold and contrasting endings resemble one another more than it may seem. If they seem arbitrary or interchangeable, it is because of their resemblance to one another; the particularity of ending is unimportant in these novels, because ending itself is subverted. Their plots are of a nonlinear construction that devalues the ending of the primary plot as culmination and closure of the whole. Thus a single novel almost always contains several of the alternate situations and endings. By their extravagant use of what are generally called "framing" techniques, the primary plot is made constantly to interrupt, extend, wrap around, and digress from itself with variant repetitions of itself. But "framing" is an inadequate term for this type of plot structure, for it implies something static and allows a clear distinction between container and contained, a distinction these novels thwart by means of the resemblance they create between "framing" and "framed." Repeating one another, the plots open out, flow into and become one another, defying the closure of one by another.

Any enclosing structure that folds in upon itself to form another enclosure "within" itself, so that the outer and inner enclosures are continuous with one another, is defined physically as an "invagination." Jacques Derrida has already used this term to designate the folding in upon itself of a text (Shelley's, Blanchot's) through internal repetition. Such repetition, forming "an inserted miniature representing the whole, . . . deprives the text of any beginning and of any decidable edge or border" ("Living On/ Border Lines," pp. 92–93). I find this a useful metaphor for the way these plots operate, even though no simple disclaimer on my part can rid the term of its physiological and thus potentially "essentialist" connotations. I adapt it here nevertheless on the assumption that "to operate within the matrix of power is not the same as to replicate uncritically relations of domination," and hope that my use of the term can constitute instead "a repetition of the law which is not its consolidation, but its displacement" (Judith Butler, p. 30). My use as a feminist critic, moreover, of a term that connotes the female body is necessarily a different speech act than Derrida's, which has been criticized as a male appropriation and exclusion of the feminine (Spivak, pp. 188–90).

In the above quotation, Derrida is speaking of repetitions on the level of diction, whereas the repetitions in women's epistolary fiction are on the level of plot. When this mise-en-abyme structure becomes the organizing principle of plot rather than of diction, the difference in effect is that it no longer deprives the text simply of any "edge or border," but more specifically, and more *directionally*, deprives it of any destination, of any ending. For use in my discussion of plot, therefore, I would revise the term as *matrix*, which retains the structural aspect of "invagination," but adds a connotation of creative energy that reproduces repetitions of itself internally, but propels them outward and forward in time. It is thus one of the covert subversions of this fiction that the last ending is not necessarily the last word of the plot. Whatever may happen in the end is, after all, a matter of chance (*l'effet du hasard*); the important and consistent fact, whatever the ending, is that it is not the heroine's fault, as demonstrated by her virtuous conduct throughout the story.

The virtuous heroine who successfully toes the brink without falling (like other women) is quite obviously exemplary, "a good example for young ladies," as Beccary puts it. After the previous chapter's discussion of exemplarity, Derrida's metaphor for the metaphor of invagination, "an inserted miniature representing the whole," must strike the reader as identical with the standard metaphor, since the Renaissance, for the rhetorical figure of example. What makes the mise-en-abyme of example a matrix when it structures novels of the later eighteenth century is its insertion in the directional frame of plot. In the first half of the century, by contrast, novels by writers like Delariviere Manley or Jane Barker were, in their extremely episodic construction, much closer to the Renaissance novellas and their medieval precursors (Chaucer, Boccaccio, *The Thousand and One Nights*) in which each tale is set like an example in the relatively static frame story of the scene of narration. John Lyons has argued that *La Princesse de Clèves* takes the novella structure and expands the frame, drawing our attention to it and miniaturizing the exemplary tales within it (p. 217). These novels inherit that device from *La Princesse de Clèves*, in the form of its miniature portraits and its miscarried letters sent and received within a larger, more elaborated main plot. They actively inherit and transform it, however, so that here it is the letter that most proliferates as the vehicle of example, whereas in *La Princesse* the image of the miniature portrait predominates (there the letter's circulation is important but empty, as the letter contains no example).[26] While the double figuration of example as portrait and letter is transmitted intact, the emphasis has shifted over the course of a century from the static, perfected quality of example to its narrative aspects, which, as we saw in the quotation opening this chapter, specifically deny perfection, closure, and destination (by which I mean unidirectional transmission according to the will of the sender) in favor of an open exchange of "interest."

Both the similarity and the shift in emphasis between Lafayette's novel and those written by women in the later eighteenth century have to do with a crucial shift in the ideological positioning of women writers in the century that had elapsed between them, one in which national differences also came into play, although even those differences reflected mutual influences. The key term in this shift is also the key term for later eighteenth-century fiction, especially sentimental fiction, and its absence from *La Princesse de Clèves, as a term* although not as an implied concept, is equally key to understanding the shift. That term is *virtue* (*vertu*). In the previous chapter, I agreed with Françoise Meltzer that in *La Princesse de Clèves* "the glory of an [aristocratic] name must indeed be upheld by virtue," and with Peggy Kamuf that the organizing metaphor of its maternal discourse is the precipice—that very precipice where "virtue incessantly hovers" in every eighteenth-century novel of sensibility (Kamuf, *Fictions of Feminine Desire*, pp. 83–84; Meltzer, p. 182). And I would agree too with Joan DeJean that Lafayette had reason, not unlike her successors, to prefer "the wages of anonymity," because they allowed her control over her story and its circulation in a social context where readers would always conflate a woman's story with its author and make it their own by making it part of the evidence against her in the perpetual trial of feminine virtue ("Lafayette's Ellipses"). Nevertheless something happened in that intervening century to the way readers viewed both novels and the women who wrote them, a something that was not so much a complete transformation as, again, a shift in emphasis.

What happened was that novels became novels, and women became women. Novels were no longer, variously, some kind of romance or *nouvelle historique*. Women were no longer, variously, aristocrats or tradespeople first, women second. Novels had become mass-produced commodities, the income from which supported relatively large numbers of women who were neither aristocrats nor tradespeople. Even in France, in the decades leading up to and following the Revolution, novels were more than ever written by and for the bourgeois class, and more than ever by women. And at the core of the ideology of that class, woman had already been placed as prisoner and protector of the domestic sphere, idol of its separation from and guarantor of the existence of the public sphere, its principal object as well as its symbolic subjectivity (one has only to think of all the novels written in the eighteenth and nineteenth centuries whose titles are simply women's names). As more women wrote novels, it also became a general assumption that most readers were women.[27] These facts of historical context are now well known, but what they imply for the form of fiction is less evident. My research shows that they did tend to result in a shift in emphasis in women's epistolary novels in contrast even to those of the male writers who made use of conventions of femininity, sensibility, and epistolarity in the novel, such as Richardson and Rousseau. That shift in emphasis involves a feminization of readers, whatever their actual sex, and a corresponding change in the relationship constructed between text and reader that demands the transmission of virtue and supplies it—along with its "faults" or subversions—through channels deliberately diverted from those of patriline kinship relations.

The maternal demand of virtue as avoidance of fault, which seemed to Lafayette's contemporaries so curiously in excess of aristocratic reality, had a century later come to be strictly applied, not only to the whole tribe of heroines, but equally to their female readers and writers.[28] Not only the discourse passed on by a mother like Mme de Chartres to her daughter—that is, from one character to another within the novel's narrative frame—but the discourse of transmission from author to reader as well, when these were read as feminine, had to convey the demand of virtue. Since an example must always be framed by a maxim in order to be understood and received as an example, the elaborated "frame" of the primary plot that conveyed the "tableau" of the heroine was now perforce a plot with a moral.[29] That moral is its end, in more than one sense of the word, the precept that gives closure to the portrait of virtue. Paula Backscheider writes that "many women's novels have been criticized for lacking satisfactory resolutions. Closure, however, is in the interest of the hegemony, and the 'conclusions' of [eighteenth-century] novelistic works are eloquent testimony to this truth" (pp. 291–92). "The hegemony" resisted by women writing in the later eighteenth century took the specific form of the imperative of "morals" in both authorial image and textual tableau. As Backscheider further comments, "By this time women and women writers had learned that their acceptance and even authority—at least what authority they were permitted—depended upon their conforming to a female script" (p. 295). The invagination, proliferation, and repetition of the matrix-plot that disturbs this larger tableau of virtue with its ostensible moral frame and end, the proliferation of examples that resemble each other *with a difference*, the repetition of miniatures re-presenting the whole *with a difference*, undoes the precept just as it undoes the ending. It undoes the wholeness of the whole not so much through fragmentation as through multiplication.

Resistance to closure, more generally conceived, is hardly a uniquely feminine preserve in eighteenth-century narrative, as no one who has read Sterne or Diderot needs to be told. While many eighteenth-century novels defied structural closure, the effect and ostensible purpose of such resistance in novels of women's correspondence is specifically gendered and politicized. By the repetition of similar plots and variant endings, the force of prescribed and prescriptive precepts about feminine virtue is undermined by the force of proliferating examples at variance with one another.[30] They provide a marked contrast with the plots of more domestic and realistic courtship novels, "whose conventions of ending usually enforce a particular ideological view."[31] Techniques of fragmentation might also be said to characterize the period to a degree; Clarissa's "mad letters" are a famous example. Nevertheless, the deliberate use of epistolary form for purposes of narrative fragmentation (before the twentieth century) is an aspect of letter-fiction that has not been adequately taken into account by students of "epistolarity," possibly because it may be a technique more characteristic of early women's fiction than of their canonical male contemporaries (Elizabeth MacArthur's work on eighteenth-century epistolary fiction in French is an important exception). Dorothea von Mücke explains the importance of the illusion of wholeness, for example, in *Clarissa*: "The pedagogical intervention of this epistolary novel is situated at the threshold of representation, at the level that effects the illusionary reading of a vast collection of individual letters as one organized whole" (p. 191).

Similarly, when Robert A. Day lists the four "advantages and improvements which the epistolary method added to fictional technique," the first three have to do with the representation of interiorized characterization, and only the last with narrative: "The ability to present a *rounded picture* of an event by recording it from several contrasting points of view" (emphasis mine). He is describing exactly the technique by which Sophia Lee, whose work is discussed in detail in Chapter 5, presented events and relationships from contrasting points of view—except that Lee's emphasis is clearly on the disjointedness, the undecidability produced by such juxtaposition, on the breaking open of the frames of viewpoint rather than on the framing of a larger, all-enclosing "rounded picture."[32]

Janet Altman, in her thorough and subtle consideration of the permutations of epistolary form, recognizes that "within the epistolary framework, frames are constantly broken, and even closural gestures have inaugural consequences." While she thus theoretically recognizes the propensity of the epistolary form to fragmentation, Altman's own bias, like Day's, is nevertheless to concentrate on the "closural gestures": "Indeed, one of the implications of this survey may be that in comparison to other early novelistic modes, epistolary literature developed relatively more codified, more formal, and more narratively integrated closural strategies." The same tendency is apparent when she turns from the subject of "Epistolary Closure" to that of "The Epistolary Mosaic," the letter considered as both separate "unity" and "unit" within a larger whole. Again, she points out that "epistolary narrative is by definition fragmented narrative," but she then proceeds to concentrate mainly on the kinds of "compensatory continuity" with which different authors have been able, "more often than not," to "produce the illusion of a continuous line from a series of points"—with the result, again, of a "rounded picture," only this time in mosaic (pp. 161, 163, 169, 171).

The shift in emphasis in women's epistolary novels after Richardson is away from a presentation of the separate letters and narratives as fragments that together form a whole, and rather towards the multiplication and interruption of wholes by other wholes that resemble each other yet mutually contradict and disrupt, not only closure and fixity, but also the hierarchy of framing that would make the "enclosing" narrative a framing precept, its ending the last (moral) word. Richardson, Rousseau, and even the ostensibly "libertine" Laclos, more protected, as men, from the social and economic retributions risked by women authors, were clearly far more interested in reinforcing the demand of feminine virtue in society, however complex their texts may be (see, for example, Mücke and Mullan). That interest comes through, as many critics have demonstrated, even though the relative immunity of these male authors to the imperative of virtue made them freer to engage in openly ironic play with the feminine convention of the transmission of virtue through example from author to reader—the prefaces of *Clarissa*, *Julie*, and *Les Liaisons dangereuses* being all three versions of the defense of the depiction of vice in the promotion of virtue—a line in general too dangerous to toe, too close to the brink, for women who signed their own names to their work.[33]

Correspondence as Sympathetic Exchange

Novels of women's correspondence in the eighteenth century tend to resist not only the "closural gestures" prevalent in contemporary uses of the form, but also the very logic of the gaze implied by the project of creating a "rounded picture" out of the epistolary "mosaic." As mentioned above, sympathy, in the eighteenth-century sense, is at once a pitying of and an identification with another person who is at a distance, a victim whose suffering is framed as spectacle—a stranger, a fictive character, an actor, an inanimate canvas. Women were supposed to have a special talent for sympathy, not surprisingly since the sympathizing person is enabled to identify with the sufferer by putting herself in the other's place, by recalling and reliving her own sufferings; therefore those who are often victims might naturally be supposed to have an easier time sympathizing with victims.[34] The demonstration of sympathy is as obligatory for a heroine as is her victimization or her virtue itself.[35] But these novels use the concept of sympathy, first developed by earlier eighteenth-century philosophers and novelists, in a significantly different way which subverts the fixing relationship of the gaze.

Calling sympathy "the anthropological 'deep value' of the eighteenth century," Mücke stresses its importance to the structuring of the "dramatic tableau" in Lessing's theory of tragedy (pp. 16, 63, 104–5). One of the most important effects of this difference in the use of sympathy is that the emphasis is no longer placed upon what Marshall similarly identifies as "the theater of sympathy," where sympathy is an effect of spectacle—whether on the stage of "real life" or as a self-consciously dramatized interplay between the roles of "spectator" and "actor," between the positions of viewer and (suffering) viewed. Indeed, recent studies of sympathy and sensibility have all concentrated on the theatrics of sympathy. But the range of conventions covered by this term has at least two distinct aspects, each with gendered associations in the eighteenth century. Both of them are discussed, but they are not clearly distinguished from each other in the critical literature. One is the tableau of the suffering female body, a transparent medium in which men (usually) can read the truth of women's virtue and the genuineness (as well as the excess) of their feeling (e.g., Mullan, pp. 61, 113). The second is "the spectacle of benign generosity" (Markley, p. 211; but see also Barker-Benfield and Mullan). This distinction really identifies two different layers of sympathetic theater: the spectacle of suffering itself and the theater that stages the act of sympathizing with, and sometimes attempting to relieve, suffering. The first is entirely passive and the sufferer most often feminine; the second active, even though the effectiveness of its agency is often dubious, and is more primarily the sign of a masculine capacity for sympathy. Pamela may bestow charity, for example, but only after she herself has suffered spectacularly for quite a few pages. Both Lovelace and Valmont, on the other hand, attempt to convince the virtuous and sentimental women they want to seduce that they themselves are really "men of feeling" by staging and starring in scenarios of charity for the benefit of the ladies. Fiction of women's correspondence, however, generally does not "offer narrative as a theatre for sympathy" so much as it enacts it as an exchange of narrations (Mullan, p. 143). The narrative demanded is that of the true, secret history (of suffering).

The structure of the sympathetic relation between women as an exchange, not simply of narrated secret histories, but specifically of written histories, already informs an early work of Eliza Haywood's, although it was published well before the post-Richardsonian period in question, and although it is not an epistolary novel. In *The*

British Recluse (1722), Cleomira and Belinda first cautiously, privately identify each other as fellow sufferers who are probably victims of similar plights (the punch line of the novel is that they are both victims of one and the same rake). Once they have established a friendship, each is anxious to pour out her own tale of woe and to know the cause of the other's sufferings, in order better to sympathize, but each is still afraid both to expose herself first and to offend the other by making an unequal narrative demand. The difficulty is at last resolved by an epistolary expedient that Cleomira ("the Recluse") suggests:

> Here (continu'd she, taking Pens and Paper) do you write, and I will do the same; and by reading what each other have set down, both will avoid the Confusion of speaking first. Agreed (said Belinda, and immediately did as the RECLUSE desir'd.) On Exchange of the Papers, Belinda read in that which the RECLUSE had writ, Undone by Love, and the Ingratitude of faithless Man. And the RECLUSE found in that which the other had writ, these Words, For ever lost to Peace by Love, and my own fond Belief.[36]

The rest of the book consists of the double histories narrated by each in turn, after which they decide to perpetuate the sympathetic pact by living the rest of their lives together in rural "retirement." The establishment of a community of women with which Haywood ends this novel looks forward to what the women novelists of the succeeding generation have done with her transformation of the "theater of sympathy" into a sympathetic exchange of narrative: they have inserted it into a system of female inheritance according to which "virtue," conceived of as the compulsory avoidance of fault or blame, is passed down from a substitute mother to a heroine in textual (letter) form as inherited exemplary history, thus establishing a moral tie that cuts across the lines of kinship, patrilineal or matrilineal.[37]

Since the substitute mother serves the heroine as educator and confidante but is no kin to her, their relationship remains entirely outside patrilineage and its indebted structure for the transmission of inheritance. It is based instead on sympathy as an equal exchange of narratives. This mise-en-abyme of textual reception implies that the novel itself is to be received as part of a similar sympathetic feminine exchange, and not as part of the *patrimoine* or received literary tradition. The feminization of the implied reader by this process also transforms the romance of patrilineage, in which a heterosexual pair enacts a courtship or seduction plot before the reader's voyeuristic gaze (often at a female character's expense). It replaces that distanced relation with a sympathetic bond, a feminized erotics in which the reader is invited to participate in an equal exchange of sympathy as (actual or potential) fellow-sufferer (on the amorous epistolary tradition, compare Benstock, pp. 92–98; Cook, and Kauffman).

If Mullan is right about "the distinctive ability of novels of the period to deal with sociability [a social "contract" based on "commendable sympathies"] as a desirable but exceptional propensity by addressing as if privately each member of a growing readership," then the novels of women's correspondence evince an ability, or at least a project, that must be further distinguished from that of works by writers like Richardson or Sterne. For the community that these novels establish by "positioning each private reader as the exceptional connoisseur" of sympathy is not simply a resistance to "the anti-social vices or insensitivities" that everyone agreed at the time to read as masculine (even in female instruments of vice like Richardson's Mrs Jewkes; Mullan, pp. 13–14). The community so established by novels of women's correspondence also, and crucially, represents a resistance to marriage and to the domestic sphere itself as an arena in which men could inflict the consequences of such "vices or insensitivities" on women in the privacy of their own homes and out of reach of the laws and other customary restraints governing vices committed in public. This is one reason why female novelists of this period turned away in such large numbers from the ancient and still vital convention of the (heterosexual) amorous epistle. Riccoboni, for example, like Scudéry before her, attempted to revise the amorous convention in her first novel, but abandoned it afterwards (on Riccoboni, see Cook, pp. 22–23; on Scudéry, see DeJean, *Sappho*, pp. 96–100). She returned in her later works to the female confidante convention in which women addressed each other in passionate language across their domestic confinements, and sometimes in the context of separate female communities.

Correspondence as Filiation

The correspondences represented in the subgenre of women's correspondence can be divided into two types. Some are exchanged between friends of the same age (the "confidante" convention). Usually these are girlhood companions who were raised together, and are now separated by plans for marriage, or sometimes by a marriage already consummated. The others are correspondences between a younger woman and an older one who has a maternal relationship to the younger (the educational or "conduct book" convention). Although the love-letter convention is notably absent from this typology, the passion of its language and connection is often preserved in the confidante convention. The confidante relationship thus preserves the erotic force of the love-letter, while stabilizing the bond it represents, which becomes much more reliable through the guarantee of sympathy. Indeed, this can be as true of the maternal or conduct book convention as it is of the confidante convention.

Jane Spencer discusses the importance of "maternal advice" to daughters in English novels by women in the later eighteenth century; she gives credit to Frances Sheridan for "setting the trend" in her *Memoirs of Miss Sidney Biddulph* (1761), in which Sheridan makes "the heroine's relationship with her mother, rather than her lover, the emotional focus" ("Of Use," p. 201). Both Sheridan and Jane West, another novelist mentioned by Spencer, may well have been aware of earlier French models such as Jeanne Marie Le Prince de Beaumont's *Lettres de Madame du Montier à la marquise de *** sa fille . . .* (1756), which, like West's *Advantages of Education* (1793), features a mother's advice to her daughter on how to adapt to the hardships of isolation in a patriarchal marriage. Le Prince de Beaumont is herself fictionalizing a conduct book convention already strong in both countries, as well as exploiting the ancient association of the epistle with education, which in the later eighteenth century came to be particularly associated with the mother's role as educator of her daughters (on the older educational valences of the letter form, see Ferguson; on the eighteenth century in particular, see Spencer, "Of Use," p. 203). As always, then, generic invagination defies categorization: confidantes are amorous educators, like substitute mothers, who are also confidantes.

In the formal subgenre of epistolary fiction in which the primary correspondences are exchanged between women, the division between the confidante and conduct book conventions is further undermined. Because the outermost structure is also repeated, in variation, as the inner structure, a novel "framed" by one type of correspondence usually contains, and is framed by, the other type as well.[38] These narratives enclosed in letters always have other, antecedent narratives enclosed within them, the sending and receiving of which are crucial to the development of the "primary" plot as it unfolds. Within the more numerous framing correspondences between friends of equal age, then, one or more of the most important plots enclosed within the main, presently unfolding plot is a maternal history. Along with the latest installments of their own presently unfolding histories, enclosed with friendly admonishments for avoiding pitfalls, the young correspondents enclose an inheritance from the elder generation.

Whether the text of the recurring mother figure, the woman who has educated, protected, and often still advises the heroine, forms part of the "enclosing" or of the "enclosed" correspondence, she is always there, and she is almost never actually the heroine's mother. The real mother is often not mentioned at all; she is one of the forgotten dead. Or she has explicitly been killed off by the narrative, usually before it properly begins. The story of her death then becomes a temporally prior narrative enclosed within the heroine's narrative (transmitted diachronically), and becomes a repeated motif and a central motivation of the heroine's plot. The first question that demands attention is this: if the figure of the mother and her relation to the heroine as educatrice and protectress is so important to these novels as to recur almost invariably in a central position, why is that role equally invariably displaced from the real mother onto a substitute? Although recent historians of women's lives in the period find that unmarried women in fact played an important role in many households as "surrogate mothers," the extremely persistent recurrence of this displacement in a subgenre more concerned with the symbolic expression of the truth of women's status under patriarchy than with any directly mimetic realism can only be partially explained with reference to such historical tendencies.[39]

The answer must be sought in the nature of what is transmitted and the mode of its transmission: in other words, in what constitutes filiation in these novels. That which is exchanged in the correspondences between the female characters, whether they appear in an "outer" or an "inner" narrative, whether they are exchanged within or between generations, is always twofold, for it has the double structure of example that always consists of both precept and example. In these novels, the precept is offered directly by the substitute mother for the heroine's education, while the example consists of a "history," a life story.[40] As exemplified by the passage from Riccoboni quoted earlier in this chapter, the status of this exchange as a maternal inheritance is consistently emphasized; it is always structurally, and often rhetorically, substituted for the inheritance of money and name that the patriline fiction prevents the mother from conferring or the daughter from receiving.[41] Miss Mancel of *Millenium Hall* is another example: her parents of both sexes having mysteriously disappeared sometime before she can remember, she is raised by an aunt (or rather by someone called an aunt, who seems to be unrelated to the heroine). This "aunt" upon her death leaves her, as her parents have once already, with neither name, connections, nor money to live on, but unlike the girl's parents, she has left her one thing that must serve in their stead for the rest of her history: "This person had bred her up with the utmost tenderness, and employed the most assiduous care in her education; which was the principal object of her devotion."[42] A host of eighteenth-century heroines are in Miss Mancel's predicament, and similarly armed.

The Value of Maternal Inheritance

The typical protagonist of the subgenre is abandoned in the world without a penny to her name, and indeed without a name to which pennies might attach themselves. Only the careful education bequeathed to her by an older woman who has befriended her can enable her to survive as an exile in a world whose boundaries are traced out by the lines of patrimonial transmission. The necessity of this educational inheritance, as opposed to sheer innocence or "native" virtue, is proven by the negative example of one Mrs Williams, a heroine who is atypically deprived of it, and suffers inordinately even though both of her parents are present to pass on both education and wealth.

Mrs Williams's father, a serious and intellectual man, is contemptuous of his fashionable wife and of the lack of education that stultifies the minds of most women. When their daughters are out of their infancy, he insists that they learn Latin, history, and everything that boys would be taught. The mother, however, protests that women "were, without education, more rational than their masters; and that learning (as she termed it) only served to render a girl ridiculous in the eyes of her own sex, and contemptible in those of the men." In resolution of this quarrel, the elder daughter, our heroine, is educated by the father, and her younger sister by the mother, from which moment the mother begins to despise the heroine, so that she is effectively left without a mother. The mother does her daughter no material harm, however; the downfall of Mrs Williams is simply the result of her purely intellectual, "masculine" education having failed to prepare her for the trial of virtue that takes place not in a court of law, but in courtship. As a result she is forced to depend, during her trial, upon "the dictates of innocence and nature" when, away from her parents in the care of an ineffectual substitute mother, she meets the irresistible Mr Williams.[43] Going courting without the proper feminine education is like going to court without legal counsel, and "the dictates of innocence and nature" only leave her open to deception. Tricked into eloping with a rake, she is consequently disowned and disinherited, while her sister, the mother's pupil, eventually marries the nice young man to whom her father had engaged the heroine. The language of the text surreptitiously justifies this escape from the paternal destination, but at the same time it dwells, for most of the novel's great length, upon the unbearable sufferings and humiliations the heroine must undergo as the effects of having had to rely on the instructions of nature and innocence when she arrived at the crucial moment—the interesting age—instead of upon the instructions of a woman experienced in the ways of the world she was about to enter. Lack of a feminine education can leave a heroine "orphaned," even if she did not begin that way.

In contrast, one of those who does begin her history as an orphan, Mademoiselle de Boismiran, does receive the priceless legacy of education from a religious "mother" who brings her up as an obscure girl of small fortune in a convent. But when at the interesting age she is let into the secret that her paternal name is not plain "Gelin," but "de Boismiran," and when she is furthermore given to believe that her father's riches will settle upon her along with his aristocratic name, she finds that the best of feminine educations still leaves something to be desired: "It is not that I have benefited so little from your precepts and your examples as to value riches beyond their worth. But, my dear good friend, how sweet it is to owe both necessities and luxuries to no one but the authors of one's days, and to be able to share them with unfortunate virtue!"[44] This passage lays open the whole economics of female filiation: to receive an inheritance is to "owe the means of living" to the "authors of one's days"—but it is to be indebted *only* to them, and thus preserved from the danger of becoming indebted to others, involved in debts multifarious and nefarious that tend to become dangerous liaisons. Inheritance seems to be a closed system, the stability and self-containment of which would provide a surplus of means and agency that the heroine would use to engage freely in other forms of exchange beyond the circle of inherited debt. Having already "profited" from "unfortunate virtue," the heroine might now "share" her inherited wealth with the personification, or, more specifically, with the *exemplar*, of the instruction she has received as a substitute for that inheritance.

The "lessons and examples" (precepts and examples) that make up both the heroine's inheritance and the reader's texts teach that virtue is both more valuable than money and "unfortunate." It is not valued highly enough by the world, does not have the proper position within the system of the transmission of "fortune," to be spared the necessity of accepting *nécessaire & superflu* even from a girl who is clearly not the author of anyone's days. Nevertheless, virtue as a substitutive inheritance does, in combination with the "fortune" transmitted as patrimony, allow the heroine to construct an alternative to the patrimonial relation of indebtedness: the desire she expresses as *partager* quite specifically deflects the notion of an implicit indebtedness to the woman by whom she has "profited," shifting its terms to those of sensibility, in which the suffering that identifies virtue also entails a capacity to sympathize with suffering. By wishing to share her fortune with "unfortunate virtue," the heroine signifies that her virtue has outlived her suffering, and substitutes for the relation of inherited debt a relation of equal and free exchange.

But if the transmission of feminine virtue as maternal inheritance can escape or invert the relations of indebtedness created by patrimonial transmission, it also fundamentally fails to confer the agency expressed in the instrument of patrimonial transmission, the "will." While this feminine legacy is assigned a positive value of its own, that value is defined in negative terms. Defining the value of feminine virtue in negative terms—namely, those of passivity—amounts to a positive valuation of the feminine exclusion from the agency of transmission. As an example of this, take the case of Miss Melvyn: "[Her mother] had no other child than this, whose education was her mother's greatest care; & she had the pleasure of seeing in her an uncommon capacity, with *every virtue* the fondest parent could wish; & *which indeed she had by inheritance*; but her mother's humility, made them appear to her, as a peculiar gift of providence to her daughter" (pp. 40–41; emphasis mine). When a mother does manage to bequeath virtue to a daughter, it is, of course, not her fault.[45] The exemplary self-effacement that prevents Mrs Melvyn from seeing herself as the willing agent of an educational inheritance is itself the essence of that inheritance.

Bernard Duyfhuizen has made a strong generalization about narratives that rely upon "documentary techniques" such as letters: he claims that "each document marks the 'will' of its writer to control the transmission of his or her life story" (which Duyfhuizen figures as an "inheritance" passed to the reader), even though he acknowledges that "every textualized attempt at control presupposes its converse" (pp. 20–21). While the concern with narrative as transmission is indeed preponderant in novels of women's correspondence, however, what is marked in them is rather eighteenth-century women's legalized incapacity to will or to act. Such narratives implicitly allow the receiving daughter or reader a degree of release from authorial control that appears from Duyfhuizen's study to be exceptional (my reading of *The Recess* especially illustrates this). Yet as feminine "inheritances," they also transmit the restraints that perpetuate and naturalize female "incapacity." As Spencer argues, conduct books and novels of this period "establish a kind of maternal line of moral worth," while at the same time "maternal authority is fundamentally divided against itself" ("Of Use," p. 204).

The text of the maternal testament is thus explosively aporetic, and the value it bequeaths equally so, as the examples of Mrs Williams, Mademoiselle de Boismiran, and Miss Melvyn have made clear. Aporia, the trope of undecidable excess, results here from the fact that the maternal legacy of verbs, of narrative precepts and examples, is indeed what the patrimonial system of names leaves (out) for mothers to pass on, but at the same time its transmission reinforces the patrilineal system itself. The receiver of such an inheritance will always be at a loss as to how to interpret and act upon its contradictory messages. Nevertheless, the maternal inheritance does escape from the system that partially engenders it and works to inscribe it within its own limits, by promoting survival within (and thus potentially beyond) that system, and by providing the sympathetic relation of freely offered exchange as an alternate model to that of the paternal will.

The two halves of the feminine inheritance, precept and example, may be merged into one text or received from one source, but often they are not merged, and whether they are or not, they constitute two quite distinct and dissonant discourses. The attempt to resolve the contradictions between them is the task of the heroine, the receiver of the irreconcilable texts inherited from mother and substitute mother. For the precept is always a lesson in survival (remember Mme de Chartres's precept), about how to maintain a female existence within the impossible system of patriarchy—impossible because it is a system within which such female existence does not substantially exist. But the example is always the history of the mother's failure to survive in that system (even Mme de Chartres only survived by putting herself into voluntary exile, and she dies soon after introducing her daughter to the world of the court).[46] It is the narrative of the mother's death; or when the exemplary history passed on to the daughter is the narrative of the mother's survival (as we glimpsed briefly in the quotation from *Lady Susan* at the end of Chapter 1), it becomes the narrative of her monstrosity.

Patrimony and Matrimony: The Monstrous Mother

There is a third category, then, besides the dead and the substitutive, into which mothers fall: the monstrous, or, more specifically, the spectral. The role of witch, so often accorded in fairy tales to stepmothers, is in these books generally reserved for biological mothers—in those cases where they have survived long enough to take on any present role in the heroine's life. Evil stepmothers do sometimes appear as a variant of this, but the essential point is that, whether mother or stepmother, the monster is always *wedded to the father*. As Spencer similarly remarks, "the maternal authority so crucial to West's oeuvre finally operates under the authority of the patriarchal system" ("Of Use," p. 204; see also my discussion in "Value"). The substitute mother, a maternal figure not married to any father, is much more consistently the beneficent figure, whether she substitutes for a dead mother or protects the heroine from the wrath or negligence of a living one.[47] Thus "the mother" is herself as fragmented and ambiguous a figure as the legacy she leaves. The representation of mother-daughter relations in these novels shares with the epistle and the tableau the structure of mise-en-abyme, as the heroine gets passed on from one substitute mother to the next at each narrative turn. The maternal role is insistently displaced from the mother onto a substitute who is nobody's mother. This displacement is too systematic and universal within the subgenre to be explainable solely by the historical facts of maternal mortality and child-rearing practices.

If exceptions are what prove rules (and exceptional examples *are* what prove maxims), they may also be useful in demonstrating how the rules operate. A notable exception to the rule of "nobody's mother" appears in one of the best known of the novels under discussion: Staël's *Delphine*. Delphine, about whose legal and biological mother not one word appears in nearly 1,000 pages, has two substitute mothers. One, her sister-in-law, Mlle d'Albémar, like most substitute mothers of the genre, has retreated from the world instead of marrying. The other is Mme de Vernon, who is actually somebody's mother—the mother of Mathilde, Delphine's rival for the hand of her lover, Léonce. And it is precisely because Mme de Vernon is a mother that she violates the role of substitute mother and uses her position as adviser to betray Delphine. Eventually Delphine discovers this betrayal and confronts Mme de Vernon, after which they become enemies until Mme de Vernon is on her deathbed and begs Delphine's forgiveness. Delphine then visits her, and Mme de Vernon gives her an apology in the form of a narration of her own education in life—not in person, but in a letter Delphine is explicitly asked to read alone, in its author's absence. Mme de Vernon's history is telling enough to reproduce here in large part:

> The circumstances that governed my education changed my natural disposition. . . . My father and mother died before I was three years old, and those who educated me did not deserve my attachment to them. . . . I soon became aware that the feelings I expressed were made fun of, and that my mind was stifled, as if it were not suitable for a woman to have one. Therefore I kept to myself all that I felt; early on I acquired the art of dissimulation, and I smothered the sensibility that nature had given me . . . I found it rather unjust that the very same men who counted women as nothing, who granted them no rights and barely any faculties, were also those who would demand of them the virtues of strength and independence, of frankness and sincerity.
>
> My guardian, rather tired of me since I had no fortune, came to tell me one morning that I had to marry M. de Vernon. . . . I examined my situation; I saw that I was powerless; a useless struggle seemed to me the conduct of a child; I renounced it, but with a feeling of hatred against a society that did not come to my defense and left me without any resources other than that of dissimulation. Since that time, my mind was irrevocably made up to make use of that re-

> source whenever I might deem it necessary. I firmly believed that women's fate had condemned them to falsehood; I was confirmed in my idea conceived since childhood that I was, because of my sex and the little fortune that I possessed, an unfortunate slave to whom all ruses were permissible with her tyrant. I never thought of morality; I did not think that it could concern the oppressed.

There are strong echoes here of the monstrous Mme de Merteuil, in the famous Lettre LXXXI of Laclos's *Les Liaisons dangereuses*. What would have happened if Mme de Merteuil had had a daughter of her own to educate? We see something of that in what happens to Cécile when Mme de Merteuil takes on the role of her adviser and teacher. Staël does not, however, make her Mme de Vernon into a disfigured she-demon like Mme de Merteuil. Instead, Mme de Vernon is a character who makes grave mistakes and helps create much of the suffering in this novel of long sufferings, who is even quite hard to forgive, but who never undergoes that transformation into a mere female incarnation of evil. The tensions within her character become especially visible, in the same letter just quoted, when she comes to the education of her own daughter:

> I had at first had the idea of raising my daughter according to my own principles, and inspiring her with my character; but I felt a kind of distaste at forming another in the art of feigning: it repulsed me to transmit the lessons of my doctrine; in childhood my daughter showed a strong attachment to me; I never wanted to tell her the secret of my character, nor to deceive her. Nevertheless, I was convinced, and I still am, that women, being victims of all the institutions of society, are destined for unhappiness if they give themselves up in the least to their feelings, if they lose their self-control in any way. After considering this for a long time, I determined to give to Matilde, whose character, as I have told you, showed itself at an early age to be quite harsh, the bridle of the Catholic religion; and I applauded myself for having found the means of submitting my daughter to all the yokes of woman's destiny without altering her natural sincerity. From this you can see that I did not love my way of life, although I was convinced that I could not do without it.[48]

Such is the legacy, an education and a narration of her own history, written upon her deathbed, that Mme de Vernon leaves to Matilde and to Delphine. Her desperate plot to spare her daughter the pain of a woman of sensibility succeeds only in creating another monster, who ends up causing interminable grief both to her mother and to Delphine (who herself becomes a kind of substitute mother to Matilde by providing her with a dowry). Staël makes explicit in this passage what Boisgiron encrypts in the one quoted earlier in this chapter: the conflict between sensibility and survival. If passively virtuous suffering and the interest it draws enable female survival, they also endanger it.

The example of Mme de Vernon, the substitute mother who is also a real mother, and who is therefore dangerous, seems an exception to the pattern according to which the substitute mother is nobody's mother, just as the heroine who comes under her protection is nobody's daughter. This is only so, however, because she belongs less to the pattern of the substitute mother than to that of the biological mother, the married and especially the widowed mother who is always, by virtue of her anomalous and dangerous position within patrilineage, an unnatural mother.[49] Delphine looks up to Mme de Vernon for guidance, looks for the care of a mother from her, but her own early education was provided by her first substitute mother, Mlle d'Albémar, whose defense against the society described by Mme de Vernon was retreat rather than dissimulation.[50] It has already been observed that natural mothers in these novels, like Delphine's, like Evelina's, and like those of a crowd of lesser-known heroines, are generally left in entire oblivion, or killed off by the narrative at a point in time before its beginning. Those who do survive into the heroine's own story become monsters, more or less blatantly depending on how much the writer is interested in complexity of interior characterization. The reason for this, as already implied in the previous chapter's reading of *La Princesse de Clèves*, is the mother's inscription within patrilineage.

How exactly does the mother's inscription, through matrimony, within the system for the transmission of patrimony turn her into a monster? It makes her potentially both an unnatural competitor with her own daughter and an unnatural usurper of patriarchal privilege. The paradigmatic "history of every woman" narrates not only women's own story but also exposes the institution of patrimony as a fictional narrative. Since the fiction of patrimony demands and states that the succession of male generations be clear and regular, the attempt to make that fiction real by demanding that men always marry women young enough to produce sufficient heirs and backup heirs to keep the paternal name and fortune attached to the paternal "blood" brings about, in the female line, a strange intergenerational confusion. In explanation of the recurrent theme of the evil mother that Ruth Perry has documented in English women's epistolary novels of the early eighteenth century, she observes that women were married off and had children at such an early age that widowed mothers and their daughters were often in competition for the same men (pp. 53–54). In agreement with this historical explanation, I would add that patriline structures bring mothers and daughters into competition, not simply for the same men, but most significantly for the possession of the same fortune, the same patrimony and the same destiny: in narrative terms, they compete for the same history. As Hirsch points out, the works of George Sand display a pattern observed also by Margaret Homans in *Wuthering Heights*, in which mothers and daughters "could not coinhabit the space of their fiction world but had to replace one another" (*The Mother/Daughter Plot*, p. 49). In the late eighteenth-century French novels surveyed by Stewart, she notes a repeated theme of mothers giving up lovers to their young daughters—a similar form of "replacement" that accentuates maternal generosity and sensibility (pp. 204–5). This is indeed what Mme de Boismiran does, as will be made clear by my discussion of *Lettres de Mademoiselle de Boismiran* in the next chapter. But Mme de Boismiran gives up her lover only after a long struggle with her daughter, literally to the death. This novel, like *Corinne*, explores the darker or Gothic side of the sexual interchangeability of mothers and daughters within patrilineage that other writers moralize and sentimentalize into a positive form of control available to the mother.

The darker side of mother-daughter competition is also dramatized in Austen's *Lady Susan*. Lady Susan tries to marry her daughter Frederica to her own cast-off suitor, Sir James, of whom a friend writes to her, "I talked to him about you and your daughter, and he is so far from having forgotten you, that I am sure he would marry either of you with pleasure" (p. 219). She herself intends to marry, for his money, the younger man with whom her daughter has fallen in love. Lady Susan, who escapes the disadvantages of her advanced age (32) by means of a lively wit and, especially, the fact that she looks only 25 (p. 214), scandalously neglects her daughter's education, as all the characters in the book, including herself, remark (e.g., *Lady Susan*, p. 216). The passage quoted in Chapter 1 presents the bad example she sets her daughter, in addition to preventing her from learning anything useful. It is remarkable that when a female character finds herself in the independent state that only widows, like the princess of Clèves, attain, it is precisely then that she becomes incapable of passing on even the ambivalent female legacy of an education that will guide her daughter through her own history. The moment a mother enters into the princess's state, she is transformed into a quasi-mythical monster—even in the hands of Jane Austen, who could give other improper women, like Mary Crawford, much more subtlety of interior characterization. Mary Poovey correctly reads the portrayal of Lady Susan's monstrosity as highly ambiguous, while Gilbert and Gubar argue that Austen enacts "a complicated dual identification both with the more compliant heroines and the subversive, capricious, powerful mothers" (Poovey, *The Proper Lady*, pp. 173–79; Gilbert and Gubar, *Madwoman*, p. 174; see also Hirsch, *The Mother/Daughter Plot*, p. 47). Nevertheless, the fact "that Lady Susan is given the sentiments and the demeanor of a monster when it comes to her treatment of her sixteen-year-old daughter" is too anomalous in Austen's fiction, and too persistent in that of female novelists before and after her, to be considered "arbitrary, even baseless" (MacDonagh, pp. 21–22). The monstrosity of widowed mothers in women's fiction is too consistent to be only a question of literary skill.

Unlike the good mothers who die young, monstrous mothers are *not* in the position of having nothing to pass on; we have seen what kind of education Mme de Vernon gave her daughter, and what example Lady Susan gave hers. It is certainly not insignificant that although both of these characters are independent widows, they both lack the princess's jewels—her movable but material inheritance—to lend agency to their independence. It is not out of sheer bitterness that Mme de Vernon plots the marriage of her son to Matilde in spite of Delphine's love, nor is it pure unmotivated ill nature—although Austen's atypically flat characterization sometimes makes it seem so—that makes Lady Susan try to force her daughter's marriage to Sir James and finagle her own union with the wealthy Reginald De Courcy. Rather, both mothers resort to such manipulation out of a need for money and a lack of respectable and active means to obtain it.[51] What is villainous about Mme de Vernon and Lady Susan is that they respond in direct, pragmatical ways—in short, in unsentimental ways—to the problem of poverty and to the problem of women's general exclusion from lines of inheritance, rather than accepting like proper heroines the substitution for patrimony of a passive, sentimental virtue passed on through the female line, and accepting the fiction that virtue can effectively substitute for these as a means of survival in the patrie. They are monsters because they refuse to suffer (virtuously); they reject the role of *la vertu malheureuse*. The lack of money emblematizes the situation of the independent mother, in particular, who has entered the patrimonial system by marrying and producing heirs to the paternal goods. Although she is left by her husband's death in sole possession of his property and sole control of what name shall receive it (at the marriage of his daughter), this only means, as mentioned previously, that she finds herself in a position to wield some patriarchal power, but without the legitimacy, the authorization, the recognition of the patriarchy.[52] She has only what her husband has left, and that has been left not to her possession, but only in usufruct.

Any mother who tries to claim possession of an inheritance in her own right is thus automatically a usurper of the rights of her child, the father's true heir. Even the child itself, while considered the father's property according to this system (in which fathers are often seen using absolute and tyrannical authority over children of both sexes) is by no means considered a mother's property.[53] Any mother, even a living, present, and wholly benevolent biological mother, *is thus in legal terms a substitute parent*. Adele's mother, who appears in *Adele et Sophie* as a foil to Sophie's mother, the book's more typical monster mother, is overtly described by her daughter as knowing her place as technically a substitute, a mere guardian appointed as a substitute for the dead father: "Mother, having been left a widow early, having no other children but myself, and a rather limited fortune, was named my guardian [*fut nommée ma tutrice*]. She always viewed herself as a mere depository of my father's wealth, the usufruct of which was hers by right, until my majority."[54]

We may at this point hazard a tentative answer to the question of why the role of passing on the ambiguous education in feminine virtue is consistently displaced onto a substitute mother who is nobody's mother. In the first place mothers, as the example above demonstrates, are always already in the position of substitutes. The mother of Adele passes on nothing of her own but her example of extreme self-abnegation. Most of these fictional mothers, as has been mentioned, go even further in their exemplary passivity, being dead before the heroine's history begins. The only successful "mother" in this fiction, as it appears thus far, the only mother who can salvage something beneficial to pass on to a daughter, is the mother who has refused to become a mother. To take on the biological and legal status of mother is, in this period, whether one looks to "history" in the modern sense of the word or to "history" in the other eighteenth-century sense—to "romance"—is ineluctably to inscribe oneself within the patrilineal system that leaves the mother with nothing to pass on. One may inscribe oneself in a way legitimated by the system (appropriate marriage), in which case one's history is simply forgotten, or one may do so in a way not legitimated (elopement or premarital sex), in which case, in the late eighteenth century, one is crushed.

The effect of the historical shift in emphasis since *La Princesse de Clèves* is that a heroine can no longer be a successor, like the princess, to a Mme de Valentinois—"a mistress of the state"—she must now be a successor to the princess herself, by attempting to live up to an impossible example of virtue. Even when a mother has refused to be forgotten, and manages to pass on the narrative of her death to a daughter who considers it her duty to preserve it and pass it on again, she herself is by virtue of this achievement no longer around to give that daughter the other half of the maternal inheritance, direct advice for her own life.[55] That missing half, the one that aids in the preservation of life instead of the repetition of death, can only be provided—sometimes—by one of those substitutes who avoid the impossibilities of existing within the patrimonial system by exiling themselves from it, either by becoming nuns, by a secular "retirement," or, if lucky enough to be independent widows who are both childless and sufficiently wealthy to remain independent, by simply living as heirs to the princess of Clèves, continually refusing offers of marriage, even from the men they love. One substitute mother of the latter category exclaims, when her good friend and former lover suggests that they marry in order to acknowledge as their own the young heroine of unknown parentage: "What! take a master, and live in Holland!"[56] Her response implies that the only alternative to exile from within the system of patrimony is another kind of exile, in which one leaves one's own country, but still fails to escape the laws of the patrie.

It is important, not only that the role of passing on the maternal inheritance is always displaced onto a substitute, but that the "real" mother herself, when she does survive, is also insistently monstrous. Surviving mothers, in exile from the patrie but still inscribed in the system of patrilineage, confuse the linearity of female lines of descent and desire, and hence of a heroine's plot. But the passing on of the inheritance of virtue by a substitute mother tends similarly to collapse the heroine's plot into the maternal destination. By framing the mother's deadly example with the precepts of passive virtue, it demands a repetition of the plot that should have been the mother's in a mirroring that reproduces the virtuous death (whether literal or figurative) required by the laws (that is, by the fiction) of patrilineage. Nevertheless, as the reading of *The Recess* in Chapter 5 will clarify, the sympathetic exchange of histories between women who are not related in the terms of patriline kinship can undermine this deadly effect by modeling an alternative form of transmission between women that resists the patrilineal system within which the mother-daughter relationship always remains inscribed. For an anatomy of the surviving mother as monster and specter laid out against a geography of the mother country as colonial exile within the patrie, I now turn to the *Lettres de Mademoiselle de Boismiran*.

Chapter 4 · · ·

The Spectral Mother; or, The Fault of Living On

She has opened my grave, and she is going to push me into it.

—Mme de Boisgiron, 'Lettres de Mademoiselle de Boismiran'

A book entitled *The Spectral Mother* was published a few years ago by Madelon Sprengnether, who explains her use of the phrase thus: "The preoedipal mother, in Freud's unsystematic treatments of her, emerges as a figure of subversion, a threat to masculine identity as well as to patriarchal culture. . . . She has a ghostlike function [in Freud's Oedipus theory], creating a presence out of absence. . . . Her effect is what I call 'spectral,' in the full etymological sense . . . related to 'spectacle,' 'speculation,' and 'suspicion'. . . . [She is] an object of fear or dread." It is a matter of chance that I happened to hit on the same phrase, and I do not undertake a discussion of "the preoedipal mother" in psychoanalytic terms. Yet the correspondence is suggestive. In eighteenth-century novels of women's correspondence, the mother is also "spectral" in that she is mostly either absent—repressed—or returns as "an object of fear or dread." But the source of terror in this fiction, as I began to outline it in the previous chapter, lies not in the mother's "threat to masculine identity as well as to patriarchal culture," but rather in the threat to feminine identity posed by her specular reproduction of patriarchal culture, as perceived by her daughter. In this overwhelming identification with the psychological position of a daughter in relation to a maternal threat, the novelists discussed in this book immediately anticipate the related phenomenon Marianne Hirsch has described in *The Mother/Daughter Plot* as characteristic of many of the best-known novels authored by French and English women in the first half of the nineteenth century (esp. pp. 46–58). In *Lettres de Mademoiselle de Boismiran, receuillies et publiées par Mme de **** (Paris and Amsterdam, 1777), Madame de Boisgiron has left us a text that maps out, in the most shockingly literalized detail, the intertwinings and collisions of the monstrous plot of maternal survival with patriline plot and with the heroine's plot. For that reason I have chosen to devote a chapter to reading it. The fact that there is no modern reprint necessitates some outlining of the novel's plot as the reading proceeds.[1]

Patriline Plots: Will and Will's Miscarriage

Mlle de Boismiran's story resembles that of other heroines of her period, as described in the previous chapter. Like theirs, it begins at the moment when her arrival at the "interesting age" exposes the lacuna in the fiction of patriline transmission. The heroine's history recounts the deviation of patrimonial transmission from the path of the father's will, so that his wealth and even his death escape his willed destination. The rhetoric of Mlle de Boismiran's letters, moreover, strikingly exposes the miscarriage of paternal will as inherent in the logic of patriarchal authority: "Merciless death did not leave him the time to choose the hand that closed his eyes. The same day returned him to his fatherland [*patrie*] and brought him to the grave."[2] After making a fortune in America, the father had destined his ducats for his daughter, and his daughter for a proper education in France. But *la mort impitoyable* operates here as an ironic subversion of Providence as apotheosis of paternal will, transforming the father's willed destination, *sa patrie*, into his grave.[3] It subverts the logic of patriarchy simply by following it to its own logical conclusion and ultimately turning its primary metaphor against itself. For the symbolic logic of patriarchy rests on the equation of authority and power, not with masculinity, but with paternity, and thereby constructs a hierarchy not simply of men over women, but also of fathers over sons, within a many-tiered hierarchy of "descent." The ultimate earthly father is the king, whose "divine right" descends from a paternal God. But this patriarchal logic is always vulnerable to being "turned on its head": if the father's power is authorized by the hierarchy of paternal authority resting ultimately in God or His Providence, that ultimate power, God or Providence, can always be invoked as legitimate authority for thwarting the earthly father's lesser authority.[4]

By equating *patrie* and *tombeau* as (unwilled) destinations, moreover, the rhetoric of the sentence quoted above takes the theme of women's exile in the patrie and turns it upon the father himself. If feminine exile is frequently literalized in women's fiction of the period as a fictional burial, her name living on in the fatherland only on a tombstone marking an empty grave, a father's return to it here becomes an actual burial.[5] Just as Providence apotheosizes paternal authority, it is also the mark of the father's absence, signifying his lack of ultimate authority, as well as the absence of any ultimately authorizing father at the top of a hierarchy that vanishes, by its very apotheosis, into the clouds. The patrie is deadly for men as well as for women, in this novel whose plot opens in the patrie as the father's grave plot, and leads through long detours to its close in the mother country as the daughter's grave plot.

The rhetorical transformation of patrie into grave robs the dead father of his will, leaving an opening for the miscarriage of patrimony, name, and heir from any legitimate path, by a competing plot of patriline "interest." At the father's deathbed, his daughter is left to a confidence man, M. de Flinonval. By the starting point of the narrative, Flinonval has had the heroine educated in a convent under the care of a substitute mother, Mme de Foncel. The heroine grows up in the belief that she is only plain Mademoiselle Gelin, without wealth or title, while Flinonval has used her patrimony to buy himself land and a title, and plans to legitimate his possession by marrying her to his son. It is this plot to divert the patrimony to another paternal line that opens the novel, with Flinonval's disclosure to the heroine that she is really the wealthy heiress Mlle de Boismiran, and that, by virtue of her arrival at the "interesting age" and her mother's decree, she is now released from the convent and has become "mistress of her fate" (pt. 1, p. 8). Like the princess of Clèves, Mlle de Boismiran inherits an illustrious patronym, but no proper name of her own. Like her, she inherits a patrimony as well, and arrives at the point (later for the princess) where she seems to be free to follow the plot laid by her own desire. Whereas by the end of her novel, the princess becomes a "mistress of the state" of private independence on her own plot of ground, Mademoiselle begins her narrative by being told that she is "mistress of her fate"—that is, of the course of her own life plot. But Mlle de Boismiran's desire, like the princess's, has no plot of its own—just as the heroines have no names of their own—for the heroine's desire is detoured from its own path by a mother's desire that survives, in both cases, beyond the grave.

It is typically in the interest of patriline plots to warn the daughter, as Flinonval does, against competing "interested" plots. He tells Mademoiselle that for her own good he will continue to conceal her true identity from the world; she wouldn't want importunate noblemen of ailing fortunes deceiving her innocence into a "marriage of interest" (in which the "interest" on her fortune, as a means of living, is what the "interested" nobleman would really be after, precluding any sentimental "interest" in the heroine). But the daughter's own interest, of course, lights upon the hero of sensibility, the young marquis d'Ornevil—handsome, romantic, noble, impoverished, but virtuous. To sum up, the conflict of plot lines that sets the novel in motion is this: in the opening left by the self-displacement of patriline will, the heroine's desire would seem to be freed to follow its own trajectory ("maîtresse de son sort"). But in fact the same hierarchical competition among patriline interests and the overarching interest of patriline hierarchy, which diverted the father's will from its proper path, diverts the daughter's desire as well. Here the crucial third plot line enters the web: the diversion of patriline will from its destination is made possible, not only by the competitive and hierarchical nature of its internal logic, but also by the passive complicity of the absent mother.

The Absent Mother

The paradigmatic heroine's plot begins not simply in the lacuna that exposes patriline transmission as fiction, but also in the absence of the mother, whose prior history is often interpolated within her own. It was mentioned in Chapter 3 that in those versions that look at first like "exceptions" or variants, where the mother is neither dead nor absent, she appears persistently as monstrous. *Mademoiselle de Boismiran* demonstrates that the present, living, surviving mother's monstrosity is, in fact, the *appearance* (*monstrum*) of her absence, of her absence-in-presence, the rearing its ugly head of the particular form of death-in-life that is maternal survival within patrilineage.

If Providence is the mark of paternal absence, the absence of the mother—and of her double, the substitute mother—shows itself in written correspondence. As the mark of absence, maternal correspondence represents the lacuna that allows for the diversion of female desire from its destination, just as the patriline hierarchy of descent allows for the diversion of paternal will from its destination. This diversion is worked out in the plot of *Mademoiselle de Boismiran* in a manner true to epistolary form: Flinonval intercepts a letter from the substitute mother in which she attempts to warn the heroine that he is an impostor, then cows the daughter into writing, at his dictation, a letter to her mother. All that she will write is simply that she "does not hate" Flinonval's son, but that is enough. Here, as throughout eighteenth-century literature—and already in *La Princesse de Clèves*, during the scene of the aveu—a woman's silence or ambiguity is interpreted according to the will of its receiver. As a result, when the heroine later refuses to marry his son, Flinonval has written evidence that enables him to induce the absent mother to view her daughter as a capricious girl with no sense of honor or duty. He persuades her literally to sign over to him all her parental authority (pt. 2, p. 7). In the most literal sense, then, the letter has here become the mark of maternal absence.

The heroine responds to her mother's letter much as if she had seen a ghost: "I was penetrated with horror at reading the decree of my unhappiness traced by her own hand."[6] The words *pénétrée*, *tracé*, and even *horreur* are almost dead metaphors in the conventionally excessive language of sensibility. Nevertheless, in representing the heroine's response to her mother's letter, they transmit a sympathetic frisson to the reader, even though neither reader nor heroine yet knows that these very same words will recover all their literal force to an uncanny degree when met with again in the mother's excessively literal country.

The miscarriage of the maternal letter effects the miscarriage of the heroine's plot, and of her person. After his interventions in women's correspondences, Flinonval manipulates the patriarchal hierarchy once more in order to divert male desire from its path by seeing to it that d'Ornevil is called away to his regiment on false pretenses. He diverts Mademoiselle just as literally and more directly, kidnapping her and imprisoning her in a convent. There he introduces her to the nuns as "a false and dissimulating person, who eludes legitimate authority only to follow the dangerous inclinations of her heart."[7] The mark of the mother's absence—her letter—thus allows for a slippage in the legitimacy of authority that can result in the very literal absence of the daughter from her own (desired) destination. But the mother's presence as substitute or legal guardian was already a mark of the father's absence, and the father's will has no authority without the direction of that great absence, Providence. The misrepresentation used by Flinonval to alienate the nuns' potential sympathy for Mademoiselle calls attention at an early stage to what will become the main problem of the novel: the conflict between desire, especially female desire, and authority. Authority, as will be remembered from the earlier discussion of maternal monstrosity, is always paternal authority, but it is also always displaced. The central question, then, is more particularly that of the legitimacy or illegitimacy of that (always patriarchal) authority, a question marked by its exercise by a female substitute.[8]

The absent mother is first represented to her daughter, through the distorting medium of Flinonval's narrative, in terms of tyranny—not, indeed, of aristocratic tyranny, but of colonial tyranny. He tells her that her mother remained behind in America when her father returned to his patrie because she could not bear the social equality that, according to him, was so characteristic of prerevolutionary France: "Being accustomed to seeing a crowd of slaves occupied with discerning and anticipating her wishes made her dread the European way of life, where the greatest pleasures are to be found in society, and thus in equality."[9] The inequality of the social organization of the patrie—that is, of monarchy as quasi-apotheosized patriarchy—is thus displaced onto the colony as "mother country," and in its displacement apparently effaced in the fatherland. It must be remembered, however, that this description is uttered by the novel's arch-villain of displacement, Flinonval. Nevertheless, he is a villain of displacement because his primary motivation is to rise in the social hierarchy, to violate the very separation of classes by which he hopes to profit. Indeed, the heroine's first objection to marrying his son is that he remains, though personally less despicable than his father, a mere *financier* like him. Her wariness of the bourgeois "interest," not in doing away with class distinctions, but in deriving greater personal profit from them, would seem to confirm the novel's investment in Flinonval's implied statement that equality is only to be achieved by maintaining the separation of classes and the hierarchy of (patriarchal) "society," rather than by leveling class distinctions. Her lover, the marquis, however, seems to display more revolutionary sentiments than our heroine, having proposed marriage to her at a masked ball in the belief that she was only Mlle Gelin.

What the novel does consistently espouse, throughout the varying views of the characters on class relations, is the substitution of the sympathetic form of "interest" for the self-interest of usury and profit, which it identifies with the bourgeoisie.[10] The latter form of interest is portrayed as requiring a maintenance of the distinctions between the bourgeoisie, the aristocracy, and the poor. The maintenance of that hierarchy, in turn, means the maintenance of clear and distinct boundaries, which reassuringly appear to allow for the stable placement and identification of each of the elements that make up the oppositions organized by the hierarchy. Those oppositions include the distinction between sympathetic interest and self-interest, which, as the discussion in Chapter 3 emphasized, is inherently far from stable. But a monolithic hierarchy based upon a logic of oppositions cannot maintain its stability as a closed system, for it can never completely contain within itself the terms to which it places itself in opposition.[11] It therefore requires as its complement another logic of excess and displacement. Thus the patrie requires the colony, the rigidly placed patriarchal hierarchy requires maternal absence and boundlessness, and the fictional character as exemplar (even as negative exemplar) of patriarchal maxims requires a double.

Doubling in the Literature of Sensibility; or, Virtue's Double Agent

Before her narrative begins, the heroine has developed both of the primary forms of female friendship in novels of women's correspondence: with a substitute mother, as has been mentioned, and also with a confidante and peer. Mademoiselle de Belvaux, rather than corresponding with the heroine after she leaves the convent, as Mme de Foncel does, follows her out instead to become her inseparable friend, her double. She infiltrates the new convent where Mademoiselle is confined, where, being a much more intrepid character than the fearfully passive heroine, she draws up a plan for escape and forces Mademoiselle to dare its execution. The contrast between the two personalities, Mademoiselle's paralyzing hesitations arising from virtuous doubts about duty, as opposed to Belvaux's clear sense of fundamental right and wrong, with prompt action upon it, is constantly stressed throughout the text. Both are virtuous, but Belvaux's virtue is closer to a masculine model of virtue. This doubling of the heroine is a standard device in novels of sensibility, showing its uncanny side in sensibility's own dark double, Gothic fiction, as it will in the second half of this novel. Doubling enables literature of sensibility to portray a female character exhibiting qualities of active strength in opposition to the patriline plots that would divert her own, while avoiding the social unacceptability under real patriarchy, the patriarchy confronted by novelists and readers, of investing a supposedly virtuous heroine with such unfeminine qualities. Our text employs the device in a particularly forceful way, not complicitously criticizing a minor character's example of female boldness, as Burney and Austen do, but making her clearly a strong double of the heroine, who takes even more part in the action of the book than does the heroine herself.[12]

Encountering many more adventures and threateningly interested suitors along the way, Mademoiselle and Belvaux (disguised as her servant) find their way to Martinique, her mother's home and her own birthplace. This journey, an immense detour in the progress of the daughter's desire to marry d'Ornevil in spite of Flinonval, is nothing other than a quest for the maternal recognition that could be so successfully alienated from the daughter by the interested plotting of Flinonval because it was never in fact hers. The only way to escape Flinonval's authority over her, now fully recognized in the patrie—authorized and evidenced as it is by the mother's letter—is to seek the recognition of an absent mother by a voyage to an uncharted and unrecognized country.

The rhetoric of the text figures the heroine's escape from the patrie to the mother country in the terms of death and rebirth. During her flight from the convent to the ship that is to carry her to America, an "accident" has occurred that has given Belvaux occasion to invent and publish the fiction of the heroine's death (through no fault of her own). This fiction has put her pursuers off her track, but has also been taken literally by her friends and her lover. The result is that Mlle de Boismiran is now fictionally "dead" in the patrie.[13]

A Voyage to the Mother Country: Displacement and the Maternal Sublime

A letter to Mme de Foncel reveals that Mademoiselle has found the means to let her friends, at least, know she is alive and safely aboard ship. She hopes "that they will not delay in reporting my fortunate and romantic resurrection."[14] "Romantic" (*romanesque*) here has the sense of "romance-like," both fictional and implausible. In effect, the heroine implausibly writes her own fictional resurrection beyond the borders of the patrie, as a sequel to Belvaux's fiction of her death within it, and asks the female friend with whom she is in correspondence to "publish" what she has written in the fatherland from which she has exiled herself. Her agency as a heroine thus exists entirely on the plane of fiction-making published through female correspondence.

At this narrative juncture a break occurs in the text, separating part 2 from part 3. This break typographically repeats and literalizes the gulf that now separates the heroine and her fiction from the place of its publication. On the other side of that gulf from the final words of part 2, *romanesque résurrection*, the first words that the reader encounters are those with which the heroine dates her letter: *En pleine mer, ce . . . 1755* (literally, "In mid-sea," but the phrase also suggests "in the pregnant mother"). The pun may sound a bit stretched here, at its first appearance, but it haunts the rest of the novel in its most crucial moments, in contexts that force its significance upon the reader (we shall soon observe some of these).[15] The last words of part 2 and the first of part 3 resonate over the gulf that divides the text with a semantic shift from "resurrection" to rebirth. The rhetoric of birth and resurrection in connection with the motion of the heroine's plot away from the patrie and into a separate country dominated by the figure of the mother revalorizes the image of female exile. It does so by rhetorically setting up a contrast between two sets of twinned ideas: "sea journey to the mother's country = resurrection as rebirth" versus the parallel rhetorically implied earlier, "father's return to his patrie" = "father's passage to the tombeau." Yet, as the plot unfolds, the reader finds that the relation of the mother's country to the patrie is considerably more ambiguous than such an opposition implies. The heroine expects that the publication of her novelistic (and secret) resurrection will save her from further unwilled plot detours. But as she leaves the patrie, the epistolary message of her "rebirth" miscarries, because its destined receiver, d'Ornevil, has himself already been diverted to the mother's country.

While *en pleine mer*, Mademoiselle has only good things to report to her substitute mother of both *mer* and *mere*: "This element, which was represented to me as so terrifying [*terrible*] and so dreadful [*redoutable*], has cast off all its impetuosity for us. . . . The peace and order that reign in your haven [*asyle*] of respectability are the image of the life we lead here."[16] *Terrible* and *redoubtable*, in English as well as in French, are ambiguous terms, whose connotations are only partly negative. This was much more true in the eighteenth century than in modern usage. Power in the abstract, whether for good or ill, is what these terms convey.[17] By linking the mother to a potentially overwhelmingly powerful force in the landscape, this description evokes the contemporary philosophical terms of the sublime. Just as Parmenides linked the opposition bounded/unbounded to that between male and female, Kant associated his opposition of the beautiful to the sublime with sexual difference. Boundlessness is an attribute of the sublime, while the beautiful is safely limited. Thus the imperfectly domesticated woman becomes boundless, a terrifyingly, redoubtably sublime maternal landscape.

But the feeling of the sublime in eighteenth-century thought crucially requires a distance from the object that inspires the feeling: a safe distance that allows the subject to perceive the sublime landscape (for example) aesthetically, and to transcend the threatened feeling of her relative puniness through a sense of the force of her own imagination. Without such a distance, sublime objects, forces, or ideas would only terrify. As long as she remains *en pleine mer*, the heroine herself cannot experience the *mer(e)* as sublime; indeed, her description as quoted denies the sublimity attributed to it by report and substitutes terms more appropriate to the beautiful and bounded (*paix*, *ordre*, *asyle*). *En pleine mer*, she remains in a transitional and immediate relationship to the maternal.

Mademoiselle has not yet encountered her mother as an actual, separate person or in a real situation. While the mother is still hidden for her in a pun, she remains an abstract "element." She can conceive of this maternal abstraction only through displacement, in the image of the *asyle*, the protective enclave of order and respectability represented by the convent and the substitute mother. If the voyage to the mother country takes place already *en pleine mer*, it is an invaginated journey, in which there is no distinct, decidable path, because the plot is collapsed into its own destination. In this immediacy, this lack of differentiation between mother and daughter, the daughter cannot herself recognize the mother; the text thus renders the mother's sublime boundlessness recognizable *to the reader alone* through a series of displacements. The first of these displaces the signified to the signifier (the pun on *mer/mere*), turning an apparently arbitrary homonymous relation between signifiers into a metaphorical resemblance in the substitution of sea for mother. This metaphorical resemblance is in turn recognized only through its further displacement—namely, the displacement of the image of the mother as "the boundless," as the ambiguous conflation of oppositional terms, onto the metaphorical image of the *substitute* mother as "calm haven." It is as if the heroine were saying, "The *mer(e)* is not ambiguous and terrifying; it has put aside its impetuosity to become a 'calm haven' like the substitute mother, just for us." Maternal ambiguity is thus displaced onto a single term of the opposition it confounds, onto the very term in which the substitute mother is here opposed to the mother, as the bounded (*asyle*) to the unbounded (*mer*). The displacement of the figure of the boundless maternal onto the figure of the substitute mother, who is in turn associated rhetorically with the bounded, thus represses maternal ambiguity. The mother's threat to the system of gendered oppositions that her ambiguity conflates is thus concealed under the sign of one of its terms: the bounded. The result is that both mother and substitute mother, mirroring one another as equivalent *asyles*, appear to be less of a threat to the patrilineality that excludes them, and to represent only a calm and separate space of escape from it.[18]

La mer as a sublime representation of maternal power is thus an ambiguous abstraction that combines and confounds the oppositions it contains. It can therefore only be grasped by means of images that figure forth one of its qualities as the mark of absence of the opposing, but equally characteristic, quality. The absent term then becomes, by virtue of its repression, more insistently significant than the term "represented," or marked as present in the figure (as in the metaphor of *asyle* for *mer*, the repressed "impetuosity" of *mer[e]* threatens to emerge). The force of the heroine's rhetoric as just analyzed is repeated in subsequent narrative representations of the mother: people on the ship represent her to her daughter as anything but terrible and redoubtable, although wielding absolute power. They tell her exemplary stories of her mother's heroic rescues of mistreated slaves, and of her protection and promotion of various other persecuted waifs. Madame de Boismiran seems to make an ideal substitute mother, in other words, using her usurped patrimony and patriarchal authority to enforce and authorize the generosity and goodwill that has so far expressed itself to her own daughter only in terms of abdication, as when she left her "mistress of her fate" before signing her over into Flinonval's power.

The rhetorical strategy of nonrecognition I have just described, which displaces in order to render a repressed term recognizable to the reader (although only as the "manifest content" of a dream can render recognizable a "latent content"), is akin to the narrative strategy of literalization that differentiates the Gothic mode from the literature of sensibility more generally. In generic terms the shift from the representational strategy of the displacement of maternal ambiguity onto rhetorical figures and internal narratives to that of its literalized enactment in the mother country is also a shift from sensibility to the Gothic.

The Literal Plot; or, The Literal as Plot

The heroine reencounters the ambiguity of maternal authority, expressed neither in rhetoric nor in narrative, but in enactment, at the very moment when she leaves the sea to set foot in the New World. From the moment of approach to the boundary of the mother country, the mother's presence there is marked again for her daughter as absence: still in the ship, about to disembark in Martinique, the heroine receives a letter from her mother, in which she purports to welcome her daughter with open arms, for she has already received the heroine's history by letter. Those welcoming arms are not her own, however; she excuses her absence by claiming that she is convalescing from a long illness, and regrets that she must "entrust you to strange hands. But what am I saying? the marquis d'Ornevil must no longer be a stranger in my home. Consider him as another me: your affection for him will become a duty."[19] It is, in fact, d'Ornevil who is convalescing from a long illness, as the unfolding plot reveals, and the mother, adopting the convalescent passivity that belongs to him, makes him the agent of her own absence. The ambiguities of language in her letter turn, once more, on the social ambiguities that riddle the logic of patriline hierarchy. Making d'Ornevil a double of and a substitute for the mother, the letter confers paternal authority upon him in terms that are ambiguous because they would apply equally whether the man married either mother or daughter, expressing the degree to which the roles of father and husband blur in the marital discourse of the period. With such blurring of generational boundaries in the male line *as it corresponds to the female line* comes the intergenerational conflation of the plots of female desire.

Mademoiselle, like a more optimistic princess of Clèves, blissfully interprets the letter's ambiguities according to her own desires. While the mother's letter puts off the maternal recognition that the daughter has come to seek, it brings about a near-fatal recognition on the part of d'Ornevil. Recognizing his long-lost beloved as he arrives to help her out of the boat, he faints so near the water's edge that, as the heroine puts it, "without the special protection of Heaven, the sea [*la mer*] would have separated him from me forever."[20] Here the function of providential intervention seems to be to protect the accomplishment of the heroine's desire, not from parental will, but from maternal desire. The return of this terrible revenant of a pun on *mer*(*e*) announces proleptically the same danger that resonated in the terms of the heroine's earlier responses to the mark of maternal absence (*pénétrée*, *horreur*). The danger is not realized in the plot, however, until after many further delays: that space of tergiversation *is* the mother country. Putting off the full, direct expression of her desire and rage—both emotions are equally monstrous in her—the mother is alternately and inexplicably cold and warm towards her daughter, now enacting the conflation of oppositional terms that before had only been narrated to the heroine or rhetorically intimated to the reader.

Mme de Boismiran begins to notice d'Ornevil's increased coldness towards herself, and then to suspect a connection between him and her daughter's double, Belvaux. Meanwhile, Mademoiselle receives for the first time the full "portrait" (*portrait*) of her mother in the "precious" or narrative sense (pt. 3, p. 33). It is the portrait of a monster, in which the mother's boundlessness is seen in action, in all its specificity as a boundlessness of sensibility, and in all its contradictory ambiguity. Passion, the negative and dangerous aspect of sensibility, is represented alongside the positive or sympathetic aspect narrated earlier: in addition to her great acts of benevolence, the mother's passions have led her to commit some equally ruthless ones. She and her own dark, Gothic double (discussed below) are together portrayed as "monstrous beings, capable of the greatest crimes and the most heroic acts."[21] Like *la mer*, and like the adjectives *terrible* and *redoutable*, *la mere* is monstrous because she is a literalization of the abstract and morally ambiguous power of sentiment dislocated from within the logic of patriline hierarchy that had domesticated it, making it look so reassuringly contained and familiar. In defamiliarizing it, in displacing it from the patriarchal family and the domestic space, the Gothic mother makes sensibility monstrous. Sentiment becomes ultimately indistinguishable from passion, from "interested" desire. But in this lack of distinction, it becomes clear that it was the patriarchal family, all along, that did not sufficiently distinguish the daughter's desire from the mother's, or the mother's from the father's.

Mlle de Boismiran came to the mother country in search of recognition: the recognition of the distinctness and legitimacy of her own desire by the authority figure she herself could recognize as legitimate in patriline terms. But in the boundless territory of the mother country, recognition itself is enacted as a blurring of boundaries. This crisis is narrated in an interpolated letter from d'Ornevil, addressed to both Mademoiselle and Belvaux (pt. 3, pp. 74–119). He asks the double (whose toleration for Gothic horror is higher than the heroine's) to intercede for him with Mademoiselle—but again willed destination is thwarted when Mademoiselle comes across it and reads it herself. This failure of epistolary destination culminates the whole series of failed destinations that make up the plot of the novel—that of M. de Boismiran's last will, that of Mademoiselle's intended message of obedience to her mother in the letter dictated by Flinonval, that of Flinonval's intended dispatching of d'Ornevil out of the path of his ward, that of Mademoiselle's published death and resurrection—with the ultimate failure of sexual desire, both female and male, to reach its willed destination. The bizarre trajectory of this failure is traced out through every turn in the plot enclosed within this diverted letter, in the plot of d'Ornevil's secret history.

We learn that upon receiving the fiction of the heroine's death, d'Ornevil fell ill of chagrin: "It was thought that the sea air was hindering the effect of the cure, and the plan was formed to remove me from it without my being consulted."[22] Passively removed from *l'air de la mer*, he finds himself transported into the house of *la mere*, where her unladylike *air* (manner) will indeed prove deadly. In this suppressed repetition of the earlier pun, the terrible ambiguity of *la mer(e)* can at last be fully identified as the element that miscarries desire from its destination. The boundary line of the mother country, then, as well as the path by which it is reached—namely, that which separates and distinguishes it from the fatherland or patrie, is *la mer*, the boundless element.[23] To the extent that it is distinct at all (for the island mother country remains a colony of the patrie, although separated from it by vast distances and outlandish social and cultural practices), it is distinguished not as one bounded and recognized state from another, but as the boundless, the indistinct and unrecognizable, in opposition to the bounded. As the opposite of the distinct, the formed, the limited, and the ordered, the boundless admits of no distinctions, whether between male and female, black and white, border and interior, old and young, living and dead, good and evil, completion and excess. D'Ornevil's story enacts the impossibility of recognizing distinctions in the boundlessness of *la mer(e)*: he cannot leave the patrie or flee the mother country, leave the border and go to the interior, or desire the daughter and not the mother, the mistress and not the slave, the white and not the black, because all are confused and conflated in *la mer(e)*.

What is paradoxical in the opposition of the boundless to the bounded is that it posits an opposite—the boundless—for the notion of opposition itself. Boundlessness therefore threatens the recognition of any distinct terms of opposition—of "any decidable edge or border." The paradox of mother-daughter recognition is thus a function of the paradox inherent in the opposition of the boundless to the bounded: as the boundless negates the distinctions that make recognition possible, the boundless itself, *la mer(e)*, can only be recognized through a series of displacements that blur those distinctions in the gesture of positing them. This accounts for the recurrence, within the invaginated series of narrations that recount the voyage to the mother country, of the complex trope that first came into play in the description of *la mer(e)*. There, maternal boundlessness was rendered recognizable to the reader through a metonymic series of metaphorical displacements that blur even the distinction between metaphor and metonymy, between resemblance and contiguity, analogy and contingency, chance and Providence, desire and will-lessness. The "blurring of any decidable edge or border" is all, in fact, that remains recognizable in that process, and it becomes spectacularly recognizable in d'Ornevil's narrative of desire.

The passive marquis finds himself in the care of Mme de Boismiran, who, like a good substitute mother, nurses him back to health. Her maternal and sympathetic feelings, however, slip dangerously (and boundlessly) into amorous ones, for she falls in love with the young man in the process. In this she is no ridiculous old lady. She has been described by this time in terms similar to those used by Austen for Lady Susan: "She is beautiful and looks uncommonly young: one can hardly believe that she is the mother of her daughter."[24] Indeed, we have just learned that she became the heroine's mother at fifteen (pt. 3, pp. 51, 55). Nevertheless the heroic d'Ornevil resists, because he cannot forget Mlle Gelin, even though he still believes her dead. But Mme de Boismiran further obliges him by preserving his patrimony: by giving his sister a dowry, she enables him to keep the last piece of real estate he has to his name. In unladylike (unheroinelike) fashion, she makes her own avowal of love, thus forcing him to choose between accepting her, as a man of honor, or humiliating a woman to whom he is indebted for the preservation of his life and fortune. Still his fidelity to the memory of the apparently desireless heroine and her virtue makes him hesitate to answer.

In the moment of hesitation, Madame's eyes flash with fierce indignation, but she controls herself immediately, regaining the air of dignity that (as d'Ornevil adds at this point in the epistolary account addressed to Belvaux) never departs from her daughter. He identifies that moment of transition as a moment of recognition: "For the first time I was struck by the astonishing similarity of their features. Transported and beside myself. . . . I threw myself down at her feet."[25] The recognition that takes place here is *not* one of the distinctness of mother and daughter, but rather of their resemblance, and this act of recognizing resemblance has the force of utterly conflating the two. The hero is "transported outside himself" into a passion for this daughterlike mother, just as passively as earlier he was transported into the mother's house. The mother responds by absenting herself, satisfied with his reply, and at that moment Zaïde enters as the double agent who must enact the plot of the absent mother and the passive lover.[26]

Gothic Doubling: The Agency of Absence

> Betrayed by that intoxicating resemblance by which I had been struck so vividly, the frenzy and fire of passion took hold of my entire being. Zaïde, the inexplicable, the dangerous Zaïde, appears at my side, in transports over the happiness of her mistress . . . . . , herself inflamed with. . . . But alas! . . . . Yes, my extreme repentance forces me to confess the shameful pleasures that the disorder of my senses made me taste in the arms of that voluptuous slave.[27]

Zaïde is the most important of the mother's substitute daughters. She is a slave who had been used for sexual purposes by her master ("It is said that in our colonies, as in those of our rivals, it is not uncommon to see women born in the fiery climes preferred to the prettiest Europeans").[28] Mme de Boismiran has saved her from a cruel death, since which time Zaïde has become Madame's devoted and inseparable servant. Just as the hierarchical logic of patriarchal authority was undermined in the patrie when divine Providence turned the father's willed destination into his tomb, Zaïde now recalls the orientalist convention of the non-Westerner whose naïve responses to European culture constitute a piquant critique to invert patriline logic in the words with which she greets her savior: "Powerful God (cried the unfortunate, falling down before my mother's knees), for the first time I behold your image!"[29]

Zaïde, as much the agent of the mother's passive absence as Belvaux is of the heroine's passive virtue, actively announces here Mme de Boismiran's usurpation of providential authority in intervening where a mortal male master had abdicated his own. Zaïde can conceive of God only in the concrete, literalized image of Madame, who for her embodies God's *puissance*, just as Mademoiselle can only conceive of her mother in the image of the *mer*, which in turn she can only comprehend as an image for the *asyle* of her substitute mother.

The "shameful pleasures" indulged in by d'Ornevil and Zaïde repeat themselves, inexplicably and quite often (to d'Ornevil's avowed degradation) during the several delays to his planned wedding with Madame. The letters of Zaïde to him during this period are enclosed at this point in his letter to Belvaux/Mademoiselle (yet another instance of failed or improper destination); Zaïde herself must narrate what went on between them, since none but an uncivilized African she-monster can knowingly allow herself to speak the unspeakable. No one else, not even a man who is also a virtuous man of feeling, could use her language of direct desire, full of blood boiling in the veins and invocations of the *chaînes de la volupté*. Only Zaïde is able to call herself *pénétrante* (pt. 3, pp. 113–19).

What d'Ornevil is addressing to Belvaux, and unwittingly sending to Mademoiselle, is a narrative whose plot needs to be repeated at this point in order to unpack the rhetorical structure at play in the pun on *la mer(e)*: D'Ornevil never recognized the resemblance between Mademoiselle and her mother until the return of the self-restrained dignity always present in the daughter revealed the contrast (a *lack* of resemblance) between the daughter's and the mother's expression of passion. It is the shift, the gesture by which the mother visibly represses her passions under the mask of "dignity," that reveals the resemblance between mother and daughter. This resemblance transmits the flash of passion to d'Ornevil. The desire created out of resemblance/contrast then continues on its virulently metonymic course, transferring itself immediately onto the next person to enter the room, who of course is not only contiguous with, but also resembles Madame in precisely the single point—the expression of passion—the *lack* of which constitutes the sole resemblance between mother and daughter.

Zaïde, who is simply the literalized agent for the plot of absent or repressed passion, succeeds and replaces the now "dignified" and absent Madame in d'Ornevil's chamber and communes in the "shameful pleasures" of d'Ornevil's passion for the dispassionate and absent Mademoiselle. Such resemblance resembles—and becomes—metonymy because the resemblance can only be established in the moment of slippage from one term to the next. The flash of passion disappears to reveal the repression of passion, which requires a slip, the momentary absence of repression and the movement of return to it, in order to constitute a resemblance between the present mother and the absent, "dead" daughter. Resemblance ought to have been directly inherited and recognizable, but instead it can only be recognized in the figurative terms of its opposite, its negation, its lack. This figuration of lack was already connected with the *mere* in the self-contradictory image of the *mer*. The strange trajectory of enclosed and enclosing stories that fail of their willed destinations has brought us to the enactment in plot of the dynamic that was "miniaturized" in rhetorical terms, in the metonymic metaphors of absence. Female desire proceeds along the same indirect and unrecognized detours—in short, along the same illegitimate paths of transmission—as does female inheritance, subverting will and ultimately, as we shall see, subverting the plot of virtue, the plot of the female inheritance itself.

Legitimating Female Desire

D'Ornevil sends the heroine his narrative, with its virulent force of contagious resemblances of lack, via the detour of her double, Belvaux. He intends it to persuade Mademoiselle to understand and forgive his passive powerlessness to resist. He does this even though he refers to her as "purity and virtue," not merely pure and virtuous, but an embodiment of these abstractions, and thus, presumably, completely outside the chain he expects her to understand (pt. 3, p. 104). But Mademoiselle is not, in fact, entirely outside the metonymic chain along which the metaphors of passion slip, for she is not entirely devoid of dangerous passion herself. Her disgust at the infidelity of d'Ornevil only adds to a difficulty that has been preventing her, since she first discovered her mother's interest in him, from complying with his plans for their escape together from her mother's control: she is paralyzed by guilt in the conflict between *amour* and *prudence*, which is nothing other than the problem, mentioned earlier, of the legitimacy of authority. She cannot bear to become an unnatural daughter by challenging her mother's natural authority. When she finally resolves to do so, unleashed desire acts out its most outlandish plots of all.

The logic that persuades Mademoiselle to rebel against her mother follows this line: maternal desire is boundless, therefore maternal authority is illegitimate (unrecognizable), because boundless desire and the plots it generates will inevitably kill the daughter and her own plot. The mother is therefore no mother at all. Passion, the heroine is warned, is already driving her mother to plot a bloody revenge on the rival of whose existence she is now certain, but whose identity is still unknown to her. "You have no mother . . . love and jealousy have annihilated every honest feeling in that heart. . . . Let us not wait until she shall have recognized her victim; it will be too late then to rescue her."[30] The heroine is also reminded that "revolt is a crime only when authority is legitimate." Her mother destroys its legitimacy by abusing her authority—but it must be remembered that whenever a mother attempts to wield the paternal power left in her hands, her act is by definition an abuse, a usurpation.[31] "Honesty" for a woman consists in matrimony (and fidelity to it), while maternal boundlessness confounds the sentiments defined by the terms of matrimony with the passions that burst forth from its safe boundaries and threaten to efface them. Simultaneously—true to her boundless nature, with its conflation of opposites—the mother is making an effort to quench her passion for d'Ornevil and give him up generously to her unknown rival. She is prepared to do so, she says, as long as the lovers have not deceived her in her own house, or lied to her in saying that the long-lost love is someone who has not yet arrived in Martinique.

Her mother's threats of vengeance against the suspected Belvaux in the event that she *has* been deceived are what convince Mademoiselle that she is justified in her revolt: "I needed to hear them, in order to resist the sentiments of nature."[32] But what finally sets her "against nature" is an instance of the unnatural force at work in this country where untamed nature seems to extend its influence to the unrepressed enactment of natural human desires. By means of this force, the desires that "the sentiments of nature" should have kept under repression—desires that should have remained in the realm of metaphor in order to keep them displaced from the realm of action—do, indeed, remain metaphoric, but are transferred directly, *as metaphor*, into the sphere of the literal, which is to say into that of action, of plot. I have referred already to this process of the literalization of metaphor, particularly in connection with Zaïde. Only Zaïde can call herself, metaphorically, "penetrating"; but at this crisis of the conflict between natural desires and the "sentiments of nature" in both mother and daughter, the mother shows herself capable, *not* of speaking the word *penetrating* about herself, yet of enacting it, of literalizing it. When her mother actually runs a sword through d'Ornevil, Mademoiselle can have no further doubts. She will enact, "against nature," her own desires.

Literalizing Female Desire; or, The Deadly Gulf

D'Ornevil is not fatally penetrated. He survives to provide the grounds for metaphors gone literally wild. There is to be a secret wedding at midnight in the family chapel before he and the heroine flee together to France—back to the patrie. The trajectory of this plot of escape literally maps out the topography of the mother country as an abyss, which, as in *La Princesse de Clèves*, opens before the daughter's feet.

Mademoiselle has to cross the garden of her mother's house to get to the chapel, while at the same time avoiding the slave quarters, home of the dangerous Zaïde. In the garden—the old topos of female enclosure transgressed by the enactment of female desire—maternal desire, displaced and literalized, again finds voice (having found one before in the letters of Zaïde). Mademoiselle and Belvaux hear "horrible howls and roars that let us know we were only a short distance from a number of enraged animals; and to increase our fright, the darkness prevented us from seeing anything distinctly. Moreover, we were caught under a vault that did not allow us to remove ourselves from the danger."[33] Darkness, like the sea, is boundlessness, effacing the visible distinctions that might determine the meaning of these inarticulate voices, just as, while *en pleine mer*, the stories Mademoiselle heard about her mother could not be interpreted correctly. The animal cries terrify even Belvaux, who has already braved many a peril with equanimity. In their fear the two hurry on to the place where Mme de V . . . , another in the series of the heroine's substitute mothers, is waiting for them. This one has aided Mademoiselle ever since she left France, and Mademoiselle now literally asks her to "act as my mother."[34]

Having safely passed through the peril of the "raging animals," who only appeared, in the obscurity, to be on the loose, but were in fact caged all the while, they arrive where the substitute mother waits to protect them with the rational language of causality: "It was there that we learned the cause of our vain terror."[35] They have merely passed over the mother's menageries, located on a terrace under the garden, another example of the outlandish and (un)natural luxury of this New World. The metaphors now become fully as unrestrained as the maternal passions: "A wide pit, by which the food is lowered to the animals caged there, lay at our feet, and allowed us to hear their cries, as if they had been ready to devour us."[36] This rhetoric is hardly in need of interpretation, so literal have the metaphors of repressed maternal passion become. The text makes the sexual imagery as blatant as possible for the reader, yet refuses to recognize its own meaning, unlike other eighteenth-century texts that make use of similarly obvious sexual metaphors.[37] The text refuses to leave such imagery on the level of the metaphoric, and thus open to interpretation on that level; rather it relentlessly turns its metaphors into literal beasts trapped in proper abysses, whose devouring desire is thus displaced from a rhetorical force to an agency of plot.

Mademoiselle and Belvaux make it to the chapel, where Mademoiselle weds d'Ornevil at last, but their earlier "terror" proves not so "vain" as they think it is: Zaïde finds out that Mademoiselle is the mysterious beloved of d'Ornevil, and learns also that d'Ornevil planned to meet his new wife under the aforementioned "fatal vault." In an elaborately constructed scene, Madame first learns that her rival and her daughter are one and the same at the moment when she is rushing to the "fatal vault," newly informed that Zaïde has quite literally opened the "trap" (*trappe*) and pushed her rival into the beasts' den. What the mother sees upon arrival there is not her daughter, but Belvaux—till this moment her prime suspect—standing safely outside the pit. What she hears, through the "trap" (which, we are informed, is still "wide open" [*toute ouverte*]), are her own daughter's "feeble human moans mixed in with the cries of those raging animals."[38] Recognition remains impossible because the daughter is still *en pleine mer*, inside the gaping trap of her mother's sexual desire. In the visual register, the mother still cannot distinguish the daughter from her double; the daughter's voice is lost in the inhuman clamor of maternal desire.

The agent of maternal desire, the mother's double, who, as "savage," blurs the boundaries that distinguish human from animal as well as female from male (*pénétrante*), is sacrificed as the figure of mother-daughter interpenetration. D'Ornevil, who has also rushed to the scene, fatally penetrates the exulting Zaïde with his sword, and leaps into the *gouffre funeste* before bothering to determine whether there is still any chance of saving Mademoiselle. Just as Zaïde was the only female who could voice the language of penetration—while the mother actually, although ineffectually, penetrated the hero—Zaïde is also the only female who can literally be penetrated, whether in sexual terms or in the terms of sexually symbolic violence. Just as the violence of repressed female desire has to be displaced onto a figure that violates the bounds of gender and of genera, the violence of male desire, while itself allowed to be construed as fully human and fully masculine, must also be diverted in its object towards that same figure.

Mademoiselle, again suspected dead, "found herself separated from those ferocious animals by a strong grate, which is hardly ever shut."[39] This happy event is attributed to the agency of Heaven (*le*

Ciel). Recall the pun that presaged all of this: "Without the special protection of Heaven [*le Ciel*], the sea [*la mer*] would have separated him from me forever."[40] Here, Providence again intervenes to protect the heroine from maternal desire. Maternal desire had destined d'Ornevil—who represents the daughter's own self-determined destination—to become *un autre moi-même*—that is, it intended to collapse the daughter's destination into the mother('s). Paternal will, under the guise of its apotheosis, Providence, must intervene as a higher power to turn the daughter out of the path of maternal destination and, apparently, back into her own. It appears to be her own, of course, only insofar as her own desire remains in the service of the patriline plot whose destination is a marriage in which the heterosexual couple lives happily ever after.[41]

Arrival at the maternal destination would have returned Mademoiselle to her point of origin, the point where her trajectory and the maternal destination are the same, by collapsing the figures of womb and tomb: *gouffre funeste, voûte fatale*. The trajectory—collapsed into its destination—of maternal desire would thus have been parallel to that of paternal will: "The same day returned him to his fatherland and brought him to the grave."[42] It was providential intervention that thwarted the trajectory of paternal will by collapsing its origin into its destination, whereas here providential intervention blocks the trajectory of maternal desire by preventing it from attaining its end—that is, from collapsing the heroine's origin into its own destination. This feat accomplished, the women seem to be replaced into a "natural" order, the proper relations reestablished, the vectors of female descent replaced into the patriline plot. One page after her fall into the *gouffre funeste*, it is announced that Mademoiselle "a retrouvé sa mere" (has found her lost mother), who now appears only too happy to have lost a lover instead of a daughter. When Mademoiselle first returns to consciousness after her fall, "the names of daughter, lover, and wife were the first words that struck her ear . . . she did not dare to trust her senses [or "their meanings"]."[43] The names designating family relationships have at last been properly assigned. It appears that the plot has at last brought us safely back from the female Gothic to the domestic—

that is, from the literal excess of the mother country to the patriarchal family structure—but, as Mme de Chartres told her daughter, in this place things are never what they seem.

Speaking Female Desire; or, The Gothic Language

With the silencing by penetration of maternal desire's voice and agent, the language of patrilineage, the language of names that distinguish family relationships and patrilineages, loses its sense for the heroine. Mademoiselle is never again to be able to believe in the senses (*sens*) of those all-important names, nor will her own senses (*sens*) any longer be able to distinguish the articulations or the linear direction (*sens*) of patriline language. The traces left by her fall into the gouffre funeste and her confrontation with the maternal *animaux furieux* cannot be erased. Mad therefore, she is tormented by the vision of the abyss that is womb and tomb, and of Zaïde, who represents the maternal desire that would have plotted out the daughter's life as a sheer fall between those two endpoints: "She has opened my grave, and she is going to push me into it."[44] Her madness consists in a permanent state of recognition of those literalized displacements of maternal desire, which in turn preclude any recognition of socially recognized reality. The heroine is now blinded to everything other than her recognition of the maternal gouffre funeste, revealed and opened. There is no more distinction between literal and figurative for Mlle de Boismiran, nor between her own beginning journey and her mother's destination. The womb *is* the tomb. The collapse of plot that reveals the womb as tomb stills narrative into a tableau, a still life that is a vision of Gothic horror.

D'Ornevil tries to soothe Mademoiselle out of one of these visionary fits by repeating the "tender names" for the sake of which she has gone through her four-volume quest. But these names only send her into a rage of indignation, in which she accuses him of addressing her thus only because he cannot distinguish her from Zaïde. Of course, Zaïde is not only the mother's double: as her substitute daughter, she is also the daughter's double. Now that the double onto whom both mother's and daughter's desire had to be displaced is no more, the heroine must herself refuse the "tender names" of patriline relations, in order to replace them with the language of Zaïde. She repeats word for word, in her delirium, the letters of Zaïde which she had read earlier, "without being halted by the indecency of a style which is so foreign to her."[45] The fall into her mother's "deadly gulf" has not obliterated her, but has left her, rather, with a deadly testament, with *traces* that make it impossible for her to go on living in the patriline fiction of romance. The maternal "deadly gulf" has left the daughter the indecent, the horrific, in short the Gothic language of Zaïde, of female desire.

Mademoiselle can no longer forget a word of the Gothic language, nor can she believe, as she did relatively successfully before, that she feels none of the rage and resentment that goes along with the recognition of one's own desire and of its systematic frustration. Yet at the same time this unleashed rage, this indelible memory, precludes normal consciousness; it blots out her recognition of all familial and domestic relations, and of the happy ending of the patriline romance plot. In her abnormal lucidity, she knows she is going to die, although to all other eyes she appears to be recovering. Her lucidity is accompanied by a new strength of character lacking in her before, a change upon which she and Belvaux remark a number of times. But this strength is of a negative kind, not the power of agency her double has possessed all along. When Belvaux admires her courage in facing death, she replies, "Cease to admire a necessary sacrifice. Once hope is destroyed, one is soon resigned."[46]

The heroine thus uses her newfound firmness in the negative to refuse ever to consummate her marriage. She conceals and defends this negative agency under the guise of deferral to maternal will. She now bows to maternal authority, not to designate a destination, but to determine the span of narrative delay by fixing the date that will lead the daughter to the patriline destination she thought was her own. "She thought it necessary to add to our ceremonies those which custom alone [*l'usage seul*] has introduced in Martinique, and that she was justified in contesting his rights until the moment indicated by her mother for the publication of their marriage."[47] "L'usage seul" implies an informal custom as opposed to a written law. Of course, all the rules native to the mother country must be considered "informal" at best when they diverge from, and put obstacles in the way of, those imposed by the ruling fatherland. Female authority is designated as "mere custom" in the terms of patriline naming, now that its only agent capable of outright transgression has been executed. Such authority cannot alter written law; it can only violate it (monstrously) or delay its execution. Therefore the heroine must continually shift her strategy of self-authorization as each delay expires in the fixity of masculine authority and its law of male desire. Her last authorial act is to send her husband away on the night she knows will be her last, saying she prefers to spend it with her friend, because they will never see each other again (she and her husband are supposed to return to France imminently, while Belvaux will stay behind in the mother country, with *her* new husband). Once d'Ornevil is gone, Belvaux, who alone knows that Mademoiselle is dying, begins to weep. Mademoiselle reminds her that the "happy ending" would have meant an equally final separation for any female relationship established outside the patrilineal "tender names": "Separated by seas [*séparées par des mers*] that neither of us would ever cross, were we not already dead to one another?"[48]

"Séparées par des mers"? The resonant displacement of this pun perfectly articulates the Gothic language of female desire, in which there is no name that does not confound the relations it names, and of which the primal name is *la mer(e)*. The polyvalence and the resonance of its punning brings together across the vastness of narrative time (four volumes of it) the complex significance of *la mer(e)*. *La mer(e)* is not simply a rival for a man or for the possession of property. The special intervention of a paternal Heaven that prevented the *mer* from separating Mademoiselle forever from her lover would only have served, even had the heroine survived, to make her "dead" to Belvaux, her strong double. On the level of representation, female friendship is clearly being valued above heterosexual relationship, at least as defined in patriline terms, which is its only possible definition here. But the literal sense of the language implies that Providence would have killed her unvirtuous double agent, that other self who acts upon her own desires against authority wielded illegitimately, and chooses whether to recognize that authority, or not, according to her own authority as its interpreter. Thus she would have lost the legacy of *La Princesse de Clèves*, the succession to the sovereignty of readership, which is even more authorizing, more sovereign, than the state of authorship.

Surviving the descent into the "deadly gulf" and the encounter with the "raging animals" trapped there would have succeeded, indeed, has succeeded, within the temporary and imperfect terms of feminine tergiversation, in reinserting the heroine, her mother, and her strong double quietly into patrilineage, whose fixed line is traced upon female self-renunciation. In order to bring about the desired happy ending, mother and daughter must renounce not only their own desire, but also any conscious expression of their rage at d'Ornevil's infidelity (his shifting desire). As his confession of it clearly echoes St.-Preux's confession of a similarly passive sexual infidelity to Julie, this novel implies a rejection of the absolving role that makes Julie a heroine of domestic sensibility. Patriline language, Mademoiselle de Boismiran emphasizes, recognizes only *his* unrestrained passion (even though it may censure it, it does not censor it), while she is expected to satisfy that uncensored, unsteady male desire, which she had earned the right legitimately to satisfy only by virtue of the conflicted repression of her own desire throughout the whole book. To bring about the happy ending, then, she is expected to follow her husband back to the patrie, to retrace her plot and redouble her exile, this time an exile from the exotic country of female authority, from that invaginated space of tergiversation where both her mother and her strong double will remain.

The reader's interest in or desire for the happy ending reflects both heroine's and mother's investment, or "interest" in and identification with the desire represented and enacted by Providence, the force of patriline will at work in the plot. All three, heroine, mother, and reader, begin the journey of female plot in the complicitous desire and expectation of arriving finally at the ending designated by patriline plot, once the tergiversations of female plot have played themselves out. Yet tergiversation is not always in vain; delay can effect a transformation, as the matrix-narrative transforms the ending through repetition, undoing its own frame. Providence saves d'Ornevil from falling into *la mer(e)* and the heroine from death in the mother's *trappe*, but in the end the heroine chooses her own end, her own destination, by refusing (like the princess of Clèves) the happy ending, the return to *la patrie*, that Providence has arranged for her.

It is important to realize that it is not active masculine oppression—as it is in Wollstonecraft's fiction, for example—that makes the tableau of domestic happiness a fate worse than death for the heroine. For in spite of his failings à la St.-Preux, d'Ornevil is the most perfectly feminized of heroes of sensibility. In fact, as for St.-Preux, the account of his indiscretion is a narrative of his passivity, and thus of his feminization vis-à-vis the "penetrating" Zaïde/Mme de Boismiran. During the brief period that the novel allows for the achievement of the domestic bliss promised by the romance plot (while the new wife is on her deathbed), d'Ornevil is described as "the least demanding, . . . , the least . . . , the least *husband* possible; . . . always of the opinion that a submissive wife has good reason to be so."[49] That the "happy ending" entails the "willing submission" of a return to exile in the patrie is not d'Ornevil's fault; just as the misfortune of exile is never the virtuous heroine's fault. It is the fault, rather, of the overarching patriline plot called Providence, which requires that the mother give up her lover to her daughter, just as mothers do in many other women's novels of the period (as documented by Stewart, pp. 204–5). Only by virtue of that gesture of repression of rage—the very act that first made it possible for d'Ornevil to recognize the resemblance between mother and daughter—can the mother survive in the plot of patrilineage. The fact that the mother will live on in her outlandish exile means that her daughter will have to return to take the place the mother has left vacant in the patrie, where, as she has now learned from her mother, a woman of feeling cannot survive.

Grave(n) Plots; or, Exemplary Remains

The mother's fate is the daughter's destiny (remember the queen of Scots) because of the impossibility of female destination within patrilineage. There is no place where a woman can go and be in one place; the strong mother has refused to return to the patrie, but she is a bewilderingly ambiguous character, both split and doubled, a monster one minute and an angel the next. The daughter, whose characteristic weakness resolves itself into a fortitude of firm passivity, can go only to her grave when faced with the exigency of exile from her own strong double. Nor do the others fare better; d'Ornevil kills himself, and the mother, buries her daughter on her own island.[50] Like the earlier "usage," or illegitimate feminine custom, this one "violates" patriline law by literalizing it, and thus speaking its Gothic truth. Maternal custom, like Zaïde's Gothic language, is "barbarous" not only in being foreign, but also in the brutality of its refusal either to submit willingly to the laws of patrilineage or to let them lie unnoticed and naturalized as dead metaphors. The language of the female Gothic thus literalizes the dead metaphor of patriline naming as an actual death that puts a dead end to *all* plots, masculine or feminine. A memorial set up on the spot of the "fatal vault" and the "deadly gulf" literally petrifies the narrative into a stone allegory. There, Mademoiselle is shown with Love and Hymen triumphing over the Passions. When d'Ornevil had erected this monument to the "happy ending" before Mademoiselle's death, he had originally depicted the triumphal procession being led by the Virtues. Before he kills himself, he effaces the Virtues and replaces them with Death (pt. 4, p. 139). Even the hero now writes the Gothic language, and all that remains of patriline plot is a petrified plot whose end is no longer marriage, but death.

Virtue becomes death: the plot of virtue is collapsed into a petrified allegory of death erected upon the plot of the mother's silenced sex. The contested lover has the last word, both in his engraving of the tombstone and in the suicide letter that ends the novel, also written in the Gothic language: "What virtuous mortal would have dared advise me to live!"[51] Any advice (lesson, precept, moral) that would have prolonged life and its narrative is no longer possible in combination with the dead, completed, perfected exemplary history—fixed now in its most compacted form upon a tombstone—of the heroine's death, of Death itself. The grave is the only destination left for a heroine who can support neither exile nor a virtuous, legitimate, "willingly submissive" place in the patrie. This is the feminine dilemma, but it equally puts an end to all possible plots for the ideal eighteenth-century "feminine" man, the hero with "a too sensible heart" who is not rendered happy by the mere privilege of power, but must passionately desire a virtuous woman, for whom desire and virtue can never be in the same place (pt. 4, p. 119).

Neither the substitute mother's apparently beneficial inheritance of virtue, nor the overtly dangerous one, the language and example of passion that come to her through her biological mother, is sufficient in itself to kill Mademoiselle. She succumbs, rather, to the fatal combination of the two. Like two substances that annihilate one another, they explode and destroy whatever contains them together in one place. Both mothers, Madame de Boismiran and Madame de Foncel, have survived, and both hand down the message of their survival to the same daughter. The life of every woman may not in fact be the same, it may have one or two possible variations, but its audience is single: the next generation must put them together, even if the attempt proves fatal. It is always a paradox to connect the substitute mother's lessons in survival through virtue with the mother's virtuous death, but when the latter becomes instead the narrative of her survival beyond the moment when the patriline narrative, the providential plot, should have killed her off, it is more than paradoxical—it is monstrous. Long after "la beauté, les graces, la jeunesse" of the heroine should have turned her mother, for all social purposes, into a "hideous cadaver," the cadaver refuses to go to its grave. It persists with a terrifying power that seems supernatural because not wholly its own, an absolute but borrowed authority added on to the uncommon strength of its own refusal to die. The scene of a mother's failure properly to "pass on," by which she obstructs and diverts the lineal "passing on" of patrimony, is the scene of the transformation of the literature of sensibility into the Gothic.

The laws of Martinique, that colony of the patrie in the New World where mothers survive in exile only to become monsters, require that a mother place her daughter with her own hands in the tomb. This gruesome image literalizes the way in which the female line of descent becomes a nonlinear, barely traceable tangle when it is forced into crooked and unmarked paths by the imperative of the patriline fiction in which the father's name is made to appear to descend in a straight and orderly succession down the generations, leaving mother and daughter to compete for one and the same history. As Marianne Hirsch similarly extrapolates from her discussion of Freudian family romance, "In order to make possible the 'opposition between successive generations' and to free the girl's imaginative play, the mother must be eliminated from the fiction" (*The Mother/Daughter Plot*, pp. 55–56). This is so in Freudian terms because the mother's identity as parent, in contrast to the father's, cannot be subject to doubt, so that the child cannot entertain the fantasy that she is only a substitute. Hirsch, like Madelon Sprengnether, is correcting the male-centeredness of Freud's family romance. Yet the psychoanalytic explanation leaves out the historical specificity of women's legal "orphanage" within patrlineage, which was being emphasized in the official discourses of the later eighteenth century. *Lettres de Mademoiselle de Boismiran* enacts the Gothic fantasy of the mother who is repressed and replaced by a benevolent substitute, but returns in all her spectral terror to occupy the narrow plot allotted to female desire within the plot of patriline succession, thus condemning her daughter to move prematurely into its plot for mothers by becoming a "hideous cadaver" and passing away.

Since both mother and substitute mother here outlive their daughter, it is the daughter who leaves the novel's last will and testament. This consists of two halves—but she, unlike her mothers, has two legatees between whom to divide her double legacy. To Mme de Foncel she leaves her patrimony, the money left by her father in the hands of her guardian, M. de Flinonval (who has since died repentant and left it all to Mademoiselle again). She leaves to her surrogate mother, in other words, the vehicle of value and power that can only be transmitted through paternal lines, and that Mme de Foncel accordingly had to do without in her exile from the patrilineage.[52] Her mother, on the other hand, in her own kind of exile, has never lacked for patrimonial goods; she has brought on death and destruction by trying to use wealth to escape the restrictions of the system by virtue of which she possesses it. To her, Mademoiselle leaves the monitory narrative of her own death, graven on the memorial that now blocks the opening to her mother's "deadly gulf."

In not having left to her daughter the narrative of her death, Mme de Boismiran can be regarded as an exceptional mother within the subgenre, but in fact this novel merely reverses the succession of generations and leaves the mother with that narrative. It leaves Mme de Foncel locked up alone in the nunnery with the money for the lack of which she was forced to retreat there. It leaves Mme de Boismiran alone on an island full of "raging animals," with neither a lover nor an heir to whom she can pass on anything, but with an unforgettable, an indestructible text, a text that literalizes the dead letter of patriline law. In Riccoboni's work, an escape from the Richardsonian (or Rousseauesque) "progress to death" (in Janet Todd's words) can sometimes be achieved through "heroines emotionally sacrificing lovers to their female friends" (*Angellica*, p. 143). In Boisgiron's novel, such sacrifices of heterosexual passion to sensibility, made in fact by both mother and daughter, cannot stop that progress. Instead, it is here literally graven in stone as the triumph of Hymen/Death over the Passions, shown to be ineluctably inscribed in the mother-daughter relationship as it is structured in the romance of patrilineal reproduction that leads to the stasis of the domestic "happy ending" in marriage.

Chapter 5 . . .

Secret Communications; or, Faults of Transmission

Virtue incessantly hovers on the verge of a precipice
a thousand ready hands would push her over.
—Sophia Lee, 'The Recess'

Lettres de Mademoiselle de Boismiran left its heroine's plot literally petrified over the surviving mother's "trap," and Sophia Lee explores an even more overtly Gothic drama of maternal inheritance within patrilineal succession. *The Recess* replaces the Gothic daughter figure into a narrative of public history, the same epoch as that inhabited by Lafayette's princess. Taking one of the key figures from Lafayette's historical setting, Mary Stuart, Lee endows her with daughters, thus endowing the daughters with a political and magnificent, but unrecognized, maternal inheritance. That inheritance prevents them from retiring to the "private state" where the princess was able, briefly, to linger. *The Recess* poses the question, "What would a daughter inherit as heir to Mary, queen of Scots? And is there not something in that situation emblematic of the possibility of female inheritance in patriline systems?" Thus it is an exemplary work for the subgenre described in Chapter 3, exploring the paradoxical blockages of both public patriline succession and private female correspondence, as well as the openings that may be made possible by such enclosures. As I argue below, *The Recess* offers unique, though characteristically Gothic, narrative solutions to these questions. It literally cleaves and twins the figure of the heroine, her plot, and the epistolary narrative frame. This doubling causes the twinned narratives to undo each other in order to enact the novel's own plot of transmission, not in representation, but in its invocation of its inscribed reader.[1]

The Gothic Dream of Sensibility

The Recess; or, A Tale of Other Times (1783–85) is one of the very first English Gothic novels.[2] That a Gothic novel should be chosen as exemplary for novels of sensibility should come as no surprise, after the shift between the two modes enacted in *Lettres de Mademoiselle de Boismiran*. I am using the term, *mode*, as defined by Alastair Fowler; "modal terms never imply a complete external form," but rather a "repertoire" (p. 107). After all, the whole machinery and the preoccupations of the Gothic were always there in the novel of sensibility. The theme of women's imprisonment and buried life is the main subject of most eighteenth-century sentimental novels, and the narrative strategies by which these themes enter into the fully developed Gothic are also already present there.[3] The situation of simultaneous entrapment and exile in enclosures that are ancient and hereditarily received, but also fractured, before it became literalized in the figure of the ruined castle, was imaged forth in the histories received in epistolary enclosures that break open by means of repetition and displacement to create an invaginated structure of narration and transmission, much as the Gothic castles crack open to reveal the fatal flaws in the patriline transmission of real estate. And the epistolary situation often implies some kind of sequestration that prevents the writer from seeing her addressee.[4]

In keeping with the conventions discussed in Chapter 3, our heroines are orphans, brought up by a substitute mother, and as usual they believe her to be their real mother until, at her death, she passes on the secret of their inheritance. Again, like the others of its subgenre, this novel is about survival in a world where daughters are denied the possibility of legitimate inheritance, where even their most basic inheritances, the lives and bodies that come to them through the "authors of their days," are so circumscribed as to have only a kind of provisional existence, neither fully legitimated nor "proper," in the sense of being properly their own, because unrecognized. Like the others, *The Recess* is about the double maternal inheritance that makes that limited survival both possible and problematic, the precepts of survival through virtue together with the exemplary history of the mother's death through virtue, both received from the substitute mother.

A true Gothic tale, *The Recess* literalizes all the conventions of the novel of sensibility, through the process described in the previous chapter. The heroine's symbolic double is a literal double, not merely a confidante or even a sister, but actually a twin; the two of them grow up, not simply within the strict confines of the home, but in a hole in the ground fitted up with the trappings of civilization, the exits of which are concealed, the windows opaque and out of reach. The enclosures in *The Recess* are inherited, and therefore always already there, forming the matrix of the heroines' doubled plot.

Maternal History as Gothic History; or, The Narrative Dynamic of the Double Bind

The whole wish and obsession of the heroines' childhood, the initial desire that drives their plot, is to get out.[5] This driving desire and the blockage it encounters constitute the double bind, or double precipice, that is their maternal inheritance. The plot is generated out of the tension of that inherited threat of fault. It takes the form of a series of attempted escapes from the maternal double bind, aided by the intrusion of a demand for narrative—"escapes" that then turn out to be displacements, repetitions, of the same enclosure. With each new enclosure that seems to open out from "the Recess" to Kenilworth Castle to Elizabeth's court, the enclosure in fact becomes tighter, because each time the heroines emerge farther out into a world of unsympathetic readers. The space for avoiding the threatened fault becomes smaller and smaller, until the act of avoiding fault becomes itself the fault to be avoided. The originary fault that will determine the cleft structure of the narrative, which in turn allows for an enactment of transmission to a sympathetic reader that escapes the logic of the double bind, is a failure of sympathy.

Early in the book, the novel's substitute mother, the literally dying Mrs Marlow, teaches her charges that she has willingly "died" all her life. Her life-as-dying constitutes the education by example she leaves to the twin heroines. The other half of the double maternal inheritance—the history of the mother's death, which always accompanies and yet is disturbingly incompatible with the substitute mother's lessons in survival—Mrs Marlow also bequeaths to Matilda and Ellinor on her deathbed. But here the mother's death is a case, particularly appropriate to the Gothic, of an uncanny survival, a form of death-in-life that repeats, with a twist, that of the substitute mother. The mother's history has been withheld until their coming of age (as usual), except for one mysterious statement, which long has haunted the heroines' minds: "Your mother lives—but not for you" (1: 19). The deathbed history communicates to the heroines their mother's identity and the meaning of this oracular statement, while it reveals to readers the historical claims of the narrative. Mary Stuart is still living as the novel begins, but for her daughters she does not live; for Mary, like Mrs Marlow, has spent much of her life "buried" in a prison (2: 131). The effect for the reader is similar: Lee borrows directly from Lafayette the effect of still life created by framing a fictional life of this historical queen within the reader's knowledge of the history of her death, leaving Mary at no point in narrative time entirely living or dead. It is around this borrowed effect, which centers on the portrait of Mary Stuart the revenant resonances of a historical narrative of unrecognized female inheritance and authority leading to Gothic imprisonment, that Lee creates what may well be the first historical novel in English, as well as the first "female Gothic" novel.[6]

Although the mother's history parallels that of the substitute mother in important aspects, there is one significant difference, which in effect (and literally) springs the trapdoor of the twins' tomb/womb/home, both freeing and binding them to abandon it for the wide world so desired and feared. Unlike Mrs Marlow's, Mary's "live burial" has been imposed by a hostile authority. Although Mary is described as a virtuous example of resignation to a fate that is not her fault, we are also told repeatedly that she would like nothing better than to get out. Nor would she mind dethroning or even killing her older "sister," Elizabeth, whose "unfeminine use of power," like Mme de Boismiran's usurpation of patriline rights, renders rebellion legitimate (2: 151, 214). Mary's male (and therefore less resigned) friends are continually plotting to aid her in fulfilling this wish. Matilda and Ellinor, as inheritors of Mary's violently circumscribed patrilineal rights to authority and agency, now inherit a new duty not fully compatible with their duty to imitate their substitute mother's example by remaining willingly entombed. It is also their duty to keep their mother and her claim alive, to support her right as actively as possible, to strengthen it too by multiplying it, by becoming mothers themselves. Mary's example is in another sense the opposite of Mrs Marlow's: far from sacrificing her life in any way for her daughters' sake, she has committed *them* from birth to grow up in a tomb in order to preserve her own life. This contrary maternal example breaks the fixity of the lesson that framed the substitute mother's example, just as the multiple plots of invaginated narratives break the fixity of the framing end.

On the one hand, the mother's history thus undoes Mrs Marlow's guilt-fostering example of voluntary retreat and self-abnegation, making it possible for Matilda and Ellinor to leave the Recess, and even to seek agency outside of it; on the other, Mary's history also reflects and redoubles Mrs Marlow's, reinforcing the stricture against will and agency even while demanding them. This conflict constitutes the double bind. Whereas Mrs Marlow's lifelong dying laid the threat of fault upon the heroines, Mary's fictional survival, set within the frame of her historical death, once again lays the threat of fault (of responsibility for their mother's death) upon them. Because Mary still lives—but not for them—they are obliged, once permanently escaped from the Recess, willingly to continue living buried lives under fictional names and conditions, to move as ghosts exiled in the world of the living, in order to preserve their mother's foredoomed life, and with it the equally foredoomed virtue necessary for their recognition by the reading public as legitimate heroines. The double frame of fictional life and historical death set around the portrait of the queen of Scots that Lee takes from Lafayette replaces the precept necessary to frame example as such with a double, self-contradictory maternal precept—with a double bind.

In *The Recess*, literal frames and related enclosures—tombs, caskets, and letters—constitute Gothic doublings of the maternal precept and example as ambiguous inheritance, at once open and enclosing. Fueled by the heroines' own desire for escape, these literalized repetitions of maternal inheritance propel the plot out of entrapment. The conception of "narrative energy" appropriate to texts like *The Recess* is quite different from that used by Peter Brooks to account for plot in masculine-centered novels of the received canon. Plot here is not conceived as energy on the model of a lineal, object-directed desire, as in "the male plots of ambition" where "the ambitious hero stands as a figure of the reader's efforts to construct meanings in ever-larger wholes, to totalize his experience of human existence in time, to grasp past, present, and future in a significant shape."[7] Rather, the energy of plot here arises out of the tension of the double bind. Without its unstable entrapment, this kind of plot could not be. An object (such as the Recess itself) or a narrative structure (such as the epistolary form) that literalizes that tension reproduces the double bind with a difference, and in doing so moves the plot out of its initial stasis—even if into another variant repetition, a mise-en-abyme, of the double bind. Literalization gives the plot of *Mademoiselle de Boismiran* its agents, but it gives the plot of *The Recess* its sites, because this novel literalizes female exile and entrapment rather than female desire and agency. Each of these literal sites, matrixlike, repeats the tension of the double bind and opens a new way through it.

Gothic Relations

The full-length portrait moral that the précieuses substituted for the exemplary portraits of the Renaissance, and that Lafayette miniaturized, has become—literalized and doubled, of course—the central fixture of the Recess. Here, paintings are often compared with or exchanged for written texts, as Matilda writes: "Being deprived of my customary resource, books, . . . we mutually agreed to invent tales from the many whole-length pictures, which ornamented the best room" (1: 7). Rather than telling any stories, however, she describes how "an awe, I could not conquer, made me unable to form any tale." Her storytelling is silenced because she feels that the eyes of the gentleman in the painting, "full of a tender sweetness," are "bent upon [her]," and because she notices "in [Ellinor's] every feature the strongest resemblance" to him. It is not the painting that resembles the sister, but the other way round. The living heroines are first silenced and then endued with meaning, speech, even life, only through the frame of reference of the dead portraits. Through their power, the sisters regain voices to exclaim, "Why do our hearts thus throb before inanimate canvas?" (1: 8–9).

The portraits' Gothic reversal of the expected relation between viewer and object expresses a continual threat of fault: "I knew not why, but we lived in the presence of these pictures as if they understood us, and blushed when we were guilty of the slightest folly" (1: 9). Their gaze is no longer tender and sweet, but judging, penetrating, and fixing. They have now become omniscient viewers, from which the heroines, trapped like inanimate canvases within the closed frame of the Recess, cannot escape.

The first time they are released from this gaze and frame, the twins are led out blindfolded, for the secret of the Recess is not yet to be communicated to them; that is, they may not yet be told of its "secret communication" to the outside world (2: 10). But release from the initial enclosure without that knowledge only leads to a repetition of their situation inside the Recess: "Unbinding our eyes, we *found ourselves* in a noble cloister. We flew in to the garden it *bordered*, and how strong was the *impression* of the scene before us!" A detailed description of the "living landscape" beyond the cloister follows (1: 5). The rhetoric of the picturesque used in the passage implies that the world is presented to their view as a framed painting, yet all the images of enclosure refer rather to the viewers themselves. Their very first sight of the world outside the Recess is that *of themselves* inside a cloister; they run out of it into an enclosed garden, "bordered" by the walls of the same cloister. Only from within this frame can they view the world as a landscape—one they still cannot enter. The landscape is "living," while the viewers are "impressed" by the scene.

When the heroines must willingly follow their substitute mother back into the tomb after their initiatory view of the world, she entrusts them at last with the "secret communication." The knowledge transmitted has distinctly sexual connotations: Matilda finds that the "so often-sought entrance" is concealed behind "that portrait which first gave me such singular sensations, and which I perceived was made to fall together, with a spring almost imperceptible" (1: 24).[8]

Gothic doubling silences the historical fictions the sisters want to relate to each other by the striking features that evidence a hidden history of historical fact—namely, their secret relationship to the historical figures, and through them to a narrative of public history. Thus the relationship signified by visible doubling initially blocks and occults narrative relation. The Gothic truth of doubling is the truth of relation(ship) unrecognized because of the sexual relations it cannot name. It silences the fictive relations the heroines wish to invent, without making its historical truth graspable until Mrs Marlow conveys it in narrative. Until they receive that narrative, they are less alive than the "inanimate canvas."

Legitimation and Recognition

The heroines do not learn that the portraits depict their parents until the moment when they receive their substitute mother's deathbed history, which contains within it the history of their mother. Once unpacked in narrative, the relationship represented by the doubling of the portraits can be recognized and thus cease to haunt the heroines. Now the portraits become simply objects to be possessed by the daughters they once possessed and objectified. When bequeathed as possessions by Mrs Marlow, the "valuable pictures" are ascribed an economic value as a material legacy, but this is outweighed and indeed voided by their "recognition value" as portraits of Mary Stuart and the duke of Norfolk. What the heroines actually inherit is, not a patrimony, but the legitimation of their status as heirs—or rather a potential for legitimation consisting of the *evidence* with which they may seek to establish the public recognition of their legitimacy. As long as the letters and portraits they inherit remain enclosed, seen by no one but themselves, the heroines themselves remain enclosed, entitled to no inheritance but their tomb. They must find the proper "readers" for their legacy, those who are willing and able to read it, to legitimate it, to assign it a value, to give or procure something in exchange; finally, to *recognize* it. The possession of this evidence constitutes both a license and a debt for the heroines to open the enclosure, to leave the Recess, to show their evidence to the proper readers, to attempt to recover the fortune and the rights to which they have inherited only an unrecognized claim.

"What new ideas, what *amazing* feelings *did her narration give birth to*? The impulses of nature taught us to *treasure* every word she uttered" (1: 80; emphasis mine). This narrative "treasure" confers a valuable legacy upon the daughters who receive it, while it gives birth to new ideas that seem to supply the place of the stories they could not invent before. Nevertheless it leaves the heroines "a-mazed" in a labyrinth, a tomb now drawn out into passages that lead neither outward nor forward.[9] Without authoritative readers to recognize their legacy, they must return willingly to the tomb with every sunset, like ghosts at sunrise, for any right to the landscape they now term their "new empire" remains unrecognized (1: 88). They have found no readers for their evidence, and their realm is therefore unpeopled; the signs of human habitation mark the boundaries beyond which they dare not wander, on threat of precipitating their mother's death. Caught within the maternal double bind that bequeaths them a "male plot of ambition" (to rule England and Scotland) together with a sentimental plot of suffering virtue, *both* imposed by the threatened fault of killing the mother, they are doomed to repeat daily both transgressive escape from and voluntary return to the tomb/womb. Only an intrusion into their enclosure from the outside, a displacement of their own will to escape onto an agent who comes from without, can break the magic circle that frames them.

Female Agency; or, Providence and the Debt of Sympathy

Before Ann Radcliffe, Lee provides her Gothic novel with extended landscape descriptions in picturesque terms. For Lee, these serve to emphasize the unbreachable distance between viewer and prospect. It is as impossible for Matilda to enter the "empire" she describes as it would be to step into a painting. The breaching of that distance is enacted as a narrative break and described as a narrative fault, for which the narrator, Matilda, on her deathbed, absolves herself by intruding to point to a male intrusion from outside: "But you reproach me with losing time in uninteresting descriptions—Ah, Madam! this wood was not always a desart. Chance, or rather I should say, Providence, led into its solitary windings, the man . . ." (1: 89–90). A man, a stranger, and most of all Providence, is the solution to the paradoxical matrix-trap. The sentimental hero arrives, himself marked by a feminine form of virtue as a faultless victim, like d'Ornevil and even the prince of Clèves, but with the important qualification that to have a will or a desire of his own is not automatically, in him, a fault.[10] The earl of Leicester intrudes upon the heroines' "empire" as a victim, chased by murderers, and he finds his way there, not through his own will, but by the will of Providence.

Providence, in the person of Lord Leicester, breaks into the matrix-trap; yet this is no narrative rape. It takes away all fault of will or desire from Matilda, but it does not remove will itself; rather it allows her will to exist, and to accomplish its desire, by expressing it as compliance to a series of paternal wills: that of Lord Leicester (who is old enough to be her father), of "Father Anthony," and of Providence, which functions here, as in *Lettres de Mademoiselle de Boismiran*, as paternal will apotheosized.

After Mrs Marlow's death, the heroines remain in the Recess under the penetrating and judgmental eye of their other guardian, Mrs Marlow's brother and former fiancé, the priest Father Anthony.[11] The authoritarian imposition of his will upon them authorizes a transgressive escape that would have been impossible in relation to Marlow's "willing" example of self-entombment: "We resolved to conceal our ramble [a step further into their prospective 'empire'], lest Father Anthony should forbid us to repeat it . . . we rejoice to escape from haughtiness or austerity, however venerable the form they assume . . . to deceive the watchful, reflects a compliment on our own sagacity, which renders us insensible of the error" (1: 88–89). The error of letting Leicester into the secret of the Recess and of their true identity, however, cannot be concealed from the watchful. The enraged Father Anthony commands Matilda, as punishment for her transgression of his will and of her obligation to preserve her mother's secret, to comply with Lord Leicester's demand to marry her, and to leave the Recess forever with him and her sister. Of course she wants nothing other than just this. Her own will is thus neatly transformed by the workings of Providence into virtuous self-sacrifice: "The peculiarity of the situation can alone excuse such a marriage, but I was born for obedience" (1: 161).

As one of the "watchful," Father Anthony is an unsympathetic receiver of the heroines' narrative. All the characters in the book, female or male, are identified as good or bad by whether or not they display sympathy. If they do not, they are automatically placed in the opposite camp, that of the penetrating watchers—the powerful, the enemy, those whose "ready hands" would push the virtuous heroine over the precipice. Penetrating readers are associated with precept, masculine and ineffectual as a form of education, and indeed Father Anthony's instruction by precept has complemented Mrs Marlow's education by example. Mrs Marlow has duly educated our heroines in sympathy through her example: "At a tale of distress her eye assumed a melting benignity rarely seen" (1: 19). A victim is *owed* the sympathy of anyone who becomes the receiver of her or his tale of woe; if that sympathy is not paid, the reader is at fault, and such a violation authorizes an equal one—a rebellion, a revenge, or at least an expression of anger—on the part of the sufferer, as in this example: "Had she generously sympathized in the cruel events which robbed me of happiness, to cast it away on her, my melting heart would have spent its last breath in wishing that happiness perpetuated" (2: 287). (As it is, Ellinor is thus justified in coveting her neighbor's husband.) The providential arrival of the stranger thus opens the pitfall before Matilda of being too lacking in sensibility to be recognizable as a heroine. The transgression that requires Matilda's obedience is itself, therefore, the fulfillment of a new debt, the debt of sympathy, and the evasion of a new threat of fault. The debt of sympathy, then, actually *demands* Matilda's agency: first in leading a stranger into the Recess, and then in following him out of it, all in order to avoid the fault of insensibility.[12]

Narrative Demand; or, Sympathetic and Penetrating Readers

The successive leaps that plot the narrative mise-en-abyme of *The Recess* are made possible each time by an intrusion from the outside, as in the providential arrival of the earl of Leicester. Such intrusion always includes a demand from a reader or narratee for the heroines' true history. In the exchange initiated by a sympathetic demand, the narratee binds herself with the narrator by *living over* his narration and redoubling it: "Lord Leicester thus concluded his story; but oh! how much of my life had evaporated during the relation! The unconquerable anxiety with which I followed him, united my heart for ever with his. . . . As the only acknowledgment for his noble frankness, I in turn related the little tale already repeated" (1: 149).[13] The escape made possible by this redoubling only leads to a repetition of the heroines' live burial, this time in Leicester's country seat at Kenilworth Castle, because Leicester as sympathetic reader can only further their inherited plot of ambition by both exposing them to and protecting them from readers more authoritative and more penetrating than he is himself.

The only real difference between the heroines' situation at Kenilworth and in the Recess is that Kenilworth is full of strangers, all of whom are potential "penetrating" readers, from whom their true history must therefore be withheld. The supreme example of the "penetrating" reader is Elizabeth. Like Zaïde in *Mademoiselle de Boismiran*, the queen of England, who stands as far outside the sphere of domestic womanhood or virtuous heroinehood as did the "savage" slave, here functions as the masculinized double of the mother, the "phallic mother," the only female character in the book to whom the word *penetrating* can be applied.[14] Elizabeth at last literally penetrates the enclosure at Kenilworth, as Leicester did that of the Recess, and forces the heroines out of it.

A "penetrating" reader demands, not only the relation of a true history, but also and especially "hard" evidence of its veracity as defined by the patriarchal laws of plausibility, as the prince of Clèves did in response to the princess's aveu. Although the heroines' true narrative is wildly implausible, they have inherited with it evidence (likenesses and letters) with which to establish its authenticity. Matilda fears her family resemblance to Mary Stuart will be as easily readable by all at court as the princess feared her desire for Nemours would be, as open as the vidame's dropped letter. Anticipating the sudden arrival of Elizabeth's court at Kenilworth, Matilda is "apprehensive . . . lest the similitude my features bore to those of my unfortunate mother, might strike some idle observer" (1: 203). When the sisters are exposed to the view of Elizabeth—hardly an idle observer—she in fact recognizes, *not* the evidence of their high birth, but rather the implausibility of Leicester's lie about their low birth. Pressed by her on this fiction, Leicester is "reduced to frame a new story" (2: 164). But this new variation of the fiction is hardly less implausible than the true history: "[Elizabeth's] mode of conduct convinced me at once that she utterly discredited the whole of this fiction; which allied us, by another branch, almost as near to the throne as we really stood. Would not a jealous, selfish soul, like hers, have demanded dates, facts, testimonials and witnesses?" (1: 214). What is evident to the penetrating reader is not the visible evidence of the heroines' legitimacy as heirs (their physical resemblance to Mary and Norfolk), but only the implausibility of the fiction offered in response to her demand for their true history.

The passage just quoted makes it possible to define a distinction that holds for novels of sensibility generally: the "penetrating" narrative demand really asks for a *plausible* history, rather than simply a true one. In response to the demand for plausible narrative, the heroines are pushed farther towards the fault they have already entered by acquiescing in fiction-making before becoming the victims of a demand for evidence. The result is only their further encryptment at Elizabeth's court, where they "constantly act under the eye of a haughty, jealous, and revengeful Sovereign" (1: 216).

If the court is the ultimate open frame (the princess of Clèves's "demeure exposée"), the ultimate closed frame is the body, frequently termed "frame" in *The Recess*. Into this ultimate frame a new stranger penetrates: a daughter, who grows within Matilda's bodily frame until the fact can no longer go unmarked by the watchful court. The pregnancy would be incontrovertible evidence of the fictionality of the story they have framed for Elizabeth; unable to frame any new fiction that could incorporate *this* evidence of their fictionalizing, Matilda and Leicester resort to flight.[15] This final attempt to avoid exposing the evidence of fault finally does expose it, and also multiplies fault again: when at the crucial moment for escape Ellinor cannot be found, she is abandoned to the interrogations of Elizabeth. There is a dangerous similarity between sympathetic and unsympathetic demands for narrative. Both the sympathetic demand and the "penetrating" one, as the unsympathetic demand is often called in *The Recess*, place the teller in the position of victim—whether through identification with the narrator's victimization or by threatening the narrator with victimization. It is therefore not always easy to distinguish a sympathetic from a penetrating reader. This ambiguity constitutes the main pitfall for both heroines, providing a fault, a double precipice, over which each of them falls. Matilda errs on the side of sympathy, confiding too easily in people of whose trustworthiness she does not have enough evidence. This weakness corresponds to her lack of agency and need for others to further her mother's plot: indeed, she abandons Ellinor, with a good deal of sympathy for her plight but no effort at active assistance, in favor of Leicester's agency on her mother's behalf. Ellinor errs, meanwhile, on the side of secrecy, creating fictions to deceive those who would penetrate her secrets, but also often creating havoc for her sympathizers, and therefore for herself.

Elizabeth's "unfeminine use of power" leads her in this novel to the fate that, for a female character, is worse than death, but the heroines' fate resembles hers in all but the possession of power. The queen is "destined to survive her youth, *her virtue*, her fame, and her happiness" (2: 61; emphasis mine), but Matilda has already suffered a similar destiny only six pages earlier, when, learning that her mother has just been executed, seemingly as a result of her own flight, she cries, "Why, why, oh God, was I permitted to survive my innocence?" (2: 55). The reason Providence permits her to survive can only be well understood by comparing Ellinor's reframing of the same story.

The instrument of torture by which Elizabeth first seeks to extract the true narrative of the heroines' identity from Ellinor is "a large book of devotion," like that associated earlier with Father Anthony and his masculine education, which she throws at Ellinor's head (2: 204). Ellinor is knocked out by this weighty precept, and in the process of unlacing, the papers that are the evidence of her birthright are exposed (for she wears them around her neck the way everyone else in the book wears miniature portraits). The true history is thus disclosed at last, and the interrogation takes a new turn: the interrogators try to force Ellinor to sign a statement asserting that the testimonials relating the circumstances of her birth were falsified, being merely part of a plot to seize power. Thus Ellinor must again consent to a fiction that would plausibly conceal her true, implausible history, in response to the demand of the interrogators. Sick (literally) with having survived her virtue by authorizing a "vilifying" fiction, Ellinor realizes that she must struggle to live on in order to attempt avoiding the fault she has already survived: "I recollected that in thus resigning myself to the stroke, I rendered the last fatal blot my own hand had fixed on my character indelible; that while I lived I had yet a chance of justifying my intention, in an act which reflected alike on myself and all dear to me" (2: 230). To survive one's virtue is, then, to extend the plot, to extend the possibility of displacing fault. Yet it seemed, in the cases of both Elizabeth and Matilda, that to survive one's virtue was to live on past the possibility of such displacement, because it was to live on in fault. Furthermore, in a novel that defines feminine virtue as the steadfast avoidance of fault, how can it be, and what can it mean, that the heroines resemble Elizabeth in surviving their virtue?

Like Matilda's plot to reclaim the throne of Scotland, Ellinor's plot of "justifying [her] intention, in an act which reflected alike on myself and all dear to me" is aimed at gaining public recognition. As should already be clear from the discussions in previous chapters, the plot of virtue is always a trial, whose goal is the production of evidence that will establish—that is, render recognizable—the heroine's virtue. But the heroine's plot for recognition, not simply of her virtue, but of her survival in virtue, cannot work on the level of representation, because the laws of representation are written in the patriline script of verisimilitude. The demand of verisimilitude or plausibility is, as we saw in *La Princesse de Clèves*, the unsympathetic demand for the whole truth, for a narrative that is whole because it includes the evidence named in the demand. Not only will the heroine's plot always be judged, by the law of verisimilitude, as implausible representation; it will also always fall short, *in representation*, of its end. In other words, the goal of the heroine's plot—survival in virtue—can never be represented.

The only possible full recognition of the heroine's plot is that which comes from the sympathetic reader, the self-selected stranger who "has ears to hear," like the elect listeners to Christ's parables, the secret communications of women's correspondence. In representation, none of these heroines survive their own histories—their deaths are the ultimate evidence with which they finally satisfy the larger cultural demand of their time for a complete narrative of virtue. But the heroine's more subversive plot is not represented. Rather, the novel transacts its plot of transmission and recognition by a sympathetic reader by invaginating that "whole" narrative, performing a fragmentation that is really a faulty mise-en-abyme, a multiplication of wholes that are *not* perfect mirror images of one another but include a "false detail" of difference.[16]

Counterfeit Representation; or, The Fault of Fiction

The "penetrating" demand for narrative in *The Recess* fits Derrida's description of what he calls simply "the demand for narrative," which, he argues, brings about the invagination of a text.[17] *The Recess* does not literalize the penetrating demand as interrogation under torture, although it threatens to: Elizabeth's threat of real torture turns into an allegorical torture, Ellinor's being struck with a book of devotion and then faced with her mother's death warrant. Nevertheless, literal torture does threaten darkly and most strangely in a seemingly unmotivated, offhand gesture, but at a climactic moment of the novel. During Matilda's flight from Elizabeth's court to France, she and Leicester need a place to hide from their pursuers en route, and they seek out the Recess. There they are captured, however, by a band of outlaws led by Williams, a treacherous ex-servant of Leicester's who had earlier been entrusted with the secret.[18] Matilda observes "a variety of instruments, nameless to me, which I considered as the means of torture and death," but Leicester soon names the instruments and their users properly, calling them a "set of coiners, for such their apparatus proved them" (2: 2, 6). The instruments thus turn out to be tools of a certain kind of fictionalizing, rather than tools of an inquisitorial demand for the concealed true narrative. The coiners are *not* what Derrida calls "police"; they are outlaws themselves. They do torture and interrogate, but as victims of their interrogations, they choose only the patriarchal interrogator himself, Lord Burleigh, along with Father Anthony, who, as we have seen, is associated with the "large book of devotion," with precept as opposed to example, and thus with the law as a fixed, constraining text. They see the heroines, by contrast, only as potential rape victims; they have no interest in their narrative, seeming to want only their bodies, as valuable goods to be wrested from the legitimate patrilineage. The difference between the police and the outlaws, when put together with the similarity between the two senses of *coiners*, elucidates the nature of the interrogators' threat to the heroines.

Coiners is a word that signifies both counterfeiters and minters of legitimate coin. What these activities have in common is a gesture of self-legitimation; a creation, on one's own authority, of an entitlement to the means of exchange. Coining is the imitation and reproduction of an entitlement that, in the economy of the law—which is the patriline law of virtue and verisimilitude—can only be legitimate if it is *not* self-authorized, but received from a higher authority: in short, inherited. To counterfeit is thus to engage in *un*authorized imitation, and by doing so to imitate the state's self-authorization. The notion of inheritance as *received legitimacy* is what is supposed to distinguish "legitimate" from "illegitimate," or usurped, authority. Elizabeth's authority, while in this sense (always precariously) legitimate, is rendered illegitimate by her attempt, through the agency of her interrogator, Lord Burleigh, to rob and then falsify the "good coin" of Ellinor's and Matilda's, and of their mother Mary's, birthright. Thus, much as when Mme de Boismiran "ceased to be a mother," she legitimates rebellion. The heroines *resemble* the coiners as outlaws, exiles within the territory of the state, unrecognized by it, hiding out in the Recess as they plot to overthrow the existing hierarchy of authority by circulating counterfeits. That resemblance is the secret of their terror for Matilda. The outlaws perform in representation what the heroines cannot by making the double patriarchs, malevolent and benevolent, interrogating and precept-slinging—Lord Burleigh and Father Anthony—the prime objects of their attack. In enacting that plot, they exactly repeat the brutality, and especially the gender biases, of patriarchy. Yet their plot further resembles the heroines' in that its aim is not to change the dominant patriarchal model for control over circulation and exchange, but only to usurp the position of those it currently legitimates.

The threat posed to the heroines by the coiners' instruments is not, then, that of interrogation by torture; rather, the instruments represent the threat of falling into the fault of coining fictions. Matilda's confusion of the two threats shows that they are in fact closely related: the heroines are repeatedly forced into the fault of coining fictions, pushed over the verge of the precipice of fictionalizing by the "thousand ready hands" of the interrogators. The coiners and their instruments, then, instead of *performing* the threat of interrogation upon the heroines, which forces and thus authorizes their fictionalizing, *represent* the still greater threat of the fault into which they fall by the act of fictionalizing. They thus create a mise-en-abyme of the fiction of *The Recess* itself, while performing for its heroines the function of a negative example, just as the "pictures of love," including the portrait of Diane de Poitiers "painted" by Mme de Chartres, function for the princess of Clèves. But the act, the fall, represented by this negative example is not a loss of sexual chastity, like that represented by Mme de Chartres's "pictures." Instead, it resembles that other act of Diane de Poitiers that Mme de Chartres leaves out of her portrait, freeing the princess to imitate it: the act of imitating and appropriating the images upon which the authority of the patriarchal state is based. The act of coining, besides being an imitation of the state's gesture of self-authorization, is also literally the imitation of a portrait: it reproduces the portrait of Elizabeth that stamps her coinage with the mark of legitimate value. Whereas the princess imitated and appropriated paintings that represented historical battles fought for the recognition of the boundaries of the state, the coiners imitate the portrait of the monarch, which not only represents but in representing constitutes the centralizing political and economic authority of the state.[19] Imitating the central figure of authority rather than the decisive historic victory for the recognition of boundaries means reduplicating that authority (a reduplication enacted, moreover, within the original tomb of the Recess) rather than shifting the gesture of the victorious fight for recognition towards the establishment of a private "new construction."

Living up to the double imperative of exemplifying passive feminine virtue and carrying out the maternal plot of patriline ambition means living on within the fault created between these two precipices. It means both "surviving one's virtue" and surviving one's fictions, surviving within the fault of disseminating fictions as "good coin." Ellinor enacts this "survival in fiction" by staging her own death. Aided by a trusty maidservant named Alithea (or "Truth"), Ellinor escapes from her prison at the Abbey, thus surviving her fictive self.[20] Her boldness in inventing and enacting fictions is read even by those supposedly sympathetic to her as evidence of madness. Passing off fictions as truth, as good coin, is a fault because it entails withholding the debt of sympathy—that is, refusing to confide truthfully in those with whom she is in a sympathetic relation. When she conceives the plan of staging her own death, she refuses to be rescued from her prison by Essex, and also refuses to confide to him her own plan of escape. As a result he, like her enemies, ends up believing her dead. (Mlle de Boismiran's staged fictional death created the same problem for her lover.) The act of preserving the evidence of true history entails the fault of concealing plots from sympathetic readers, which is in turn read as madness in a paradoxical mixture of sympathy for the mad sufferer and an unsympathetic, distancing judgment. Thus in staging her own death with the aid of Alithea, Ellinor literally survives her virtue as a deceptive plotter and fighter in male disguise.

Both heroines survive everything, so much so that it is no

longer virtue, but survival, that characterizes them as heroines. Both survive mother and virtue; Matilda also survives her husband, her daughter, and the narrative; Ellinor survives her lover, her fictionalizing, her sympathy, and her own consciousness, hence even herself. She does not, however, survive the sight of a painting of the storming of Cadiz that contains a portrait of her lover, Essex. That the historical painting literally kills Ellinor is significant, especially since she is the "fictionalizing" sister. The primary symptom of her madness is her inability to recognize anyone, including her lover, her substitute mother, and her sister—the ultimate failure of sympathy. In a rhetorical sense, this means she has survived the grave, since she had told Essex earlier that she would cease to recognize him only in the grave (2: 292). It is thus an "undead" Ellinor who much later inherits that painting of the storming of Cadiz, long after she has lost the ability to know anyone. When she comes upon it in a moment of lucidity, recognition kills her. Not having appropriated it by her own will, but having received it from her substitute mother while in an utterly will-less state, the truth it represents penetrates first the space of her own estate and finally the mad state into which she has withdrawn. Rather than her winning recognition through an active appropriation and recontextualization of this historical painting, as the princess of Clèves does with her painting of the siege of Metz, the moment comes in which Ellinor is obliged to recognize the historical truth it represents: the whole killing truth of official patriarchal history, fixed in its violence. This forced recognition annihilates her.

Ellinor has only been able to survive herself by fictionalizing to the point of madness, refusing to acknowledge the fixed historical truth of Essex's death, or to open herself to the recognition demanded by sympathy. Her madness can be read as a strategy to resist the whole, ordered, complete—that is, *plausible*—narrative demanded by the interrogators. For Ellinor simply does not possess the whole narrative of the twin heroines' plot. The only form in which she ever does possess a "whole narrative" is that of the inherited painting of the storming of Cadiz. No character in the book possesses the whole story, and when anyone, on either side of the act of interrogation, acquires the missing piece that completes a story, the effect is "killing" (e.g., 2: 203–5). Just as Ellinor dies instantly upon recognition of the likeness of the dead Essex within the rigid frame of history, male honor, and violence, Matilda's recognition of the truth about her daughter similarly kills her.

Surviving Representation (in the Fault of Fiction)

The very demand for order, for wholeness in narrative, creates disorder in the mind of the victim who is supposed to provide it, as Ellinor writes while under interrogation: "Unable to command a single moment of solitude and silence to regulate my thoughts or actions, the past, the present, and the future, presented only one wild chaos to my mind, which hardly the breath of Heaven, seemed able to bring into order" (2: 200–201). Not even Providence, in other words, can put order, wholeness, or closure into this narrative. In it, even Providence operates through the escape vents, the faults in narrative enclosure.

The operation of Providence through faults is literalized in the heroines' escape from the outlaws in the Recess. Matilda and Leicester are imprisoned together in one of the chambers, considering suicide, that ever-tempting method of escape, which is a dangerous fault because it involves taking matters into one's own hands, the sin of not relying on Providence or accepting paternal destination.[21] In the episode where they become the coiners' captives in the Recess, Leicester finds himself incapable of "saving" Matilda from the coiners/rapists by killing her, and is blaming Providence for abandoning her to this fate, when suddenly

> a peal of thunder, which shook the ruins to their foundation, seemed to reprove his boldness. The livid lightning pervaded our dungeon through many a time-worn aperture. . . . Suddenly glancing around, I gave a cry which startled even myself—glowing, gasping, transported, yet still unable to speak, I sunk before my Lord, and clasping both his hands, alternately prest them to my heart, and lifted them, with mine, towards Heaven. "What means my beloved? exclaimed he . . . has pitying providence deprived her of her senses?" "Ah no, it is God himself who has illumined them, faltered I at last." (2: 9–10)

"Providence" penetrates through the "time-worn apertures," enabling Matilda to recognize the "secret communication," the way out of the Recess, in the very spot upon which she is imprisoned. To recognize the secret communication is literally to recognize the ancestral portraits concealing it. Whereas recognizing Essex's portrait kills Ellinor, here recognizing the portraits of their parents leads Matilda back out of the trap. The daughter's recognition of the doom of her own desire is more immediately deadly than her recognition of her mother's plot/desire. But these differences are undermined in representation, because Matilda's escape only leads, ultimately, to a repetition of Ellinor's death by recognition (this time, of her daughter's death and rebellious desire). The opening out of these dead ends of repetition comes rather in what they allow the reader to recognize: that Matilda's providential illumination is so akin to the madness that will affect Ellinor as to be mistaken for it.

What madness and illumination have in common is a faultiness, a fragmentation, that makes survival possible. Ellinor's madness, showing its first symptoms under Elizabeth's interrogation, does not allow her to put order into her narrative, not even into the one she writes for Matilda. That narrative is broken into frequently by disconnected, "mad" fragments, which violate the orderly course of the *sjužet* (the plot as it is narrated, in Russian Formalist terms), to address openly the problems or faults of the narration itself, as in this example: "Oh, these cruel wanderings!—but I dare not attempt to correct or avoid them, lest in the very effort reason evaporate, and one inconsiderate stroke should confuse my whole story" (2: 244). The attempt to correct the faults, the breaks, in her narrative, endangers it because the attempt to order the narrative, to "frame a fiction," is itself an attempt to conceal the narrative's truth; it is to literalize the "latent content" into an unreadable allegory, a dream that will protect the reader and the writer from having to understand its killing truth. It is to cover over with a plausible fiction the faulty truth it is trying to narrate: "Something strangely intervenes between myself and my meaning" (2: 243). Ellinor's "meaning" is the truth she wishes to narrate, the private truth of her own history that she wishes to offer to a sympathetic reader, and that truth is the fault in which a heroine survives her virtue—that is, the fault of narrating fault—whether by telling the truth of her survival of her virtue, or by framing fictions in response to a penetrating demand. That which intervenes between the female narrator of her own history and her truth, or narrative desire (for ultimately these are identical) is the double bind: the abyss between the double precipice of narrative desire and narrative demand. There is no ground shared by the desire to narrate the abysmal truth of her survival of her virtue in fault, on one side, and on the other, the penetrating demand for a whole, coherent, hence *plausible* account of, or accounting for, her virtue and her legitimacy. There is only the deathly fall, and the strange survival, undead, motherlike, within it.

The introduction of the portrait of Essex framed within the historical painting of the storming of Cadiz establishes feminine madness in *The Recess* as the hysterical speechlessness between the desire to speak truth and the demand for plausible narrative. Lee rewrites Nemours's attempt to penetrate the princess's pavilion as follows: Ellinor has been married off to a noble but foolish husband by Elizabeth in order to separate her from her plotting lover, Essex. Ellinor's second substitute mother, Lady Pembroke, possesses a new painting of the storming of Cadiz, which contains the portrait of Essex, just as Diane de Poitiers had one of the siege of Metz that included a portrait of Nemours. Although virtue has required Ellinor to repel all Essex's efforts to see her since her marriage, she writes, "I did not think virtue herself would refuse me one little satisfaction, I could not but desire"—that is, to view this portrait (2: 288). To deceive the husband's vigilant jealousy, Lady Pembroke arranges for Ellinor to visit the gallery alone, when everyone else is away—as they are when Nemours comes to Coulommiers—at a court function. The fiction they frame together is that Ellinor is going there to copy a portrait of Lady Pembroke. "In this project there was nothing dishonorable or unsafe, and I embraced it readily," writes Ellinor (2: 289).

Yet framing fictions remains a fault, however seemingly honorable or safe: "How disdainful of mystery is a truly noble soul! I stopt short on the threshold, and could I without singularity have ventured immediately to return, I had not entered the house" (2: 290). Acting both of the gender roles in *La Princesse de Clèves* alternately,

Ellinor here hesitates on the threshold like Nemours at Coulommiers. She, too, must cross it, not, like him, because of the force of her own desire, but because she has already entered the fiction, and must thus uphold its plausibility or else reveal it to the ever-watchful penetrating gaze as a fiction. Once inside, she gazes at Essex's portrait, like the princess, but unlike her, she moves from the language of the gaze to that of speech. She addresses the portrait aloud, to hear the voice of Essex himself in response. Like Nemours, he is in the window frame, but unlike Nemours, he is already in the room, sitting in the window seat behind a curtain. She finds him already inside the enclosure that she had to enter because she found herself already inside it. But this guilty situation is nobody's fault. Chance alone is at fault, he assures her: "Believe me I come not an artful, black seducer—chance, and chance only has crowned wishes so long submitted to your will." Where Matilda had displaced the fault for following her own desire in inviting Leicester into the Recess onto "chance, or rather I should say, Providence," Essex similarly maintains his own feminized virtue, his entitlement to be received with more trust than Nemours was, by displacing the fault onto chance, and making an appeal similar to that made earlier by Leicester to Ellinor's sympathy. And in displacing the agency of his desire onto "chance only," he again echoes Nemours, who, to reach Coulommiers, "allowed himself to be led by chance." But the discourse of "chance," although it seems here to absolve even Providence of the fault of plotting against virtue, lacks the latter's patriarchal authority. That lack of authority enables Ellinor, unlike Matilda with Leicester, but like the princess of Clèves, to refuse Essex's demand for sympathy: "Though my eyes surveyed his form," she writes, "my heart for the first time shut him out" (2: 292).

Ellinor's heart may shut Essex out, but she cannot retire, like the princess of Clèves, to "le lieu où étaient ses femmes," to the place where the presence of the female witnesses of her female virtue preclude any meeting between them. There is no space of virtue into which she can escape, no witness to validate the evidence of her virtue, no "space of reception" that she can transform into her own state, no pavilion.[22] Where the princess's "heart of glass" is defended within by the female witnesses of virtue, Ellinor's sympathetic heart is the last stronghold from which to maintain her virtue's evidence—which, however, she cannot do without witnesses. She is already locked in with Essex, enclosed in a fault within which she can maintain her virtue in fact, but without the means to establish the evidence that would make it recognizable to penetrating and powerful masculine readers like her husband.

Ellinor has no pavilion, no estate, and no state; nor does she possess the painting at which she gazes. The double bind that requires her to keep her mother alive by concealing her true history, yet also gain public recognition for her mother's right to patriarchal authority, allows her no possible space of her own *outside* the public and patriline order. No negotiation like that of the princess's aveu is possible here; Ellinor is caught in *fictionalizing instead of confessing* because the revelation of her desire to her husband would (and does, when he literally catches her in her fiction) only result in imprisonment, not the *liberté* the princess asked for. Instead of transforming the jeweled frame of her maternal inheritance into a pavilion from which she can rule her own (e)state, Ellinor is forcibly sent back to the tomb of the Recess, which is devoid now even of its protective, womblike aspects, for she can only gaze on the distant prospect of the ruins around it (with their association with female genitalia, noted earlier) from her place of imprisonment. Because the maternal destination inscribes the heroines unrelentingly within the patriline order, because it aims at succession to the chief patrilineal office, they cannot negotiate in representation, like the princess, for a new kind of evidence upon which to establish the recognition of their virtue. They must, instead, play by the rules of plausibility: it is in order to do so that Ellinor goes in to the gallery after hesitating over the virtuousness of entering. Without the princess's negotiation away from the laws of plausibility, the estate becomes a prison, and the state remains under the rule of the "phallic mother" who kills off the mother. The historical paintings remain solely in the possession of a substitute mother, whose portrait could plausibly be copied, but who can never be imitated in the nonmimetic way that the princess imitated Diane de Poitiers.

While Ellinor lacks testimony to establish her marital fidelity, the princess lacked the late eighteenth-century sentimental heroine's imperative of demonstrating sympathy to establish feminine virtue. As a sympathetic relationship between Essex and Ellinor has already been established through a ruse of Lady Pembroke's, it now poses its own threat of fault: Essex's demand for sympathy requires a return. Trapped again in the double bind, Ellinor has not even a narrow space in which to retreat, and is forced instead to inflict the violence of male honor upon herself, thus stifling the simultaneously ambitious and sympathetic voice with which she had been able to address the painting:

> "Alas, my Lord . . . those dear wishes, a higher power has annihilated:—nor while the tie which robbed you of this trembling hand subsists, can I suffer it to be thus pressed in yours. Yet recollect at the same moment, the influence you still have over my heart—an influence virtue alone contests with you—Ah, gentle Essex, *fix* not an angry eye upon me—you know not the wound you give—the horrors you may occasion."—The wild accent of my voice struck even my own ear, and not daring to trust it with another syllable, I strove to bury my agitation and sensibility in a silence. . . . A suffocation more painful than fainting ensued. (2: 295–96; emphasis mine)

As she is choking on this early *globus hystericus*, a live repetition of the bloody scene of conflict she deplored earlier in the painting forms itself around her: her husband storms in, and in an instant she sees both men with drawn swords. Lacking the space to maintain the distance of a spectator, she ends the duel by throwing herself between them and getting pierced through the shoulder by her husband's weapon. She thus acts to escape the scene of violence, but turning herself into a victim is the only form of action available to her, and she can only escape into her own weakness: "Extreme weakness blended for once objects ever before so distinct, and I ceased to feel for the lover, or dread the husband." This phase marks her descent into permanent madness and live burial.

The essential difference between the two scenes around historical paintings, in *The Recess* and in *La Princesse de Clèves*, is the response of the husbands—both of them maternal doubles—as interpreters who insist on judging the evidence of their wives' virtue according to the code of plausibility. For both husbands, the truth of their wives' virtue is of no consequence; only its plausibility matters. That Ellinor's heart actually does shut Essex out, and that the princess walks away from Nemours, is immaterial. Ellinor would have ended up in the same prison, and the prince of Clèves would have died of chagrin, whether the heroine acted virtuously or not. Plausibility is against them either way, simply because they are already "framed" in the scene, the same masculine field of vision, with their lovers. The difference is that the prince's vengeance is to die, like the mother he represents, abandoning his wife to her haunted guilt, while Ellinor's husband, as instrument of Elizabeth and thus of the patrilineal agency to which her mother aspires, entombs her alive. The princess internalizes her mother's ghost with her virtuous prohibition, but Ellinor internalizes the double bind of her undead mother's virtuous prohibition combined with her claim on what Peter Brooks has called "the male plot of ambition."[23]

Resemblance and the Fault of Sympathy

Ellinor's determination to enact her mother's "male" plot of ambition causes her to withhold the confidence required by (feminine, virtuous) sympathy not only from men but from women too—including her twin sister. Ellinor's first-person narrative, enclosed within Matilda's and addressed to Matilda, opens a cleft in the center of Matilda's narrative with these words: "Oh you! much loved, but little trusted, dear sister of my heart" (2: 158). This address seems contradictory, but its contradiction is the key to understanding how this novel leaps out of its own double bind through a "secret communication" that, like the princess's nonmimetic imitation of Diane de Poitiers, refuses resemblance in constructing its correspondence.

While Ellinor is imprisoned as mad because she enacts fictional plots instead of offering her true history even to sympathetic readers, Matilda is open to sympathy, moving through a parallel series of imprisonments, from which she is rescued by a series of intruders, some sympathetic, others unsympathetic and deceptive. She trusts them, putting herself into their power even when she perceives that they are not capable of sympathy. The events lived by both heroines together, up to Matilda's flight to France, are narrated by Matilda. She then pursues her separate narrative until her return to England from imprisonment in a colony.[24] Here, at the exact midpoint of the novel, she receives and encloses for her reader the separate narrative addressed to her by Ellinor, who by then has already survived her own consciousness of self in madness. It is at this point that the reader's attention is drawn to the fact that neither sympathy nor resemblance is as simple as it may at first have seemed.

What looks like fragmentation in this novel is rather a reduplication into multiple wholes. While the characters have been "reduced to frame a new story," the text expands in order to do so. With the introduction of Ellinor's narrative, it repeats the story that has already been read from a different point of view. This doubled perspective makes it possible to read that too much readiness to enter into the bonds of sympathy, too much willingness to see a resemblance with the other, actually destroys sympathy. Lee uses the epistolary form to give a jagged edge to the apparently "rounded picture" of Matilda's memoir-letter by dividing it in the middle with the insertion of Ellinor's mad account of her own plotting. In this doubling fragmentation, each epistolary piece does indeed constitute, as Altman points out, both an individual unit and a fragment within the larger whole (p. 186). But it does so in a formal move unique in the eighteenth century. It sets doubled memoir-letters in correspondence with one another by undercutting the wholeness of the memoir, by performing the tear, the hole, that makes of the whole text a matrix for the reader.[25]

In her final classification of all theoretically conceivable epistolary types, Altman wonders at the lack of any novels that do what *The Recess* does: "We note, for example, that the 'type Marianne' exists but there seem to be no novels composed by two or more correspondents removed [temporally] from the action. This is largely because *La Vie de Marianne* and *La Religieuse*, like John Cleland's *Memoirs of Fanny Hill* (1745), grafted epistolary traits upon the memoir model, in which a single narrator recounts his life. Yet nothing precludes our imagining a novel that would interweave autobiographical letters or combine several correspondents' memoirs of the same past incident" (p. 204). By doing exactly that, Lee's doubled memoir-letters combine, moreover, the extreme forms of what Elizabeth MacArthur calls the "metaphoric" and "metonymic" axes of narrative, defined as the "desire for the end," closure or stable meaning, and the "valorization of desire and expanse," respectively. Although MacArthur cautions that "all narratives depend on both tendencies," nevertheless the memoir, for her, exemplifies the "metaphoric" tendency, while letters exemplify "metonymy": "Retrospective narratives . . . often produce a stabilizing sense of inevitability," whereas in both real and fictional letters "narrative drives forward to an open future instead of looking back over a completed past." Lee's unique technique for combining these two axes of narrative at their extremes preserves the "energy and movement" of metonymy within the most retrospective type of narrative (*Extravagant Narratives*, pp. 25, 32–33). It destabilizes meaning, closure, and their implied "moral order" by first creating a voice whose sympathetic appeal seems to give it authority to tell a story that represents "the whole truth" for both sisters, and then suddenly setting their double narratives in uneasy correspondence with (and against) one another.

The extreme tension produced by this technique is precisely what creates the demand on the reader that MacArthur defines as a hallmark of metonymic epistolarity: "Real and fictional epistolary narratives require the reader's active participation, whether to replace the absent narrator or to share in producing an exchange. The reader necessarily enters into dialogue with the epistolary text, a dialogue that is never resolved and never completed" (p. 273). Lee's doubled memoir-letters ensure both that dialogue and that openness by invoking and maintaining the reader's sympathy over time before radically questioning the reliability of sympathy as a social bond. The questioning is especially effective since it casts doubt upon exactly the mechanism of identification by which the reader's *interest*, in the full sympathetic sense, has been so long maintained—for, as Frances Ferguson remarks, "the letter, precisely because it lays claim to a reply, registers an attempt both to generate and to enforce resemblance between the correspondents" (p. 111). Having invoked sympathy through resemblance in the voice of Matilda, the novel suddenly undermines the possibility of such identification by introducing the voice of Ellinor. This narrative structure works to make the reader not only understand, but intensely *feel*, after sympathizing with Matilda's narrative for a volume and a half, what Mücke calls the "dark side" of sympathy as a discourse of identification through resemblance: "The relation of similarity can be established only by rejecting that which is asserting an otherness" (p. 105).

Matilda's great capacity for sympathy is suddenly cast in a most dubious light by the introduction of her sister's perspective. She appears, in this new light, repeatedly to sympathize with men so exclusively that she ceases to offer sympathy to her own sister and daughter, forcing them to withdraw their confidence from her, since they perceive that their own true stories will not meet with her sympathy. At the same time, these sympathies with men prevent Matilda from penetrating the true stories that are being withheld, stories of the sister's and daughter's differently placed sympathies with men. Ellinor gives a portrait of Leicester that is entirely at odds with Matilda's, as a selfish man who uses Matilda for his own ambitious ends; she also reveals her own attachment to Essex, which Matilda never noticed because of her absorption in Leicester.

A similar failure of sympathy characterizes Matilda's return to her role as narrator. Towards the end of the novel, she finally finds the perfect reader, both sympathetic and a recognized heir to the throne of Scotland: her own nephew, Prince Henry, son of James I. She and Henry indulge in sympathetic communications every day, in which they confide their whole histories to each other and decide between them that he will marry Matilda's daughter Mary, thus finally legitimating and actualizing the right to power that Matilda has now carried through three volumes. Young Mary herself is sent out riding during these conversations, in order to keep the appearance of her virtue intact as evidence in the code of plausibility. Daughters, however, like stories, have a way of following their own paths, regardless of the will of their authors. Mary can't stand Henry herself. While out riding she falls in love with his bad double, who seduces her into betraying her own sexual purity and her mother's political plot. Caught between her lover's selfish seductions and her mother's failure to sympathize with her real desires, she commits suicide. This novel of sympathy thus demonstrates a dangerous pitfall of sympathy, which seems to be associated with a problem of gender: the sensibility with which women bind themselves to men renders them insensible to their sympathies with women, precisely because of their shared status of exile within patriarchy. This basis for division is the same one that so frequently grounds sympathy between women, as in novels like *The British Recluse.* After reading Ellinor's narrative, Matilda herself observes this through her use of a telling adverb: "I could not help imputing her blindness to the same cause she assigned for mine. . . . I saw but too plainly . . . how much a woman *insensibly* adopts of the disposition of him to whom she gives her heart" (3: 195; emphasis mine). To adopt, sympathetically, the disposition of one's male lover is to become, insensibly, insensible to female relations.

This apparent absorption in men, however, is really a self-absorption, or rather a forgetting both of self and sympathy in the plot to make good the maternal inheritance through the agency of men as the only authorized readers capable of legitimating a patriline birthright. Sympathy with men can be problematic too, as in the scene in the gallery where Ellinor's heart "shut out" Essex, as well as in a parallel passage involving Matilda and Leicester (2: 54–62). But there is a special problem with sympathy between "little-trusted" sisters, between mothers and daughters, and it is the same as the problem of maternal inheritance, as outlined in chapters 2 and 3. Female relations are always already contained within the same enclosure of exile. They have inherited the same history, and any demand for that history by one from another can only produce a repetition, a reframing of the same history, whose difference can be disturbing, because it discloses the failures of sympathy by re-creating, rather than bridging, the gap between them. Not being strangers, but co-inheritors, they can neither intrude upon their inherited enclosure from without nor break out of it from within, but only reduplicate it. Because of this failure of maternal sympathy and inheritance, the history that would have been the maternal legacy can only be successfully passed on to a stranger through a form of transmission less fixedly inscribed within patriline relations.

Living Over

After the failure of her plot to use her daughter to legitimate her mother's birthright, Matilda exiles herself in France to die of chagrin, coming to rest in the "narrow asylum" of an inn. This is neither the princess of Clèves's pavilion nor a substitute mother's estate, nor even the Recess, but an equally confined space, which is not inherited but foreign and borrowed. Into this space, Providence penetrates once more with "a second angel," a sympathizing replacement for her dead daughter, but like this last asylum, foreign and borrowed (3: 354). In contrast to the true daughter, whose death in fault has killed Matilda, this substitute daughter is able to make her live on by a sympathetic demand for maternal history. Matilda acknowledges this after fulfilling that demand: "That my decline has been prolonged till this narrative is concluded, I do not regret; and by compliance, I have evinced my sense of your friendship:—I have now only to die" (3: 354–55). The whole narrative we have just read thus turns out to be a survival beyond the point when the heroine ought to have died, a long tergiversation conjured forth by the demand for true history from a sympathetic stranger.[26] From the beginning, then, the text has constituted a strange form of repetition, a survival from the brink where the grave should have opened. The grave literalizes that metaphorical precipice on the verge of which virtue incessantly hovers (3: 150–51) from the very first page of the novel: "I turn my every thought toward that grave *on the verge of which I hover*. Oh! why then, too generous friend, *require me to live over* my misfortunes?" (1: 1). Why, then? The sympathetic reader represented by Adelaide demands a "living over" in narrative representation because it is necessary for the narrative transaction of the text's transmission to its reader through the secret communication of sympathy.

The Recess*'s Secret Communication*

The Recess counts on its readers' willingness to perform in reading a plot of escape from the feminine entrapment in repetition that it tries repeatedly to represent as performative text. The only way in which a heroine in *The Recess* can write her "meaning" is as a performative, rather than as a constative narrative, of her own history. The performative force of this "passionate vocation" of the reader, to borrow Kauffman's words, is represented in Lee's text in a double mise-en-abyme: once in Ellinor's attempt to write her "mad," fragmentary meaning and again in an episode in Matilda's narrative.[27]

In their final imprisonment, Matilda and her daughter are incarcerated in the library of a castle, where they are surrounded by books but not allowed writing instruments:

> Involved in a thousand plots, the want of pen and ink seemed to condemn them all to inhabit only my brain, when at once I discovered a substitute for those useful articles. From the middle of a *large book*, which we had unmolested possession of, I took some of the printed leaves, and from the conclusion a blank one; out of the first I cut such words as simply conveyed my meaning, and sewed them on the last. (3: 309–27; emphasis mine)

The "large book" here recalls the "large book of devotion" that Elizabeth threw at Ellinor's head, the Derridean "torture" that enforced her unsympathetic demand for Ellinor's whole history and brought on the first symptoms of madness. Matilda's plot of writing takes that book of patriarchal precepts and fragments it, undoing its imperative meaning to turn her own from a plot condemned to "inhabit only her brain" to a performative of escape. She finds that the "conclusion" of the large book is not an end but a blank flyleaf, an open space upon which she can use the domestic instrument allowed her to sew letters. Cutting fragments of leaves out of the book's solidly printed pages, she creates a secret communication.[28]

Yet to "simply convey her meaning" is to write with, by, and for the patriline plot from whose library she is trying to escape. Matilda's meaning can be simply conveyed because it does not, like Ellinor's, attempt to represent her history. It is a sheer performative that relies for its enactment on the sympathetic agency of the male guard who stands outside her door. Matilda's performative does get her out, but her escape serves only to get her to the scene of her daughter's suicide in time to behold that killing spectacle. In its reliance on male agency, her plot still follows the logic of the substitute, which changes the content of the message without changing the structure of transmission, just as the substitution of widowed mother for father, or of a female inheritance of virtue for a proscribed patrimony, fails to effect more than a tergiversation in the patriline plot, because it in fact reduplicates it.

While *The Recess* cannot enact its heroines' plot successfully in representation, it counts on the reader to perform its parable of reading and writing: to operate on the books of the library of tradition, not by looking for the whole story, but by cutting the significant holes that create the secret communications of women's correspondence. As plotted by these novels, reading is, like writing, a matter of reordering, choosing and cutting out fragments and individual letters and juxtaposing them in a different order to convey the secret communications within works and among works, the smoothed-over breaks and leaps that generate meaning. *The Recess* performs its plot, and plots its enactment for the reader, by cutting up both its own narrative and the books in the library: not only the tomes of patriline history and patriarchal devotion, but those of Lee's female predecessors outside her national tradition, notably Lafayette.[29]

The "time-worn apertures" through which providential lightning penetrates to allow Matilda to recognize her ancestral portraits and the opening they conceal are repeated in the outermost frame of the novel. This repetition opens an invagination into the text, through which the voice of the fictional editor of the letters intrudes to address the reader. The editor frames her fiction as implausible, and therefore true: "The depredations of time have left chasms in the story, which sometimes only heightens the pathetic. An inviolable respect for truth would not permit me to attempt connecting these, even where they appeared faulty" (Advertisement, unpaginated). The prevalent fiction in eighteenth-century epistolary novels is of the editor who performs on private correspondence the same operation that Matilda performs on the library. The device of apologizing for its faults generally refers either to faults of a feminized, naive-sentimental style or to gaps created by the editor's cutting.[30] Lee's editor insists that in offering this history to the reader, she cannot attempt to close up its faults, any more than mad Ellinor could those of her fragmented history, because the truth of the narratives both editor and character are trying to pass on resides in and is evidenced by its faultiness. With the fiction of the editor, concerned with preserving historical truth rather than with coining fictions unified and plausible enough either to deceive or to satisfy a penetrating (unsympathetic) demand, Lee locates that truth in the literal, textual faults, in "the depredations of time" that have made the manuscript into a broken ruin, in her fragmentary *sjužet* rather than in the *fabula*, or imaginary "whole story" behind narrative representation.

On the other hand, the dedication that precedes the Advertisement, signed by the author, has already announced the book as a fiction. Lee sets this double frame around her work, announcing it as a fiction in the dedication while maintaining the fiction of its historical truth in the Advertisement, in order to authorize herself and the fictional author-heroines of her text in the ultimate fault that both she and they are passing on: the fault of writing as a woman at all, but especially and specifically, the fault of rewriting history in the feminine.[31]

With her double fictional/historical frame, Lee achieves a self-authorization for "coining" fictions that, by virtue of its doubleness, is neither that of the law of plausible truth nor that of the outlaw. She does so by arguing the plausibility of her historical manuscript's existence on the basis of the very implausibility of the narrated events: "A wonderful coincidence of events *stamps* the narration at least with probability, and the reign of Elizabeth was that of romance" (Advertisement; emphasis mine). By recalling the metaphor of coining in her Advertisement, Lee imitates *La Princesse de Clèves* "en abyme." She makes of *The Recess* a gesture of non-mimetic imitation, like that by which the inimitable princess chose herself as the successor of Diane de Poitiers, and precisely as her heroines are unable to do.

Lee does not imitate *La Princesse de Clèves* in representation: her heroines' double plot diverges from that of the princess, and fails precisely where the princess's succeeds—namely, in the construction of the heroine's plot as the heroine's own state. What Lee does imitate mimetically, in "stamping" her counterfeit "coin" with Elizabeth's portrait, is the same historical period represented by Lafayette in the creation of her *nouvelle historique*—just as the princess copied the historical paintings from Diane de Poitiers's estate. Thus engaging in a secret communication with the French novel, through which she translates its perspective on the representation of history across the Channel towards the state of England, she also translates its fictional framework—Lafayette's "new construction," the genre of the *nouvelle*—into the quintessentially English genre of Gothic romance. In fact, Lee's novel ushered in the vogue of the "female Gothic," thus creating a "new construction" out of representations of ruin and "time-worn" fragmentation.[32]

More important, Lee's allusion in her "Advertisement" to the outlawed "coiners" who hide out in the Recess and threaten the heroines with their instruments of forgery creates another mise-en-abyme structure that allows her, as author, to evade the threat of fault their example holds out to her fictionalizing heroines. For the metaphor of coining prefigures the mise-en-abyme structure she creates within the narrative itself by representing the coiners and their instruments at the center of a novel about the necessary faults of passing on fictions. Mise-en-abyme structures in narrative reinforce the invocation of readers that MacArthur and Ferguson, as mentioned above, attribute to the epistolary form. As Marie Maclean argues, mise-en-abyme structures "provoke reader participation in the construction of the text. . . . It is also a way of reminding us of the true nature of the currency we are using in the fictional transaction. . . . Self-reflexivity, by foregrounding the special status of the narrative 'act,' is one device which maintains the 'gold standard' of literature" (pp. 83, 87). By claiming the reader's recognition of the text's very fictiveness, which Lee "advertises" when she points to its faults, and alluding to its status as "counterfeit" history, she invites the reader to accept it, nevertheless, as "good coin," a signifier of true, though unauthorized, value.

Counterfeit History; or, Telling Portraits

In the "Advertisement" that frames *The Recess*, Lee further compares written history to a static and stylized portraiture, contrasting it to the revelation of character from a sympathetic perspective. The sympathetic depiction of character may be faulty, Lee admits, in comparison with the objective stance of history, for it may "veil a fault, or irradiate a virtue." Yet the fault of veiling faults is here "advertised" as the prime virtue of sympathetic representation. A history that takes sympathy and sensibility as its touchstone of truth, as opposed to demanding the "hard evidence" recognized by the discourse of rational objectivity, avoids the pitfalls inherent in painting as a mode of representation: "History, like painting, only perpetuates the striking features of the mind; whereas the best and worst actions of princes often proceed from partialities and prejudices, which live in their hearts, and are buried with them." The gesture of framing her text as "one of the first recognizable historical novels in English" involves a new strategy for tackling one of the dominant problems of Enlightenment thought: how to negotiate the chain of rhetorical oppositions that includes sentiment versus reason ("heart" versus "mind"), the private versus the public spheres, feminine versus masculine.[33] In placing her text on the side of sentiment, faultily concealing potential faults, Lee places historiography as we have come to know it, along with painting, on the side of reason, of the masculine, the public sphere, and the graver fault of expecting whole truths from hard evidence.

The visual metaphors Lee uses to describe her text's gestures ("veil" and "irradiate") recuperate the visual register, and with it the whole series of terms with which she has aligned the visual (the masculine, the public). What Lee "advertises" to her readers is not a text as painting, which would fix and preserve "striking features," but rather a text as "moving picture," a revival or animation of precisely that living aspect of history and its figures that *has not been passed down* to posterity, but has been buried. That aspect is sentiment, that which *moves* readers, aligned here with the private and feminine. The transformation she effects amounts to a narrativization of portraiture. The fixed text of example (in the terms of which history had been understood at least since the Renaissance), translated into the private terms of exemplary feminine virtue, blocked the maternal "trap" at the close of *Mademoiselle de Boismiran*; Lee now unpacks it as plot. This strategy for representing historical character was highly successful in Lee's own time as a competitive genre of history. "The truth of character is here preserved," wrote a reviewer for the *Gentleman's Magazine* in 1786, "for the peculiarities of Elizabeth and James are not delineated with more exactness in Hume or Robertson."[34]

Two pleas for sympathy, addressed to the reader in the novel and to readers of the novel, map out the trajectory over which the new genre of history Lee authorized herself to coin is to be kept in circulation. In the last paragraph of the novel, Matilda addresses the young foreigner to whom she bequeaths her narrative:

> Dear and lovely friend, you are now in England—Already perhaps your feet have trod lightly over those spots where my happiness withered.—Ah! if sensibility should lead you more thoughtfully to retrace them, check every painful emotion, by recollecting I shall then be past the power of suffering.—Yet, when your noble father reconducts you to the home you was born to embellish, grant a little to the weakness of mortality, and linger once more on the spot where we met: the pious De Vere will there attend your coming—Accept from his hand the casket I bequeath, and suffer him to lead you to the nameless grave where he shall have interred my ashes: drop on it a few of those holy tears with which virtue consecrates misfortune; then raise your eyes with those of your venerable conductor, and in a better world look for MATILDA.

Matilda asks her reader to sympathize, but not too much, not to succumb to the deceptive illusion that she can feel what Matilda feels—for Matilda will in fact feel nothing. It is significant that she asks Adelaide to shed these few tears of sympathy in France, but not in England. As long as Adelaide is in Matilda's own country, in the place marked with the traces of Matilda's sufferings, she should only "retrace" them without "painful emotion." It is only when Adelaide is in her own country that she is asked to provide the measured dose of sympathy, the repayment of an equal exchange, without the excess of accumulated interest, that Matilda wishes to exact. The reception of the inheritance is to occur there, at the "nameless grave," neither circumscribed, claimed, nor named as the writer's own.

The reader, in other words, is not to put herself in the place of the writer, but rather to carry the text into her own place. That place is designated as the location of the exchange of sympathy for the textual legacy in the casket. Lee's innovative use of the epistolary form replaces the relation of inheritance through patriline kinship with one of *distanced* sympathy. An intergenerational exchange between women who are not relations, but foreigners, replaces the relation of sympathetic resemblance between twin sisters that has been shown to be so dangerous. The ending of Lee's novel together with the "Advertisement" thus creates a framing mise-en-abyme that establishes a narrative contract guaranteed by the sympathy of a feminized, although not necessarily female, reader who is no relation to the figure of the writer and shares no domestic space with her. The true history it transmits is available only to the proper readers, whom the "editor" defines at the close of the "Advertisement": "To the hearts of both sexes nature has enriched with sensibility, and experience with refinement, this tale is humbly offered." Such inheritance cannot be willed, for its inheritors must be already "enriched" with the quality that will enable them to receive their enrichment.

The proper receiver thus invoked carries the book into her own place of silent and private reading, where women's epistolary culture could become a public bond crucially resistant to the patriarchal culture of the emerging middle class that dominated the larger society of readers.[35] Deborah Kaplan's historical research into actual epistolary correspondences between women of the period has revealed an English "women's culture" uneasily contained within and critical of "the gentry's patriarchal culture." Kaplan stresses that "the women's culture's" criticisms of patriarchy "functioned to accommodate the women to their subordination and maintain it" because "they communicated these sentiments *only to one another* (*Jane Austen Among Women*, pp. 78, 82). By publishing epistolary critiques in the spirit of those that historical women were sending each other, novels of women's correspondence radically changed the status of these critical acts of communication between women from strictly private to publicly private. Literariness thus lends the critique considerably greater force.

Novels of women's correspondence do not resolve, in representation, the problems they explore; their subversive potential is rather in the narrative transaction they invite. Matilda asks her reader to look for her "in a better world," but neither she nor Lee wish to depict such a world, even in the frame of a romance. The fixed facts of their historical frame are closed and simply do not allow for such a revolution.[36] Instead, the writers of this fiction restructure the linear narrative of the progress of Virtue towards Death as a matrix-narrative of survival. For the enactment of this narrative, they now rely upon readers who, coming upon it in another country and in a wholly different historical frame (as Lee's fictional editor comes across the manuscript of *The Recess*), have the sympathy to read a text whose faults may enable them to "give birth to new ideas," to build new constructions through its secret communications. Such readers can still be created through an education that would include reading novels like *The Recess*, an education that can become possible only with a reconception of models of narrative form and literary tradition.

Chapter 6

Corinne's Correspondences; or, The Fault of Passing On

The unhappy Corinne had only to take one step to plunge into eternal oblivion.
—Germaine de Staël, 'Corinne, or Italy'

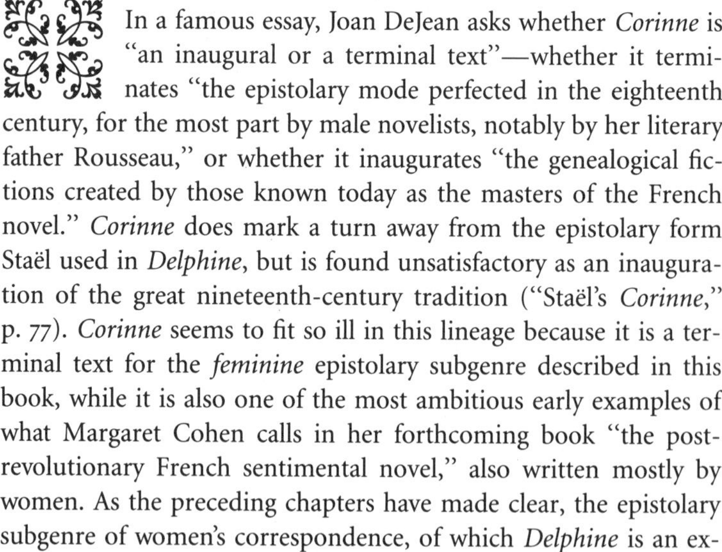

In a famous essay, Joan DeJean asks whether *Corinne* is "an inaugural or a terminal text"—whether it terminates "the epistolary mode perfected in the eighteenth century, for the most part by male novelists, notably by her literary father Rousseau," or whether it inaugurates "the genealogical fictions created by those known today as the masters of the French novel." *Corinne* does mark a turn away from the epistolary form Staël used in *Delphine*, but is found unsatisfactory as an inauguration of the great nineteenth-century tradition ("Staël's *Corinne*," p. 77). *Corinne* seems to fit so ill in this lineage because it is a terminal text for the *feminine* epistolary subgenre described in this book, while it is also one of the most ambitious early examples of what Margaret Cohen calls in her forthcoming book "the post-revolutionary French sentimental novel," also written mostly by women. As the preceding chapters have made clear, the epistolary subgenre of women's correspondence, of which *Delphine* is an example, was always concerned with "genealogical fictions"—specifically, the fiction of patrilineage that excluded women from patrimonial succession and female authors from participating in any recognized way in national tradition.

Like Sophia Lee's *The Recess*, Germaine de Staël's *Corinne, or Italy* revises received conceptions of both national and gender boundaries. Working out the same interconnected problems of transmission—represented as inheritance, education, literary tradition, and history—as well as of women's place in the modern nation-state, it revises Lafayette's *La Princesse de Clèves* via Lee and the English "female Gothic." By reading the first woman's novel to be included as constitutive of the borderlines that define French nationalism alongside one of the first English historical novels, Staël participates in and perpetuates the gestures of her predecessors in both nations towards an alternative feminine cross-generational form of literary transmission, one that differs both from a patrilineal model and from any notion of maternal legacy inevitably defined by patrilineage. Yet she accomplishes this through a move that is markedly different from those of her eighteenth-century predecessors, who kept their plots within the formal limits of the subgenre of women's correspondence. Moving from the figure of epistolary exchange to that of public performance, Staël writes the tragedy of a heroine who exchanges virtue for talent, accepts as a result of that choice a literal exile from her patronym, her fatherland, and the domestic sphere, and then attempts to reinscribe herself within the system of patriline legitimacy—not, this time, as a usurping mother, but as a father in her own right. In so doing, Staël creates a Romantic version of national and gender identity, and of female transmission in particular, ultimately resisting, despite her heroine's failure, the boundary lines of patrie and of literary tradition as patrimoine. In her own Corinne-like effort to enter the paternal lineage of "the French novel now referred to as great," Staël also helped end the production of the formal subgenre of women's correspondences in France, as Austen did at the same time in England ("Staël's *Corinne*," p. 77).

· · ·

As a reformulation of the solutions offered in *La Princesse de Clèves* to the problem of female transmission within a patrilineal society, *Corinne* retains the earlier novel's primary couple, the mother-daughter dyad, in the relationship between Lucile and her mother, but replaces it squarely within a patrilineal frame of reference. The description of Corinne's foil as the English exemplar of feminine virtue resembles nothing more than its French model, Lafayette's princess. Physically, Lucile presents the same perfect blank of fair skin and blond hair that make up the nondescript princess, distinguished by the same excessively modest reserve and described in the same terms of "brilliance," even in her name. For both characters, the culmination of a secluded education by a widowed mother comes with their entrance at the age of sixteen into a public arena (for Lucile, the London opera house instead of the royal court) as the greatest heiresses of their respective nations, and the central focus of society's collective gaze (Balayé, pp. 480–83; Goldberger, pp. 341–43; Adam, p. 53).[1] What first attracts the hero of Staël's novel to Lucile is precisely that unbroken and exclusive connection to her mother, consisting of a severe education in virtue, for which the princess of Clèves is famous (e.g., "He was lost in a dream of the celestial purity of a young girl who, always at her mother's side, knows nothing of life but daughterly affection" [Balayé, p. 450; Goldberger, p. 317]). And in fact the function of Oswald's marriage to Lucile is to preserve that maternal connection unbroken—just as the prince of Clèves is chosen by his mother-in-law to continue in her role as educator in feminine virtue after her death. Lucile secures Oswald's "interest" (*intérêt*) when she agrees to the marriage, not by expressing any desire for it, but by demanding that it not separate her from her mother. The mother, meanwhile, expresses her satisfaction with the match by pronouncing herself "well replaced" (Goldberger, p. 379, Balayé, p. 533).

While Lucile resembles the princess of Clèves in the primacy of her relationship to her mother, Staël's most important revision of the earlier work is to replace this mother-daughter relationship within the very patrilineal frame that Lafayette had deemphasized as much as possible. Lucile, unlike the princess, is heiress to a real patrimony. She is specifically named as heiress to her father's estate, and when her future husband first catches sight of her, alone and unchaperoned like the princess when first seen by Clèves at the jeweler's shop, she is on that heritable estate rather than in a public place of exchange. Instead of seeking to match the incomplete set of jewels that form the princess's maternal inheritance, she is absorbed in reading a book (pp. 317, 353). The book she is reading is not named, but only one of Lucile's books is ever named, and that is her copy of the same volume of paternal precepts that were handed down to Oswald by his father. Lucile's copy forms the focal point of her private funerary shrine to this, her "second father," who praises her feminine virtues and designates her as the perfect wife in his inscription to her (p. 350). The book is thus the paternal parallel to the princess's maternal jewels; it is movable property that is passed down but does not constitute a patrimony proper, an inheritance that will remain incomplete unless the daughter fulfills its destination and lives up to its image of perfect feminine virtue.

In relation to Lafayette's novel, then, *Corinne* performs the reinscription of maternal inheritance within a patrimonial system. Lucile is literally *inscribed* in the father's will, not only in the dedication to the memorial book of precepts, but also in the other apotheosized form of inscription that traces the patriarch's ghostly word over all the novel's landscapes: the providential signs that seem to spell out the fate of Corinne and her relationship with Oswald. At the same moment when he first sees Lucile reading the book in the park of her estate, she is marked in his imagination as the tableau of feminine virtue where the gaze of male desire must come to rest: "His imagination set in motion just a short time ago by eloquence and passion, enjoyed the picture of innocence, and seemed to see around Lucile some sort of modest aura that was deliciously restful to the eye" (p. 319). This "aura" that settles around Lucile evokes the "cloud" that Corinne has just read as the expression of a paternal heaven's condemnation of her love, and that will appear again, as she predicts, at the moment of her death. This providential writing is the international language that all three protagonists know how to read.[2]

Staël reinscribes the characters' relations, more specifically, in the writing of the father's will *as providence*—which again includes that word's other early sense, "inheritance." In both senses, "providence" is precisely the writing that Lafayette had suppressed. Not only do M. de Chartres's presumable real estate and will go entirely without mention; as was argued, the organizing force of events in *La Princesse de Clèves* is neither the providence that drives romance nor the chance whose operations distinguish other early novels, like *Don Quixote*, from romance; rather the sense of fatality that pervades it derives from the foregone conclusion of maternal history and its endless specular repetition in the process of its transmission from mother to daughter. The daughter as mirror of speculation, one that gives back the mother's image *with interest*, survives in *Corinne* in the relationship between Lucile and her mother. Thus Lucile repeats every night *her mother's prayer* that she remain unsoiled by a single thought or feeling not in keeping with her duties (*devoirs*—what one *owes*), in order that her dying mother's own sins may be forgiven (Goldberger, p. 320; Balayé, p. 455). While this relation of speculation resembles Mme de Chartres's demand that her daughter be *more* perfect than any other woman (including, by implication, herself), it has here been reinscribed into the *devoir*, the debt, of a specifically *paternal* will that is written in the heavens, in the grave that is also a graven book, and in the landscaped park of the estate. In *La Princesse de Clèves*, an opening for the free play of the daughter's desire just large enough to effect a displacement of maternal destination is created in the terms of compliance with a maternal demand that requires at least the action of *going out and seeking* the matching patronym that will bring the real estate with it. Here, that "space of reception" is closed off by the fixed boundaries of the patrimonial plot.

While in *Corinne* the paternal estate as the daughter's inheritance returns from its repression in *La Princesse de Clèves*, that estate is anxiously preserved from the ruin characteristic of Gothic patrimony by the Gothic strategy of doubling. Ruination, and the paternal threat it expresses, is displaced onto the stepmother, who serves as the father's dark (female) double, just as her castle doubles the civilized paternal estate: "Living quite close to the seashore [*bord de la mer*], we often felt the north wind in our castle: at night I used to hear it whistle through the long hallways, and by day it marvelously fostered our silence when we were together" (Goldberger, p. 255; Balayé, p. 367). In this sentence, Staël reunites all the traits of the Gothic mother in the description of her castle: the pun on *mère/mer* survives from *Lettres de Mademoiselle de Boismiran*, associating the maternal with the tempestuous, overwhelming and dangerous force represented by the sea, the silencing of the daughter by this dark maternal force, the fragmentation of its enclosure, the mournful monotony of a domestic life that is compared to an imprisonment and a haunting. Lady Edgermond is a Gothic Mme de Chartres, who not only controls a daughter through education in virtue, but dramatically "kills" a stepdaughter, staging Corinne's exile from the fatherland (*patrie*) as a literal entombment within it.

The Gothic reinscription of the maternal order into the paternal framework of Providence constructs the boundaries of that framework as those of empire, as it did in *The Recess*, where the heroines go in search of the "match" needed to realize their maternal inheritance, wandering to Jamaica, to Ireland, and to their own maternal kingdom of Scotland, only to find that they can never escape England's political enclosure. Much has been written about the association in *Corinne* of England and the north with the paternal, and of Italy and the south with the maternal, of Corinne's (or *Corinne*'s) effort to reconcile the two or to return to a utopian life in the mother country. But the problem is not one of an opposition or separation between the two "places." The solution, therefore, is neither one of reconciliation between the two worlds nor of retrieval of a lost maternal paradise.[3] For the problem of *Corinne*'s geography is the problem of empire, one of paradoxical boundaries that enclose the "mother country" within the patriarchal empire as a place of exile. Although patrilineal borderlines define both gender and nationality, they also enclose and appropriate aspects of what they define as other, while inevitably leaving open possibilities of transgression.

What distinguishes the roles of the primary characters in *Corinne* from one another is thus no longer as much a matter of difference of sex as it was in *La Princesse de Clèves*, where the situation of a daughter as receiver of a problematical maternal inheritance was set in contrast with the agency of possession and transmission belonging to a Clèves or a Nemours within the masculine bias of the feudal social order.[4] While Oswald plays both of Lafayette's masculine roles—Clèves and Nemours—to Corinne's and Lucile's differing interpretations of the princess, his most significant role in Staël's rewriting of the earlier novel is actually that of the princess.[5]

Oswald's response to Corinne echoes that of the princess to Nemours, when he argues that he cannot be hers, notwithstanding that he is unattached, because to marry her would be to transgress the plot laid out for him by his father (Balayé, pp. 394, 397; Goldberger, pp. 275, 277; Adam, p. 172). And he gives that response because the same curse, nearly word for word, has been laid upon him by his father as is laid by Mme de Chartres upon her daughter: "Seeing that his wife would not be happy in England, my son would soon find himself uncomfortable here. He has all the weakness sensitivity [*la sensibilité*] inspires, I know that. So he would go off to settle in Italy, and *if I lived to see that expatriation, it would make me die of grief*" (Balayé, p. 467; Goldberger, p. 330; emphasis mine). After the father's death, the son reads the paternal declaration that his own expatriation would have killed his father, had he still been alive to see it; just as the princess hears her dying mother declare that her daughter's "fall," were she to live to see it, would be the one thing that could make her glad to be dead (Adam, p. 68).

The threat that transmits the paternal debt is thus patterned on Lafayette's model of maternal transmission—which itself, however, had been modeled on a patriline transmission already structured like a debt. The effect of this detour, this doubling back of fictions of patrimony, is to debunk the patrilineal transmission of property as a fiction of the perpetuation of agency or empowerment, and to expose it as a bond of indebtedness upon which the interest due is perpetually increasing. In *La Princesse de Clèves*, maternal transmission models itself upon patrimony in being also structured like a debt; indebtedness itself becomes the only legacy transmissible through maternal lines in the absence of the property and agency that is the content of patrilineal transmission. *Corinne*'s retranslation of maternal indebtedness into the terms of patrimony offers the Gothic revelation that it, too, finally *constitutes*, and is not simply structured as, a debt. This retranslation entails a shift from the terms of a "fall" from feminine virtue into those of "expatriation"—of exile from the patrie.

The fatherland, like its son and heir, bear in *Corinne* the marks of Staël's translation from the terms of femininity. The reason given by the old Lord Nelvil for fearing his son's expatriation is the weakness of sensibility. Although in the "moral geography" of Richardson's *Sir Charles Grandison*, one of Staël's favorite books, Italy is the country of sensibility, "a location for the excesses of feeling" according to John Mullan, this only shows how little those excesses are capable of containment by the boundaries of national character (Mullan, p. 112). For sensibility is a weakness that is one of the chief distinguishing marks, not only of Italy in *Grandison* and of Oswald's character in this novel, but of English national character in European eighteenth-century discourse more generally. This "weak," feminine sensibility is precisely the quality in Oswald that makes him not merely comply with, but *exceed* the father's will, pay back the debt of patrimony with the interest of sensibility. M. Dickson, by showing him the letter in which Oswald's dead father translates the curse of Mme de Chartres, "assaulted the most sensitive [*sensible*] places in Oswald's heart" (Goldberger, p. 331; Balayé, p. 469). The son's response to this attack on his sensibility is, like the princess's, to exceed the demand made: "However fleeting that wish may have been, I wanted to comply before I knew you, as a kind of expiation, as a way of extending the power of his will [*l'empire de sa volonté*] beyond death" (Goldberger, p. 235; Balayé, p. 341; note *l'empire*). The interest paid by (feminine) sensibility on the debt of inheritance complicitously locates agency in the "will" (*volonté*) of the dead, and thus legitimacy in the inheritance itself. As the agency of the dead extends beyond the grave, it also extends the patrie beyond the limits of the plot of real estate and the borders of the nation, so that it becomes an *empire* whose law of patrilineal transmission extends even over those countries excluded by its borders.

Italy, "deprived of independence by unfortunate circumstances," has thus come under the dominion of the law that lays down the simultaneously inclusive and exclusive borders of the patrie as empire.[6] Its association in the novel with the maternal and with the feminine generally, far from separating it from the fatherland, is in fact the very quality that "pays the interest" that supports the fatherland as empire. Paternal will and feminine sensibility come together to produce the *circonstances malheureuses*, the plot that continues to deprive Italy of her independence. These "circumstances" appear to be ineluctably decreed by a paternal providence, but at the same time they require, in order to maintain that appearance, the determination of a reader who will authorize the ambiguous signs that patriline writing traces upon the heavens. Corinne—or Italy—is just such a reader, as is evident from her insistence on determining the meaning of what she reads in the heavens as the paternal writ of her own banishment:

> "As I was gazing at the moon, it hid behind a cloud, and that cloud had a deathly look. I have always known the sky to look paternal or angry, and *I tell you*, Oswald, tonight it condemned our love."
>
> "Dear friend, the only omens on man's life are his good or bad deeds, and have I not this very evening sacrificed my most fervent desires to a feeling of virtue?" (Goldberger, p. 196; Balayé, pp. 289–90; emphasis mine)

Oswald here seems to oppose an order of active self-determination to Corinne's order of a paternal fatality, but the terms of his reply undermine the force of his own assertion and secretly reinforce Corinne's. He begins by stating that the only auguries of the life of *man* (*l'homme*) are his own actions; Oswald seems to mean the "generic man," but in fact only masculine virtues would have been "actions." The example with which Oswald supports his precept about "gender-neutral" virtue is that of his own avoidance of action in the name of "sentiment" and "virtue." Like a typical eighteenth-century sentimental hero, then, Oswald adopts a feminine virtue that denies female desire and passively preserves female chastity in order to maintain patrilineage intact.[7] By "proving" his precept of gender-neutral virtue with the example of his own feminine virtue, Oswald demonstrates that the feminization of masculinity actually brings both genders all the more rigidly into the terms and under the law of the dead father whose will is apotheosized as Providence—and thus proves Corinne too sure an augurer, for what she has prophesied is above all her own final act of readerly complicity.

Italy's relation to the masculine order represented as empire and as English must, as I have said, be understood in the terms of the Gothic, that mode of sentimental fiction as characteristically English as sensibility itself was said to be. In her chapter on *Corinne* in *Literary Women*, Ellen Moers asks a basic but important question: "Why Italy?" She points to eighteenth-century conventions about English and Italian national character in *Sir Charles Grandison*, and concludes convincingly that Staël and Richardson are working with the same conventions of national character: "For married happiness and domestic virtue, England is undoubtedly the place; but for love outside of marriage, go to Italy." She notes in passing that Radcliffe, like her predecessor Walpole, but without his personal experience of the place, also chose Italy as the setting for her Gothic novels, even though the Gothic style in architecture is not much in evidence in Italy's landscape, as compared with that of the northern countries. Moers closes with a reference to the fact that *Corinne* winds up in *northern* Italy, "cold as the rest of Europe," and like the north even graced with a Gothic cathedral—precisely *not* the Italy of sunshine and free love that was Moers's answer to the question of setting (Moers, pp. 200–203, 210). But Radcliffe's interest in Italy had nothing to do with either sunshine or free love, for that matter, and even *Corinne* seems rather to be in pursuit of a fusion of "northern" with "southern" characteristics. I would agree that Staël's Italy is, as Moers suggests, an English Italy—in that it is an ambiguous territory split between the Italy of Richardson and the Italy of Radcliffe. This ambiguity does not, however, as Moers further implies, repeat in simple geographic terms the same line of division between north and south that separates Italy from England on the map of Europe. For the central Gothic ruin in *Corinne* is not the cathedral in Milan, nor the paternal estate in Scotland; rather it disintegrates at the heart of Rome itself, appearing to Corinne's imagination in her vision of St. Peter's in ruins (Balayé, pp. 409–10; Goldberger, p. 286).

The key to the significance of Corinne's seemingly unmotivated vision comes near the novel's close, when Oswald and Lucile, touring northern Italy, visit the cathedral of Milan, "Italy's masterpiece of Gothic architecture, just as St. Peter's is for *modern* architecture." At that point the narrator actually quotes Horace Walpole, the first Gothic novelist, on the difference between Gothic and modern churches: "To build modern temples, the popes used the wealth they had obtained through the piety inspired by the Gothic churches" (Balayé, p. 556; Goldberger, p. 396; translator's emphasis). In other words, St. Peter's represents a kind of "interest" on the Gothic; it is built with the financial interest (*richesses*) paid in expression of the spiritual interest (*dévotion*) inspired by Gothic architecture. The accumulation of this interest creates a legacy that replaces and destroys the "real" estate inherited—the Gothic churches themselves. The proleptic vision of St. Peter's in ruins is a device similar to that used in *La Princesse de Clèves* to doom Mary Stuart and other historical characters, by which Staël projects the English Gothic associations of Catholic abbeys falling into ruin after the dissolution of the monasteries onto the central edifice of both the Roman Catholic Church and the Holy Roman Empire under Napoleon.

As argued above, the patrilineal script in *Corinne* translates "fault" from feminine to masculine terms. The fall from virtue that would entail upon the daughter the responsibility for the mother's death is replaced by the fault of expatriation that would entail responsibility for the father's death upon the son. It is a Gothic writing that simultaneously translates the moral fault, the fall from a feminine virtue, to which both sexes are now subject, into the literalized cracks that ruin the edifice of patriline transmission. That Oswald, just as much as Corinne, is threatened with the abyss of exile from within the patrimony is dramatized in his act of narrating his own history: he concludes the story and the chapter by lamenting his inability to escape the "conscience" that is his introjected dead father. He is thus contained within the fatherland as empire even when he is standing in sunniest Italy. Mount Vesuvius, the scene of this narration, is a phallic abyss that is called the "fatherland" (*patrie*) of the Neapolitans—that is, of the quintessential southern Italians in this novel, the inhabitants of the "country in Europe most favored by the sun." On the same page, it is also referred to as "the empire of death" (Goldberger, p. 206; Balayé, p. 303).[8] To the extent and in the moment that the sunny south becomes a patrie, it too becomes just another territory of the paternal empire of death from which Oswald cannot escape, lying as it does under the continual threat posed by the uncontainable abyss of the volcano.

And yet, standing within its domain, Oswald remains in exile from this paternal empire of death: the scene closes with his anguished wish that the ground would open up to let him enter (*pénétrer*) into the land of the dead—which is the true fatherland, since the volcano as patrie has just been equated with the "empire of death" (Goldberger, p. 231; Balayé, p. 336). The abyss is *itself* the patrilineal script: Oswald compares the words he reads in the public papers at the moment of his return to England, "Lord Nelvil has just died," to the threatening fire of the volcano. The referent of those printed words, necessarily uttered after the death of Oswald's father and thus after his own succession to the title, contains an inherent ambiguity that simultaneously includes Oswald himself in the reported death. He has become at once the haunted and the haunting. The fiery letters are always before his eyes, "haunting [him] like a ghost," yet the effect of this haunting paternal script is to transform *him* into a ghost, the shade of his dead father. Incapable of speech, Oswald can only repeat his father's written words: "Next to the vivid colors we use to paint their blessed halo, we would find ourselves obliterated in the very midst of our golden days, in the midst of the triumphs that most dazzle us" (Balayé, pp. 332–35; Goldberger, pp. 228–30). The death of Oswald's father—his penetration into the empire of death, his eternal inaccessibility to dialogue—gives his words the fixity of a written will, and so makes a specter of the son left behind to wander the map like a restive and gibbering ghost.[9]

Corinne is in exactly the same position within the paternal empire as Oswald, differences of gender and nationality notwithstanding; the only real difference between them is that she resists. What makes that difference? The difference of gender, although confused and challenged throughout the novel, does momentarily ground Corinne in Italy, even if that ground is only a platform or state formed by the verge of a precipice. Her maternal inheritance consists of a position within the empire of the father that, while it is not her own ground, nevertheless allows her to stage a fiction of escape. This ground is precisely what Oswald lacks, as he explains to her at the end of his story: "How could courage triumph, when it cannot even hold out against conscience which is its source?" Courage—will, self-determined action—*virtus*—needs the ground of "conscience" to stand on, by which is here meant freedom from the threat of the abyss, of those fiery fixed characters announcing the father's eternal removal beyond the reach of the son's own discourse. By naming this missing ground "conscience," Oswald is again not using his own language but repeating that of Corinne, who has just suggested that he use her heart—her feminine sensibility—as the grounding that might replace conscience: "Judge yourself in my heart, take it for your *conscience*" (Balayé, pp. 332–36; Goldberger, pp. 228–31; emphasis mine). Yet the difference made by maternal inheritance is an unreal estate, a precipice that cannot provide either of them with a sure foothold.

The question of what Corinne has that Oswald lacks leads to the question of what Corinne wants. Attempts to answer that question have been almost as various as the speculations in response to Freud's question about women—and perhaps they are versions of the same question. The suggestions of recent feminist critics tend to characterize Corinne's desire, one way or another, as a nostalgic wish for wholeness. Carla Peterson observes that Staël invented, with the Schlegels, the Romantic project of a reconciliation between northern and southern aesthetic sensibilities, and argues that Corinne fails to enact with Oswald, or to embody within herself, that ideal union of opposites; instead she both enacts and embodies her failure by falling into madness and fragmentation (Peterson, pp. 38–39). Nancy Miller puts forth that the wholeness for which Corinne struggles is specifically a lost maternal wholeness: "The unconditional love of the mother, the dead mother who named her and who mapped out her destiny . . . a lost maternal plenitude." She echoes Peterson in blaming Corinne's failure to realize her desire in part on the lack of the very thing she is supposed to be seeking, "maternal support."[10] This would in fact amount to a nostalgia for the princess of Clèves, who haunts *Corinne* as the daughter whose dead mother both named her and mapped out her destiny by appointing as her husband that very "man who could love like a mother," the ideal male Miller proposes as the obscure object of Corinne's desire (Miller, *Subject to Change*, pp. 186–87).

To understand Corinne's desire as nostalgia for a plenitude that never was, however, is to mistake the ground of her resistance to patriarchy. Moers answers the question of her desire more obliquely, with the remark that "all she gets is what she deserves—Italy." But Corinne certainly doesn't get the Italy of free love that Moers identifies earlier in her essay; she ends up instead with the Gothic Italy, as Moers herself implies at the end of her chapter. Quoting Lucile's question to Oswald, "Où donc est votre belle Italie?" she leaves the reader free to follow through its implications on her own (Moers, pp. 209–10). The answer that Moers leaves out is written in that patriarchal script associated with Lucile, and its logic is that of empire. That the north (England) is associated with the father and with the patriarchal order, while the south (Italy) is an idealized mother country, and that Corinne, her own origins divided, seeks in her relation to Oswald to chart a union between the two, cannot be denied. But the charter she would enact is not one to establish a reunion out of separation, or unity out of opposition, but rather one that would renegotiate the boundaries defining the union that already exists under the patriarchal "empire." For just as the north is fatherland and the south mother country, they are both, finally, the same place of exile, borderlands of a single empire united in imagination, first by the tradition of Rome, then by the ambition of Napoleon, and always in the ruinous Gothic edifice of patriarchy. The system of patrimonial transmission that holds edifice and empire together conceptually does so by writing "maternal plenitude" out of existence, and rewriting it as a myth of paradise (happily) lost. The mother as "the perfect *destinataire*," as Miller calls her, the ideal addressee who names her daughter and plots her destiny, is already inscribed by the patriarchal writing as a substitute father, a pretender—like Lady Edgermond, like Lafayette's Mme de Chartres, like Mme de Boismiran and like both Mary Stuart and her daughter Matilda, whose naming and destination of their daughters put dead ends to the daughters' own plots. Maternal destination is of a piece with patrimonial transmission, and Corinne's "failure" in fragmentation, while hardly a happy fall, is, as Staël may have learned from Lee, the only possible form of her resistance to the wholeness of its empire.[11]

Corinne does and must fail in that she opposes the order of paternal will without being able to escape it—she can go nowhere to escape from exile, because exile is the state of being a woman within the patrie.[12] Like the princess of Clèves, she is in a position only to attempt to renegotiate the terms upon which she inhabits the patrimonial real estate; she cannot make it a maternal ground. In this she proves herself true heir to the princess, not by resembling her, as Lucile does, but by adopting, as DeJean argues, her strategy of negotiation by confession (*aveu*)—but with a difference ("Staël's *Corinne*," pp. 84–86). Corinne already has at the outset what the princess fought for: before the novel begins, she has given up her life in the fatherland rather than exist on its terms, and she has accepted an exclusively movable inheritance by way of renouncing her interest in the patrimonial real estate, in order to become the mistress of her own state of exile (p. 264).[13] But Corinne wants more than what the princess left her. The princess was able to own her desire only by renouncing its object, and Corinne wants to have her desire and to satisfy it too.

Rather than paying interest on inherited debt, as does the princess's mere speculative double (Lucile), Corinne makes use of the princess's radical strategy to refuse the terms of patrimonial debt and replace them with the terms of female desire. The secret life histories exchanged by Oswald and Corinne are *both* explicitly announced as *aveux* (Balayé, pp. 304, 360). Their narrative transaction begins with a demand on his part for her true history, paralleling the demand by the prince of Clèves that prompts his wife's aveu. Corinne responds with the tergiversation of the travelogue, which she compares to Scheherazade's narrative strategy of delay, while simultaneously writing the history she plans to offer him once delay becomes impossible (Balayé, p. 133; Goldberger, p. 81). What finally does preclude further delay is Oswald's offer to transform the structure of their transaction from one of masculine demand and feminine fulfillment of it to one of exchange—he will tell her his own story first.

Corinne's strategy of delay allows Oswald's offered exchange to revert to the structure of debt. This becomes clear, not only through the terms in which she asks him to put off the moment ("I beg you, eight days more of grace"), but again when he makes an offer that preempts her narrative (p. 236). Mistaking her recognition of his father's image (in another miniature portrait) as a sign from Providence, he gives her the ring that at once binds him in debt to her and imposes a debt upon her, using the very language of sympathetic exchange to transform that exchange into an indebted relation:

> And from this moment on, I am not free. . . . I make this solemn commitment before I know who you are: it is your soul I believe in, for your soul has disclosed everything to me. . . . Therefore, my dear Corinne, tell me your secrets; *you owe it* to him whose promises have come before you confided in him. (Balayé, p. 359; Goldberger, p. 249; emphasis mine)

Just as the princess's narrative of desire was not finally acceptable to her husband as an aveu (pledge of fidelity), so that he pressed her for an aveu (confession, evidence) of the "whole" truth, located by him in the name of her lover, Oswald's reference to his father's wish that he marry Lucile gives Corinne to understand that the written aveu of the secret history she is about to offer him will not constitute the whole truth for him, *as it does not include the name of her father* (p. 236). She specifically refers to the act of naming the father as the *aveu* that "must surely decide my fate" (Goldberger, p. 251; "l'aveu qui doit décider de ma vie," Balayé, p. 360). Although Oswald is a "man of feeling," capable of a sympathetic exchange of private histories, both he and Corinne remain within the order of patrimonial debt; thus within their indebted exchange of narrations, Corinne's aveu reverts to the sense of a courtroom confession, offered in the expectation of a judgment. She can attempt to sway that judgment by the strategy of evoking sympathy, but it remains a judgment, with authority lodged in the masculine position.

Oswald's response in fact expresses a conflict between his own sympathy and the "rational" judgment he feels compelled to make in accordance with his father's will. Because he is all sensibility—as his father well knew—and has no will that does not come from his father, his departure for Scotland is a journey made explicitly in search of his dead father's judgment on the subject of Corinne (Belayé, p. 394; Goldberger, p. 275). He finds exactly what he was looking for, and what Corinne dreaded: a letter from beyond the grave, textual evidence that his father had "pronounced against her." His father's response to her youthful display of talent was to judge her as if the performance were a trial of her virtue, rather than an improvisation requiring a sympathetic response in order to achieve its aesthetic effect. In pronouncing this judgment, he simultaneously pronounced upon his son Mme de Chartres's curse, already mentioned, of responsibility for the parent's death (Balayé, p. 468; Goldberger, p. 331).

Corinne's radical renegotiation of the terms of patrimonial debt into those of female desire is doomed to failure because both she and Oswald lack any other ground than that of the patrie, any other language than the terms of indebtedness in which to engage in their narrative transaction. Inhabiting the system of patrimonial relations more centrally than Corinne, desire and debt have become indistinguishable to Oswald. Thus the narrator repeatedly informs us how much he needs to be commanded by honor (*devoir*) to do that which he desires (Goldberger, p. 136; Balayé, p. 207). His life history shows that "passion"—what he feels for women—and "duty" (*devoir*)—what he feels for his father—are mirror-images of one another, finally becoming so confused as to be indistinguishable. That is why the symmetrical and conflicting claims made upon him by his father and his French mistress leave him in an impossible double bind (Balayé, p. 325; Goldberger, p. 223). Corinne, too, is confronted with patrimonial debt by her stepmother: "You *owe it to your family* to change your name and pass for dead." But Corinne translates this demand out of the patrimonial language of debt and into the terms of desire, reading in it no legitimate obligation of her own, but only the *desire* of Lady Edgermond ("she had confessed her heart's hidden wish" [Balayé, pp. 382–83; Goldberger, pp. 267–68]). This defiant translation wins Corinne the ability to enact a plot of escape: death in the fatherland, and life in Italy.

Why then does Corinne leave Italy to return to the country that she can only haunt as a ghost? She does so in keeping with the terms of a desire that, as in *La Princesse de Clèves*, takes for its object a representative of the very order that would deny the legitimacy of its terms. In Italy, Corinne is in "the Italian state": the state, not of one who possesses one's own country, but of one who wanders dispossessed among the ruins of empire (Balayé, p. 48; Goldberger, p. 18). She is in the situation of the Roman widows mourning their husbands, haunting the sunny landscape as if it were they who were the shades, grieving over their own imprisonment on the wrong side of the river Styx, in exile from the land of the dead heroes (Balayé, p. 353; Goldberger, p. 244). By going to haunt the patrimonial estate in Scotland, therefore, Corinne does not change her state, but only gives plot and place to the state she is already in.

If the estate at Coulommiers is the "state" of exile of which the princess of Clèves makes herself mistress, Staël has inherited it through the narrative relation she sets up between *La Princesse de Clèves* and *Corinne*. As an inhabitant of that state of exile, Corinne has inherited no example of active female desire. When the strategy of the confession as sympathetic narrative exchange fails, she attempts to base her resistance to the patrilineal empire upon the masculine example that comes literally framed in the opening (at once window and door) of the estate at Coulommiers. Staël transforms Coulommiers, the baroque pavilion of glass, into a Gothic castle, reinscribes the "fall" as its patrimonial ground, and puts her heroine into the position, not of the mistress of the estate, but of the male intruder whose desire leads him to trespass on another man's property: Nemours. Like Nemours, Corinne arrives at the estate unannounced and allows her steps to be guided by chance (*au hasard*) through the park, concealing herself in the garden, as he does, from the view of those within (Goldberger, p. 353; Balayé, p. 499; Adam, p. 120). Whereas this attitude allows Nemours on both of his visits to *watch* the princess through the architectural frame formed by her pavilion, as well as to overhear her aveu, Corinne's perception of what is passing within the castle is confined to the sense of hearing. While giving her Nemours's active, "masculine" desire, Staël does not give Corinne his mastery of the gaze, his strategy of fixing the object of his desire in a visual frame. Through this rewriting of the Coulommiers scenes, she is attempting to articulate female desire in a language other than the specular.

A servant tells Corinne what she cannot see: Lord Nelvil has opened the ball with Lucile, "*the heiress to this castle*" (Balayé, p. 498; Goldberger, p. 353; emphasis Staël's). The reader, however, gets a full description of what Corinne cannot see, which turns out to be another scene rewritten from *La Princesse de Clèves*, in which the duc de Nemours dances with the princess, the great heiress who is making her first court appearance (Adam, p. 120). Staël's narrator characterizes this dance as an unremarkable performance, in which Lucile's reserve detracts from her dancing and bores Oswald—quite a contrast to the spontaneous murmur of admiration caused by the spectacle of the princess dancing with Nemours at their first meeting. Lafayette, with a narrator elsewhere quite capable of reporting interior events, frames the dance entirely from the perspective of its spectators (Adam, pp. 53–54). Whereas Staël also makes her dancers the focus of a collective gaze, she does not report their audience's response, concentrating instead on the thoughts and feelings of the dancers. What becomes crucial in Staël's rewriting, then, is not the gaze, but rather a sensibility unavailable to the senses. "Corinne would have tasted some moments of happiness still could she have known what he was feeling then." If she could have known the feelings of the beloved separated from her by the walls of the estate, she would have had the pleasure that the duc de Nemours takes from overhearing his beloved's confession of her secret feelings, or from watching her gazing at his own portrait and wrapping his tournament colors around his cane—all spectacular evidence of how he is loved (Adam, p. 155). But Corinne remains aimlessly wandering the garden paths, feeling herself a foreigner on paternal soil, where neither Providence nor maternal destination guides her steps towards the evidence she seeks. In the logic of paternal plot—upon the grounds of which Providence and real estate become one—it makes perfect sense that without paternal authority for her destination (the castle, with Oswald in it), the very ground beneath her feet falls away (Balayé, p. 499; Goldberger, p. 353). In the absence of the paternal plot and its specular language of evidence, there is simply an abyss, the epistemological paradox of sensibility.

Lacking the grounds for desire that allows Nemours to "steal" the evidence of the princess's love for him, Corinne is rather in the position of Lee's heroine, Ellinor, in that author's rewriting of the Coulommiers episodes: the position in which "virtue incessantly hovers on the verge of a precipice" (*Recess*, 3: 150–51). Thrown instantly into the uncertainty in which Nemours finds himself only later, Corinne begins as he does his *second* trip to Coulommiers, wandering passively in the garden and hoping that the beloved will come out. Whereas Nemours then gets a view of the princess that gives him a feeling beyond description ("ce qui n'a jamais été goûté ni imaginé par nul autre amant"), Corinne finds herself literally on the verge of the princess's (and Lee's) precipice, where mothers place their daughters in the very act of teaching them how to avoid the fatal faux pas ("Corinne had only to take one step to plunge into eternal oblivion" [Balayé, p. 499; Goldberger, p. 354; Adam, p. 155]). In that position, she not only hesitates, like Nemours, over what strategy to pursue, but hesitates even over her own desire, just as Ellinor does on the threshold of Lady Pembroke's gallery, her own desire lost in the hesitation between the precepts of virtue and the fiction she had framed to conceal her desire to see her lover's portrait (p. 354: "She herself did not know what she wanted"; cf. *Recess*, 2: 288). Moving nevertheless, like Nemours, from hesitation in the garden to a determination to break through the architectural frame and speak with the beloved, Corinne approaches the window where, unlike him, she finds her view blocked. Like Lee's heroine, on the other hand, instead of the expected sight, she encounters the living voice of her lover. The sound of Oswald's voice gives Corinne a joyous emotion that is described in the same terms of ineffability as that which Nemours feels on catching sight of the princess ("The voice of the one we love: indescribable thrill!" [p. 355]).[14] Here the evidence of passion is no longer the name, the verbal signification of speech, but rather the pure sentiment conveyed by the tone of the lover's voice.[15]

The language of sensibility is the only one by means of which

Corinne *could* know what Oswald was feeling, and it does indeed convey to her a pleasure parallel to that experienced by Nemours. But the effort to translate Nemours's active desire from the specular language of masculine desire into the audible one of feminine sensibility only turns Corinne definitively into a ghost. At the moment that Corinne becomes a specular object, a *vue* glimpsed by Lucile, she becomes a specter. Recognizing Corinne as the sister who is dead in and on the patrimonial plot, Lucile is convinced that she has seen a ghost, and the whole scene, with its potential for a translation that would transcend, through the communication of sensibility, the need for patrimonial ground and the framework of its real estate, is closed again, in the twinkling of an eye, within the patriarchal frame of reference: "She was convinced that her sister's image had appeared walking toward their father's grave to approach her for forgetting it." Corinne's "apparition" has the same frightening effect as Nemours's appearance does upon the blonde beauty within the château, who in both cases causes the servants to flock around her, thus precluding communication between the lovers (Balayé, p. 501; Goldberger, p. 355; Adam, p. 156). And no wonder, since for the princess the sight of Nemours breaking into her pavilion also raised the specter of her censorious mother/husband. The heroine's transformation into a ghost thus completes Staël's Gothic reinscription of female desire into the patrimonial plot through a double translation of Lafayette via Lee: the plotting masculine subject whose agency is thwarted by the woman's transformation of him into a painting is first translated by Lee as a plotting feminine subject (Ellinor) whose agency is thwarted by her ghostly position of survival in virtue's fault, and then by Staël as a plotting feminine subject whose agency is thwarted by her ghostly position *as* the dead mother (in relation to Lucile) whose death works in the service of paternal will to keep both daughters toeing virtue's faultline.

What Corinne wants is named in a single word: she identifies it herself as *sympathy* (*sympathie*). Sympathy is at once what she offers and what she elicits through her improvisational art; sympathy is also what she says she needs from her lover (e.g., Balayé, pp. 56, 84, 520; Goldberger, pp. 24, 44, 369).[16] Staël's use of sympathy is not a simple borrowing from earlier women writers. She not only invented *romanticism* as a term, but here also invents what I would identify as one of its central moves: the shift in emphasis to *imagination* from the feminized Enlightenment term, *sensibility*, as the primary concept set in uneasy opposition to *reason*.[17] Imagination is "the source of her talent," and for Corinne imagination cannot be separated from sensibility; this is what keeps Corinne's imagination feminine, even while the talents to which it gives rise place her in the prophetic and heroic role that the Romantics would typically gender masculine. This "gender confusion" causes her deep suffering, because imagination, as a more actively creative sympathy, is here already a masculine-identified property (Balayé, p. 125; Goldberger, p. 74). The feminine sensibility inseparable from Corinne's imagination is what binds her to the patriarchal relations that define sensibility as feminine, making her susceptible to a fall from the heroic masculine heights into the abyss of female fault: "He has hurled me from the triumphal chariot into the unfathomable depths of sorrow [*l'abîme des douleurs*]" (Goldberger, p. 347; Balayé, p. 489).

It is because of her radical refusal to dwell in the patrimonial plot or enter into its economy of debt that Corinne fails to get what she wants. She loses Oswald because he cannot take her conscience as his ground, named and destined as he is entirely by his dead father. She loses herself as well because, although her maternal legacy has placed her literally outside the patrie, so that unlike Oswald she has a position from which to refuse patrimonial debt, the ground of her critique nevertheless remains contained within the empire she seeks vainly to escape. Her own realm is only an abyss within it, and the language of her resistance continually lapses back into its terms. Rather than rejecting the notion of debt, she only recasts it as a contract between the self and "another destiny," the term with which she attempts to replace the dead father, or Providence, as paternal destiny. "Can it be true that duty [*devoir*] prescribes the same rules for everyone? Do not people capable of great thoughts and generous feelings owe it to the world to share them?" (Goldberger, p. 255; "Les grandes pensées, les sentiments généreux ne sont-ils pas dans ce monde les *dettes* des êtres capables de les acquitter?" [Balayé, p. 366]). Corinne has no language in which to voice her refusal of patriline debt, other than that of debt; not only does she adopt its terms in her critique of it, but she even adopts its medium of writing. Her refusal to engage with Oswald within its economy is expressed most strongly in her twice writing to him the message of forgiveness of debt, "*You are free*"—twice attempting to "leave him his liberty" (this was also the princess's demand of her husband in making her aveu; Adam, p. 122). Thus she is attempting to take on what was necessarily a masculine role in *La Princesse de Clèves*, and remains so in the world of *Corinne*. She cannot leave Oswald what she (still) does not truly possess. This becomes very clear the third time Corinne offers Oswald his freedom in writing: "Be free then, Oswald, now and every day, free even if you were my husband: for if you no longer loved me, I would free you by my death of the *indissoluble* ties that bound you to me" (emphasis mine). In leaving him this paradoxical freedom from bonds that are "indissoluble," she repeats exactly the paternal threat of responsibility for her death that keeps Oswald in eternal debt—and in the end, even the narrator will refuse to forgive him that debt (Balayé, pp. 390, 493, 587; Goldberger, pp. 272, 349, 419).

Sympathy, as Staël develops the concept, is a deep interpersonal *recognition* that would transcend the means of its conveyance, whether specular or narrative. This is what Corinne wants, and yet she finds herself obstructed from its transaction by the very thing she wants to transcend: her exile from the patrimonial site and its frameworks of sight, her lack of a language that could circumvent the terms of debt—that is, of patriline writing. What means of conveyance is left, if any, beyond the character's dead end, beyond the meaning of her last utterance: the silent signing of her hand towards the same clouded moon she had earlier identified to Lord Nelvil as the expression of a "paternal" heaven that condemned their love? The improvisational poet loses her voice, and with it the romantic, heroic talent with which she had taken up the border wars begun by the princess of Clèves against patrimonial empire. Having lost her battle, she closes the frame on her own history by setting herself at the center of a final tableau constructed to elicit the sympathy of an audience through the spectacle of suffering, and with her last gesture she refers the meaning of that tableau to the frame of patriline writing. Does this closural gesture of signification in fact cut off all possible openings for a sympathy that would escape the voyeuristic spectacle of victimized femininity? Not if the frame itself, the ceiling or *ciel* of patrimonial writing, can be found to open, like the ancestral portraits in *The Recess*, into some secret communication.

Silenced and displaced from any possible ground of resistance, then, Corinne as a character is reduced to writing. Yet her writing is not reducible to the patrimonial script that encloses her personal narrative. The imprisonment and isolation of her feminine exile can still allow for one form of conveyance and performance: correspondence. Correspondence, while it can become the dead letter of absence—patriline writing—or be seized as the evidence demanded by unsympathetic readers, can also recuperate writing for a sympathetic narrative exchange. A communication personally addressed to the sympathetic reader and concealed from the demand for evidence, its transmission transcends the isolation of exile (see Balayé, pp. 520–24, 582–83; Goldberger, pp. 369–71, 416–17). Much attention has been devoted recently to the role of the narrator of *Corinne* in recuperating the heroine's failure for the reader, but not enough has been said about how Staël's text uses correspondences with the narratives of earlier women writers to move itself out of the frame of patriline writing in which Corinne herself is finally trapped.

Corinne's last act corresponds with the princess's: both leave their ambiguous legacies to the reader as they disappear into a final frame. It is a correspondence, however, that emphasizes difference. Corinne does not follow the princess's example in leaving examples of virtue; Oswald is the one condemned to mirror that exemplarity in the novel's final lines (Balayé, p. 587; Goldberger, p. 419; Adam, p. 180).[18] Instead, Corinne leaves the example of her talent—the new, Romantic term she thus successfully substitutes at last for eighteenth-century feminine virtue.[19] But the transmission of female talent, like that of inimitable examples, is a paradox, as is all transmission through female lines within a patrilineal framework: where the only model of transmission is patriline debt, how can maternal transmission escape the terms of debt and speculation, escape becoming the mere specular image, the reflection, the horrid specter of patrilineage? What Staël gets from Lee's reading of Lafayette is first of all the refusal to recognize bloodlines as the proper path of inheritance. The princess does not reproduce motherhood; she leaves her inimitable examples to the reader alone. Lee represents her own novel's transmission by closing it with an exchange transacted between the dying Matilda and an unknown young woman. Staël further elaborates Lee's strategy of female transmission by detailing and doubling the means through which Corinne manages to transmit, not exemplary virtue, not her own fictional plot of escape, but her talent—what she hoped would enable her to enact a successful female plot, and may still help the strangers who receive it.

Having failed in her own plot, Corinne's first plot of transmission is to become, not a substitute father—for that would mean becoming a Gothic mother like Lady Edgermond, Mme de Boismiran, or Mme de Chartres—but rather a Gothic father: a ghostly father who reduces Oswald to his/her mere double. Lucile's anxiety on first introducing their daughter to Oswald, "as timidly as if she had been a guilty woman," takes on its full significance only when considered in the context of the sentence that follows, which explains little Juliette's resemblance to Corinne by informing us that Lucile's thoughts have dwelt upon her sister during pregnancy (Balayé, p. 542; Goldberger, pp. 385–86). John Mullan identifies as part of the eighteenth-century culture of sensibility the widespread medical belief that the thoughts and desires of a pregnant woman could physically "mark" the fetus in the womb, and comments, "The improper and volatile 'Desire' raised in the woman by reading the wrong books or thinking the wrong thoughts intervenes in the process of the reproduction of a social order" (p. 223). This is clearly what has happened to Lucile's pregnancy, thanks to Corinne's educational interventions. Moreover, the resulting "mark" of physical resemblance to someone other than her husband is the primary evidence, in romance particularly, of a wife's infidelity. No wonder Lucile is timid.[20] The force of Lucile's *imagination*—the very source of Corinne's talent with which she wanted to replace feminine virtue, and that she alone has developed in Lucile—has thus made Corinne the true *father* of Juliette.

Corinne's subsequent transmission of her talents to the child through education operates entirely within the terms of specularity and speculation: Juliette imitates Corinne's playing so perfectly as to become her portrait in miniature, which *spectacle* has the calculated effect upon Oswald of a sentimental haunting.[21] Corinne lets the child see how much her educational efforts "cost" her and demands in exchange a payment of interest in perpetuity, exacting the promise that on a certain date every year, the child will repeat the performance for Oswald. The character of the *héritage* she transmits to Juliette is thus tainted with possession (Balayé, p. 575). Lucile understandably objects, relying on the argument of maternal debt: her daughter's affection "is due [*due*] to her in her misery" (Balayé, p. 576). It is striking that all Corinne has to do to win Lucile over in spite of this objection is to use her in a way that parallels her usage of Juliette: she emphasizes her maternal relation to Lucile by renewing the relation of educational debt through the transmission of some more of her talents, so that Lucile, too, willingly submits to Corinne's plot to haunt Oswald in exchange for inheriting some specular affection: "You will have to be you and me at the same time . . . my only personal desire is that Oswald find some traces of my influence in you and your daughter, and that at least he can never enjoy feeling without remembering Corinne" (p. 413).

This is Corinne's terrible revenge upon Oswald: first, she robs him of paternity; he has no son, and Corinne is the father of his only daughter, so that he becomes a dead end to his own sacred patrilineage.[22] Having diverted his family from the patrilineage, she binds them to herself through relationships that remain outside the patrilineal script: she is Juliette's illegitimate father and Lucile's substitutive mother, without being a "substitute father" because, neither wife nor mother, she is not wedded to any father.[23] In this way, she contrives to exert a form of agency, although it is only a ghostly agency, an act of haunting. But the ghostliness of her agency is essential to it, for two reasons. On one side it makes her truly resemble the father—all fathers are ghostly in this book, and therefore armed with a supernatural agency. Corinne's very last communication to Oswald is her mute act of pointing, on her deathbed, to "the moon covered by the same cloud that she had pointed out to Lord Nelvil when they stopped along the sea's shore on the way to Naples" Goldberger, p. 419; Balayé, p. 586). Even more surely than when she first pointed out and interpreted that portent, Corinne here arrogates to herself the act of uttering the father's curse. On the other side, Corinne is still a woman, and therefore the ghostliness of her agency presents her claim to the paternal sympathy without which she would lose her title to a favorable judgment, and with it, to agency itself. By disowning her own agency she is able to claim absolution from the heavenly Father on the grounds that she herself has wreaked no active vengeance. Although she thus adopts the patrilineal strategy of transmission (debt) used by Lady Edgermond and Mme de Chartres, she nevertheless uses it to interfere with the specular reproduction of virtue by substituting talent for virtue as the legacy thus transmitted.[24] As with the princess's imitation of Mme de Valentinois, Corinne adopts the gesture of a powerful maternal figure to whom she bears no relation, while taking care not to resemble her.

Corinne's strategy of transmission, like that of Lee's heroine, is not a closural gesture but an open one, created out of the reader participation provoked, as Maclean argues, by mise-en-abyme (p. 83). Her plot for passing on her talent to Lucile and Juliette is doubled and contrasted with the act of intergenerational transmission she stages in the performance of her last song. Although Corinne and Staël use their art and the figure of the daughter, Juliette, to get revenge on patrilineage as represented in the novel and, as DeJean argues, on literary patrilineage through allusion to Rousseau's *Julie*, both heroine and novelist have other heirs besides Juliette, and other legacies besides "turning female literary creation into a revenge fantasy" ("Staël's *Corinne*," p. 86). Juliette is heir to Corinne as vengeful Gothic father, but the true heir to Corinne as artist is the figure of the unnamed young girl in white (*blanc*). Her face is a blank upon which suffering has yet to leave any trace, and it tempers, instead of retracing, the song's *sombre* words. Corinne's improvisations have always been interpretations of the ruins of patriline history, and her last one becomes the performance of a silence as ghostly, as fragmentary, and as *written* as the paternal curse she brings down on Oswald. It is the record of the wreckage she has made of her body, voice, and talent in the mad attempt to reinsert herself into a ruinous patrilineage by becoming its interpreter and exponent. But the young girl in *blanc* sings in Corinne's place, already engaging in the public display of her own talents for which Corinne had to give up both her fatherland and its feminine solace, domestic life.

Thus, while the performance is a memorial at once of Corinne's talent and of the suffering that has robbed her of it, it simultaneously avoids imprinting that history of loss upon the next generation. Although the girl repeats Corinne's words, her blank face cannot mirror her history of suffering, and seems too fresh even to receive the *impression* of pleasurable sensibility that her performance makes on the fictive audience. This last spectacle is staged so that Oswald alone, seeing only a "cruel apparition," will be compelled to mirror the suffering it represents (Balayé, p. 581; Goldberger, p. 415). If the members of her audience see a ghost in the veiled figure hovering behind the girl, they see it from a Gothic distance that allows them to enjoy the horrid apparition, assured that *they* are free of its curse.[25]

The next chapter argues that Austen also transformed the eighteenth-century fiction of women's correspondence to the point of ending it as a formal subgenre, through an invocation of a "gender-neutral" consensus of reading that could only appear neutral because it was in fact understood as generically masculine. In so doing, she integrated the themes and paradigms of her eighteenth-century female predecessors with the formal strategies of the type of realism that came to dominate the nineteenth-century novel. Staël, writing in post-revolutionary France of the impossibility of inscribing oneself, as a woman, into what DeJean calls "the male script," cannot make the same move ("Staël's Corinne," p. 86). Staël had the French revolutionary discourse of public and private spheres to work with, but she did not have a Humean consensus of gentlemen to invoke, nor could she invoke it with the particular moral authority, as described by Armstrong, of a woman enshrined within domesticity. While the English reading public was able to imagine itself as participating in a consensus represented by that hybrid class, the gentry, Staël's public consisted of a much more awkward hybrid. The mixture that went into her literate public, of disillusioned Jacobin republicans affecting aristocratic values in reaction to the Reign of Terror with aristocrats confused about what those values were, formed anything but a consensus.[26] Thus women's fiction in France during Staël's time and until about 1830, as described in Margaret Cohen's forthcoming work, tends to use settings that are private, indeed, but more aristocratic in tone than in English domestic realist fiction. Staël clearly locates the domestic sphere as an English—and Gothic—place, tracing its boundaries with the paternal name and script. She has Corinne reject the very place that Austen's works embrace so entirely, in order to explore instead the possibility of the public performance of female talent—only to find, like every English Gothic heroine, that it is a place with no outside, even though it has no real "inside" either in France (or in the fantasy "Italy"). Because women writing in France after the Revolution lacked Austen's combination of female domestic authority and a gentlemanly consensus of shared national experience to be invoked by and centered in that authority, their works were not and could not be recognized as contributions to the realism developed after Austen by Englishwomen like the Brontës and Eliot.[27] For Staël unambiguously rejects the domestic sphere as a theater of female authority, and thus she continues, like her eighteenth-century predecessors in both England and France, to resist its containment of women. Yet at the same time she could not simply continue writing epistolary fiction of women's correspondence, as she had done in *Delphine*, because, like Austen, she was reaching for an authority unavailable to that feminine subgenre because it was understood as masculine. The reason Staël drops the epistolary form is not to avoid a genre "perfected by male writers" but to avoid a female-dominated and feminized one. The opposition between the oral and written in *Corinne* thus turns out, like those between north and south or paternal and maternal, to be no simple one. Writing is certainly a "masculine script," but it is also the letter of women's correspondence in the eighteenth century.[28] Without the first, Corinne is illegitimate—but with the second, Staël, like the feminine subgenre from which she attempts in that novel to dissociate herself, is also illegitimate. Therefore Staël attempts to reject *both* forms of writing—not only in favor of salon conversation on the model of "Sapho," but in favor of the public performance of her talent on the model of Corinna, the poet who allegedly prevailed over Pindar in competitions and "wrote in the language of Epic poetry."[29] The modern Corinne also celebrates patriline history, but one that is Gothicized in that, like St. Peter's, it lies already in ruins.

Jane Austen's Drawing Room; or, Framing Common Faults

"You will hurt yourself, Miss Bertram," she cried, "you will be in danger of slipping into the ha-ha."
—Jane Austen, 'Mansfield Park'

Jane Austen's work creates the illusion of fully inhabiting the domestic sphere, and that agenda distinguishes it from all the novels given full-scale readings in this book. Without fully entering the public sphere, Lafayette, Boisgiron, Lee, and Staël nevertheless plot the private as a "mother country," a state of exile within the empire of the fatherland.[1] The domestic space as such appears in these and other works discussed in Chapter 3 as a blank within the map of a fatherland that is elaborated as an ever-expanding frame around that diminishing space. Austen has inherited the private "state" of which the princess of Clèves made herself mistress, in which the isolation of a private space from the public or political arena allows its historian to construct it symbolically as both a state of sovereignty and a centralized state. But she inverts the relation of private to public in the work of her predecessors by shifting the emphasis from framing "empire" to framed "drawing room." The patrie, the nation-state, the court, the rest of Europe and the colonized world beyond become mere asides—although significant asides, of course—in her drawing-room conversation.[2] Thus Austen's work represents a crucial turning point in the exploration in fiction of women's correspondence of the problems of female filiation and transmission within patrilineage. Those explorations continued well into the first half of the nineteenth century at least, as Marianne Hirsch's work in *The Mother/Daughter Plot* has demonstrated. But they took a different form in fiction, abandoning the epistolary form and focusing more than ever on representations of the domestic sphere. Barker-Benfield describes the beginnings of this shift in England in the 1790's, the context in which Austen began writing: "Literate women consolidated their claim to mind and domesticity at the expense of politics and the sexual promise in sensibility. This story . . . set the stage for Victorian separate spheres and further fruitful conflict" (p. xxviii). In France, meanwhile, Staël's work, with its outright rejection of a Gothic and foreign domestic sphere and greater willingness to explore forms of public and political agency for women, seems to have set the stage for what Margaret Cohen calls "the French social novel" of the first half of the nineteenth century. I would have to add that the construction of women's correspondence, the imagined community of female and feminized readers connected through a sympathy that transgressed the bounds of the domestic sphere and heterosexual marriage in letters, was also sacrificed in the terms of this historical shift. Nevertheless, the sacrifice itself required that Austen, like Staël, "correspond" with the eighteenth-century novelists of women's correspondence.

"To suppose that a manuscript of many generations back could have remained undiscovered in a room such as that, so modern, so habitable!" (*Northanger Abbey*, p. 137). Some of the best recent work on Austen has emphasized the importance of reading her fiction in relation to that of roughly contemporary English women novelists (especially Maria Edgeworth, Amelia Opie, Frances Burney, Mary Wollstonecraft, and Ann Radcliffe), while championing her "moderate feminism" against a recently prevailing view of her as a conservative or anti-Jacobin writer.[3] Without quarreling with these needed representations of Austen, I would like to end by exploring why the literary traces of the international correspondence of women novelists discussed in this book have been less clearly legible in her work than are those of the English Jacobin and radical feminist novels of the 1790's. I would also like to take this opportunity to ask what it is, exactly, that "moderates" Austen's implicit feminism.

All of the elements mentioned in Chapter 3 as characteristic of novels of women's correspondence recur in Austen. We find young, marriageable heroines who are in some sense orphaned or disinherited in most of her novels. Even though they never discover a concealed aristocratic lineage, and they are more often educationally or financially "orphaned" while their parents are present, nevertheless their exclusion from lines of inheritance makes marriage an economic necessity, and their financial situation is spelled out in detail.[4] They have dead mothers or mothers threateningly alive, who usurp patriarchal rights and vie with heroines for marriage partners—although the monstrous mother has generally become simply a negligent mother.[5] Substitute mothers abound, although they, too, have become much more lackadaisical than they generally were in the eighteenth century.[6] There are framed stories in which a dead mother's history or a substitute mother's advice is passed on to a daughter.[7] Female friendships and romantic retirements, sympathy, Gothic conventions, and the epistolary form are all important subjects of Austenian experimentation.[8] With a method almost formulaic in its consistency, Austen dislocates, domesticates and ironizes every feature of the eighteenth-century novel of women's correspondence.

The particular "manuscripts" read in previous chapters have continued largely "undiscovered" in the room of Jane Austen's domestic fiction because they are so dislocated, while it is "so modern, so habitable." It is designed to plaster over its own Gothic foundations so that they look comfortable even to an English gentleman, to confine the wandering plots of romance to familiar spaces, and to combine the fragmentation of epistolary wholes into an apparently singular (although inevitably multivalent and complex), consensual public point of view, focused squarely on the new private center of the nation. The "Gothic" aspect of Jane Austen's drawing room is that it is designed in part as a fitting tomb for her literary foremothers, burying them even as it keeps them alive with its praise, respectfully invoking their "genius" in order to dismiss their representations as unreal.

Austen's strategy in addressing her readership is to appropriate the "feminine" genres of eighteenth-century fiction: the literature of sensibility, including the Gothic (*Sense and Sensibility*, *Northanger Abbey*), and the epistolary form (*Lady Susan* and other early works and drafts), and to "realize" them—that is, to render them more recognizably in the terms of what we have come to call "realism," by framing them within a domestic representational space. That Austen's shift away from earlier feminine novelistic conventions begins as a domestication has previously been pointed out by Claudia Johnson, who writes that *Northanger Abbey* "domesticates the Gothic and brings its apparent excesses into the drawing rooms of 'the midland counties of England'" (p. 47). But here a distinction should be made that tends to be forgotten, between specifically "domestic" fiction and the literature of sensibility more generally, whose larger geography draws upon romance antecedents. Burney, Edgeworth, and Opie, the English female predecessors most often discussed in relation to Austen, are, like her, more domestic writers than the ones I have given the most attention to here—but even they, as Franco Moretti's recent research has shown, are literally "all over the map" when compared to Austen.[9] They had not turned as far as Austen would from romances of sensibility like those described in the preceding chapters, which more explicitly mapped a feminine territory in relation to the larger boundaries of nations, continents, and colonies.

But if Austen "realizes" the novelistic conventions marked as feminine in the eighteenth century by framing them, more narrowly even than Opie or Edgeworth, within the domestic space, she does so with a continual ironic wink at the reader that seems to subvert the feminine generic attributes she adopts. To domesticate and to ironize are equally to make use of the first common elements most frequently cited as those of "realism," or at least of the version of it now recognized as culminating in the nineteenth century's high realism. Thus *Don Quixote* is often considered the first "novel" because of its "realism," whereas what constitutes that "realism," its emphasis on the quotidian, is identical with its ironic parody of chivalric romance. Austen in *Northanger Abbey* is obviously taking a similar approach to the "female" Gothic romance. Considered in the more local context of eighteenth-century fiction, Austen's oeuvre does to the feminine genres of her youth something like what Fielding does to Richardson (e.g., in *Shamela* and *Joseph Andrews*): it performs a gesture of laughing off the feminized sentimental representation of social relations in favor of a strongly imagined consensus among the middling "gentleman" class about what is plausible, and, consequently, what is real.

As Alistair Duckworth points out, Austen is following Shaftesbury in using ridicule to illuminate truth, as "that Manner of Proof, by which we discern whatever is liable to just Raillery."[10] One of the truths she puts to the test of ridicule is that of the eighteenth-century feminine literary conventions. In order to manipulate her audience's perception of truth by this light, she must appeal to its sense of humor. For the refutation of any expressed point of view by giggling is effective only when a strong contingent of one's addressees giggles along. Austen's extended giggle at sentimental romance makes ingenious use of the same support that Hume had been able to invoke against the existence of miracles: the "uniform experience" of English gentlemen, or what Mary Evans refers to as "the common sense of the age."[11]

By implicitly invoking Hume's imagined consensus of gentlemanly readers, Austen effects a transformation vis-à-vis the earlier fiction of women's correspondence so fundamental as to put an end to it as a formal subgenre. Mullan has argued persuasively that Hume's theory of sympathy modeled "society as a scheme of consensus and unanimity" specifically by eliding "two distinct meanings of 'society' [the experience of particular contacts and the consistency of political structure]. . . . Sympathy with 'another' is made congruent with sympathy with 'the interest of society'" (pp. 25, 30, 34). Hume's theory of sympathy constructs what Mullan calls "sociability" by (uneasily) conflating the principle of individuals sharing sentiments through identification, on the one hand, with the idea of "society as a scheme of consensus and unanimity" on the other. This model works well in Mullan's argument about the reader relations constructed by the novels of Richardson, Sterne, and Mackenzie. Precisely because Mullan is right when he says that "the novel of sentiment in the eighteenth century . . . elaborates pathos from exactly the disconnection of special experiences of sympathy from dominant patterns of social relationship," however, novels of women's correspondence specifically resist the Humean construction of sympathy as participation in a dominant social consensus. But Austen takes it up. In relying on the force of a conservative readership, however, Austen toes an almost miraculously fine line. If recent critical representations of this much-contested author as a "moderate feminist" have any truth to them, and I think they do, she was performing the amazing trick of getting gentlemen to giggle with her, not just at sentimental conventions, but simultaneously at the same conservative "commonsensical" world-view they themselves sustained, in the very midst of the well-documented backlash against 1790's Jacobin feminism.[12]

Janet Todd makes the important point that Austen's project is primarily an antisentimental one, specifying as her target exactly the conventions of sensibility, including plot conventions, that characterize the literature of women's correspondence.[13] Although Todd seems to be arguing against critics like Claudia Johnson, who defend the feminist implications of Austen's work, nevertheless her description of Austen as antisentimental is very much in line with Johnson's references to Austen's "skepticism," a term Johnson uses to distinguish Austen's stance from both conservative and Jacobin partisanship.[14] While Staël moved away from the passive femininity of eighteenth-century notions of sensibility by shifting towards a Romantic conception of "imagination," Austen's reaction against romance and sensibility is an exact echo of Wollstonecraft's, including all the ambivalences evident in the theorist's own novelistic practice. Sulloway, like many modern critics, adopts Wollstonecraft's view of "the cult of sensibility" as a historically objective one: "It guaranteed that women's mental faculties would remain attenuated" (p. 118). Wollstonecraft's word for these vulnerable "mental faculties" was *reason*, which she understood, following Rousseau, within the terms of an unstable opposition to *sensibility* or *sentiment* that was pedagogically powerful, and thus potentially dangerous to any educational project. Rousseau, like all writers of sensibility, held that education by example is education through sentiment rather than through reason, and thus more effective as a form of instruction (*Emile*, p. 379). But the other term most commonly set in opposition to *reason* in the rhetoric of the Enlightenment was *prejudice*. Both *sensibility* and *prejudice* were obviously terms of importance to Austen, and it is in their dangerous proximity, which had already alarmed Wollstonecraft in regard to the education of women, that her skepticism of sensibility arises.[15]

Austen's antisentimentalism, although directed against the conventions of a feminized literature, nevertheless worked in the service of a cultural project that has with some truth been called "feminist" by many recent critics. Insofar as that term has been applied to Austen in reference to her fiction's indirect critique of the constraints upon women, social and representational, that predominated in her society, it is used meaningfully, although perhaps anachronistically. But the point I wish to emphasize is that Austen's apparent antisentimentality actually works to recuperate the literature of sensibility's critique of the gendered world-view represented by the dominant consensus of gentlemen with which Austen's work aligns itself, and upon which it depends for its representational force. Her ironic undermining of the feminine conventions is precisely what enables her to recuperate the force of their critique.

Austen pulls off her trick of manipulating the gentlemanly consensus on reality and common sense to "feminist" ends, I shall argue, by dramatizing the idea that "sense" is hardly common. She frequently ironizes the voice of "common sense" and surreptitiously validates the truth of the feminine-identified conventions of sensibility. But in order to make such ironic hints effective, she had first to represent a world recognizable to "gentlemen" in and on their own terms. She achieves her appeal to the most powerful readership available to her through the extreme confinement of her represented world and of the women (especially) who inhabit it to the domestic space and to private conversation.[16]

The debate between Richardson and Fielding defined the stakes of fictional representation for the latter half of the century in a version of the tension between realism and romance that was linked to a gender opposition.[17] The success of Austen's strategy, in the wake of that debate, of recuperating the "feminine" genres by satirizing them lies in the fact that she can claim to comprehend both terms of the masculine/feminine opposition as it was being negotiated on the field of literature. By adopting an ironic and quotidian discourse strongly identified in the eighteenth century with Fielding, with the critique of sensibility, and overtly with masculinity, she successfully reappropriates the "feminine," antirealist or romance discourses associated with Richardson and lady novelists at a time when these were becoming increasingly discredited.[18] This strategy is especially apparent in *Northanger Abbey*, in which Austen most intensively and overtly works out her authorial relation to the earlier feminine literary codes. For that reason I shall discuss it in more detail than the other novels, although it is my purpose in this chapter only to sketch Austen's relation to the literature of women's correspondence in general terms, making no pretense of doing interpretive justice to any of her individual works.

· · ·

In a novel where she parodies the "female Gothic" yet aligns herself with the "injured body" of female novelists of sensibility, Austen surreptitiously signals the gender-neutrality of sentimentalism by coding her omniscient narrator's commentary in terminology borrowed from *Paul et Virginie*, one of the most popular and most sentimental novels of her time, but written by a male author (*Northanger*, p. 21).[19] Austen's narrator obliquely slips in an aphoristic description of Catherine Morland, the antisentimental heroine, as "always distressed, but always steady" (p. 76). This is a direct and literal translation of the ultrasentimental Virginie's maxim for feminine virtue: TOUJOURS AGITÉE, MAIS CONSTANTE (Mauzi, p. 103).[20] The terms of Virginie's precept continue to frame feminine conduct throughout Austen's novel: Isabella is "unsteady," whereas Catherine, in her weakest Quixotic moments, is only "agitated," like the "steady" Virginie (*Northanger*, pp. 117, 121, 153). The adjectives, *unsteady* and *agitated*, which might in other contexts be considered synonyms, are thus coded as moral opposites, for in the formulation Austen quotes from Jacques-Henri Bernardin de Saint-Pierre, "unsteadiness" signals a lack of virtue, while "agitation" is its requisite trial and proof.

At the climax of Catherine's Gothic trials, just before the moment of truth represented by the revelation of the laundry list, she is briefly both "agitated" and "unsteady": "She seized, with an unsteady hand, the precious manuscript. . . . With a curiosity so justly awakened, and feelings in every way so agitated, repose must be absolutely impossible" (*Northanger*, p. 135). Here Austen is emphasizing the distinction between conduct and feeling implicit in Virginie's maxim: "unsteady" describes Catherine's condemnable *conduct* (as it does in the case of Isabella), while "agitated" and "distressed" refer to the state of her feelings. Conduct is again emphasized at the end of the same episode: "She got away as soon as she could from a room in which her conduct produced such unpleasant reflections" (p. 138). Since Isabella is condemned as a treacherous and selfish—that is, *unsympathetic*—female friend, while Catherine learns better conduct through the trials to which her agitated feelings have made her susceptible, Austen is valorizing the codes of feminized literary sensibility, while signaling that they are not only to be identified with the "injured body" of women writers, but also with successful literary men like Bernardin.[21]

The notions of plausibility, realism, and common sense rely upon making constructed categories for reality perception seem neuter or unmarked. One such category is that of gender difference. When Catherine Morland and Henry Tilney discuss reading, they try to divide literary genres according to categories that are very much marked in terms of gender difference, but falsely so. The praise of Gothic romances as literature of sensibility that may be written by women but is read by men too, if often on the sly, gives way to the famous debate about the other primary genre of historical narrative prevalent at the time, which Catherine identifies as "real solemn history," with its "men all so good for nothing, and hardly any women at all" (p. 84). If the private histories proffered by Gothic romances are too feminized, "real solemn history" is too masculinized. When the gendered characterization of these two narrative genres is compared with the narrative in which they are delivered, it becomes clear that a claim is implied for the superiority of Austen's own genre, which we might identify retrospectively as "the realist novel," one that claims to transcend constructed oppositions, neither sentimental romance nor real solemn history, neither feminine nor masculine. As Henry Tilney says, "In every power, of which taste is the foundation, excellence is pretty fairly divided between the sexes," proceeding immediately to demonstrate this truth by exhibiting his understanding of muslins (pp. 13–14).[22]

Catherine's argument against history further confuses the mapping of generic distinctions onto gender roles with more borrowing from *Paul et Virginie*. In it, Paul describes himself as "hardly interested" in history, where he finds "only general and recurring calamities without apparent cause, wars without motive or object, obscure intrigues, nations without principles and princes without humanity." Catherine very similarly describes her own lack of "interest" in "the quarrels of popes and kings, with wars or pestilences, in every page" (p. 84). And like Catherine after him, Paul "preferred the reading of novels, for in their greater concern with human interests and feelings he sometimes discovered situations that resembled his own" (Donovan, p. 91).[23] If the literature of sensibility feminized its heroes while still granting them masculine active virtues and relative freedom from constraint, Austen seems to want to model her realist heroine on the example of such a *hero* by identifying her with Paul's mixing of gender and generic stereotypes.[24] Catherine has ostensibly put aside her early preference for "boy's plays" and gone into "training for a heroine" by reading "all such works as heroines must read to supply their memories with those quotations which are so serviceable and so soothing in the vicissitudes of their eventful lives" (*Northanger*, pp. 2–3). But the quotation she is made to use in the important vicissitude of her debate with Henry about gender and genre surreptitiously undoes the explicit identification of her critique of history with a specifically female viewpoint, by identifying the female speaker with the male hero she echoes. In the figure of Catherine Morland, Austen effectively couples the example of Paul with the precept of Virginie, thus deftly salvaging her own heroine's virtue within the codes of sensibility, yet deeply modifying it by negating the fatal example of Bernardin's popular sentimental heroine. (Virginie drowns in her crinolines rather than accepting rescue from a shipwreck, because that would have involved removing her dress and trusting herself to the arms of a naked sailor before a crowd of spectators.) At the same time, Austen salvages her new genre from the implausibly modest wreckage of the late eighteenth century's literature of sensibility.

Austen's own recognition as an author depends upon her claim of gender neutrality in literary genres. That claim is based in turn upon a balance between romance and history, which Austen achieves through her manipulation of the discourse of plausibility. When Henry Tilney admonishes Catherine, in another famous passage, for perceiving reality through the lens of romance, he employs an argument that refers her not to the direct observation of facts, but to the notion of plausibility: "Consult your understanding, your own sense of the probable, your own observation of what is passing around you." The rhetoric of sound empiricism with which Henry seems to recommend to Catherine "her own observation" is preceded, however, by a reminder that her "own sense of the probable," by which she should interpret her observations, should consist first and foremost in her full participation in *Henry's* sense of plausibility—that is, in what Hume had called the "uniform experience" of English gentlemen: "Remember that we are English, that there can be no such secrets because there are roads, newspapers, and neighborhoods full of voluntary spies" (*Northanger*, p. 159).

Claudia Johnson has pointed out the supreme importance to Henry of *his* sense of plausibility, referring to his earlier reaction to Catherine's assertion that she keeps no journal: "Perhaps you are not sitting in this room, and I am not sitting by you. These are points in which a doubt is equally possible" (*Northanger*, p. 13).[25] Henry does finally succeed in persuading Catherine, not to rely on her own sense, but to reformulate her own sense of the probable along the lines Henry has given her: "But in the central part of England there was surely some security for the existence even of a wife not beloved, in the laws of the land, and the manners of the age. Murder was not tolerated, servants were not slaves, and neither poison nor sleeping potions to be procured, like rhubarb, from every druggist." Several critics have adequately demonstrated already that this is Austen in her best ironic mode, and that she means just the opposite of everything Henry Tilney says here.[26] But since other intelligent feminist critics are still capable of seeing those interpretations as revealing more about "ingenious modern readers inspired by feminist sociology and psychoanalysis" than about the irony undercutting what Catherine learns of life in the Midland counties of England, I venture to add two small points, an intertextual and a historically contextual one, to the demonstrations of others.[27]

First, Austen still seems much later to have entertained some doubts as to whether "servants are not slaves," given that Jane Fairfax likens the "misery of the victims" of the "governess-trade" to those of the slave trade (*Emma*, p. 946). Secondly, not only *were* poison and sleeping potions (laudanum) available "from every druggist"—as Austen's Romantic contemporaries so well knew—but even rhubarb, which sounds to modern readers so harmless and domestic, was in Austen's time an exotic plant, and was known on occasion to be fatally poisonous. It was sold as a drug by men dressed up in Turkish costume.[28] Catherine's sense of the familiar and the plausible has indeed been altered *in spite of* her own and her readers' perception of facts. The governance of that sense has simply been shifted from one set of conventions to another: from those of the literature of sensibility in Gothic romance, marked as feminine, to those of "the uniform experience" of gentlemen, (un)marked as gender-neutral.

The final ironic blow is dealt to Henry's more general argument about England as a nation of plausibility by another intertextual allusion: his argument is itself a convention of Gothic romance. Radcliffe set her novels in the "Alps and Pyrenees" because she had to write about female domestic distress while preserving the convention of the safety and sanctity of the English home. But Henry's articulation of it in his exhortation to Catherine to "remember that we are English" is borrowed specifically from one of the "horrid novels" mentioned by Isabella: Eliza Parsons's *The Castle of Wolfenbach* (*Northanger*, pp. 24, 159).[29] In that novel, the distressed heroine is more than once similarly reassured. Early on, her French suitor observes that "the English . . . enjoy the blessings of a mild and free government; their personal safety is secured by the laws," while her substitute mother later assures her that in England she is safe from being hauled off back to the Alps by her pursuing foster-father: "Here are no lettres de-cachet, the laws will protect you from injury; compose yourself, therefore, my dear girl—in England no violence can be offered to you in any shape" (Parsons, pp. 51, 95). By reproducing this discourse, what Henry truly and primarily demonstrates is his vaunted superior depth of reading in "horrid novels" ("Do not imagine that you can cope with me in a knowledge of Julias and Louisas" [*Northanger*, pp. 82–83]).

Austen's modifications agree with the original passages from Parsons in implying that private relations cannot escape public governance. Parsons emphasizes that the state's legal system will protect the heroine from the private despotism of her foster-father by virtue of its reliance upon only "the clearest proofs." Austen's shift is to emphasize the importance of plausibility over that of proof. Catherine does not need proofs, Henry argues; she should not be looking for any, because there is no domestic space or relation so private as to escape the technologies of public surveillance. Since we know everyone is constantly watching, we do not need to look for ourselves. That argument is at the foundation of the logic of plausibility. Austen, following Parsons and by means of alluding to her work, proves that statement wrong. The heroine of Wolfenbach finally has to flee England, whose legal system is effective, not so much at protecting young women from fathers, but rather, if anything, at protecting fathers from the fears of young women. This is in fact the reason for which the French suitor originally praised it: the stringent requirements of English legal proof are beneficial because "no man can be punished for an imaginary crime" (Parsons, p. 51). Now, an "imaginary crime" is exactly what Henry accuses Catherine of laying at his father's door, a crime for which no man in England can be punished. The informal system of private surveillance for the public good thus helps to establish domestic abuses as beyond unprovable, for it renders them implausible, and thus in effect imperceptible. The Humean "uniform experience" Henry invokes relegates such abuses to the realm of "imaginary crimes," to the Alps and Pyrenees of everyday English perception.

In moving toward a mode of representation that we would now recognize as "realism," Austen tries to deconstruct the gender coding of the opposition between the feminine sentimental "histories" and a masculine history that is more "real" because more public and more validated by the Humean version of sympathy based on a gentlemanly consensus of common sense. She puts forward her own realistic fiction as superior to both: it is a form of history that presents a feminine perspective on private life *as central to the public interest*, while rendering such a perspective recognizable, and thus capable of validation, by that gentlemanly consensus. If the project of realism is to unmark, to make what it describes appear natural rather than constructed, there is only one way for Austen to accomplish that with the conventions and experience with which she is working, already marked as feminine. She must make them recognizable from the perspective of another set of conventions about experience, which had already succeeded in making itself seem unmarked by the time Hume was able to call it "uniform experience." But she is not inhabiting "uniform experience"; she is only impersonating it. If Catherine Morland's education suffers from what Duckworth calls her parents' "too complacent common sense," and Henry's education in common sense is equally exposed as too complacent, the narrator undermines the authority of common sense even as she invokes it (Duckworth, p. 5). Only the ironic tension in Austen's version of the discourse of plausibility leaves open the crucial room to believe that General Tilney did murder his wife, not à la Montoni, but through a plausible combination of neglect and ill-temper invisible as anything but an "imaginary crime" to the public gaze of "uniform experience" and its code of legal evidence. Austen's irony thereby salvages, although only surreptitiously, the critique of domestic arrangements implied in feminine literature of sensibility, a critique that the discourse of plausibility would deny.[30]

· · ·

The importance of *Northanger Abbey* in establishing Austen's stance toward her female predecessors also affected its form, as noted by Epstein and others: "*Northanger Abbey* was probably the first of Austen's major novels conceived with a third-person narrator from the outset; indeed, Ian Jack persuasively suggests that *Northanger Abbey* is fundamentally 'an anti-epistolary novel'" (Epstein, p. 404). By rejecting the epistolary form from *Northanger* on in favor of a return to an internalized indirect discourse more akin to Lafayette's, Austen performs a gesture on the level of narrative technique that parallels and reinforces her thematic recuperation of the feminine genres of sensibility.

Whereas the women writers of the previous generation used the familiar letter to establish sympathetic narrative exchange, for the skeptical Austen it became, as it had been for Laclos, the genre of deceit and thus of suspect sensibility.[31] While identifying it thus, she also sought to disassociate it, like the genres of history and novel, from its conventional gender identification. At least twice she refers ironically to the familiar letter's conventional associations with femininity. In addition to the passage in *Northanger Abbey* (p. 13) where Henry finally pronounces the equal distribution of taste and its powers between the sexes, there is another famous passage in *Mansfield Park* where the narrator appeals to the reader to identify with Lady Bertram *qua* letter-writer: "Everybody at all addicted to letter-writing, without having much to say, which will include a large proportion of the female world, *at least*, must feel with Lady Bertram" (p. 729; my emphasis). This passage seems at first to collude with the convention Henry Tilney refuted, were that collusion not undermined by the tellingly inclusive "at least." Austen's readers are here invoked as "assumed females," in that they are generally assumed to be women, but may include many men assuming a position conventionally designated as feminine, like the readers of Gothic fiction according to Henry Tilney. Thus Austen repeats her earlier text's critique, although far more subtly, and indeed almost imperceptibly, of the gender coding of literary genres.[32]

A critique of conventional gender codes could only be enunciated, however, by invoking them, and with them their already well-entrenched position in the "common sense of the age." For a woman writing, therefore, dropping these marked forms enacted a far more effective critique of the mapping of gender onto literary genre than could be achieved in the mere enunciation of critique. By the time she was writing *Mansfield Park*, Austen was almost purely enacting and barely enunciating her critique of the convention that associated the familiar letter with femininity. Yet I would argue further that Austen's motivations for dropping the epistolary form were at least equally in line with the literature of women's correspondence and of sensibility as they were with their critique. She had to drop the form because, unlike Laclos, but like the writers of the fiction of women's correspondences, she was ultimately more interested in exploring the communicative and epistemological possibilities of sensibility, including its pitfalls, than in monstrous feats of epistolary deception à la Mme de Merteuil or Lady Susan.[33]

Consolidating the narrative voice and perspective in an omniscient narrator allows Austen, furthermore, to slip a closural and normative frame around her text, a unified moral commentary that will hardly be noticeable for what it is: a framing precept. Her formal strategy in confronting the problem of writing a literature of sensibility that would be skeptical of sensibility is thus the opposite of Sophia Lee's, who, as discussed in Chapter 5, was struggling with a version of the same problem. Lee enacted her skepticism of sympathy by splitting her epistolary memoir into two mutually contradictory narratives, dramatizing how the fantasy of perfect sympathy drives apart and destroys women who are also bound by the closest ties of kinship (twin sisters; mother and daughter), and then invoking a reader who would sympathize from a geographical, temporal, and above all an imaginative distance. Austen's single narrator, by contrast, invites her reader to enter into a more unified "we" of common sense based rhetorically in the notion of common experience. Thus Austen not only enacts the disassociation of the female writer from the feminine modes and genres (romance, sensibility and the Gothic, the epistolary form) but actually impersonates "common sense" or "uniform experience" and usurps its authority.

Concomitantly, Austen's turn to free indirect discourse in place of the letter form used by her immediate predecessors frames for the reader the interiors inhabited by her heroines. Rather than eliciting the reader's own sympathetic imaginary narrative, as did Lee and all the writers of sensibility, omniscient narration of characters' thoughts focuses the reader's "gaze" on the private space from which the heroine gazes out, thus fixing her more squarely in its exemplary frame than letter fiction ever could. The normative gaze represented by the unified narrator is an essential aspect of Austen's shift away from the literature of women's correspondence, and of sensibility generally. Its aesthetic effect is to present readers with a fully imagined world, rather than inviting them to supply the fictional world from their own private and exceptionally sympathetic imaginations (although sympathy was guided, of course, by the reader's familiarity with the conventions of sensibility, one of those conventions was that sympathy was an exceptional capacity; see Mullan, p. 13). Claudia Johnson is certainly right when she argues that "Austen draws attention to the artificiality, rather than the *vraisemblance*, of her conclusion" in *Northanger Abbey* by "declining to describe Eleanor's new-found husband because 'the most charming young man in the world is instantly before the imagination of us all'" (pp. 47–48). It is important to add that the specific artificiality emphasized (and mocked) here is that of sentimental literature's conventional invocation of the reader's individual and private sympathetic imagination.

The importance for Austen of parodying the conventional invocation of the reader's imaginative sympathy is underscored by the fact that Henry Tilney not many pages before had borrowed exactly the same artificial conclusion to his own parody of Gothic fiction, in one of his allusions to Sophia Lee: "But Henry was too much amused by the *interest* he had raised, to be able to carry it farther . . . and was obliged to entreat her to use her own fancy in the perusal of Matilda's woes" (*Northanger*, p. 126; emphasis mine). Henry's paraphrase does not at all imply the Radcliffean "convention of the happy ending," but rather a quite different version of the Gothic—Lee's—that refuses to provide one.[34] As discussed in Chapter 5, Lee's Matilda makes exactly the entreaty Henry makes to Catherine as she bequeaths her manuscript to her young reader ("Oh! thou—whomsoever thou mayst be, into whose hands these memoirs of the wretched Matilda may fall—"), while the editor of Lee's "ancient manuscript" makes an earnest appeal to the sympathetic imagination of the reader of *The Recess*. The parallelism Austen sets up between her own ironic invocations of the sympathetic reader and Lee's sincere ones emphasizes Austen's gently mocking yet sympathetic turn away from the device of invoking the reader's sympathy.[35]

The appeal to a reader's sympathy demands that the reader participate in a sympathetic exchange much like those represented in the literature of women's correspondence, in order to affirm and validate its codes as reality. As it establishes the nature of the relation between text and reader, it is just as essential to the literature of sensibility as Austen's rejection of it is to her own. The trope of inexpressibility, in which the narrative declines to describe either emotions or events but rather bids the reader imagine, is just that, a trope, and one that serves the essential function of creating the reader's sympathetic participation. It is not, as has often been asserted, a fault of basic writing skills. What Austen did instead has now been reinforced by two centuries of dominant novelistic practice, which has accustomed us to her alternate strategy of providing readers with worlds ready-imagined.[36]

Austen's move away from the convention of sympathetic appeal to readers is not only concomitant with but crucial to her abandonment of both the epistolary form and the overtly didactic stance. If the epistolary form crosses the boundary between public and private spheres, free indirect style evades entirely the problems of distinguishing between the public and the private by letting the reader inside someone else's head. The epistolary "blur" consists in the gesture of exposing private documents to a public readership that is asked to be moved by or to judge them, to prove or to falsify private truths (truths of feeling, action, or both). But the illusion of omniscience, even partial omniscience, means giving readers far surer "evidence" of such private truths, by making them privy to characters' innermost thoughts.[37] Omniscient narration sacrifices the "documentary status," as Julia Epstein calls it, that eighteenth-century fiction strove to achieve, in favor of providing the sympathy or judgment of its audience with evidence about the truth of character that seems more immediate and therefore less ambiguous (Epstein, p. 415). The result is that narratorial voice exerts tighter control over readers' judgment and sympathies, even when it preserves, as in Austen's practice, the gesture of deferring to their final authority. Thus Austen has received much credit from readers from her day down to this "for declining the didactic posture—which assumes the ambition as well as the authority to teach the public," but her unified narrator and use of indirect discourse unobtrusively frame events and characters with implied precepts.[38]

Jan Fergus observes of Austen's didacticism that "although she accepts the eighteenth-century doctrine that literature should educate the emotions and judgment, she rejects most of the literary conventions associated with the doctrine, and particularly the exemplary character" (p. 5). I would argue rather that Austen domesticates the exemplary heroine, just as she does the other conventions of sensibility—romance plot and setting, epistolary form, and sympathetic exchange—not rejecting them altogether but modifying them profoundly in accordance with the skepticism of "common sense." To "domesticate" is in this sense to train upon the exemplar the normative gaze of that common sense, through the vehicle of the single, ironic narrator.

In domesticating sentimental romance, Austen domesticates both feminine virtue and its faults. Heroines in her works whose perceptions of social reality are formed by the conventions of women's novels of sensibility rather than by those of "the uniform experience" of gentlemen are poised, much like the heroines of sensibility themselves, for a fall. But here the frightful precipice of the literature of sensibility—virtue's fault—becomes the "danger of slipping into the ha-ha," the danger of becoming nothing more than a ridiculous and unredeemed butt of the omniscient narrator's ironic derision.[39] The fall into the "ha-ha" is one that neither threatens literal annihilation nor elicits the sympathy that could redeem earlier fallen heroines for their readers. The fall in Austen results only in the kind of quotidian misery that Maria Bertram Rushworth suffers after failing to heed Fanny Price's warning: that of living alone "in another country" with Mrs Norris (an unmistakable dystopic parody of the retirements of female "Romantic friendships"), where "their tempers became their mutual punishment." The omniscient narrator here asks the reader to consider, "What can exceed the misery of such a situation?"—implying that it is in fact a worse fate than the tragic sentimental falls it parodies. The redemptive endings of the feminine fiction of sensibility, which lead their heroines to a shared retirement in female friendship and sympathy, are thus rendered highly suspect in accordance with the "common sense of the age."

Yet Maria's fate *is* an annihilation from the perspective of the world Austen represents, an exile to its unrepresented margin ("another country"), which is not only "private" but also, crucially, "remote": cut off at once from pleasant and *meaningful* society.[40] Without the Gothic literalization that characterizes sentimental representations of feminine social suffering from *Clarissa* onwards, however, such suffering cannot lay the same claim to its reader's sympathy and absolution: "The indignities of stupidity, and the disappointments of selfish passion, can excite little pity" (*Mansfield Park*, pp. 423–24).

But of course it is Fanny Price, not Maria, who is the true descendant of the eighteenth-century heroines of sensibility. What seems in the last quotation like a direct attack upon the conventions of sympathy is in fact a direct echo of prefaces like that in which Mme Beccary presented her "tableau of a heroine, whose unfailing virtue is put through every trial without ever proving false." It will be remembered that she also explained the necessity of such virtue for the eliciting of sympathy: "It is through virtue alone that love is pardonable and interesting; without virtue, it is nothing but the most vile and contemptible of weaknesses."[41] Austen condemns Maria Bertram with as heavy a didactic hand as Mme Beccary dismisses the woman who loves without virtue, while Fanny Price is as unfailing in trials of virtue as any of Beccary's heroines. I do not at all mean by this to deny the complexities of Fanny's character. These are brought out, for example, in D. A. Miller's persuasive discussion of the "hysterical" disruptions complicating her moral condemnations of other characters' indiscretions. But those psychological disruptions only prove her virtue all the more surely, since they dramatize her struggles and her triumph in its trials. The trial of virtue has simply been psychologized and interiorized by Austen, rather than enacted in plot.

The emblematic framed portraits that pervade Austen's work likewise perform a function that is the inverse of their role in Lee's. Portraits in *The Recess* always slip from their frames to create narrative breaks: the fascinating portraits of the heroines' parents prevent their imaginative storytelling and at last move by means of a secret spring to reveal the "secret communication" with the outside world; the miniature that slips from the bag around Ellinor's neck reveals the heroines' identity and precipitates both the flight of one twin and the imprisonment of the other; the portrait of Essex at the storming of Cadiz, transported into Ellinor's sight, brings on the final break in her insanity, her life, and her narrative. Although Austen seems to refer to Lee's portraits, portraits in Austen tend to center textual perspective rather than fragmenting and reduplicating narrative.[42] They become iconic (and ironic) literalizations of the invisible normative frame provided by the unified narrator.

If *Lady Susan*, as mentioned in Chapter 1, has gossiping letter-writers present a tableau of Frederica gazing out a window at the dangerous example of her mother walking in the shrubbery with Reginald, Austen's more famous works continue to place her heroines significantly at windows. Two important examples are the final prospects that close the courtship plots of Fanny Price and Elizabeth Bennet. At the end of the series of cautionary conclusions to the lives of the various sinners who populate *Mansfield Park*, Fanny's moral surveillance at last controls the manor house all the more surely because, no longer occupying it, she holds it perfectly in view from within the frame of her beloved window at the parsonage. And when Elizabeth enters Pemberley at the culminating moment of *Pride and Prejudice*, she surveys the prospect it commands, with the portrait of its owner, as future "mistress both of his person and of the estate," to paraphrase Lafayette. Both of these moments are crucial to the fixing of a moral frame around the bewildering contradictions in the relations among characters, events, and narrative voice in their respective works.[43] According to Katrin R. Burlin, "Elizabeth in all her human imperfections" is necessary to bring the Bingleys to life, frozen as they are in the frames of their portraits and their property (p. 166). Similarly, Rachel Brownstein emphasizes Elizabeth Bennet's "partial creation" of Darcy through her manipulation and interpretation of his portrait, an act of interpretive authority that parallels what she does with his letter (p. 130). Thus the salubriously imperfect Elizabeth is the inverted mirror-image of the exemplary Fanny, her double as manipulator of the interpretive frames that can contain disturbing behaviors.

Like Staël's Lucile in her naïve blonde rectitude, Fanny corresponds to the princess of Clèves, framed at the last within "the picture of good" at the Mansfield parsonage as an inimitable example of virtue—inimitable, indeed, like the princess and Lucile, because readers could hardly be tempted to mirror her. Like the princess, Fanny retreats from the estate proper into her own new version of the "demeure exposée," described in the novel's final sentence as "*within the view* and patronage of Mansfield" (*Mansfield Park*, p. 432; my emphasis).[44]

Certainly, Fanny Price stands out in her inimitable exemplarity from the rest of Austen's heroines, but none truly approach the brink except Marianne Dashwood, whose dangerous activity requires the virtuous double of her sister Elinor as much as any eighteenth-century antiheroine's would. The difference, the distance of these Austen heroines from Lafayette's, is that neither can ever properly inherit their estates, as Austen repeatedly makes clear, for reasons of class as well as of sex. This transformation of Lafayette's aristocratic literary model evinces Austen's correspondences with the intervening writers: "Soon the self in Jane Austen's world loses its birthright," Alistair Duckworth notes, as did the orphaned heroines of the later eighteenth century (pp. 2–3). Austen's transformation of those more immediate precursors is to make the heroine's education, rather than the heroine herself, exemplary. Austenian heroines are made, not born; the trope of feminine education in virtue as maternal inheritance that connects Lafayette with the eighteenth-century writers of sensibility is yet another inherited convention that Austen radically transformed. Her heroines receive little or nothing in that line from either mothers or substitute mothers—just as, with one exception, they receive little or nothing in the way of material inheritance.[45] The romance of virtue as a feminine inheritance whose plot must be mapped across national boundaries has been domesticated as the novel of education, the prime vehicle, later, of nineteenth-century realism. But it is still the novel of a feminine education, which in Austen's work must take place within a narrow, domesticated space whose boundaries identify nation and empire.

The private estate in which the princess of Clèves established her sovereignty marks Austen's correspondence with Lafayette, as it does that of her female contemporaries in France, such as Germaine de Staël. The princess's private house and "heart of glass" is more fully domesticated in Jane Austen's drawing room than in any of its French avatars, and thus differently a "demeure exposée." But it is once again peered into through its picture window by a reader whose voyeuristic authority is as necessary to the text as it is ironized and undermined by it. The voyeuristic authority invoked is no longer that of a self-interested aristocrat like Nemours, but rather participates in the public consensus of "neighborhoods full of voluntary spies." The real business of the nation is still inseparable from the business of love, and once again, as in Lafayette, it occurs in the interplay and competition among observers who are also constantly observed. But now it takes place in the private space, rather than in the court from which the princess wanted to retreat.

Austen's replacement of the aristocratic court with a prototype of the bourgeois domestic sphere as the center of the nation, however, leads her to a turn, in terms of narrative technique, back in the direction of Lafayette's practice and away from the epistolary fiction of women's correspondences that prevailed in both countries during the latter part of the intervening period. Lafayette's use of omniscient narration gave her courtly readers a peek, such as Nemours steals, into her heroine's private "heart of glass," lending irrefutable evidence and thus authority to the otherwise unacceptable "implausibility" of free female confession. In Austen omniscient narration invokes a similarly dominant cultural authority that is also linked to a discourse of plausibility. For it borrows and mimics the authority of the "uniform experience" of the English gentry, even while the play of irony continually undermines that "uniformity." Whereas the female novelists of women's correspondence had worked to replace the voyeuristic emphasis of the amorous epistolary tradition by modeling a relationship between reader and text that was based on a sympathetic exchange between women, Austen invites a more apparently voyeuristic response in order to use it, as Lafayette does, against itself. In its reliance upon the culturally dominant fiction of public unanimity about private experience, Austen's omnisciently observed and plausible domesticity contains the germ of nineteenth-century high realism. Because she so successfully negotiates her feminine correspondences as a writer into the dominant (and "masculine") mode of the succeeding century—a "masculine" mode precisely in that it claims gender universality—we as twentieth-century readers are still very much inhabiting Jane Austen's drawing room (so modern, so habitable!). It is our inheritance as readers of novels, and that is why the works that allow us to inhabit it so comfortably appear to us the most real, the most valuable, and the most faultless.

Reference Matter

Notes

Chapter 1

1. This phrase comes from Sophia Lee's *The Recess*, where it refers to the literal passageways that connect apparently isolated enclosures.

2. In this method I am following Nina Baym, who wrote of the nineteenth-century American genre she identifies as "woman's fiction": "I would like at least to begin to correct such a bias [regarding their literary value] by taking their content seriously" (pp. 14–15).

3. See Jehlen, p. 73: "We need to acknowledge, also, that to respect [the] integrity [of the literary subject] by not asking questions of the text that it does not ask itself, to ask the text what questions to ask, will produce the fullest, richest reading. To do justice to Shelley, you do not approach him as you do Swift." Yet Jehlen goes on to pass judgment on the novels of nineteenth-century American "scribbling women" as simply "awful" (p. 81). But perhaps the "awful" is precisely what these texts demand that we read, a fault that must be approached differently in them than in Richardson or Rousseau.

4. I use the word *feminine* here to describe a subject position that is culturally defined as feminine-gendered, and not to designate either biological sex or a self-conscious position of active or unambiguous protest against the dominant patriarchal social order.

5. This "subgenre," which I have briefly described elsewhere ("The Value of a Literary Legacy"), is completely exclusive neither to France and England nor strictly, perhaps, to writers who were biologically female. I concentrate on England and France in this book because the relations of gender boundaries to national boundaries are among the central issues being worked out in the subgenre; the German examples tend to be derivations that complicate those relations in ways specific to a tradition not centered in a nation-state. A discussion of them would be beyond the scope of this work, but I have begun to do so in "Of Haunted Highlands." On eighteenth-century epistolary fiction by women in Germany, see Meise. Men obviously wrote epistolary novels, and a few even concentrated on women's correspondence—I think of *Clarissa* and *La Vie de Marianne* in particular. Because they are more recognized within their respective national traditions, they may even appear to inaugurate the subgenre, although Eliza Haywood and others precede them in innovating its central conventions (see Day, Richetti, and Backscheider). The prevalence of men's attempts to write with a feminine persona, including the use of female pseudonyms and of an anonymity that is in this context also marked as feminine, while fascinating, does not in itself concern me here, except insofar as it indicates the association of this fiction by mid-century with a feminine subject position. Janet Todd describes how the prevailing assumption that novelists, novel readers, and novels themselves were "feminine" provoked anxiety over the possibility of authorial gender masquerade (*Angellica*, pp. 125–28, 138). For a compelling discussion of eighteenth-century English male authors' uses of feminine masquerade, see Kahn. But the use of male pseudonyms by women was extremely rare until the nineteenth century (cf. Ezell, *Literary History*, p. 36).

6. I owe this characterization of the dominant critical view to Paula Backscheider. As this book was going to press, I had the privilege of reading in draft some of Michael McKeon's work on Burney and Smollett, as well as Sterne, in which he offers a compelling analysis of what their "anomalous purposes" may be. He describes their replacement of diachronic patrilineal inheritance with synchronic communities that are formed outside relations of kinship, in terms uncannily similar, at times, to those I use. If his paper, "Replacing Patrilineage: Thoughts on the Novel After Its Origins," had appeared in print by the time of this writing, I would have thought it appro-

priate to take up McKeon's discussion in more detail. I can say at least that I think that the writers I interpret here are generally resisting the historical trend McKeon describes.

7. On the relation of entailed patrimony to indebtedness, see J. P. Cooper, p. 304, and E. P. Thompson, pp. 346–48, in Goody, Thirsk, and Thompson, eds., *Family and Inheritance.*

8. Some of the formal and thematic patterns described here appear also in the exploration of the position of women in patrilineage in many other eighteenth-century novels written by women that do not fit strictly within the formal limitations I am describing here; see Margaret Anne Doody's introduction to *The Female Quixote* and Janet Todd, "Jane Austen," pp. 76–77. Half of the subsequent chapters are devoted to novels that do fit these limitations, and half to novels that do not (Lafayette, Staël, Austen). Other relatively well-known examples include Frances Burney's *Evelina*, Charlotte Lennox's *The Female Quixote*, Elizabeth Inchbald's *A Simple Story*, and Mary Wollstonecraft's *Maria; or, The Wrongs of Woman*. See also Carolyn Woodward: "[Sarah] Fielding's critique of the oppressive world of *David Simple* centers in the system of patrilineal inheritance" (p. 68). Yet of these only *Evelina* comes close to following the formal pattern of the subgenre, and it, as Spacks observes, is "different from the others [eighteenth-century epistolary novels by women] in virtually all respects" ("Female Resources," p. 97). I think actually that all of its differences can be accounted for in its main formal difference, which is also profoundly a thematic difference: Evelina (like Burney herself, and like Evelina's dead mother) addresses her epistolary narrative to a *father* figure. For astute interpretations of the relationship between *Evelina*'s invocations of fathers and its maternal inheritances, see Susan Greenfield, "Female Authorship," and Margaret Anne Doody, *Frances Burney*, pp. 32–33.

9. I have chosen the word *subgenre* to refer to the set of correspondences that characterize the texts I am discussing as a coherent group because it is a set simultaneously within and excluded from a multiplicity of genres and modes: the novel, the novella, romance, history, the letter, the Gothic, historiography, the literature of sensibility, the *portrait moral*, the lyric; even, in some instances, the cookbook and the medical compendium. On gender and the transgression of genre, see also Langbauer; Kauffman, pp. 17–27; Derrida, "La Loi du genre," and Kamuf, "Writing like a Woman," pp. 284–99 (both cited by Kauffman as well).

10. See Chapter 2, n. 12.

11. See also Claudia Johnson: "Fielding's efforts to elevate his own fiction by affiliating it with the classical tradition bespeak his nagging doubts about

its status" (p. 28). Janet Todd also comments on the polarization of the novel along gendered lines, so typical of the mid eighteenth century, that was organized around the debate between Richardson and Fielding (*Angelica*, p. 141). Although there are Hellenistic precursors for the novel, even in ancient times it was a low, bastard genre, as in the eighteenth century. On the literary status of the Greek novel, see Reardon.

12. For further discussion of this point, see Alliston, "Value of a Literary Legacy," pp. 109–12.

13. The construction of the state as *patria* or "fatherland" already defines women's position in relation to it as one of exile at the origin of the concept in classical times: "The fatherland is, of course, the land of the fathers. From Hesiod on, most [Greek] authors used the expression 'the female race' (*genos gunaikon*) to speak of women; on one side the Athenian people (*demos*) made up of the men of its tribes; on the other, a race from nowhere, which is solely a sex. And since in Athens citizenship derives from being a native, the equation between femininity and uprooting had to be proposed. Women do not and cannot have a fatherland; and so that everyone will know it myths of origin are there to justify it irrefutably" (Monique Saliou, in Coontz and Henderson, eds., pp. 193–94). Saliou cites Nicole Loraux, *Les Enfants d'Athéna* (Paris, 1981).

14. I intentionally avoid the imaginary construction of a "mother country" of women's writing such as that nostalgically envisaged by Gilbert and Gubar in *The Madwoman in the Attic*, or similar "strategies that figure a utopian beyond" to the "masculine hegemony" of literary history, to borrow Judith Butler's words (p. 34).

15. See, for instance, DeJean, "Lafayette's Ellipses," p. 884; Jehlen, pp. 75–81; Nancy Miller, *Subject to Change*, pp. 4–5; Schor, "La Pérodie," p. 85.

16. See Brooks, *Reading for the Plot*, pp. 11–12.

17. Cf. DeJean: "In France . . . the female tradition has a history incomprehensible through reference to either that of the novel or that of English women's writing—and this despite the fact that French women writers were no more likely than their English counterparts to explore forms other than the novel." She further dismisses French women's writing of the later eighteenth century as "less forceful" than either seventeenth-century French or contemporary Englishwomen's fiction, in order to emphasize the difference between the two national traditions (*Tender Geographies*, pp. 6–8).

18. What Mary Jacobus says about the exchanges that can be read between passages from Wollstonecraft and Irigaray is pertinent to the way women's correspondence works within and among the texts of the subgenre described above, with which Wollstonecraft's *Maria* is itself in uneasy correspondence (Jacobus, pp. 280–81).

19. As Jacobus acknowledges: "Yet the existence of these chain letters is what makes it possible for the feminist reader to create (and read) her 'tradition.' She is its reading effect" (p. 291).

20. For related discussions of the interrelationship between female-authored texts as escaping models of specular resemblance, as well as of patriline versus matriline descent, see Irigaray, *Speculum de l'autre femme*; de Lauretis on the contemporary Italian feminist concept of *affidamento*, in *Différence: Feminist Theory in Italy, the United States, and Great Britain* and in her introduction to her translation of *Italian Feminist Writers*; DeJean on "the female web of literature" in "Staël's Corinne"; and Kamuf, "Writing Like a Woman."

21. See Tania Modleski quoting and commenting on Annette Kolodny's now classic argument: "Such a [feminist theoretical] pluralism would be 'responsive to the possibilities of multiple critical schools and methods, but captive to none'—a salutary objective at a time when much feminism seems indeed to be captive of various methods generated by male theorists" (p. 122). See also Kauffman on the authors of *The Three Marias: New Portuguese Letters*: "They also write without the exclusive endorsement of any one language system (Marxism, feminism, psychoanalysis)" (*Discourses of Desire*, p. 287).

22. In this book I quote one novel published anonymously, *Adele et Sophie*, and devote a chapter to one about whose author months of research have yielded no biographical information (Mme de Boisgiron). This opens the possibility of male authorship; as argued in n.4 above, however, what is significant for me is rather the act of writing in the feminine. See Kamuf, "Writing Like a Woman," and Kahn, *Narrative Transvestism*.

23. See Backer; MacArthur (pp. 43–44); Mavor; Perry; Stewart (p. 6).

24. By the Sieur Du Plaisir in "Sentiments sur l'histoire" and by Delariviere Manley, *The History of Queen Zarah* (preface), as well as, in the later eighteenth century, by Clara Reeve in *The Progress of Romance*, to name only a few. See also Ballaster's discussion.

25. See Jackson on gender, sensibility and epistolarity in women's lyric poetry of the nineteenth century.

26. See n.8 above.

27. Brooks, *Novel of Worldliness*, p. 48.

28. See Gallop, *Daughter's Seduction*; Irigaray, *Speculum*; Jacobus, *Reading Woman*; and Nancy Miller, "Performances of the Gaze," in *Subject to Change*.

29. On the specularity of sympathy, see Marshall, *Surprising Effects*.

30. Freud, *Dora*, p. 28.

31. A notable exception is Joan Hinde Stewart's recent study of French

novels by women of the later eighteenth century. The majority of the novels she has chosen to discuss are quite different in form and theme from those mentioned here, however, although she notes that many of her selected authors also wrote "historical novels and epistolary novels of sentiment" (p. 200).

32. A few examples of epistolary novels by women, translated by women who also wrote original epistolary novels: Mrs Cartwright's *The Platonic Marriage, a novel in a series of letters* (1786–87), translated by Cornélie Petroneille Bénédicte Wouters, baronne de Vasse (author of *Les Aveux d'une femme galante, ou Lettres de la marquise de *** à milady Fanny Stapelton* [1789]); Georgiana Cavendish's *The Sylph*, translated by Isabelle de Montolieu (author of *Caroline de Lichtfield*); Marie-Jeanne Riccoboni's *Lettres de Milady Juliette Catesby à Milady Henriette Campley, son amie* (1759), translated by Frances Brooke (author of *The History of Lady Julia Mandeville* [1763]). Other women who were both writers and translators of epistolary fiction, or writers of it who spent considerable periods in exile in France, include Frances Burney, Jane Barker, Eliza Haywood, and Mary Collyer. Stewart informs us that Riccoboni, having lived in England, "embodied and fostered the anglomania characteristic of the early part of the second half of the century" (p. 199). In fact a certain obsession with England continues to characterize later novels Stewart discusses, such as Souza's *Adèle de Sénange* (1794; see p. 152), as it certainly does *Corinne*. Le Prince de Beaumont also spent fourteen years there in mid-century (p. 25), while Montolieu corresponded with major figures of the English literary scene (p. 137), as did Staël.

On the importance of the French tradition to English epistolary fiction in particular, see Altman, p. 10; Day, pp. 27–47; and Kany.

33. For the harshness of the laws on religion, there was of course in France the revocation of the Edict of Nantes (1685), the importance of which for early French women's writing is noted by DeJean (*Tender Geographies*, p. 12). The severity of the English laws against "popery" was hardly less (see Blackstone, 1: §451–§452 (pp. 424–25), although persecution of Catholics in eighteenth-century England was in practice certainly less than that of Protestants in France at the same time. Nevertheless, the proposed weakening of some of the penalties imposed on Catholics provoked the Gordon Riots of 1780 in London. See Ellis, p. 207.

Two novels that deal overtly with the issue of religious intolerance are: Elizabeth Griffith, *The Delicate Distress* (1769), and Marie Gacon-Dufour, *Le Préjugé vaincu, ou Lettres de madame la comtesse de *** et de madame de *** refugiee en Angleterre* (1787). Most, however, simply treat foreign settings and religion sympathetically and without reference to any intolerance, except for an occasional remark about the evils of prejudice. The use of images of exile and the idea of the "fatherland" (*patrie*) is discussed in detail in subsequent chapters.

34. I cannot escape the conclusion, from the specificity of their textual allusions, that Lee, Staël, and Austen all read *La Princesse de Clèves*, or that Austen also read Lee and Staël, and vice versa. Beyond that, however, and the evidence of the translations (n.32 above), I do not care to venture, as it would only divert attention from the type of correspondence I wish to emphasize.

35. Including Germany as well, although a treatment of that literature is beyond the scope of this book. See Meise.

36. Cf. DeJean, "Lafayette's Ellipses," p. 884: "In France, women's writing acquired a history and a tradition long before it did in England." Although this statement forms part of an argument whose implications run counter to my own about women writers' relation to national tradition, it nevertheless offers an insight into why the first Englishwomen to become professional writers placed themselves in a cross-national correspondence with Frenchwomen more particularly than with the male writers of their own national tradition.

37. See Day, pp. 27–47, and Ballaster, pp. 191–92.

38. "On the Most Charming Galecia's Picture," in *Poetical Recreations*, part 2: p. 36 (1688), cited in McBurney, "Edmund Curll, Mrs Jane Barker, and the English Novel," p. 389.

39. Janet Todd's comprehensive *Women's Friendship in Literature* neglects the influence of these early Frenchwomen on both English and French traditions of literary female friendships. This is a strange oversight, considering that Todd otherwise has much to say about the French. In her later *Sign of Angellica*, however, she acknowledges the influence of the French seventeenth-century letter writers and of Katherine Philips on the Bluestockings and other literary women of the English mid eighteenth century (pp. 136–38). *Women's Friendship in Literature* is a comparative study of the "borderlines" traced by both English and French, men's and women's, writing, and thus a study of the kind Jehlen calls for, but Todd tends to give short shrift in her account to the importance of women writers by beginning the history of female friendship in literature with *Clarissa*. Some of Eliza Haywood's works in particular *precede* those of Richardson, Cleland, and Diderot of which hers are said to be derivative (see p. 308, e.g.).

40. Mongrédien, p. 16.

41. *Letters from Mrs E. Carter to Mrs Montagu* (1817), 4: 33, cited in Ma-

vor, p. 82. On the similarities between the language of women's (actual) correspondences in seventeenth-century France and mid-eighteenth century England, see also Janet Todd, *Sign of Angellica*, p. 137. For an in-depth discussion of the language of the précieuses, see Domna Stanton.

42. Backer, p. 35: "It was already possible [in the reign of Henri IV, c. 1600] and not uncommon for a rich entrepreneur to buy a pedigree. But no one quite believed this was happening."

43. This coincides precisely with the "crisis of 'status inconsistency'" that Michael McKeon identifies in *The Origins of the English Novel* as the condition for the rise of the English novel, the need for a new conception of virtue and its transmission, and for a new type of narrative to convey it, to evidence and authorize its truth. Although the "problem of persistence" of aristocratic and romance values may have been greater in France than in England, the "crisis of 'status inconsistency'" clearly existed, even in France, by the beginning of the seventeenth century.

44. Backer, pp. 188, 237–56; Mongrédien, pp. 16–18; Mitford, introduction to her translation of *La Princesse de Clèves*, pp. 7, 11, 14.

45. See also DeJean, *Tender Geographies*, pp. 6–10.

46. On the English situation, Sulloway quotes Mary Astell (p. 55); this is also discussed by Perry.

47. "Dès que la *préciosité* se répandit dans le milieu bourgeois, on conçoit aisément que toutes ces mal mariées aient confronté leurs malheurs, leurs déceptions, se soient échauffées à les évoquer en commun et aient fini par mêner une véritable croisade contre le mariage, qui n'était pour elles qu'un asservissement perpétuel" (Mongrédien, pp. 16–17). On the increased "crassly acquisitive nature of marriage" associated with the rise of the bourgeoisie in England as well, see Perry, p. 55.

48. DeJean, *Tender Geographies*, p. 10; Schiebinger, p. 218.

49. See also Sylvia Myers (pp. 93, 11, 120) and Janet Todd (*Sign of Angellica*, pp. 123–24) on the English bluestockings' attitudes towards marriage, as well as Sulloway: "The moderate [feminists] thought no more highly of marriage than their radical predecessors" (p. 70).

50. Cited in DeJean, "Lafayette's Ellipses," p. 899.

51. Riccoboni, *Histoire de Miss Jenny Revel, écrite et envoyée par elle à Milady comtesse de Roscommond* (Paris, 1764); *Emma; or, The Child of Sorrow* (Dublin, 1776).

52. Faith Beasley quotes Montpensier and other members of *précieuse* culture condemning marriage "as a form of slavery" (pp. 50–51).

53. Mavor, p. 80.

54. Hester Thrale, *Thraliana: The Diary of Mrs Hester Lynch Thrale, 1776–1809*, ed. Balderston (1951), quoted in Mavor, p. 78.

55. See also Backer's discussion of Scudéry's persona as "Sapho."

56. See Hampton and Lyons; also Armstrong, pp. 61–63, and Faith Beasley, who refers to the "pedagogical function" of seventeenth-century history in offering beneficial models (pp. 12, 18–19, 22).

57. See Armstrong, p. 61, and Hampton, e.g., p. 15.

58. On the relation of example to the figure of the portrait, see Hampton, pp. 21, 26–27; and Lyons, p. 10; on the importance of the figure of portraiture in seventeenth-century epistemology, see Foucault and Marin; also Meltzer, pp. 176–78.

59. Foucault, pp. 63–71.

60. See Meltzer's discussion of *La Princesse de Clèves*, where she cites Marin extensively (pp. 177–78).

61. See Backer; also Meltzer, p. 179.

62. Faith Beasley emphasizes the "reversal of [gender] roles" in the salons as one in which women, in the words of the abbé de Pure, "exercise a glorious and spiritual influence" over men by judging their literary works (p. 48).

63. DeJean argues that the writings of Lafayette and Scudéry were perceived by contemporaries as constituting a threat to "manly, virile virtue" (*Tender Geographies*, p. 14), while Faith Beasley claims that the *précieuses* not only invented the literary portrait but elevated it as a serious historical genre and related it in that respect to painted portraits (pp. 48–50).

64. Steiner describes a similar device in the Albertian Renaissance model of painting, which she associates with literary romance: "The viewer creates a meaning by interpreting the painting. The painting does so by modeling an ideal observer. . . . The Renaissance model suggests an educative role for the painting and a training in response for viewers, who should come to match the response or responses they witness" (p. 44). Thus the link to pictorial structures of interpretive framing is another element that eighteenth-century women's novels derive from their romance inheritance, which passed to them via the précieuses.

Chapter 2

1. Mme de Clèves's control of her daughter through exemplary education is discussed by Hirsch ("Mother's Discourse"), Kamuf (*Fictions of Feminine Desire*, pp. 67–96), Lyons (pp. 222–27, 236), Meltzer (pp. 182–89), and Stone.

2. Page references to *La Princesse de Clèves* in the text of this chapter are to Adam's French edition, unless specified otherwise. Where possible, however, I quote Cobb's English translation. References following quotations list the reference to the translation as "Cobb," followed by the reference to the French text as "Adam."

3. In later works—Richardson's, for example—an education in virtue would actually make the daughter more marriageable. See also Armstrong.

4. I quote Faith Beasley, p. 199.

5. See also Meltzer, p. 181.

6. On this function of dowry in archaic and classical Greece, see Coontz and Henderson, eds., pp. 184 and 187. On a similar function of dowry for both daughters and younger sons (*enfants dotés*) in France, see Goody, Thirsk, and Thompson, eds., *Family and Inheritance*.

7. In her brilliant reading of Mlle de Chartres's meeting with the prince de Clèves in the jeweler's shop, where she is trying to match some stones, Kamuf equates the inherited jewels with the princess's name, which must be matched with another name equally illustrious; this missing name sought for as a match is described by Kamuf as "something left out of the mother's will" (*Fictions of Feminine Desire*, pp. 72–73). "That part" of her inheritance, within the convention and custom of the period, would in fact have materially constituted the entirety of her maternal inheritance. Like Kamuf, Meltzer identifies the princess's family name with her maternal inheritance. She locates that inheritance, not in the material legacy of the jewels, but in the virtue the princess receives through her mother's education (pp. 181–82). I agree that virtue is the princess's maternal inheritance, which converges in structure and function with both the portrait and the incomplete set of jewels, precisely because the name is *not* part of the maternal inheritance.

8. Hampton (pp. 25–27) describes how, in Renaissance literature, the classical exemplar's name comes to encode the exemplary narrative of the hero's completed life, and likens the name to both portrait and body, from which the narrative is unpacked. Meltzer also equates the figure of the portrait with the name (she is speaking of the princess's maiden name), and maintains that neither can be distinguished (i.e., exemplary) without virtue: "The glory of a name must indeed be upheld by virtue—this is the lesson Mme de Chartres repeats over and over again to her young daughter" (pp. 181–82). Specifically, "the name maintains the hierarchy on the one hand, and is something to be 'lived up to' by its bearer on the other"; "the portrait then becomes the idealization, the fiction, of the embodiment of the name" (p. 187).

9. Both Meltzer (p. 183) and Stone (p. 254) mention this detail of the retouched portrait, and read it similarly.

10. See also Meltzer: "In a court entirely composed of nobility, it is virtue that will distinguish one 'glorious' personage from the others" (pp. 181–82).

11. For other discussions of the difficulties of locating the princess's desire, see Hirsch, "A Mother's Discourse," pp. 71–73; Kamuf, *Fictions of Feminine Desire*, pp. 74–76; and Stone (pp. 249–51). The difficulty of speaking about the princess's desire—or not—appears when the same writers who question the possibility of her desire seem in other places to identify it as if it were rather unproblematic (e.g., Kamuf, pp. 95–96; Stone, p. 255). DeJean ("Lafayette's Ellipses") and Miller (*Subject to Change*) describe the heroine as a full, desiring subject. I read the princess as maneuvering her maternal inheritance, *eventually*, into the location of her own desire.

12. Resemblance between father and son has long been the locus of both the legitimacy of patrilineality and anxiety over its illegitimacy, as expressed in the earliest Western literature: Telemachus is repeatedly told in *The Odyssey* that he looks and speaks just like Odysseus; but when he is asked directly whether that hero is indeed his father, he tellingly replies, "I'll try, my friend, to give you a frank answer. / Mother has always told me I'm his son, it's true; / But I am not so certain. Who, on his own, / Has ever known who gave him life?" (Homer, *The Odyssey*, trans. Robert Fagles [New York: Viking Penguin, forthcoming]).

13. Kamuf argues that Nemours, rather than Clèves, is the true "match" the princess seeks, on the basis of his being described in the same terms of *éclat* as is the princess herself. The name of Clèves, however, with which the princess is quickly "matched," is on the other hand clearly the "destination" left out, but plotted for her by her mother's will (*Fictions of Feminine Desire*, p. 86).

14. Littré, s.v. *cliver*.

15. See also Kamuf on the precipice, *Fictions of Feminine Desire*, pp. 83–84.

16. That the princess continues to see her husband in the role of an educator is shown when, during a later section of the novel, she repeatedly begs him, "conduisez-moi" ("guide me"; Adam, p. 112). Hirsch ("A Mother's Discourse," pp. 78–79), Kamuf (*Fictions of Feminine Desire*, p. 81), Lyons (p. 227), and Stone (p. 249) also see the prince as supplementing and replacing Mme de Chartres as educator in his relation to his wife.

17. Littré: "*Providentia* a donné, dans l'ancienne langue, *pourveance* ou *prouveance*, avec les sens de providence, prévoyance et provision" (s.v. *providence*). Thomas Pavel argues that the literature of French classicism

generally evinces a loss of the divine Providence that previously guided the heroes and heroines of romance. For Pavel the absence of this benevolent ordering force in society explains the retreat of many protagonists of the period, including the princess of Clèves, into private spaces clearly separated from the public world of dissimulation ("La Fin du romanesque" [unpublished MS]).

18. Hampton discusses the importance of this Aristotelian notion in the Renaissance (pp. 23–26).

19. Faith Beasley also notes that Mary Stuart's recounting of history "complements the maternal discourse," as warning both against marriage and "the danger of founding one's power on passion" (p. 220).

20. Traditionally, the "digressions" or "intercalated stories" are those of Diane de Poitiers, Anne Boleyn, and Mme de Tournon, plus the vidame de Chartres's story about the queen (see Stone, p. 251). Lyons adds a fifth to that list: the story of Marie de Lorraine, the dauphine's mother (pp. 217–18). Mme de Tournon stands out in this group as being a purely fictional character, and is discussed separately. But the series pullulates with extratextual repetitions evoked by allusion: Mary Stuart, Elizabeth I—even, perhaps, Mme de Chartres, whose own portrait may be glimpsed in the story she tells about the woman who "fell" but was so discreet she deserves to remain anonymous (Adam, p. 59). The vidame's story supplements the series by portraying a woman high enough in rank to ruin the vidame but prevented by her sex from using the power of her rank to realize her own desire.

21. For an analysis of *alieni juris* in Roman law and its meaning for the position of women, see Chevillard and Leconte, "Slavery and Women," in Coontz and Henderson, eds., p. 166.

22. "After this predicted misfortune recounted by the king, those who had supported the science of astrology abandoned their former position, agreeing that he ought not give any credence at all to this fantastic story" (Cobb, p. 59).

23. The queen can be seen as occupying the ultimate position in the novel's hierarchy of mother figures, just as the king is its ultimate father (its patriarch). For the queen, then—to elaborate further on Kamuf's reading—the stakes in the game of legitimacy, the object of which is to establish the truth of female virtue and to expose its mere simulacra, are the highest, as she occupies the highest maternal position by virtue of being wedded to the ultimate father.

24. The princess makes a similar move of displacing fault again when each spouse believes the other has spread the story of her aveu: "N'ayez

point la dureté de m'accuser d'une *faute* que vous avez faite" (Adam, p. 136; emphasis mine). "Don't be so hardhearted as to accuse me of something which you yourself did" (Cobb, p. 114).

25. See Hirsch, "Mother's Discourse," pp. 77–82, and Kamuf, *Fictions of Feminine Desire*, pp. 83–84.

26. Stone (p. 253) says that the fiction of Nemours as addressee of the letter teaches the princess "the truth of her own jealousy." Since the princess is already aware of her own jealousy before this point, as, for example, when she fears that Nemours will accept Queen Elizabeth's offer of marriage, I would differ by claiming that what the fiction teaches her is rather the truth of Nemours's power to frame narratives, his superior status, by virtue of his masculinity, as one of what Stone calls "the agents of the story, the inventors of narrative" (p. 252). The heroine's only defense against his narrative agency and the truth it invents is to arrogate to herself the only power greater than masculine agency: the power to determine *interpretation*, to read or *uncover* plots—a position, in the princess's world, superior to that of the plotters, as the examples of Henry VIII and the queen both show.

27. Cf. Stone, pp. 252–53 (see previous note), and Lyons, who argues that the disjunction between the examples the princess encounters and the framing maternal precept "undermines . . . the reader's confidence in the heroine's ability to learn from the narratives of others" (p. 221).

28. Lyons, pp. 225–27; Stone, p. 252.

29. Cf. Joan DeJean, who first read the princess's aveu in terms of feudal relations. She argues that the aveu should not be understood as a "confession" in the later legal sense of an admission of guilt, but rather as a vassal's pledge of fidelity to the feudal lord, in exchange for feudal authority and a heritable estate. It is thus an entry into a "male script" in order to bid for "a male prerogative: to rule as lord over an estate." This bid fails, according to DeJean, because the prince tries to turn her aveu into the new kind of confession by insisting that she confess the name of her lover ("Lafayette's Ellipses," pp. 896–97). I read her "bid" as much more modest in terms of the material bases of social power, but both more ambitious and more successful as representation.

30. The wife's absorption into the husband's legal identity is called *coverture*. In English law, the Norman terms, *baron* and *feme*, as well as the feudal relation of lord to vassal they designated, persisted well beyond the demise of actual feudal class relations. A husband's murder of his wife was thus a lesser crime than a wife's of her husband, because the latter was defined as a "class crime" of vassal against lord, hence a form of treason

deserving extreme suffering and humiliation in the execution of justice (Blackstone, 1: §433–§459). The pre-Napoleonic French law from which the English derives defines the marital relation similarly, so that the term *baron* designates not only the lord of a walled city, but also "le mari, chef de la communauté conjugale" (Lepointe, pp. 38–39). See also Coontz and Henderson, eds., p. 146.

31. This is referred to as "legal incapacity." Cf., e.g., Chevillard and Lecomte, "The Dawn of Lineage Societies: The Origins of Women's Oppression," in Coontz and Henderson, eds., p. 82.

32. "Quelque dangereux que soit le parti que je prends, je le prends avec joie pour me conserver digne *d'être à vous*" (Adam, p. 122; emphasis mine). Cobb translates Lafayette's "worthy to belong to you" with the more ambiguous "worthy of you": "However dangerous is the decision I am now making, I make it with joy that I might prove myself worthy of you" (p. 98).

33. Littré, s.v. *aveu*.

34. See Nancy Miller quoting and commenting on Genette (*Subject to Change*, p. 26).

35. See n.12.

36. I am not the first to make a connection between the two kinds of fidelity in this novel. For a different analysis of that connection, see Stone, p. 252.

37. Miller, *Subject to Change*, p. 26.

38. On the paradox of exemplarity, see Lyons, pp. 32–33.

39. Hampton, pp. 19–28.

40. I quote DeJean, "Lafayette's Ellipses," p. 897.

41. Cf. DeJean on the heroine's efforts to control the circulation of her story by falling back on the convention of verisimilitude ("Lafayette's Ellipses," pp. 897–88).

42. Lyons discusses the etymology of *exemplum*, pp. 3, 18.

43. Cobb translates: "What road did he discover to find your love?" (p. 98).

44. Cobb translates: "She asked herself why? Why had she done such a foolhardy thing? And she discovered that she had done it without really intending to" (p. 101).

45. See also DeJean, "Lafayette's Ellipses," where she translates *s'engager* as "to pledge" in her discussion of the aveu as a feudal bond (p. 897).

46. Cobb translates: "But when she thought that this acknowledgment offered her the only means of protecting herself against Monsieur de Nemours, she was not sorry for the risk she had taken" (p. 101).

47. The appearance of being guided by chance serves the identical func-

tion to that of Providence in later novels about female desire: both serve as a disguise for the paths deliberately cut ("faites avec soin") by desire, and leading always to the heart's own destination. Providence as a mask for female desire is discussed further in the chapter on Sophia Lee's *The Recess*, which in many respects rewrites *La Princesse de Clèves*.

48. The construction by both heroine and author of an anonymous "signature" that will allow them a measure of control over their own narratives is the main subject of DeJean's discussion in "Lafayette's Ellipses."

49. See Sahlins on the permeability of the geographical boundaries of the French state in the same period.

50. The establishment of the princess's claim is signified, however, by the construction of some physical defenses, making access to the pavilion much more difficult for Nemours on his second attempt to enter it. Not only does the new fence slow him down, but the French windows of the pavilion itself are not as effortlessly penetrable as they were the first time. The fence is made up of a double row of stakes bound together (according the definition of *palissades* in Littré), with enough space between for him to get through with a little determination. But when he gets caught in the window frame, it is as if the opening itself, at once window to look through and door to enter through ("fenêtres qui servaient de portes"), were the real obstacle, even more than the wall within which it is set (Adam, p. 154).

51. Faith Beasley, pp. 240–41. Cf. Butor, pp. 76–77; Miller, *Subject to Change*, pp. 37–38; and Schor, "Portrait of a Gentleman," pp. 118–19.

52. Cf. Faith Beasley, p. 241: "Public history serves to create particular history, as the princess transforms her historical props with a vision that comes from female models."

53. "L'empereur Charles Quint avait vu finir sa bonne fortune devant la ville de Metz, qu'il avait assiégée inutilement avec toutes les forces de l'Empire et de l'Espagne" (Adam, p. 39). Cobb inverts the relation of viewer to viewed here: "He saw the tide change against Charles Quint outside the town of Metz which this king was vainly besieging with all the forces of the empire and of Spain" (p. 6).

54. Faith Beasley notes that these paintings are in the possession of the fictional Diane, but never graced the home of the historical one (p. 241).

55. Mme de Valentinois's paintings imitate in turn the series of tapestries ordered by Louis XIV, which Faith Beasley describes as a "pictorial history" that "immortalizes a succession of military victories" and other notable events of his reign (p. 10).

56. Thus the princess does not "internalize her mother's historical discourse and take Diane de Poitiers as a model for her own heroic actions"

(Faith Beasley, p. 219). It is not the "figure" or life of Diane de Poitiers as presented by Mme de Chartres that "indirectly provides the fictional princess with an example of a woman's self-determination" (ibid., p. 215). As example, Diane's *vie* is as inimitable in its own way as the princess's will become, because her enjoyment of the king's favor is as unique in its longevity as it is standard in its precarious dependency and inevitable fall. It is only as historian, in the register of purely representational acts, that Diane provides a model for the princess's actions.

57. Cf. Faith Beasley, who emphasizes the influence exercised by women in Lafayette's representation of the French court, noting that while women were "occasionally dependent upon male authority in Lafayette's history, they nonetheless dominate men." She claims further that this dominant position was "passed on from one woman to another—from the duchesse d'Estampes to Diane de Poitiers to Catherine de Médicis," and that women "pull the strings guiding history" (p. 218). The first statement is an exaggeration, given the force of the examples Marie Stuart relates to the princess; the second disregards the fact that the transmission of power "from one woman to another" was anything but willed by them; and the third is true only of the women acting as historians, not as historical actors.

58. Miller, *Subject to Change*, p. 29.

59. Faith Beasley characterizes "public history" in Lafayette's time as a "static" narrative that emphasizes "acts of sovereignty," citing Louis XIV's tapestries as an example (pp. 10–13). My reading of Lafayette coincides with Beasley's historical speculation: "Perhaps the political activism embodied by the *frondeuses* and expressed in the social and intellectual discussions of the salons inspired and was ultimately replaced by another form of expression, primarily a literary one" (p. 52).

60. See Coontz and Henderson, eds., pp. 145–54.

61. As Madeleine Bertaud has observed, the marks of public history—such as the painting of the siege of Metz—disappear from the narrative as the princess progressively retires into her private world (lecture at Princeton University, 1993).

62. This reading concurs with the views of Madeleine Bertaud, André Aciman, and Thomas Pavel that *La Princesse de Clèves* is a fundamentally pessimistic work, in contrast to the longer *romans* of Scudéry and Urfé (Bertaud, lecture at Princeton University, 1993; Pavel, *L'Art de l'éloignement*; Aciman, unpublished discussion).

63. In this construction of the relation between hero and audience, the idea of literary tradition comes together with that of patriline descent in the founding myth of both. On the connections between ancestor worship and

the dominance of patrilineal, patrilocal societies, see Coontz and Henderson, eds., pp. 127–29.

64. See DeJean, "Lafayette's Ellipses," pp. 888–91; Miller, *Subject to Change*, pp. 25–26, Genette, quoted in Miller.

65. "Resuscitating the mother is at once the subversion of patriarchy and its reinscription. . . . The liberating promise of the maternal fiction soon becomes as tyrannical and oppressive as the patriarchal regime it had tried to subvert," Maryline Lukacher similarly concludes in her book on modern French literature (p. 15).

66. See also Lyons, pp. 235–36.

Chapter 3

1. "Eh bien, me dit-elle, puisque vous vous intéressez à moi, je vous donnerai quelques lignes que j'avais écrites, non pour raconter ma vie, car, selon moi, l'histoire de toutes les femmes se ressemble, mais pour me rendre compte des motifs qui m'ont déterminée au parti que j'ai pris: cela n'est pas achevé, parce qu'on ne finit jamais ce qu'on écrit pour soi; mais il y en a assez pour satisfaire votre curiosité et pour vous prouver ma confiance" (Staël-Holstein, *Delphine*, 2: 209; my translation).

2. See also Chapter 1, n. 16.

3. For discussions of the concept of sympathy in eighteenth-century philosophy and fiction, see Barker-Benfield; Markley; Marshall, *Surprising Effects*; Mücke; Mullan; Janet Todd, *Sensibility*; and Sedgwick, who, referring to Mullan, emphasizes that "the emphatic allo-identifications that were supposed to guarantee the sociable nature of sensibility could not finally be distinguished from an epistemological solipsism" ("Jane Austen," p. 820). Markley and Marshall also argue that the sympathetic identification of self with other ultimately placed the emphasis on the self and its distance from the other.

4. See too, e.g., Jane Austen's *Emma*: "Mr Knightley did not make due allowance for the influence of a strong passion, at war with all interested motives" (*Complete Novels*, p. 802).

5. I take this phrase from the title of one of the very first epistolary novels, Delariviere Manley's *A Lady's Packet of Letters Broke Open* (London, 1707), because it succinctly expresses the preoccupation, present in the early novel generally and imaged in its frequent use of the epistolary form, with the making public of "private" writing. See also Goulemot, pp. 386–87.

6. As Patricia Meyer Spacks has written of women's fiction of this period: "Through the conventions of romance women tell themselves and each other the meaning of their fate" (*Imagining a Self*, p. 65).

7. Compare the American genre of "woman's fiction" identified by Nina Baym: "They thought of every woman as representative of all women" (p. xxxiii); as well as Rachel Brownstein's statement about heroines in eighteenth- and nineteenth-century English novels generally: "The main thing about the heroine is that hers is always the same old story" (p. 82).

8. Shorter summaries of the paradigmatic plot in women's fiction of the later eighteenth century have previously appeared in my "Value of a Literary Legacy" and in Janet Todd's "Jane Austen: Politics and Sensibility," p. 77.

9. See also Baym, p. x.

10. See also Tzvetan Todorov: "Un des premiers traits de la démarche scientifique est qu'elle n'exige pas l'observation de toutes les instances d'un phénomène pour le décrire; elle procède bien plutôt par déduction. . . . Quel que soit le nombre des phénomènes étudiés (ici, des oeuvres), nous serons toujours aussi pas autorisés à en déduire des lois universelles" (p. 8).

11. For the presence of such details as common names, real places, and a concern for the financial underpinnings of characters' lives as definitive of early realism's break with romance, see Richetti and English Showalter. Richetti's book itself tends to judge the value of eighteenth-century fiction by how far it has proceeded along an evolutionary path towards nineteenth-century realism, despite his own critique of Watt's "teleological bias."

12. Ballaster, Langbauer, and Spencer (*Rise*, p. 186) all identify "a relatively stable association of the romance with female readers and writers" (Ballaster, p. 189). Canonical male novelists like Richardson and Fielding were of course also rewriting romance in a realistic mode; it is not the combination of the two so much as the manner and use of that combination that tends to distinguish feminine from masculine conventions of novelistic realism in the period, with Richardson obviously placing himself within the "feminine" conventions. Armstrong and McKeon (*Origins*) have recently commented cogently on the struggle between Richardson and Fielding, but the question of women authors' placement and reception in relation to the masculine or the female-impersonating modes of realism in romance are not addressed there.

13. On the laws and customs regarding marriage and the transmission of property in England, see Blackstone, *Commentaries*, 1: §433–§459 (pp. 397–434); Goody, Thirsk, and Thompson, eds., *Family and Inheritance*; Perry; Spring; Staves. For France, see Cook (pp. 30–32); Lebrun (pp. 74–75); and Pocquet de Livonnière (pp. 38–39). The main difference between France and England in this area of law is the greater variety in French regional custom, but Lebrun comments that the custom of Paris dominated (most

similar to English law in its exclusions of women), and that although marriage contracts existed that could theoretically circumvent customary law, they tended to adapt legal custom, not to contradict it.

14. Lebrun quotes the sentiment of an aristocratic French suitor addressing the powerful father of his desired bride in 1694, saying that it was neither the duke's wealth that had drawn him to make proposals, nor even his daughter, whom he had never seen, but that it was the duke himself who had charmed him and whom he wished to marry. Lebrun's research indicates that this attitude was typical of the professional and bourgeois classes as well, and that even among the lower classes marriages were most often arranged by parents (pp. 23–25). The age of 17 was in reality about the average marriage age for women of the upper aristocracy or for great heiresses, while, according to Lebrun, the average age for the general French population was just over 25 (pp. 31–33). See also McKeon (*Origins*, pp. 156–57), who invokes Lévi-Strauss's account of the incest taboo and exogamous marriage as an "exchange of women aimed at the establishment of kinship relations between men," and notes that "in the English kinship system, one of the most important kinds of relation between men is the transmission of property by the direct descent of patrilineage." This being the case, it is clear that what Claudia Johnson argues for the 1790's was perhaps intensified then, but nothing new: "Female modesty . . . is no less than a matter of national security" (p. 14). Janet Todd also emphasizes the importance of Blackstone's *Commentaries*, published in mid-century, with its emphasis on "the empire of the father" and the ancient definition of the male heir as "the worthiest of the blood" (*Sign of Angellica*, p. 111).

15. In patrilineal, patrilocal societies, women are always "orphaned" in the sense that marriage for them means exile from their own families and communities. This situation is referred to by anthropologists as "alienation." See Chévillard and Leconte, "The Dawn of Lineage Societies," in Coontz and Henderson, eds., p. 81: "For a woman, marriage is akin to a disappearance"; also ibid., pp. 92–93. On references to the problem of alienation in Greek literature (the Homeric hymn to Demeter and Sappho's lyrics), see Foley.

16. These various fictional representations of the position of women in relation to the transmission of patrimony are sometimes extreme, but by no means altogether false, representations of the legal realities of the time, although these varied among regions and classes. As mentioned above, they and I are primarily concerned not with historical fact but with a culture's symbolic truths—these are by far the most persistent and therefore the most cogent for our own time.

17. Some examples of these paternal variations are Anne de Colleville, *Alexandrine de Ba***, ou Lettres de la princesse Albertine, contenant les aventures d'Alexandrine de Ba***, son aïeule, trad. de l'allemand* (Paris, 1786); Suzanne Bodin de Boismortier, *Une Correspondance épistolaire entre deux dames* (London and Paris, 1768); Mlle Poulain, *Lettres de Madame la comtesse de La Riviere à la baronne de Neufpont, son amie* (Paris, 1776); Marie-Jeanne Riccoboni, *Histoire de Miss Jenny Revel, écrite et envoyée par elle à Milady comtesse de Roscommond* (Paris, 1764). All the examples I have found of this kind of extreme aristocratic prejudice in husbands are French, which seems to be one of the few illustrations offered by this type of fiction of the differences in the course and degree of the "rise of the bourgeoisie" in the two countries before the French Revolution. In France, the legal right of fathers of great families to disinherit offspring who married contrary to their parents' wishes (which canon law permitted) had begun with an edict of Henri II in 1556 (Lebrun, pp. 13–14). However, Claudia Johnson (p. 7) also refers to the last variant listed here as a "characteristic plot" in Jane West's *Tale of the Times* (1799).

18. See also Hirsch's remarkably similar discussion in *The Mother/Daughter Plot* of novels written by women of the first half of the nineteenth century: "Because of the difficulty the maternal role [as formulated by Rich] poses for women in the Victorian period, multiple and surrogate mothers, like Jane Eyre's, are better able, at least in fictional representation, to help daughters" (p. 46). The several variant ways, important but less frequently occurring, in which a heroine can be a "motherless woman" are discussed fully in the next two chapters. Sometimes she is left instead in the clutches of an evil mother or stepmother who fails to educate her in any way except by giving her a negative example, as in the case of Lady Susan quoted in Chapter 1. Further texts containing examples of this motif are: *Adele et Sophie, ou Les Deux amies, par Mlle S**** (Paris, 1798); *The Rencontre: or, Transition of a Moment* (Dublin, 1784); Madame de Boisgiron, *Lettres de Mademoiselle de Boismiran, receuillies et publiées par Mme de **** (Paris and Amsterdam, 1777); "The Story of Miss Melvyn," in Sarah Scott's *A Description of Millenium Hall, and the Country Adjacent . . .* (London, 1762); Mme Levacher de la Feutrie, *Minna, ou Lettres de deux jeunes vénitiennes* (Paris, 1802); Susannah Minifie Gunning, *The Histories of Lady Frances S——— and Lady Caroline S———* (London, 1763).

In previously published work ("Value of a Literary Legacy"), I have referred to the recurrence of substitute mothers in women's fiction using the phrase "surrogate mother," as Hirsch has done (*Mother/Daughter Plot*, p. 46), but its use since to denote the recent practice of women hiring themselves to couples for the bearing of children has forced me to replace it with the more neutral term *substitute.*

19. Thus far, this paradigmatic plot bears a striking resemblance to the "overplot" described by Nina Baym for the "woman's fiction" written in America between 1820 and 1870: "It is the story of a young girl who is deprived of the supports she had rightly or wrongly depended on to sustain her throughout life and is faced with the necessity of winning her own way in the world" (pp. 11–12). The most significant transformation that "woman's fiction" wrought on the earlier fiction of women's correspondence is that the American heroines "overcome obstacles through a hard-won, much tested 'self-dependence,'" which replaces the function of feminine virtue as female inheritance (p. ix).

20. "J'ai pensé que le tableau d'une héroine, dont la vertu soutenue est mise à l'épreuve de tout, sans s'être jamais démentie, étoit toujours un bon exemple à représenter à des jeunes personnes. . . . C'est par la vertu seule que l'amour est pardonnable et intéressant; sans elle, il n'est que la plus vile et la plus méprisable des foiblesses" (Mme Beccary, *Mémoires de Lucie d'Olbéry, traduits de l'anglois* [Paris, 1770], Avis au lecteur). I have translated *jeunes personnes* as "young ladies" because in eighteenth-century usage that was generally the connotation; young men being more frequently *jeunes gens*. In this and subsequent chapters, where I am quoting from eighteenth-century editions because no modern edition exists, I have not modernized the spelling or punctuation in either French or English.

21. See also Backscheider on eighteenth-century fiction: "If the woman participating in courtship is not exactly guilty, she is, at least, on trial" (p. 282). The trial of virtue is an essential aspect of traditional romance plot, which, again, goes back at least to the earliest surviving Greek romance (Chariton's *Chaereas and Callirhoe*) and reappears regularly in all the major transformations of romance, from *Erec et Enide* to *The Winter's Tale*, although the details of the conception of feminine virtue may vary.

22. In her summary of the paradigmatic feminine sentimental plot, Janet Todd also notes the importance of the tableau as accompanying technique "in which the response of the reader was described and demanded in the text" ("Jane Austen," p. 77). See also Marshall, *Surprising Effects*; Mücke (p. 104); Mullan.

23. This interpretation of virtue as a maternal "inheritance" that substitutes for a lacking patrimony, passed on by means of an educative example between generations of women who are not genealogically related, corroborates Michael McKeon's reading of early novels and prose narratives, whether "progressive" or "conservative," as revisions of the old aristocratic

(romance) ideology of the patrimonial transmission of both wealth and "nobility," or virtue. Both the "conservative" Swift and the "progressive" Defoe maintain, against the aristocratic conception, "that whatever portion of virtue or merit is inborn or 'natural' is certainly not genealogically linked, and that nurture is in any case crucial for its flourishing" (*Origins*, pp. 169–70).

24. "L'éleve d'une femme respectable conservera du moins le *précieux heritage* qu'on ne peut lui ravir, un attachement inviolable à ses devoirs & la consolante certitude de se dire dans tous les tems, mon malheur est l'effet du hasard, il n'est point celui de ma propre imprudence" (Marie-Jeanne Riccoboni, *Lettres d'Elisabeth-Sophie de Valliere* [1772], p. 155; emphasis mine). Laclos seems to be playing ironically on the convention of the heroine whose misfortunes are "not her fault" in the dénouement of *Les Liaisons dangereuses*, caused by Valmont's sending the letter in which he repeats that his heartlessness towards his mistress is "not his fault."

25. Its manifold endings are another way in which this paradigmatic plot contrasts with Baym's "overplot" for woman's fiction. In their persistence in a primary ending of "happy marriage," the American writers of the next century were more optimistic and much more single-mindedly domestic in their representations, but less inventive of ambiguity in their narrative structures (Baym, p. xxvi).

26. The association between letter and example that makes this shift of emphasis slide so easily is strong and multifarious: both devices emphasize gestures of framing as well as of transmission, so that what Janet Altman says about the double transmission enacted in epistolary fiction equally describes any representation of the transmission of an example: "(A) [the author] must make his letter writer (B) speak to an addressee (C) in order to communicate with a reader (D) who overhears" (p. 210). The two rhetorical devices also share an association, going back to classical Greece, with education (on the letter's educational associations, see Ferguson).

27. See, for example, Armstrong; Perry; Todd, *Sign of Angellica*, pp. 121, 127–28.

28. The effect of this "imperative of virtue" on the implied female reader is made clear, not only by Mme Beccary's quoted *avis* (a "notice," but also a "warning,") to the reader, but also in the prefaces and dedications, in the authors' and "editors'" notes of most of the novels written in the century, forgotten or canonical, from Richardson to Rousseau and Laclos. The biographies, as well as the oeuvres, of every woman writer of the period were certainly affected by it as well, but it can be traced and dated exactly, almost as if in an archaeological stratum, in the long career of Eliza Haywood, who

began as a novelist writing the "scandalous histories" of the early eighteenth century and ended writing novels of virtue and sensibility, having suffered some harsh blows to her reputation both as a woman and as a writer when the tide of "taste" turned, a moment marked by her *History of Miss Betsy Thoughtless* (1753). See Spencer, pp. 75–81; Todd, *Sign of Angellica*, p. 104.

29. See Lyons, p. 23, and the previous chapter.

30. See also Johnson, MacArthur, Stewart, and Watson. MacArthur (*Extravagant Narratives*, p. 22) and Watson (p. 15) make similar points about the epistolary form's potential for the subversion of a "moral order" oppressive to women, while Stewart makes a related one on the basis of content rather than form: "In both Cottin and Genlis . . . partially repressed content sometimes overwhelms stated morals" (p. 198). Compare Johnson on English women's fiction of the 1790's: "They dutifully denounce reformist zeal, only to tuck away parallel plots which vindicate liberty, private conscience, and the defiance of authority. . . . Under the pressure of intense reaction, they developed stylistic techniques which enabled them to use politically charged material in an exploratory and interrogative, rather than hortatory and prescriptive, manner" (p. xxi; see also p. 22). The use of the same stylistic techniques by women writing in both France and England well before the period of the English anti-Jacobin reaction demonstrates that they had already been developed in response to the reactionary attitudes towards women in the domestic ideology of sensibility.

31. Kaplan, *Jane Austen*, p. 152. She says this, citing Joseph Boone's and Rachel DuPlessis's emphasis on the ideological function of narrative endings, by way of explaining why so many of Jane Austen's juvenilia were left without any.

32. An emphasis on discontinuity rather than on the unity of the "rounded picture" cannot be seen as one of the "advantages" of epistolary technique from Robert Day's perspective, because he attempts to frame his own rounded picture of the development of fictional technique, a frame that makes it possible for "Richardson's work to be viewed historically as the culmination of a process or development rather than as a literary eruption" (Day, p. 7).

33. Very few women published satirically libertine writings. In the later eighteenth century, I know of only Suzanne Bertrand-Quinquet (Giroust de Morency) and Sophie Cottin in revolutionary France, and in Germany, Sophie Mereau. On Cottin, see Stewart, pp. 171–98.

34. See Barker-Benfield; Marshall, *Surprising Effects*, pp. 12–13; Mullan, e.g., pp. 4–5.

35. See also Spacks, "Female Resources": "A good woman can be defined by her emotional capacity; female authors, evoking characters of sensibility, thus insist on their own female virtue" (p. 93). See also Mullan, pp. 111–13. "Sympathy" is a subset of, and often used interchangeably with, "sensibility"; see Barker-Benfield; Marshall, *Surprising Effects*, p. 10; Mullan; Todd, *Sensibility*.

36. Eliza Haywood, *The British Recluse* (London, 1724 [1722]), p. 10.

37. Baym seeks to distinguish Victorian "woman's fiction" from eighteenth-century "sentimental" fiction on the grounds that the American writers emphasize the "public sympathy" of the Enlightenment, which "makes sentimentality compatible with universal Reason" and creates a bond between "individuals who are not kin," while avoiding the "private, excessive, undisciplined, self-centered emotionality" they associated with the word *sentimental*, as well as the feminine passivity they associated with "Richardsonian fiction." She identifies "sentimental" or Richardsonian fiction, on the other hand, with the "seduction novel." But no such simple dichotomy existed in European women's practice. *The British Recluse* is a good example of a seduction novel *before* Richardson in which a strictly private sympathy creates a bond between women "who are not kin" that saves them from the (later) typical ruin of a seduced heroine. Women writers after Richardson continue to reach back in spite of him to such feminine paradigms in fiction, and in fact most of their heroines maintain their virtue, as those of "woman's fiction" do their agency, by *avoiding* the traps of seduction (Baym, pp. xxix–xxx, 29–30).

38. I shall sometimes, for the sake of clarity, be forced to continue to use the term *frame*, which I have attempted to discard and replace; it is always to be understood, however, as mentioned in the first chapter, *sous rature*.

39. Kaplan argues that surrogate mothers were historically important in the women's culture she identifies in England in the late eighteenth and early nineteenth centuries (*Jane Austen*, p. 32). Hirsch, on the other hand, argues that "Biographical parallels are not enough to explain the thoroughness with which the figure of the mother is silenced, denigrated, simply eliminated, or written out of these Victorian fictions [including Austen's]. Maternal absence and silence is too much the condition of the heroine's development, too much the basis of the fiction itself; the form it takes is too akin to repression" (*Mother/Daughter Plot*, p. 47).

40. Compare Lyons, p. 23.

41. The quotation from Riccoboni appears on p. 87 and p. 266 (n.24). See also my "Value of a Literary Legacy," pp. 110–12.

42. Sarah Scott, *Millenium Hall*, p. 35. The long epistle that provides the

frame for this novel is written and received by male characters, and the series of women's histories that it contains are told by them to the male letter-writer. One of the special themes of this novel is the transmission of women's histories to more powerful male receivers whose sympathy is won over, which explains, I think, the formal anomaly. Aside from this interesting idiosyncratic twist, *Millenium Hall* exhibits the same themes and plot structures as do epistolary novels of women's correspondence, and so I include it among my examples.

43. Miss Godwin (Mrs Vigor), *Letters Between an English Lady and Her Friend at Paris* (London, 1770), 1: 60–61, 93.

44. "Ce n'est pas que j'aie assez mal profité de vos leçons & de vos exemples, pour chérir les richesses au-delà de ce qu'elles valent. Mais, ma chere bonne Amie, qu'il est doux de ne devoir qu'aux auteurs de ses jours son nécessaire & son superflu, & de pouvoir le partager avec la vertu malheureuse!" (Mme de Boisgiron, *Lettres de Mademoiselle de Boismiran*, pt. 1, p. 2).

45. Chapters 4 and 5 lay out more fully how Providence works as an apotheosis of the paternal will to allow female action—in this case Mrs Melvyn's passing on of a maternal inheritance to her own daughter—while preserving the virtuous fiction that no willed action is involved. The effects of such action are legitimated by the will of the heavenly Father, just as, in the passage cited earlier, the systematic exclusions and oppressions of patrilineal society are written off as "l'effet du hasard."

46. In fact, the example of Mme de Chartres seems to conceal a history that is not transmitted, or rather not owned (*avoué*) to her daughter: the history of her own fall, which she relates to the princess under the guise of fiction, as one of those "histories of my time" or negative examples of her contemporaries, like that of Diane de Poitiers (see Chapter 2, n.20). The substitution of her example for her history—that is, the replacement of her own antecedent history by her example as a mother who survives into her daughter's history—creates the indebted structure of its transmission to her daughter. The daughter must live up in reality to the *fiction* of the mother's virtue, in order to exceed, to pay interest on, the mother's exemplary legacy, her survival of her own virtue for the benefit of her daughter.

47. Compare Hirsch, *Mother/Daughter Plot*, p. 46. The figure of the substitute mother in this fiction thus provides an emphatic denial of the "horror of older spinsters not under a husband's discipline," which Sulloway describes as prevalent in English culture but "decried" by women writers of the 1790's (p. 24). The horror of the mother and idealization of substitute mother figures is also the inverse of what happened later in American

"woman's fiction," where abusers of power are most often aunts who have replaced biological mothers, and least often the mothers themselves (Baym, p. 37). This element seems to be particularly characteristic of the subgenre of epistolary fiction of women's correspondence in the later eighteenth century, since Elizabeth Bergen Brophy, in her survey of eighteenth-century fiction, claims that *Millenium Hall* is unique in the importance it accords to spinsters and widows (p. 199). *Millenium Hall* is also the only novel mentioned by Brophy that is akin to the subgenre discussed here.

48. Staël-Holstein, *Delphine*, pp. 330–34 (my translation).

49. In anthropological usage, the term *patrilineage* properly refers only to a "lineage society" organized patrilineally, as distinct from a "patriline" society, like those of France and England in the eighteenth century, which were not "lineage societies" because they were organized along "lines" of transmission from individual father to individual son (as designated by the father). "Lineage societies" hold and transmit property and offices within broader kin groups. In this text, however, I use *patrilineage* simply as a nominative form of, and synonymous with, *patriline*.

50. The strategy of the princess and her mother was a combination of the two.

51. See also Deborah Kaplan, who emphasizes in "Female Friendship" that all female characters in *Lady Susan* "are keenly aware of the social and economic vulnerability of unmarried women," and use "networks of women," enacted formally in the preponderance of letters exchanged between women in this novel, in order to engage in "marriage 'plotting' . . . against men" (pp. 159–60).

52. For the great danger to patriline transmission posed by widows with children and the often stringent measures against their freedom, see Goody, Thirsk, and Thompson, eds., *Family and Inheritance*, and Blackstone, 1: §456–§457 (pp. 430–31); Barbara J. Todd.

53. See Blackstone, 1: §453 (p. 427): "A mother, as such, is entitled to no power, but only to reverence and respect."

54. "Maman, restée veuve de bonne heure, n'ayant que moi d'enfans, & une fortune assez bornée, fut nommée ma tutrice. Elle ne s'est jamais regardée que comme la dépositaire du bien de mon pere, dont la jouissance lui étoit acquise de droit, jusqu'à ma majorité" (*Adele et Sophie* [Paris, 1798], pp. 2–3; my translation). Lebrun attests that one of the protections afforded widows by the legal customs of most French regions was the usufruct of one-third of the husband's estate (pp. 75–76). This is quite similar to English practice of the time.

55. Burney's *Evelina* follows this pattern in its plot, although it does not

fall into the category of epistolary novels that primarily represent correspondences between women. Other notable examples of the pattern are Anne de Colleville, *Alexandrine de Ba**** (Paris, 1786), Marie-Jeanne Riccoboni, *Histoire de Miss Jenny* (Paris, 1764), and Sophia Lee, *The Recess* (London, 1783–85).

56. "Quoi! prendre un maître, et vivre en Hollande!" (Riccoboni, *Lettres d'Elisabeth-Sophie de Valliere*, p. 42).

Chapter 4

1. The printed text of *Lettres de Mademoiselle de Boismiran* survives, to my knowledge, only in the Bibliothèque nationale, Paris. I have obtained a microfilm of that copy, which is now in the Firestone Library of Princeton University. "Mme de Boisgiroux ou de Boisgiron" is listed by Des Essarts simply as the author of the *Lettres de Mademoiselle de Boismiran* and of *Les Suites d'un moment d'erreur* (1775); uncharacteristically, he gives absolutely no biographical information. A considerable amount of research on my part has turned up nothing, so far, to supplement Des Essarts's work in this respect. Joan Hinde Stewart has written an eloquent passage about the obstacles to finding even the most basic information about eighteenth-century women writers in French, to which I wearily refer my reader (pp. 15–19). Not being much concerned with authorial biography in the present work, I acknowledge this lacuna with regret, and with the hope that I may draw to Mme de Boisgiron's work the interest of other readers who may pursue her traces further. The translations in these pages are my own.

2. "La mort impitoyable ne lui a pas laissé le temps de choisir la main qui a fermé ses yeux. Le même jour l'a ramené dans sa patrie, & l'a conduit au tombeau" (pt. 1, p. 114).

3. Even where Providence appears as the apotheosis of paternal will, it is a covertly subversive force, authorizing the heroine to exercise her own will, to act on her own desires, by making her action appear to be an acceptable compliance to the authority of paternal will. Sophia Lee's *The Recess* provides a beautiful example of this gesture (see Chapter 5).

4. The fact that John Locke had argued in 1690 against divine right established according to this patriarchal logic (as set forth in Filmer's *Patriarcha*) gave impetus to English women writers such as Charlotte Smith in the debates spurred there by the French Revolution (see Johnson, p. 13). The influence of English thought (and its revolutionary history), with that of Rousseau, is clearly perceptible in this novel of the years of French involvement in the American Revolution, leading soon to the revolution at home.

5. The theme of female exile is literalized as fictional burial not only in

Lettres de Mademoiselle de Boismiran, but also in both Lee's *The Recess* (1783–85), and Staël's *Corinne*, to which I turn in the next two chapters of this book. It also occurs in a number of other novels, including Mlle Poulain's *Lettres de Madame la comtesse de la Riviere* (1776), Elizabeth Griffith's *The Delicate Distress* (1769), Radcliffe's *The Mysteries of Udolpho* (1794), Rowson's *Charlotte Temple* (1794), and Sophie von la Roche's *Geschichte des Fräuleins von Sternheim* (1771). I discuss the idea in more detail in "Of Haunted Highlands."

6. "Je vis la signature de ma mere, et ju fus pénétrée d'horreur, en lisant l'arrêt de mon malheur tracé de sa propre main" (pt. 2, p. 7).

7. "On craint la société d'une personne *fausse*, *dissimulée*, qui se soustrait à l'autorité légitime pour ne suivre que les dangereux penchans de son coeur" (pt. 1, p. 131).

8. The question of the legitimacy of the (always already) substitutive representatives of divine patriarchal authority, and hence of the legitimacy of rebellion against them, links the problem of women's place within patriarchy to that of the nonaristocratic classes under monarchy by "divine right," as outlined in Filmer's *Patriarcha*. The fact of this novel's publication in 1777, in France, with its American settings, is enough to remind us that even such subtle and implicit treatments of these issues as we find here would have had a highly volatile political significance. For the English novel's relation to the general questioning of authority that marked the period from the mid seventeenth through the eighteenth centuries, see, e.g., Hunter, *Before Novels*, pp. 138–39, 196–97. A similar questioning of received authority occurred in France. See Welsh, pp. 11–12. English Showalter's discussion of French romances and *nouvelles* in the context of a seventeenth-century crisis in historiography illuminates the early novel's relation to problems of authority (pp. 53–55).

9. "L'habitude de voir une foule d'esclaves occupés à deviner & à prévenir ses volontés, lui [faisait] redouter la maniere de vivre d'Europe, où les plus grands plaisirs se trouvent dans la Société, & par conséquent dans l'égalité" (pt. 1, p. 7).

10. In this view, the novel follows Rousseau.

11. This is one of the oldest problems of oppositional logic; it was this contradiction, for example, that kept St. Augustine so long from becoming a Christian. For him the problem expressed itself as that of locating evil in a world in which everything descends unilineally from a single, paternal creator who is identified with the good in *opposition* to evil.

12. See Spacks on Burney's *Evelina* in *Imagining a Self*, p. 179. In Austen's work, I am thinking, for example, of Mary Crawford.

13. See n.5 above.

14. "Je me persuade qu'ils ne tarderont pas à publier mon heureuse & romanesque résurrection" (pt. 2, p. 123).

15. Littré notes this usage of *pleine* in literature in the sixteenth century: "Lorsque ta mere estoit preste à gesir de toy, Si Jupiter, des dieux et des hommes le roy, Lui eust juré ces mots: l'enfant dont tu es pleine" (s.v. *plein*). Rousseau had already used the pun on *mer* and *mère*: a few lines after invoking his own mother ("O ma mère, pourquoi vous donna-t-il un fils dans sa colère?"), St.-Preux invokes the sea on which he is about to embark, personifying it by giving it a maternal body: "Mer vaste, mer immense, qui dois peut-être m'engloutir dans ton sein" (*Julie*, p. 293).

16. "Cet élément qu'on me représentait si terrible & si redoutable, s'est dépouillé pour nous de toute son impétuosité. . . . La paix & l'ordre qui regnent dans votre respectable asyle, est l'image de la vie que nous menons" (pt. 3, p. 1). The graphic resemblance between *mer* and *mère* is especially striking in this text, which retains the old spelling (*mere*) without marking the distinction with an accent.

17. Littré, s.v. *redoutable, terrible*; *Oxford English Dictionary*, s.v. *redoubtable, terrible*.

18. The substitute mother, as noted earlier, is not wedded to the father, not engaged in matrimony, nor, therefore, in the transmission of patrimony; thus she is neither a usurper of patriarchal rights like the mother, nor a potential disruption of the patriline fiction. In the logic of patriarchy, any being not masculine that does not participate in patriline reproduction is not feminine either. Hence the term *virgin*, or *vir-gin*, the never-wed woman as man-woman, and the dread that surrounds her in mythology.

19. "La suite d'une maladie, qui n'a plus rien de dangereux, me force à vous confier à des mains étrangeres. Mais que dis-je! le Marquis d'Ornevil ne doit plus être étranger dans ma maison. Regardez-le comme un autre moi-même: votre affection pour lui va devenir un devoir" (pt. 3, p. 23).

20. "Il tombe si près du bord, que sans une protection particuliere du Ciel, la mer l'eût pour jamais séparé de moi" (pt. 3, p. 25).

21. "Ces maximes [le dévouement total, l'abnégation entiere des esclaves] . . . produisent . . . des êtres monstrueux, capables des plus grands crimes & des actions les plus héroïques" (pt. 3, p. 63).

22. "On pensa que l'air de la mer nuisoit à l'effect des remedes[, et] on projetta de m'en éloigner sans me consulter" (pt. 3, p. 88).

23. In *Corinne*, Staël uses the image and the pun in a related way: Corinne describes growing up with her oppressive stepmother in a Gothic setting "au bord de la mer" (Goldberger, p. 255; Balayé, p. 367); through-

out the novel the sea is described as the element that effaces all traces, in contrast to the land, whose geography is elaborately drawn in the borders between patriarchal states, paternal estates, regions, and historical epochs, marked everywhere by monuments to great men.

24. "Elle est belle & paroit singulierement jeune: on a peine à croire qu'elle soit la mere de sa fille."

25. "Pour la premiere fois je fus frappé de ce rapport étonnant qui se trouve entre leurs traits. Transporté hors de moi . . . je me jettai à ses pieds."

26. Zaïde bears the name of the eponymous heroine of Lafayette's romance.

27. "Trahi par cette énivrante ressemblance dont j'avois été si vivement frappé, l'égarement & le feu de la volupté s'emparerent de tout mon être. Zaïde, l'inexplicable, la dangereuse Zaïde, arrive auprès de moi, transportée du bonheur de sa Maîtresse . . . , brûlant elle-même des. . . . Mais hélas! . . . Oui l'exces de mon repentir me force à avouer les honteux plaisirs que le désordre de mes sens me fit goûter dans les bras de cette voluptueuse Esclave" (pt. 3, pp. 94–104).

28. "On dit que dans nos Colonies, ainsi que dans celles de nos rivaux, il n'est pas rare de voir préférer aux plus jolies Européennes, les femmes nées dans un climat brûlant" (pt. 3, p. 10). The master's wife finds out, he abandons the slave to her jealous wrath, and she is about to put her to death by torture, when Madame saves her. (The master's cruelty by abdication resembles Mme de Boismiran's abandonment of her own daughter: her absenting herself constitutes the essence of her actual [as opposed to reported and distorted] cruelty towards her daughter.)

29. "Dieu puissant (s'écria cette infortunée, en tombant aux genoux de ma mere), pour la premiere fois j'apperçois ton image!" (pt. 3, p. 15).

30. "Vous n'avez point de mere . . . "l'amour & la jalousie ont anéanti tout sentiment honnête dans ce coeur. . . . N'attendons pas qu'elle ait reconnu sa victime, il ne seroit plus temps de la lui dérober" (pt. 4, pp. 19, 28).

31. "La révolte n'est un crime que quand l'autorité est légitime" (pt. 4, pp. 19, 28).

32. "J'eus besoin de les écouter, pour résister aux sentimens de la nature" (pt. 4, p. 40).

33. "Tout-à-coup nous entendîmes des hurlemens & des mugissemens horribles, qui nous apprirent que nous étions à une très-courte distance de plusieurs animaux furieux; & pour augmenter notre effroi, l'obscurité nous empechoit de distinguer les objets. De plus, nous étions engagées sous une voûte qui ne nous permettoit pas de nous éloigner du danger" (pt. 4, p. 60).

34. "Daigner aujourd'hui me servir de mere: prononcez sur mon sort" (pt. 4, p. 48).

35. "Ce fut là où nous apprimes la cause de notre vaine terreur" (pt. 4, p. 61). The dispersal of supernatural terror with the deus ex machina of rational or scientific discourse is another strategy characteristic of Gothic fiction in general.

36. "Une large trappe par laquelle on descend la nourriture aux animaux qui y sont renfermés, se trouvoit sous nos pas, & nous laissoit entendre leurs cris comme s'ils eussent été prêts à nous dévorer" (pt. 4, p. 61).

37. Sterne's noses in *Tristram Shandy* and Diderot's fable of "le couteau et la glaive" (the knife and the sheath) in *Jacques le fataliste* come to mind, as two prominent examples.

38. "Nous entendîmes de foibles gémissemens humaines se mêler aux cris de ces animaux furieux" (pt. 4, p. 81).

39. "Elle se trouvoit séparée de ces féroces animaux, par une forte grille qui ne se ferme presque jamais" (pt. 4, p. 82).

40. "Sans une protection particuliere du Ciel, la mer l'eût pour jamais séparé de moi" (pt. 3, p. 25).

41. See Boone on the paradigmatic plots of "wedlock" versus the "open forms" that resist its closure.

42. "Le même jour l'a ramené dans sa patrie, & l'a conduit au tombeau" (pt. 1, p. 114).

43. "Les noms de fille, d'amante & d'épouse furent les premiers mots qui frapperent son oreille . . . elle n'osoit croire ses sens" (pt. 4, p. 85).

44. "Elle a ouvert ma tombe, elle va m'y précipiter" (pt. 4, pp. 98–99).

45. "Sans être arrêtée par l'indécence d'un style qui lui est si étranger, elle ne cessa de parler . . ." (pt. 4, p. 104).

46. "Cessez d'admirer un sacrifice nécessaire. Dès que l'espérance est détruite, on est bientôt résigné" (pt. 4, p. 108).

47. "Elle croyoit devoir d'ajouter à nos cérémonies celles que l'usage seul a introduites à la Martinique, & qu'elle se croiroit fondée à lui contester ses droits, jusqu'au moment indiqué par sa mere pour la publication de leur mariage" (pt. 4, p. 119). This, like everything from Mademoiselle's fall into the "deadly gulf" to the end of the novel, is written by Belvaux to Mme de Foncel, since Mademoiselle is unable to write. The inability to communicate in the traces of writing, associated as it is with patriline law, with the visual, the boundary line, and with the frame and its fixity (as opposed to *la mer[e]* which effaces any trace momentarily inscribed in it, see nn.15 and 23 above) is a function of her inability to hear patrilineal language or to speak anything but the Gothic language.

48. "Séparées par des mers qu'aucune des deux ne devoit jamais franchir, n'étions-nous pas mortes l'une pour l'autre?" (pt. 4, p. 108).

49. "C'est pourtant le meilleur des maris . . . . . , le moins exigeant, ... , le moins . . . . . , le moins *mari* possible; . . . toujours d'avis qu'une femme *soumise* a raison de l'être" (pt. 4, p. 108).

50. "Il l'a suivi à ses côtés, & auprès de Madame de Boismiran, qu'un barbare usage contraint ici à placer elle-même sa fille dans le tombeau (pt. 4, p. 139).

51. "Quel mortel vertueux eût osé me conseiller de vivre!" (pt. 4, p. 142).

52. The deprivation of patrimony as a result of a refusal of matrimony is a circular problem; it is implied in references to Mme de Foncel's misfortune in having no fortune, that it was exactly this lack that forced her to retreat to a convent in the first place.

Chapter 5

1. Altman found no work that doubled the memoir-letter form before 1974 (p. 204).

2. Sophia Lee, *The Recess; or, A Tale of Other Times* (London, 1787 [1783–85]). All further references will be to this, the third edition. This edition is the copy-text for my new edition of the novel, forthcoming shortly from the University Press of Kentucky. At present, however, the facsimile reprint of the text (New York: Arno Press, 1972) is almost as difficult to find as the eighteenth-century editions, so that it will be necessary for me to summarize some of the plot in order to clarify my reading, as in the previous chapter. For biographical data on Sophia Lee and partial plot summaries of *The Recess*, see my introduction to the Kentucky edition; Ellis, pp. 68–74; Robertson, pp. 74–76; Katharine Rogers, biographical entries on the Lee sisters in Janet Todd, ed., *Dictionary*, pp. 193–95; Spencer, pp. 194–201; Spender, pp. 232–33; and Devendra P. Varma's introduction to the Arno Press reprint, pp. vii–xlviii. Margaret Anne Doody calls it "the first fully developed English Gothic novel" ("Deserts," p. 559).

3. On *The Recess*'s combination of sentimental and Gothic elements, see also Ellis, p. 70. On the Gothic as a variant of the literature of sensibility, see also Kelly, pp. 48–49, and Barker-Benfield, p. 318.

4. The direst threat of the Harlowes against Clarissa is one of imprisonment in a gloomy mansion. Imprisonment in an old mansion or medieval fortress is, after all, only a small step from imprisonment in a convent, a favorite theme of the earliest epistolary novels (to name the most famous example, *Lettres d'une religieuse portugaise*). The lack of convents (along

with the extremes of dispossession caused by the law of primogeniture) clearly encouraged this shift towards the Gothic in England; this idea is supported by the fact that a large number of the ruinous mansions of the English Gothic, including that in *The Recess*, are supposed to be monasteries that have been partially converted into residences (see also Ellis, p. 47). This did not prevent English writers from cloistering their heroines in French convents, however—as *The Recess* shows—nor French novelists, a few at least, from producing Gothic fictions. In addition to *Lettres de Mademoiselle de Boismiran*, see Madame Mérard de Saint-Just, *Le Château noir, ou Les Souffrances de la jeune Ophelle* (Paris, 1799).

5. See also Spacks, *Desire and Truth*, p. 171.

6. Doody ("Dreams," p. 554) identifies *The Recess* as one of the first English historical novels.

7. Brooks, *Reading for the Plot*, p. 39. I return to the issue of the reader's role towards the end of the present chapter.

8. I read the heroines' transgressive impulses to escape from the maternal womb of stone as a repetitive, masturbatory exploration. The "so often-sought opening . . . which I perceived was made to fall together, with a spring almost imperceptible" is an image of female genital exploration repeated a volume later in the twins' transgressive play around the ruins that conceal the other, outside opening to the "secret communication" (1: 24; 2: 10). The latter image has a long history in the narrative genres preceding the modern novel: compare the *Decameron* and *Don Quixote*. In the famous novella of Guiscardo and Prince Tancredi's widowed daughter, the lovers meet in a cavern in the mountain on which her father's palace stands. "But since the cavern was no longer used, the mouth of the shaft was almost entirely covered over by weeds and brambles. There was a secret staircase leading to the cavern from a room occupied by the lady, . . . but the way was barred by a massive door. So many years had passed since the staircase had last been used, that hardly anybody remembered it was still there; but Love, to whose eyes nothing remains concealed, had reminded the enamoured lady of its existence" (p. 333).

Don Quixote explores a similarly "overgrown" cavern in the Cave of Montesinos episode: "They arrived at the cave, and found the mouth broad and spacious, tho' overgrown with thorns, weeds, brambles and brakes, so thick and intricate, that it was almost quite covered and concealed. . . . He found it would be impracticable to slip down, or make way for entering, without the strength of arms . . . he therefore, unsheathing his sword, began to lay about him, and mow down the bushes that grew around the mouth of the cave" (p. 550).

9. *Oxford English Dictionary*, s.v. *amaze*: "*Amaze* and *a maze* were often identified."

10. Cf. Spacks, "Female Resources," p. 93. The necessity for a hero, like a heroine, to be a faultless victim, is apparent in the way Lee plays with history here. The historical earl of Leicester was suspected of having poisoned his wife in order to pursue his ambition of marrying Elizabeth. Lee turns this around and shows Leicester fleeing from the henchmen of his wife, whom he discovered willingly and knowingly engaging in the same sin from which Mrs Marlow narrowly escaped (incest), and who has just swallowed the poison she had prepared for him.

11. Mrs Marlow's fatal example of virtue is itself ambiguous. Her self-burial seemed to come from within, of her own will, and she says she has done it for the heroines' sakes. In her own history, however, we and they learn that it is in fact a result of the restrictions imposed by society, through *her* mother. On the eve of Mrs Marlow's wedding to the man she loves, a letter arrives from her missing mother, bearing, within the mother's own life history, the information that her fiancé is really her brother (Father Anthony). This letter, along with a sum of money, constitutes the legacy Mrs Marlow's mother leaves to her. While saving her from a fault so great that no amount of innocence could have expunged it, and thus preserving her virtue from a disastrous fall, it also imposes on her the obligation to give up the object of her own desire. It is in fact because of this dead end to her own plot, inherited from her mother, that she "voluntarily" retires from the world, *before* the birth of the twins. The insistent Gothic theme of incest shows itself here as another version of the collapse of the plot of female desire into its point of origin, the failure of desire to move the desiring heroine out of the maternal bond (with her maternal half-brother as substitute) and toward a new destination of her own determination.

12. Another female correspondence with *The Recess* that must be left in the margins of the present discussion takes place in *Wuthering Heights*. Brontë rewrites this passage from *The Recess* specifically when she has Heathcliff make use of the same strategy, involving a debt of sympathy, to force the younger Cathy to invite Linton Heathcliff into her home against her father's orders, which ultimately results in the marriage of the two children, according to Heathcliff's wishes (pp. 243–45). The marks of Emily Brontë's correspondence with Lee are numerous: broadly, she was still working within the terms of Gothic convention, and also quite intensively with the problem of sympathy. More specifically, though, Brontë also wrote her novel around the problem of female and maternal inheritance, with a plot that is unusual in that it, like Lee's, includes both the mother's and the daughter's histories (Matilda later has a daughter, Mary, to whom I am

referring here; her mother, Mary, has only a ghostly presence within the narrative frame). The structural peculiarities of *Wuthering Heights* also strikingly resemble those of *The Recess*, for both are doubled: Brontë devoting one of the split halves to each Cathy, while Lee devotes one half of her strangely split narrative to each of her twin heroines. Ellis remarks a further point of correspondence between the two novels: "the lack of reward [for female plotting in *The Recess*, or for 'initiative,' as Ellis calls it] comes, as it does in *Wuthering Heights*, from the unworthiness of the world from which a reward might be expected and in which it would be lived out" (p. 71).

13. See Chapter 3 on the idea of "sympathetic exchange of narratives."

14. On Elizabeth as "phallic mother," see Ellis, p. 70.

15. See also Ellis, p. 72.

16. See Janet Altman's conception of epistolary form as constructing a mosaic of fragmentary units that are each also unities in themselves (p. 186).

17. According to Derrida, invagination in Blanchot is brought about by an inquisitorial demand for narrative, made by "police" and complied with under torture. This demand cannot be satisfied by just any narrative, but only by the whole truth, a narrative that is ordered and complete ("Living On / Borderlines," pp. 94, 98).

18. Both Godwin in *Caleb Williams* (1794) and Schiller in "Der Verbrecher aus verlorener Ehre" (1786) may be referring to Lee's work with their own use of bands of counterfeiting outlaws in their Gothic fictions. I am grateful to Ellen Brinks for drawing the similarity to my attention.

19. See Marin and Chapter 2.

20. Recall here that Mlle de Boismiran was enabled to throw off her pursuers by the same means, except that in her case the fiction of her death was not plotted by herself, but thrown faultlessly in her way by Providence and then disseminated by Mlle Belvaux. See also Chapter 4, n.5.

21. This sin is committed by one of the heroines' foils, hopelessly in love with Leicester. See also St.-Preux's reflections on suicide in Rousseau's *Julie*, pp. 278–85.

22. Lafayette, *La Princesse de Clèves*, pp. 155–56.

23. Brooks, *Reading for the Plot*, p. 39.

24. Matilda and her daughter have been rescued from a prison in Jamaica by a sympathetic former slave, now the governor's favorite mistress, who watched them through their prison window and gave her daughter an inheritance in a casket—along with its contagion of unrestrained female desire. Compare the similar representation of the privileged and passionate slave, Zaïde, in *Mademoiselle de Boismiran* (see Chapter 4).

25. See the opening of this chapter and n.1.

26. Yet another unusual feature of this book is that it extends the history of its heroine (Matilda) so far into motherhood that it includes her daughter's history. This happens also in Frances Sheridan's *Memoirs of Miss Sidney Biddulph* (1761) and Elizabeth Inchbald's *A Simple Story* (1791), but the overwhelming majority of novels were only concerned with a heroine's courtship and marriage, at most showing the heroine in young motherhood as she irons out the wrinkles in the first years of marriage.

27. Cf. Linda Kauffman writing on the nature of heroines' epistolary discourse in novels that take Ovid's *Heroides* as subtext, i.e., where the heroine addresses her letters to an absent lover: "Her discourse is written in extremity and lies at the extremes of telling, so far removed from mere mimesis that the diegetic and performative aspects of narrative dominate the discourse. . . . In each text, the heroine transforms the ordeal of abandonment into a passionate vocation that might be called the vocation of iterative narrative. Ceaselessly repeated in the aftermath of abandonment, it is a powerful reenactment of pleasure and desire, related less to the mimetic than to the diegetic qualities of narrative, for the narrating heroine is intensely, constantly present as analyst, catalyst, and creator of her own desire" (pp. 24–25). Kauffman is specifically discussing *amorous* epistolary discourse; what love letters perform is at once the seduction of the absent lover and a certain "iteration" or recreation of the past event, as well as a "self-creation" that makes the possibility of the lover's actual return secondary, if not superfluous. In fictions of correspondence between women, what the letters perform is always a plot of transmission, and thus of escape and survival. In the few moments when the letters are addressed to men, as here, they are performatives that persuade a reader endowed with an agency of which the heroine has been deprived to enact the plot of escape she cannot enact alone. The novels as a group can be conceived of as performatives along the same lines, addressed to men and women of future generations, who may be able to enact what the author cannot. But primarily they perform their plot to escape from the stasis of resemblance, to survive the killing repetitions of mimesis and its law of verisimilitude, by undermining that law. They, like the novels Kauffman describes, are antimimetic, not in avoiding mimesis, but in subverting it and its double, example, through the technique of mise-en-abyme and an aesthetics of implausibility.

28. Thus Matilda both exposes the openness and the possibilities for motion of the "large book" of patriarchy, and turns to her own ends its marginalization of woman as "a cipher in patriarchal culture, the quintessential blank page, waiting to be filled." I quote Linda Kauffman (p. 290) describ-

ing a recent epistolary fiction of women's correspondence, *The Three Marias: New Portuguese Letters*. On woman as "cipher," see also Gilbert and Gubar, p. 9.

29. Thus the act of reading modeled by Lee's text in particular presents a contrast to that described by Altman as characteristic of epistolary novels generally: "As readers of epistolary narrative we are often called upon to act as detective-collators, to perceive continuity from one letter to the next" (pp. 186–87, 161). In other words, Altman sees the reader in the position of Blanchot's police, demanding the "whole story." We have already seen how Lee's heroines respond to that demand; Lee's own text evades the necessity of responding to it by inscribing within itself both the scene and the plot of escape from the demand for a "whole story."

30. See the prefaces and editor's notes to any of the canonical texts of the period: Richardson's *Clarissa*, Rousseau's *La Nouvelle Héloïse*, Laclos's *Les Liaisons dangereuses*.

31. On *The Recess* as a rewriting of history in the feminine, see also Spencer, *Rise*, pp. 195–201, and Ellis, p. 69.

32. See J. M. S. Tompkins and Varma in the Arno Press reprint of *The Recess*.

33. Doody identifies *The Recess* as not only the "first fully developed Gothic" but also one of the first English historical novels ("Deserts," 554).

34. Quoted by Varma in the Arno Press reprint of *The Recess*, xxv. Clearly eighteenth-century readers were able to appreciate the way in which Lee could "metonymize metaphor," to return to MacArthur's terms. If "metaphoric" narrative valorizes "the collapse of time into the perfect instant," exemplary painting is the perfect metaphor for it, yet Lee's stated project is to restore the energy, "mobility and desire" characteristic of "metonymic" narrative to the static truths of history (*Extravagant Narratives*, p. 33).

35. On the importance of the increasing practice of private and silent reading, as the eighteenth century progressed, in establishing a relationship between text and reader that relied on current conceptions of sympathy, see Mücke (e.g., pp. 15–16) and Mullan (e.g., pp. 13–14).

36. The revolutions taking place during their time were akin to the siege of Metz and the storming of Cadiz; they were male-dominated struggles that made the domestication of women one of the prime foundations of their discourse of liberation for and equality among men, often actually worsening the political situation of women. See Sullerot, Poovey, *Uneven Developments*, and Cohen, "Most Suffering Class," pp. 22–46. Monique Saliou remarks: "'Democracy' could not accept the status of women who had 'a right to speak up' because it would have had to extend it to all citi-

zens' wives. It is significant that women's status in Sparta during the classical period was far higher than in Athens: Sparta had kept an aristocratic government. Similarly, the French Revolution of 1789 deprived all women of political rights, whereas the old régime accepted women holding fiefs and the rights that derived from it" (in Coontz and Henderson, eds., p. 192).

Chapter 6

1. See also Nancy Miller, who notes the echo of *La Princesse de Clèves* in Lucile's entrance into the opera house as the focus of the collective gaze (*Subject*, p. 183). Miller grounds her reading of *Corinne* in its revisions of *La Princesse de Clèves* and, with reference to Carla Peterson's work, of the *Aeneid*: "Lafayette's exquisitely crafted novel of a daughter's desire and a mother's match would seem to be radically refigured through what might properly be called an epic of female vocation: the extravagant staging of a woman's performance (demonstration) of what she wants" (p. 163). I take off from that reading because the resonance of Staël's correspondences with Lafayette needs the third note of female Gothic romance—of women's writing from Corinne's fatherland—to be fully heard.

Page references for English quotations from *Corinne*, unless otherwise indicated, are to Avriel Goldberger's English translation. I refer to the French text in Simone Balayé's edition. All references in this chapter to *La Princesse de Clèves* are to the Adam edition.

2. Writing is in general associated with the will of the dead father throughout *Corinne*, as has also been observed by Peterson (p. 48), and Miller (who argues that the novel opposes a new feminist writing to patriarchal writing [*Subject*, pp. 171, 195]).

3. Cf. Miller, *Subject to Change*, pp. 186–87; Moers, pp. 200–203; Peterson, pp. 42–44. I am in disagreement with the majority of criticism on *Corinne* in denying that Italy represents a maternal country and heritage, significantly distinct from England as fatherland, which allows its daughter the possibility of escape from the order of the paternal will. Yet at the same time I do see the undermining of that distinction throughout the novel as one of the keys to the meaning of Corinne's fate.

4. Reading the novel as a revision of the *Aeneid*, for example, Carla Peterson notes that Corinne alternates among the roles of the Cumaean Sibyl, of Dido, and of Aeneas (p. 55). Staël's characters do not simply repeat, but rather combine and transform the personae of the texts they invoke, and they do so across traditional gender norms.

5. On Oswald performing both roles with Corinne, see also Miller, *Subject to Change*, p. 166.

6. Goldberger, p. 113; see Balayé, p. 175, where it is Italy that has been deprived of independence, and not the Italians, as in the translation.

7. See also Moers, who compares Oswald to Richardson's Grandison (p. 201).

8. See Moers, p. 202: "Both Oswald's values and the secret behind his melancholy derive from his worship of his dead father, as he explains to Corinne halfway up the slope of Mount Vesuvius, where 'all that has life disappears, you enter the empire of death, and only ashes shift beneath uncertain feet.'"

9. If, according to Terry Castle, *The Mysteries of Udolpho* represents "the spectralization of the Other," *Corinne* performs a spectralization of the self. The fact that this is true of other Gothic and sentimental fiction as well complicates her general claims, I think.

10. See also Peterson, p. 44: "She has lost that sense of continuing relation with the mother, or with mother surrogates, that is so important to the maturing young woman."

11. Recent feminist psychoanalytic theory strongly supports the idea that the integration of the self has as much to do with separation as with connection, especially for daughters, who have more difficulty than sons in separating from the mothers they more closely resemble. This model of separation seems a fruitful one to me for understanding fragmentation in women's fiction. See, e.g., Chodorow and Benjamin.

12. See also Miller, *Subject to Change*, p. 187, and Peterson, p. 49.

13. On cash inheritance as compensation for renouncing interest in land, see Emmanuel Le Roy Ladurie in Goody, Thirsk, and Thompson, eds., *Family and Inheritance*, p. 42.

14. "Inexprimable émotion, que la voix de ce qu'on aime! . . . Ce soupir et l'accent mélancolique de sa voix causèrent à Corinne une vive joie" (Balayé, pp. 500–501).

15. On sound and inflection as a specifically maternal language in opposition to writing and signification, see Homans, *Bearing the Word*.

16. Goldberger translates *sympathie* as "empathy," in accordance with modern English usage.

The suggestion that Corinne wants maternal love can be comprehended in the idea of sympathy, but to substitute the idea of maternal love for it is to idealize maternal love in a way that Staël and her predecessors quite emphatically do not. It is true that Rousseau specifically identified the feminine character of sympathy with the immediacy of the mother-infant bond (see Bloom's introduction to Emile, pp. 10–11). Nevertheless sympathy was never reduced to that particular connection in eighteenth-century discourse. Indeed, as has been discussed in earlier chapters, women's fiction tends to represent the relationship between mothers and marriageable daughters in patrilineage as one of specularity, the *false double* of sympathy (cf. Miller; Peterson).

17. The rhetorical opposition of *sentiment* to *reason* was a commonplace of Enlightenment discourse, although a more problematic and contested one, probably, than the opposition between *prejudice* and *reason*. This point is discussed further in the Epilogue. Moers mentions that Staël invented the term *romanticism* (pp. 206–7).

18. See also Miller, *Subject to Change*, p. 196.

19. See Moers on the reception of this example by women writers of the nineteenth century (pp. 173–210).

20. The reliance on resemblance to the father as a mark of legitimacy goes back in literature to the *Odyssey*, where Telemachus is repeatedly reassured that he must indeed be his father's son, not because his mother says so—no woman's word is reliable here—but because he resembles Odysseus. There hardly exists a work in the Gothic tradition that does not centrally play upon the epic/romance topos of paternal resemblance (or sometimes, especially in the female Gothic, maternal resemblances also). See Chapter 2, n. 12.

21. "Ses petits bras et ses jolis regards *imitaient* [Corinne] parfaitement. On croyait voir la *miniature* d'un beau tableau, avec la grâce de l'enfance de plus, qui mêle à tout un charme innocent. Oswald, à ce *spectacle*, fut tellement ému, qu'il ne pouvait prononcer un mot, et il s'assit en tremblant" (Balayé, pp. 575–76; emphasis mine). DeJean also argues that Corinne "makes the child over into a miniature of herself" (Staël's *Corinne*, p. 86).

22. For a discussion of Corinne's revenge on Oswald in its Sapphic associations, see DeJean, *Fictions of Sappho*, pp. 185–86.

23. See also Miller, *Subject to Change*, pp. 192, 195.

24. Lucile would have resembled Matilde in *Delphine*, who has all of Lucile's coldness with none of her saving graces, were it not for Corinne's influence upon her education. Matilde's name, although a common one in Gothic romances since *The Castle of Otranto*, may indicate a correspondence with Lee's Lucile-like character, Matilda.

25. The pleasurable distancing of spectator from specter is characteristic of the Gothic. See also Susan Wolstenholme on Radcliffe: "The reader assumes the position of voyeur from a safe perspective" (p. 18).

26. The general confusion in post-revolutionary France over the discourses of class and of the public and private spheres is discussed in depth

in Cohen's forthcoming book, as well as in the essays collected by Melzer and Rabine. My formulation of the relationship between *Corinne* and novels by women writing in French after Staël is entirely indebted to Margaret Cohen's work.

27. The greater divergence between the works written by women in France and England after the French Revolution—and after Staël and Austen—may explain why Hirsch, who deals in *The Mother/Daughter Plot* with women writing in both countries during the nineteenth and twentieth centuries, nevertheless concentrates almost entirely on English novelists for her discussion of the earlier nineteenth century.

28. Cf. DeJean, "Staël's *Corinne*."

29. *Greek Lyric Poetry: A Selection*, ed. David A. Campbell (Glasgow: Macmillan, 1967), p. 410.

Epilogue

1. This argument is worked out in more detail with respect to Lee and Staël in Alliston, "Of Haunted Highlands."

2. For the significance of Jane Austen's drawing room to the state, see esp. Evans and Johnson; to the empire, see Said.

3. See, e.g., Evans, p. 62; Hutcheson; Johnson, pp. xix–xxv, 21–27; Kirkham, p. 84; Sulloway, pp. 16, 23.

4. See, e.g., Duckworth, pp. 3–5; Evans, p. 8; Sulloway, p. 82; Briganti, pp. 131–32.

5. On "strong mothers or mother-substitutes" in Austen, see Auerbach, pp. 50–53; on Mrs. Ferrars in *Sense and Sensibility*, Sulloway, p. 80; on *Lady Susan*, Horwitz; on substitute mothers, Todd, "Jane Austen," pp. 79–80; on bad and rivalrous mothers, Robbins, pp. 216, 221; Gilbert and Gubar, p. 174; Hirsch, pp. 47–48.

6. See also Benson, p. 121: Fanny Price (like any heroine of women's correspondences) has multiple substitute mothers and no real one.

7. On *Sense and Sensibility*, which encloses the transmission of a maternal history just like the one that begins Riccoboni's *Miss Jenny*, see Fergus, pp. 52–53, and Briganti, pp. 135–38; also Knuth, p. 67, and Robbins, p. 220, on the transmission of a substitute mother's history and advice as negative example to an unrelated daughter in *Love & Freindship*.

8. On female friendships, see Brownstein, Kaplan, Knuth, and Todd, *Women's Friendships*; on romantic retirement in *Love and Freindship*, see Todd, "Jane Austen," p. 82, and Fergus, pp. 56–58. Many writers have offered explanations for Austen's uses of the epistolary form, including Epstein, Kaplan, and Todd, "Jane Austen," p. 81.

9. Moretti, unpublished research.

10. Duckworth quotes Shaftesbury in his discussion of *Pride and Prejudice* (p. 135).

11. Evans, p. 81; Hume, e.g., pp. 30–31, 37, 44. On Hume's imaginary consensus, see also François, Marshall, "Arguing by Analogy," and Mullan, p. 25.

12. See Evans; Johnson; Sulloway.

13. Janet Todd writes, "The main motivator of Austen, beyond any party political purpose, is her opposition to sensibility in all its forms, whether it be romantic fantasy in young girls, spontaneous feminine understanding or intuition, political aspirations or plot expectations." The letter as "*the* sentimental form" is added to the list of target symptoms of sensibility, as is the figure of the tableau to evoke reader response and a sketch of "plot expectations" very similar to those discussed in Chapter 3 of the present work. See Todd, "Jane Austen," pp. 76–77, 81.

14. Todd also concludes with a characterization of Austen's "scepticism" ("Jane Austen," p. 86).

15. On Austen's skeptical relation to sensibility, see also Evans, pp. 40–41; Johnson, p. xxii; Knuth; Sedgwick, p. 820; and Todd, "Jane Austen," pp. 76–77. Johnson and Todd both note the fluid political valences of sensibility. Todd also compares Austen to Staël, speculating on the possibility of reading Austen's work as "partly an answer to [Staël's and the late Burney's] *romantic permutation of sensibility*" (p. 85; emphasis mine). For a detailed discussion of Wollstonecraft's role in the reaction against women's culture of sensibility, see Barker-Benfield.

16. This argument is supported by Deborah Kaplan's compelling historical research, which leads her to assert that Austen lived at the intersection of two different cultures, which Kaplan calls "the women's culture" and "the gentry's culture," that often involved conflicting experiences and outlooks. As a result, she argues, the early works are fragmentary and inconclusive because in them Austen "drew on the resources of both the gentry's and women's culture" for "familiar versions of womanhood," while the success of her "shift from private to public writing" was based upon a shift of emphasis from the women's to the gentry's culture, so that the major novels "evince traces of the women's culture and amplify the gentry's culture."

As Claudia Brodsky has pointed out, Austen's contemporary Walter Scott was able to see that "Austen narrows the scope of narrative representation in order to effect a new universality of narrative comprehension. . . . In limiting their objective focus of representation to a new middle class, Austen's novels effectively represent a 'new' encompassing 'class,' that of understanding, belonged to by all those whose comprehension of life as they live it and 'observe' it lived by others is itself modeled on their reading of representational fiction" (p. 145).

17. My thinking here is informed by the work of McKeon; see, e.g., *Origins*, pp. 418–19; also Todd, *Sign of Angellica*, p. 141.

18. On the discrediting of feminized discourses, see Sulloway.

19. Many writers, especially women working in sentimental or romance modes, referred to Bernardin de Saint-Pierre's wildly popular and influential *Paul et Virginie*; it is an important subtext in Edgeworth's *Belinda*, and its plot and themes inform such novels as *Wuthering Heights* and George Sand's *Indiana*. The vagaries of canon formation can be noted in the fact that an American high school textbook on *World Literature* in 1935 still excerpted *Paul et Virginie* alongside Rousseau, Goethe, Fielding, Swift, Voltaire, Richardson, and Defoe.

20. Bernardin de Saint-Pierre, *Paul and Virginia*, ed. Donovan, p. 62: "*Shaken always, but constant*" (Donovan's italics).

21. See also Knuth, who makes a similar argument about Lucy Steele's false sentimentalism as foil to Marianne's sensibility (p. 68).

22. Evans argues similarly that Henry Crawford's appeal to female characters is "that he combines in one person both masculine and feminine qualities" (p. 49).

23. "Il n'y voyait que des malheurs généraux et périodiques, dont il n'apercevait pas les causes; des guerres sans sujet et sans objet; des intrigues obscures; des nations sans caractère, et des princes sans humanité. Il préférait à cette lecture celle des romans, qui, s'occupant davantage des sentiments et des intérêts des hommes, lui offraient quelquefois des situations pareilles à la sienne" (Bernardin de Saint-Pierre, *Paul et Virginie*, ed. Mauzi, p. 131).

24. On the feminization of the sentimental hero, cf. Todd, "Jane Austen," p. 77, and Spacks, "Female Resources," p. 93.

25. "Henry, believing, as he says here, that reality itself is sooner doubted than the infallibility of his own prescriptions, will with magisterial complacence lay down the law" (Johnson, p. 37).

26. See Barker-Benfield, pp. 320–21; Brownstein, pp. 93–94; Fergus, p. 36; Johnson, pp. 35, 40–41; Sulloway, pp. 125–26; Wilt, pp. 126–29.

27. I quote Todd, "Jane Austen," p. 79.

28. Austen means the root used medicinally for irritations of the bowel, but the choice of rhubarb is complex. By Austen's time, rhubarb was just beginning to be eaten as a vegetable: "A few years after [1810], Rhubarb had

become established in public favour as a culinary plant." This was a result of domestic English cultivation, begun in 1777, of this Chinese herb. In that year it was first grown by an Oxfordshire apothecary named Hayward, who "raised [it] from seeds sent from Russia in 1762, and produced a drug of excellent quality, which used to be sold as the genuine Rhubarb, by men dressed up as Turks. . . . It was, however, soon realized that the use of Rhubarb as food was sometimes attended with some risk to health. . . . Potassium oxalate is present in quantity in Rhubarb *leaf-stems*, and certain persons who are constitutionally susceptible to salts of oxalic acid, show symptoms of irritant poisoning after eating rhubarb stewed in the ordinary manner . . . fatal and injurious effects having resulted from eating the leaves cooked as spinach" (Grieve, pp. 677–79).

29. I owe the discovery of this particular correspondence to Ellen Brinks.

30. Contrast Austen's technique to that of the truly conservative Jane West's *A Gossip's Story* (1796). Claudia Johnson describes West's novel as "exploding the silly 'romantic' notion that behind every deceased wife is a tyrannical husband," while she notes elsewhere of *Northanger*: "alarms concerning the central gothic *figure*, the tyrannical father, [Austen] concludes, are commensurate to the threat they actually pose" (Johnson, pp. 8, 35).

31. Julia Epstein accurately describes Austen's turn away from the epistolary form as fundamental to her skeptical critique of the literature of sensibility: "It is precisely the letter's failure to communicate and to represent exchange or trust that makes it, for the young Austen, a useful scaffolding on which to support her critique of eighteenth-century narrative subterfuges." My only quarrel with this perceptive essay is that it seems to accept Austen's critique too uncritically. While it is certainly true that "both swoons and letters may be forged," as Epstein puts it, they may also be genuine, although conventional (p. 407). Austen's critique emphasizes one side of an ambiguity inherent in the letter form, as her female predecessors had emphasized the other, so that neither standpoint can claim greater truth about the nature of the form. The reason for Austen's shift is much more political than Epstein's essay implies. Nicola Watson argues that "the rapid disintegration of the epistolary novel in the late 1780's and 1790's, far from being the 'natural' consequence of the increasing sophistication of the novel (as critics have too often casually assumed), was . . . intimately bound up with the problematic political resonances of its narrative mode in the revolutionary and post-revolutionary period"—"resonances" chiefly suggestive of female disruptiveness. Ironically, then, Austen's rejection of the epistolary form in order to explore the possibilities of genuine sensibility

meant engaging in formal "manoeuvres to contain the subversiveness of illicit correspondence and thus the heroine's related insurrection," which Watson sees most consummately performed in *Emma* (pp. 17, 19).

32. Janet Todd further notes that most letters in Austen's major novels are written by men ("Jane Austen," p. 81).

33. Cf. Epstein, p. 415.

34. Cf. Johnson, pp. 47–48.

35. This analysis leads me to disagree with Jan Fergus's statement that *Northanger Abbey*, unlike the later novels, is limited to the exploration of conventions that elicit "suspense and distress," to the exclusion of those that elicit "judgment and sympathy" (Fergus, p. 7).

36. Cf. Spacks, "Female Resources," p. 94.

37. I have made this argument in "Female Sexuality."

38. The quotation is from Johnson (p. xv) referring to Archbishop Whately's praise of Austen in 1821. On Jane Austen's unobtrusive didacticism, see Fergus, esp. pp. 3–8.

39. See also Todd, "Jane Austen," p. 80: "When a woman falls she does so trivially like Lydia or stupidly like Maria or even down the hill like Marianne." And see Evans's discussion of Maria and the ha-ha (pp. 72–74).

40. See also Evans, p. 25.

41. See Chapter 3.

42. The portrait of her unknown father that first enthralled Ellinor makes its way into *Northanger Abbey* as "the portrait of some handsome warrior, whose features will so incomprehensibly strike you, that you will not be able to withdraw your eyes from it" (p. 125). This could also be read as an allusion to Walpole's *The Castle of Otranto*, but Catherine Morland generally resembles Lee's heroines much more than Walpole's.

43. See also Evans, who, echoing Alistair Duckworth and others, calls Fanny the "moral centre" of Mansfield Park (p. 25).

44. My reading of Fanny Price as corresponding to Staël's Lucile is further supported by the connection Janet Todd observes between Mary Crawford and Corinne. She describes *Corinne* as "in plot something like *Mansfield Park* if the author had decided to applaud the harp-playing Mary Crawford and had intended setting her perfections off against the narrow rigidity of the country house" ("Jane Austen," p. 85).

45. See also Duckworth, pp. 3–5, Briganti, pp. 131–32, and Benson, p. 117.

Bibliography

English and French Novels of Women's Correspondence

*Adele et Sophie, ou les Deux Amies, par Mlle S****. Paris, 1798.

Adeline de Courcy. London, 1797.

The Adopted Daughter; or, The History of Miss Clarissa B———. London, 1767.

Aïssé, Mademoiselle. *Lettres de Mademoiselle Aïssé à Madame de C****. Paris, 1787.

Austen, Jane. *Lady Susan*. In *Northanger Abbey, The Watsons, Lady Susan, and Sanditon*, edited by John Davie. The World's Classics. Oxford: Oxford University Press, 1985.

Beccary, Madame. *Les Dangers de la calomnie, ou Mémoires de Fanny Spingler, histoire angloise*. Paris, 1770.

———. *Mémoires de Lucie d'Olbéry, trad. de l'anglois*. Paris, 1770.

———. *Lettres de Milady Bedfort*. Paris, 1769.

Bennett, Agnes Maria. *Agnes de-Courci, A Domestic Tale*. London, 1789.

Bertrand-Quinquet, Suzanne Giroust de Morency, dame. *Euphémie, ou les suites du siège de Lyon*. Paris, 1802.

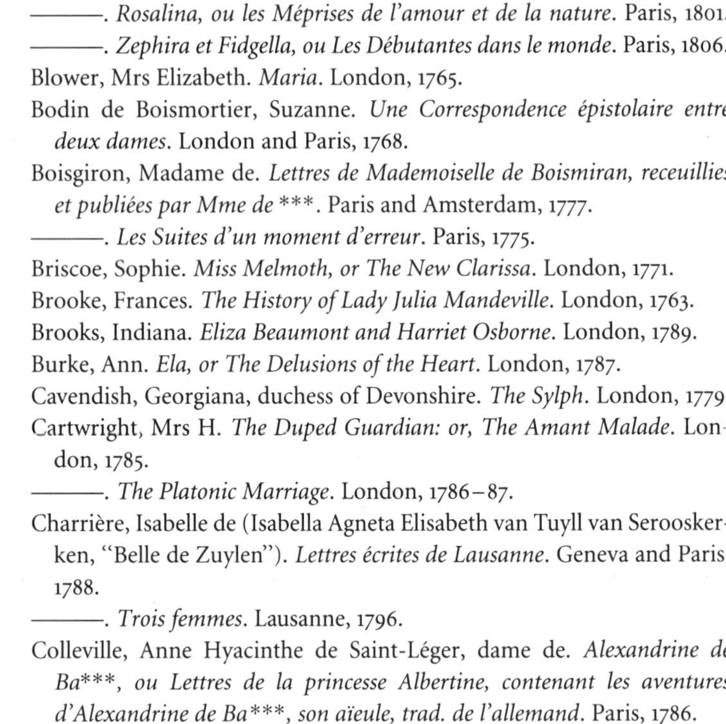

———. *Illyrine, ou l'Eceuil de inexpérience*. Paris, 1800.

———. *Lise, ou les Hermites du Mont Blanc*. Paris, 1801.

———. *Rosalina, ou les Méprises de l'amour et de la nature*. Paris, 1801.

———. *Zephira et Fidgella, ou Les Débutantes dans le monde*. Paris, 1806.

Blower, Mrs Elizabeth. *Maria*. London, 1765.

Bodin de Boismortier, Suzanne. *Une Correspondence épistolaire entre deux dames*. London and Paris, 1768.

Boisgiron, Madame de. *Lettres de Mademoiselle de Boismiran, receuillies et publiées par Mme de ****. Paris and Amsterdam, 1777.

———. *Les Suites d'un moment d'erreur*. Paris, 1775.

Briscoe, Sophie. *Miss Melmoth, or The New Clarissa*. London, 1771.

Brooke, Frances. *The History of Lady Julia Mandeville*. London, 1763.

Brooks, Indiana. *Eliza Beaumont and Harriet Osborne*. London, 1789.

Burke, Ann. *Ela, or The Delusions of the Heart*. London, 1787.

Cavendish, Georgiana, duchess of Devonshire. *The Sylph*. London, 1779.

Cartwright, Mrs H. *The Duped Guardian: or, The Amant Malade*. London, 1785.

———. *The Platonic Marriage*. London, 1786–87.

Charrière, Isabelle de (Isabella Agneta Elisabeth van Tuyll van Serooskerken, "Belle de Zuylen"). *Lettres écrites de Lausanne*. Geneva and Paris, 1788.

———. *Trois femmes*. Lausanne, 1796.

Colleville, Anne Hyacinthe de Saint-Léger, dame de. *Alexandrine de Ba***, ou Lettres de la princesse Albertine, contenant les aventures d'Alexandrine de Ba***, son aïeule, trad. de l'allemand*. Paris, 1786.

Collyer, Mary. *Felicia to Charlotte. Being Letters from a Young Lady in the Country to Her Friend in Town*. 1744. New York: Garland Press, 1974.

Constantia; or, The Distressed Friend. London, 1770.

The Convent: or, The History of Julia. Dublin, 1767.

Cooper, Maria Susanna. *The History of Fanny Meadows*. London, 1775.

———. *Letters Between Emilia and Harriet*. London, 1762.

Dalibard, Françoise Therèse Aumerle Saint-Phalier, dame. *Le Portefeuille rendu, ou Lettres historiques par Mademoiselle S****. London, 1749.

Edgeworth, Maria. *Letters for Literary Ladies*. London, 1795.

*L'Eleve de la Nouvelle Héloïse, ou Lettres de Mme la marquise de *** à Mme la comtesse de ****. Paris, 1761.

Emily; or, The Fatal Promise. London, 1792.

Emma; or, The Child of Sorrow. Dublin, 1776.

The Faithful Fugitives. London, 1766.

Fielding, Sarah. *The History of Ophelia*. London, 1760.

La Fille, ou Histoire de Miss Emilie Royston et de Miss Henrietta Ayres. London, 1776.

Fontette de Sommery, Mademoiselle de. *Lettres de Mademoiselle de Tourville à Madame la comtesse de Lenoncourt.* Paris, 1788.

Fuller, Anne. *The Convent, or The History of Sophia Nelson.* London, 1786.

Gacon-Dufour, Marie. *Le Préjugé vaincu, ou Lettres de madame la comtesse de *** et de madame de *** réfugiée en Angleterre.* Paris, 1787.

Gibbes, Phoebe. *The American Fugitive, or Friendship in a Nunnery.* London, 1784.

Griffith, Elizabeth. *The Delicate Distress.* London, 1769.

———. *The History of Lady Barton.* London, 1776.

Gunning, Susannah Minifie. *Barford Abbey.* London, 1768.

———. *The Cottage.* London, 1769.

Gunning, Susannah Minifie, and Margaret Minifie. *The Histories of Lady Frances S——— and Lady Caroline S———.* London, 1763.

Hamilton, Lady Mary. *Letters from the Duchess of Crui.* London, 1776.

Haywood, Eliza. *Epistles for the Ladies.* London, 1776.

Helme, Elizabeth. *Clara and Emmeline.* London, 1788.

The History of Lavinia Rawlins. London, 1761.

The History of Melinda Harley. London, 1779.

The History of Miss Indiana Danby. London, 1772.

The History of Miss Oakley. London, 1764.

Hortense et Mathilde. London and Paris, 1789.

Keir, Susanna (Harvey). *The History of Miss Greville.* London, 1787.

———. *Interesting Memoirs.* London, 1785.

Kendall, A. *Derwent Priory.* London, 1798.

Le Prince de Beaumont, Jeanne Marie. *Lettres de Madame du Montier à la marquise de *** sa fille, avec les réponses.* Lyons, 1756.

Lee, Harriet. *Clara Lennox.* London, 1797.

———. *The Errors of Innocence.* London, 1786.

Lee, Sophia. *The Life of a Lover.* London, 1804.

———. *The Recess; or, A Tale of Other Times.* London, 1783–85.

Lennox, Charlotte. *Euphemia.* London, 1790.

———. *Hermione; or, The Orphan Sisters.* London, 1791.

*Lettres de la Marquise de Bremont à Eugénie, publiées par la comtesse de ***.* Paris, 1788.

*Lettres de Mlle de Jussy à Mlle de ***.* Paris and Amsterdam, 1762.

Levacher de la Feutrie, Madame S. M. *Minna, ou Lettres de deux jeunes vénitiennes.* Paris, 1802.

Malarme, Charlotte Bournon, comtesse de. *Les Trois soeurs et la folie guérie par l'amour, ou Les Heureux effets de l'amour filial*. Paris, 1796.

Maple Vale; or, The History of Miss Sidney. London, 1791.

Margaretta, Countess of Rainsford. London, 1769.

Marivaux, Pierre Coulet de Chamblain de. *La Vie de Marianne, ou Les Avantures de Madame la comtesse de* ***. Edited by Frédéric Deloffre. Paris: Garnier Frères, 1957.

Marshall, Mrs James. *The History of Alicia Montague*. London, 1767.

Masquerades; or, What You Will. By the Author of Eliza Warwick. London, 1780.

Mérard de Saint-Just, Anne Louise Félicité d'Ormoy, dame. *Le Château noir, ou Les Souffrances de la jeune Ophelle*. Paris, 1799.

Norman, Elizabeth. *The Child of Woe*. London, 1789.

Palmer, Mrs *Female Stability; or, The History of Miss Belville*. London, 1780.

Parsons, Eliza P. *Ellen and Julia*. London, 1793.

Polier de Bottens, Mademoiselle J. Fr. *Félicie et Florestine*. Geneva, 1803.

———. *Lettres d'Hortense de Valsin à Eugénie de Saint-Firmin*. Paris and Lausanne, 1788.

Poulain, Mademoiselle. *Lettres de Madame la comtesse de La Riviere à la baronne de Neufpont, son amie*. Paris, 1776.

Purbeck, Elizabeth. *Matilda and Elizabeth*. London, 1796.

Purbeck, Misses. *Neville Castle*. London, 1802.

Reeve, Clara. *The Two Mentors*. London, 1783.

The Rencontre: or, Transition of a Moment. Dublin, 1784.

Riccoboni, Marie-Jeanne Laboras de Mézières, dame. "Histoire de deux jeunes amies." *Mercure de France*, 1 Apr. 1786: 5–42; 8 Apr. 1786: 64–88.

———. *Histoire de Miss Jenny Revel, écrite et envoyée par elle à Milady comtesse de Roscommond*. Paris, 1764.

———. "Lettre de Madame la marquise d'A*** à sa soeur." *Mercure de France*, 12 Nov. 1785: 53–67.

———. *Lettres d'Elisabeth-Sophie de Valliere à Louise-Hortense de Canteleu, son amie*. 1772. Neuchâtel, 1783.

———. *Lettres de milady Juliette Catesby à milady Henriette Campley, son amie*. Amsterdam and Paris, 1759.

Scott, Sarah. *A Description of Millenium Hall, and the Country Adjacent. . . .* London, 1762.

Sheridan, Frances. *Memoirs of Miss Sidney Biddulph*. London, 1761.

Skinn, Ann Masterman. *The Old Maid; or, The History of Miss Ravensworth*. London, 1771.

Smith, Charlotte. *Letters from a Solitary Wanderer*. London, 1798–1801.

Spencer, Sarah E. *Memoirs of the Miss Holmsbys*. London, 1788.

Staël-Holstein, Germaine de. *Corinne, or Italy*. 1807. Translated and edited by Avriel H. Goldberger. New Brunswick, N.J.: Rutgers University Press, 1987.

———. *Corinne, ou l'Italie*. 1807. Edited by Simone Balayé. Paris: Gallimard, 1985.

———. *Delphine*. 1802. Edited by Claudine Herrmann. Paris: Des Femmes, 1981.

Tomlins, Elizabeth Sophia. *The Victim of Fancy*. London, 1794.

Tott, Claire de. *Pauline de Vergies, ou Lettres de Madame de Stainais*. Paris, 1788.

Vasse, Cornélie Wouters, baronne de. *Les Aveux d'une femme galante, ou Lettres de la marquise de *** à milady Fanny Stapelton*. London and Paris, 1782.

Vigor, Mrs [Miss Godwin]. *Letters Between an English Lady and Her Friend at Paris, Containing the Memoirs of Mrs Williams*. London, 1770.

Warton, Jane. *Letters Addressed to Two Married Ladies*. London, 1782.

———. *Peggy and Patty*. London, 1783.

Other Works Consulted

Adburgham, Alison. *Women in Print: Writing Women and Women's Periodicals from the Restoration to the Accession of Queen Victoria*. London: Allen & Unwin, 1972.

Allen, Walter F. *The English Novel: A Short Critical History*. London: Phoenix House, 1954.

Alliston, April. "Female Sexuality and the Referent of Enlightenment Realisms." In *Spectacles of Realism: Gender, Body, Genre*, ed. Margaret Cohen and Christopher Prendergast. Minneapolis: University of Minnesota Press, 1995.

———. "Of Haunted Highlands: Mapping a Geography of Gender in the Margins of Europe. In *Cultural Interaction in the Romantic Age*, ed. Gregory Maertz. Forthcoming.

———. "The Value of a Literary Legacy: Retracing the Transmission of Value Through Female Lines." *Yale Journal of Criticism* 4, no. 1 (Oct. 1990): 109–27.

Altman, Janet. *Epistolarity: Approaches to a Form*. Columbus: Ohio State University Press, 1982.

Armstrong, Nancy. *Desire and Domestic Fiction: A Political History of the Novel*. New York: Oxford University Press, 1987.

Auerbach, Nina. *Communities of Women: An Idea in Fiction*. Cambridge, Mass.: Harvard University Press, 1978.

Austen, Jane. *Mansfield Park*. 1814. Edited by James Kinsley and John Lucas. Oxford: Oxford University Press, 1970.

———. *Northanger Abbey, Lady Susan, The Watsons, and Sanditon*. 1818, 1871, 1925. Edited by John Davie. Introduction by Terry Castle. Oxford: Oxford University Press, 1990.

———. *Pride and Prejudice*. 1813. Edited by Tony Tanner. London: Penguin Books, 1972.

———. *Sense and Sensibility*. 1811. Edited by James Kinsley. Introduction by Margaret Doody. Notes by Claire Lamont. Oxford: Oxford University Press, 1990.

Backer, Dorothy Anne Liot. *Precious Women*. New York: Basic Books, 1974.

Backscheider, Paula R. *Spectacular Politics: Theatrical Power and Mass Culture in Early Modern England*. Baltimore: Johns Hopkins University Press, 1993.

Baker, Ernest. *The History of the English Novel: The Later Romances and the Establishment of Realism*. 1929. London: H. F. & G. Witherby, 1942.

———. *The History of the English Novel: The Novel of Sentiment and the Gothic Romance*. 1929. London: H. F. & G. Witherby, 1942.

Ballard, George. *Memoirs of Several Ladies of Great Britain, Who Have Been Celebrated for Their Writings or Skill in the Learned Languages, Arts and Sciences*. 1752. Edited by Ruth Perry. Detroit: Wayne State University Press, 1985.

Ballaster, Ros. "Romancing the Novel: Gender and Genre in Early Theories of Narrative." In *Living by the Pen: Early British Women Writers*, ed. Dale Spender. New York: Teachers College Press, 1992.

Barker, Jane. *A Patch-Work Screen for the Ladies; or Love and Virtue Recommended: In a Collection of Instructive Novels*. London, 1726.

Barker-Benfield, G. J. *The Culture of Sensibility: Sex and Society in Eighteenth-Century Britain*. Chicago: University of Chicago Press, 1992.

Baym, Nina. *Woman's Fiction: A Guide to Novels By and About Women in America, 1820–70*. 1978. Urbana: University of Illinois Press, 1993.

Beasley, Faith E. *Revising Memory: Women's Fiction and Memoirs in Seventeenth-Century France*. New Brunswick, N.J.: Rutgers University Press, 1990.

Beasley, Jerry C. *Novels of the 1740s*. Athens: University of Georgia Press, 1982.

Benjamin, Jessica. *The Bonds of Love: Psychoanalysis, Feminism, and the Problem of Domination*. New York: Pantheon Books, 1988.

Benson, Mary Margaret. "Mothers, Substitute Mothers, and Daughters in the Novels of Jane Austen." *Persuasions* 11 (1989): 117–24.

Benstock, Shari. *Textualizing the Feminine: On the Limits of Genre*. Norman: University of Oklahoma Press, 1991.

Bernardin de Saint-Pierre, Jacques-Henri. *Paul and Virginia*. Edited and translated by John Donovan. London: Penguin Books, 1989.

———. *Paul et Virginie*. 1788. Edited by Robert Mauzi. Paris: Garnier-Flammarion, 1966.

Blackstone, William. *Commentaries on the Laws of England*. 1765–69. Edited by William Draper Lewis. 2 vols. Philadelphia: Rees Welsh, 1898.

Boccaccio, Giovanni. *The Decameron*. Translated by G. H. McWilliams. Harmondsworth, Middlesex: Penguin Books, 1972.

Boone, Joseph Allen. *Tradition Counter Tradition: Love and the Form of Fiction*. Chicago: University of Chicago Press, 1987.

Briganti, Chiara. "Austen's Shackles and Feminine Filiation." In *Politics, Gender, and the Arts: Women, the Arts, and Society*, ed. Ronald Dotterer and Susan Bowers, 130–49. Selinsgrove, Pa.: Susquehanna University Press, 1992.

Brodsky, Claudia J. *The Imposition of Form: Studies in Narrative Representation and Knowledge*. Princeton, N.J.: Princeton University Press, 1987.

Brooks, Peter. *The Novel of Worldliness: Crébillon, Marivaux, Laclos, Stendhal*. Princeton, N.J.: Princeton University Press, 1969.

———. *Reading for the Plot: Design and Intention in Narrative*. New York: Knopf, 1984.

Brophy, Elizabeth Bergen. *Women's Lives and the Eighteenth-Century English Novel*. Tampa: University of South Florida Press, 1991.

Brownstein, Rachel. *Becoming a Heroine: Reading About Women in Novels*. New York: Viking Press, 1982.

Burlin, Katrin R. "'Pictures of Perfection' at Pemberley: Art in *Pride and Prejudice*." In *Jane Austen: New Perspectives*, ed. Janet Todd. New York: Holmes & Meier, 1983.

Burney, Frances (Madame d'Arblay). *Evelina; or, The History of a Young Lady's Introduction into the World*. 1778. Edited by E. A. Bloom and L. D. Bloom. Oxford: Oxford University Press, 1984.

Butler, Judith. *Gender Trouble: Feminism and the Subversion of Identity*. New York: Routledge, 1990.

Butler, Marilyn. *Jane Austen and the War of Ideas*. Oxford: Oxford University Press, 1975.

———. *Romantics, Rebels, and Reactionaries: English Literature and its Background, 1760–1830*. Oxford: Oxford University Press, 1982.

Butor, Michel. "Sur *La Princesse de Clèves*." In *Répertoire*. Paris: Minuit, 1960.

Castle, Terry. "The Spectralization of the Other in the Mysteries of Udolpho." In *The New Eighteenth Century: Theory, Politics, English Literature*, ed. Felicity Nussbaum and Laura Brown. New York: Methuen, 1987.

Cervantes Saavedra, Miguel de. *Don Quixote*. Translated by Tobias Smollett. New York: Farrar, Straus & Giroux, 1986.

Chodorow, Nancy. *The Reproduction of Mothering: Psychoanalysis and the Sociology of Gender*. Berkeley and Los Angeles: University of California Press, 1978.

Cohen, Margaret. "The Feminine Origins of the Social Novel." In *Spectacles of Realism: Gender, Body, Genre*, ed. Margaret Cohen and Christopher Prendergast. Minneapolis: University of Minnesota Press, 1995.

———. "'The Most Suffering Class': Gender, Class, and Consciousness in Pre-Marxist France." *Boundary 2* 18, no. 2 (Summer 1991): 22–46.

———. *Why Was There No French Women's Realism?* [working title]. Princeton, N.J.: Princeton University Press. Forthcoming.

Coleman, Patrick. "Exile and Narrative Voice in *Corinne*." In *Studies in Eighteenth-Century Culture* 24 (1994).

Cook, Elizabeth Heckendorn. "Going Public: The Letter and the Contract in *Fanni Butlerd*." *Eighteenth-Century Studies* 24, no. 1 (Fall 1990): 21–46.

Coontz, Stephanie, and Peta Henderson, eds. *Women's Work, Men's Property*. London: Verso, 1986.

Cross, E. A. *World Literature*. New York: American Book, 1935.

Damrosch, Leo, ed. *The Profession of Eighteenth-Century Literature: Reflections on an Institution*. Madison: University of Wisconsin Press, 1992.

Day, Robert A. *Told in Letters: Epistolary Fiction Before Richardson*. Ann Arbor: University of Michigan Press, 1966.

DeJean, Joan. *Fictions of Sappho, 1546–1937*. Chicago: University of Chicago Press, 1989.

———. "Lafayette's Ellipses: The Privileges of Anonymity." *PMLA* 99, no. 5 (Oct. 1984): 884–902.

———. "Staël's *Corinne*: The Novel's Other Dilemma." *Stanford French Review* 11, no. 1 (Spring 1987): 77–87.

———. *Tender Geographies: Women and the Origins of the Novel in France*. New York: Columbia University Press, 1991.

DeJean, Joan, and Nancy Miller, eds. *The Politics of Tradition: Placing Women in French Literature. Yale French Studies* 75 (1988).

De Lauretis, Teresa. "The Essence of the Triangle or, Taking the Risk of Essentialism Seriously: Feminist Theory in Italy, the U.S. and Britain." *Differences: A Journal of Feminist Cultural Studies* 2 (1989): 3–37.

———. "The Practice of Sexual Difference and Feminist Thought in Italy." In *Italian Feminist Writers*, ed. Patricia Cicogna and Teresa De Lauretis. Milan: Libreria delle donne, 1990.

Derrida, Jacques. *La Carte postale: De Socrate à Freud et au-delà*. Paris: Flammarion, 1980.

———. "Living On / Border Lines." In *Deconstruction and Criticism*, ed. Harold Bloom, 75–176. New York: Seabury Press, 1979.

———. "La Loi du genre / The Law of Genre." *Glyph* 7 (Spring 1980). Translated by Avital Ronell, *Critical Inquiry* 7 (Autumn 1980): 55–81.

Des Essarts, Nicolas Toussaint Lemoyne. *Les Siècles littéraires de France*. Paris, an VIII–an IX [1800–1801].

Diderot, Denis. *La Religieuse*. 1796. Edited by Robert Mauzi. Paris: Gallimard, 1972.

Doody, Margaret Anne. "Deserts, Ruins and Troubled Waters: Female Dreams in Fiction and the Development of the Gothic Novel." *Genre* 10, no. 4 (Winter 1977): 529–72.

———. Introduction to *The Female Quixote*, by Charlotte Lennox. Oxford: Oxford University Press, 1989.

———. *Frances Burney: The Life in the Works*. New Brunswick, N.J.: Rutgers University Press, 1988.

———. *A Natural Passion: A Study of the Novels of Samuel Richardson*. Oxford: Oxford University Press, 1974.

Douthwaite, Julia V. *Exotic Women: Literary Heroines and Cultural Strategies in Ancien Régime France*. Philadelphia: University of Pennsylvania Press, 1992.

Duckworth, Alistair. *The Improvement of the Estate: A Study of Jane Austen's Novels*. Baltimore: Johns Hopkins University Press, 1971.

Du Noyer, Anne Marguerite Petit, dame. *Lettres historiques et galantes de deux dames de condition*. Cologne, 1704.

Du Plaisir, le Sieur. *Sentimens sur les lettres et sur l'histoire*. Paris, 1683.

Duyfhuizen, Bernard. *Narratives of Transmission*. Rutherford: Associated University Presses, 1992.

Eagleton, Terry. *The Rape of Clarissa: Writing, Sexuality and Class Struggle in Samuel Richardson*. Oxford: Blackwell, 1982.

Eliot, George. "Woman in France: Madame de Sablé" and "Silly Novels by Lady Novelists." In *Essays of George Eliot*, ed. Thomas Pinney. New York: Columbia University Press, 1963.

Ellis, Kate Ferguson. *The Contested Castle: Gothic Novels and the Subversion of Domestic Ideology*. Urbana: University of Illinois Press, 1989.

Ehrlich, Victor. *Russian Formalism: History—Doctrine*. New Haven, Conn.: Yale University Press, 1981 [1955].

Epstein, Julia L. "Jane Austen's Juvenilia and the Female Epistolary Tradition." *Papers on Language and Literature* 21, no. 4 (Fall 1985): 399–416.

Evans, Mary. *Jane Austen and the State*. London: Tavistock Publications, 1987.

Ezell, Margaret. J. M. *The Patriarch's Wife: Literary Evidence and the History of the Family*. Chapel Hill: University of North Carolina Press, 1987.

———. *Writing Women's Literary History*. Baltimore: Johns Hopkins University Press, 1993.

Fergus, Jan. *Jane Austen and the Didactic Novel: "Northanger Abbey," "Sense and Sensibility," and "Pride and Prejudice."* Totowa, N.J.: Barnes & Noble, 1983.

Ferguson, Frances. "Interpreting the Self Through Letters." *Centrum*, n.s., 1, no. 2 (Fall 1981): 107–12.

Foley, Helene. *The Homeric Hymn to Demeter*. Princeton, N.J.: Princeton University Press, 1993.

Footerman, Sharon B. "A Neglected Source for Fanny Burney's *Evelina*." *Notes and Queries* 222 (1977): 274–76.

Foucault, Michel. *The Order of Things: An Archaeology of the Human Sciences*. New York: Random House, 1970.

Fowler, Alastair. *Kinds of Literature: An Introduction to the Theory of Genres and Modes*. Cambridge, Mass.: Harvard University Press, 1982.

Francois, Anne-Lise. "To Hold in Common and Know by Heart: The Prevalence of Gentle Forces in Humean Empiricism and Romantic Experience." *Yale Journal of Criticism* 7, no. 1 (Spring 1994): 139–62.

Freud, Sigmund. *Dora: An Analysis of a Case of Hysteria*. Edited by Philip Rieff. New York: Macmillan, 1963.

Gallop, Jane. *The Daughter's Seduction*. Ithaca, N.Y.: Cornell University Press, 1982.

Gilbert, Sandra M., and Susan Gubar. *The Madwoman in the Attic: The Woman Writer and the Nineteenth-Century Literary Imagination*. New Haven, Conn.: Yale University Press, 1979.

Giraud, Yves F. A. *Bibliographie du roman épistolaire en France: Des Origines à 1842*. Fribourg: Editions universitaires, 1977.

Goldsmith, Elizabeth C., ed. *Writing the Female Voice: Essays on Epistolary Literature*. Boston: Northeastern University Press, 1989.

Goody, Jack, Joan Thirsk, and E. P. Thompson, eds. *Family and Inheritance: Rural Society in Western Europe, 1200–1800*. Cambridge: Cambridge University Press, 1976.

Goulemot, Jean Marie. "Literary Practices: Publicizing the Private." In *A History of Private Life: Passions of the Renaissance*, ed. Roger Chartier. Translated by Arthur Goldhammer. Cambridge, Mass.: Harvard University Press, 1989.

Greenfield, Susan C. "'Oh Dear Resemblance of Thy Murdered Mother': Female Authorship in *Evelina*." *Eighteenth-Century Fiction* 3, no. 4 (July 1991): 301–20.

———. "Veiled Desire: Mother-Daughter Love and Sexual Imagery in Ann Radcliffe's *The Italian*." *The Eighteenth Century: Theory and Interpretation* 33, no. 1 (Spring 1992): 73–89.

Grieve, M., F.R.H.S. 1931. *A Modern Herbal: The Medicinal, Culinary, Cosmetic and Economic Properties, Cultivation and Folklore of Herbs, Grasses, Fungi, Shrubs and Trees with all Their Modern Scientific Uses*. Reprint. New York: Dorset Press, 1992.

Guetti, Barbara. "The Old Regime and the Feminist Revolution: Laclos' 'De l'Education des femmes.'" *Yale French Studies* 63 (1982): 139–62.

Hampton, Timothy. *Writing from History: The Rhetoric of Exemplarity in Renaissance Literature*. Ithaca, N.Y.: Cornell University Press, 1990.

Harkin, Maureen. "Smith's *Theory of Moral Sentiments*: Sympathy, Women, and Emulation." In *Studies in Eighteenth-Century Culture* 24 (1994).

Harris, Wendell V. "Canonicity." *PMLA* 106, no. 1 (Jan. 1991): 110–21, 191.

Haywood, Eliza. *The British Recluse*. 1722. London, 1724.

Hirsch, Marianne. *The Mother/Daughter Plot: Narrative, Psychoanalysis, Feminism*. Bloomington: Indiana University Press, 1989.

———. "A Mother's Discourse: Incorporation and Repetition in *La Princesse de Clèves*." *Yale French Studies* 62 (1981): 67–87.

Hirsch, Marianne, and Evelyn Fox Keller, eds. *Conflicts in Feminism*. New York: Routledge, 1990.

Hobby, Elaine. *Virtue of Necessity: English Women's Writing, 1649–88*. London: Virago Press, 1988.

Homans, Margaret. *Bearing the Word: Language and Female Experience in Nineteenth-Century Women's Writing*. Chicago: University of Chicago Press, 1986.

Homer. *The Odyssey*. Translated by Robert Fagles. New York: Viking Penguin. Forthcoming.

Horwitz, Barbara J. "Lady Susan: The Wicked Mother in Jane Austen's Novels." *Persuasions* 9 (1987): 84–87.

Hunter, J. Paul. *Before Novels: The Cultural Contexts of Eighteenth-Century English Fiction*. New York: Norton, 1990.

Hutcheson, John. "Subdued Feminism: Jane Austen, Charlotte Brontë and George Eliot." *International Journal of Women's Studies* 6, no. 3 (May–June 1983): 230–57.

Irigaray, Luce. *Speculum de l'autre femme*. Paris: Minuit, 1974.

Jackson, Virginia. "'Faith in Anatomy': Reading Emily Dickinson." In "*Dwelling in Possibility*": *Essays on Gender, Genre and Poetry*, ed. Yopie Prins and Maeera Shreiber. Ithaca, N.Y.: Cornell University Press, 1997.

Jacobus, Mary. *Reading Woman: Essays in Feminist Criticism*. New York: Columbia University Press, 1986.

Jardine, Alice. *Gynesis: Configurations of Woman and Modernity*. Ithaca, N.Y.: Cornell University Press, 1985.

Jehlen, Myra. "Archimedes and the Paradox of Feminist Criticism." In *The Signs Reader: Women, Gender and Scholarship*, ed. Elizabeth Abel and Emily K. Abel, 69–95. Chicago: University of Chicago Press, 1983.

Johnson, Claudia L. *Jane Austen: Women, Politics and the Novel*. Chicago: University of Chicago Press, 1987.

Jost, François. "Le Roman épistolaire et la technique narrative au XVIIIe siècle." *Comparative Literature Studies* 4 (1966): 397–428.

Kahn, Madeleine. *Narrative Transvestism: Rhetoric and Gender in the Eighteenth-Century English Novel*. Ithaca, N.Y.: Cornell University Press, 1991.

Kamuf, Peggy. *Fictions of Feminine Desire: Disclosures of Heloise*. Lincoln: University of Nebraska Press, 1982.

———. "Writing like a Woman." In *Women and Language in Literature and Society*, ed. Sally McConnell-Ginet, Ruth Borker, and Nelly Furman, 284–99. New York: Praeger, 1980.

Kaplan, Deborah. "Female Friendship and Epistolary Form: *Lady Susan* and the Development of Jane Austen's Fiction." *Criticism* 29, no. 2 (Spring 1987): 163–78.

———. *Jane Austen Among Women.* Baltimore: Johns Hopkins University Press, 1992.

Kany, Charles E. *The Beginnings of the Epistolary Novel in France, Italy, and Spain.* Berkeley: University of California Press, 1937.

Kauffman, Linda. *Discourses of Desire: Gender, Genre, and Epistolary Fictions.* Ithaca, N.Y.: Cornell University Press, 1986.

Knuth, Deborah J. "'We fainted Alternately on a Sofa': Female Friendship in Jane Austen's *Juvenilia.*" *Persuasions* 9 (1987): 64–71.

Laclos, Pierre Choderlos de. *Oeuvres complètes.* Paris: Gallimard, 1951.

Lafayette, Marie-Madeleine Pioche de la Vergne de. *La Princesse de Clèves.* 1678. Edited by Antoine Adam. Paris: Garnier-Flammarion, 1966.

———. *The Princess of Clèves.* Translated by Walter J. Cobb. Introduction by Nancy K. Miller. New York: New American Library, 1989.

Langbauer, Laurie. *Women and Romance: The Consolations of Gender in the English Novel.* Ithaca, N.Y.: Cornell University Press, 1990.

Lathuillère, Roger. *La Préciosité: Etude historique et linguistique.* Geneva: Droz, 1966.

Le Brun, Annie. *Les Châteaux de la subversion.* Clamecy, France: Garnier, 1982.

Lebrun, François. *La Vie conjugale sous l'ancien régime.* Paris: Armand Colin, 1975.

Lepointe, Gabriel. *La Famille dans l'ancien droit.* Paris: Domat Montchrestien, 1947.

Lettres portugaises, Lettres d'une péruvienne, et autres romans d'amour par lettres. Edited by Bernard Bray and Isabelle Landy-Houillon. Paris: Flammarion, 1983.

Littré, Emile. *Dictionnaire de la langue française.* Paris: Pauvert, 1956.

Lougee, Carolyn C. *Le Paradis des femmes: Women, Salons, and Social Stratification in Seventeenth-Century France.* Princeton, N.J.: Princeton University Press, 1976.

Lukacher, Maryline. *Maternal Fictions: Stendhal, Sand, Rachilde, and Bataille.* Durham, N.C.: Duke University Press, 1994.

Lyons, John. *Exemplum: The Rhetoric of Example in Early Modern France and Italy.* Princeton, N.J.: Princeton University Press, 1989.

MacArthur, Elizabeth J. "Devious Narratives: Refusal of Closure in Two Eighteenth-Century Novels." *Eighteenth-Century Studies* 21, no. 1 (Fall 1987), 1–20.

———. *Extravagant Narratives: Closure and Dynamics in the Epistolary Form.* Princeton, N.J.: Princeton University Press, 1990.

MacCarthy, B. G. *Women Writers: Their Contribution to the English Novel, 1621–1744*. Oxford: Blackwell, 1944.

MacDonough, Oliver. *Jane Austen: Real and Imagined Worlds*. New Haven, Conn.: Yale University Press, 1991.

Maclean, Marie. *Narrative as Performance: The Baudelairean Experiment*. London: Routledge, 1988.

Manley, Delariviere (Mary). *The Secret History of Queen Zarah, and the Zarazians*. Albigion [London], 1711.

Marin, Louis. *Le Portrait du Roi*. Paris: Minuit, 1981.

Markley, Robert. "Sentimentality as Performance: Shaftesbury, Sterne, and the Theatrics of Virtue." In *The New Eighteenth Century: Theory, Politics, English Literature*, ed. Felicity Nussbaum and Laura Brown, 210–30. New York: Methuen, 1987.

Marshall, David. "Arguing by Analogy: Hume's Standard of Taste." *Eighteenth-Century Studies* 28, no. 3 (Spring 1995): 323–43.

———. *The Surprising Effects of Sympathy: Marivaux, Diderot, Rousseau, and Mary Shelley*. Chicago: University of Chicago Press, 1988.

Mavor, Elizabeth. 1971. *The Ladies of Llangollen*. Harmondsworth, Middlesex: Penguin Books, 1981.

May, Georges. *Le Dilemme du roman au XVIII*[e] *siècle*. New Haven, Conn.: Yale University Press, 1963.

McBurney, William M. *A Checklist of English Prose Fiction 1700–1739*. Cambridge, Mass.: Harvard University Press, 1960.

———. "Edmund Curll, Mrs. Jane Barker, and the English Novel." *Philological Quarterly* 37, no. 4 (1958): 385–99.

McKeon, Michael. "Historicizing Patriarchy: The Emergence of Gender Difference in England, 1660–1760." *Eighteenth-Century Studies* 28, no. 3 (Spring 1995): 295–322.

———. *The Origins of the English Novel, 1600–1740*. Baltimore: Johns Hopkins University Press, 1987.

McMullen, Lorraine. "Frances Brooke's Early Fiction." *Canadian Literature* 86 (1980): 31–40.

Meise, Helga. *Die Unschuld und die Schrift: Deutsche Frauenromane des 18. Jahrhunderts*. Berlin: Guttandrin & Hoppe, 1983.

Meltzer, Françoise. *Salome and the Dance of Writing: Portraits of Mimesis in Literature*. Chicago: University of Chicago Press, 1987.

Melzer, Sara, and Leslie Rabine, eds. *Rebel Daughters: Women and the French Revolution*. New York: Oxford University Press, 1992.

Miller, D. A. *Narrative and Its Discontents: Problems of Closure in the Traditional Novel*. Princeton, N.J.: Princeton University Press, 1981.

Miller, Nancy K. "Changing the Subject: Authorship, Writing, and the Reader." In *Feminist Studies / Critical Studies*, ed. Teresa de Lauretis, 102–20. Bloomington: Indiana University Press, 1986.

———. *The Heroine's Text. Readings in the French and English Novel, 1722–82*. New York: Columbia University Press, 1980.

———. *Subject to Change: Reading Feminist Writing*. New York: Columbia University Press, 1988.

Miller, Nancy K., ed. *The Poetics of Gender*. New York: Columbia University Press, 1986.

Modleski, Tania. "Feminism and the Power of Interpretation: Some Critical Readings." In *Feminist Studies / Critical Studies*, ed. Teresa de Lauretis, 121–38. Bloomington: Indiana University Press, 1986.

Moers, Ellen. *Literary Women: The Great Writers*. 1963. New York: Oxford University Press, 1985.

Moi, Toril. *Sexual / Textual Politics: Feminist Literary Theory*. London: Methuen, 1985.

Mongrédien, Georges, ed. *Les Précieux et les précieuses*. Paris: Mercure de France, 1963.

Mücke, Dorothea von. *Virtue and the Veil of Illusion: Generic Innovation and the Pedagogical Project in Eighteenth-Century Literature*. Stanford, Calif.: Stanford University Press, 1991.

Mullan, John. *Sentiment and Sociability: The Language of Feeling in the Eighteenth Century*. Oxford: Oxford University Press, 1988.

Myers, Mitzi. "Daddy's Girl as Motherless Child: Maria Edgeworth and Maternal Romance." In *Living by the Pen: Early British Women Writers*, ed. Dale Spender. New York: Teachers College Press, 1992.

Myers, Sylvia Harcstack. *The Bluestocking Circle: Women, Friendship, and the Life of the Mind in Eighteenth-Century England*. Oxford: Clarendon Press, 1990.

The New Cambridge Bibliography of English Literature. Cambridge: Cambridge University Press, 1969–77.

Newton, Judith L. *Women, Power, and Subversion: Social Strategies in British Fiction, 1778–1860*. Athens: University of Georgia Press, 1981.

Nussbaum, Felicity, ed. *The Politics of Difference. Eighteenth-Century Studies* 23, no. 4 (Summer 1990).

Nussbaum, Felicity, and Laura Brown, eds. *The New Eighteenth Century: Theory, Politics, English Literature*. New York: Methuen, 1987.

Parke, Catherine. "Vision and Revision: A Model for Reading the Eighteenth-Century Novel of Education." *Eighteenth-Century Studies* 16, no. 2 (Winter 1982–83): 162–74.

Parsons, Eliza. 1793. *The Castle of Wolfenbach*. Reprint. London: Folio Press, 1968.

Pavel, Thomas. *L'Art de l'éloignement: essais sur l'imagination classique*. Paris: Gallimard, 1996.

Perry, Ruth. *Women, Letters, and the Novel*. New York: AMS Press, 1980.

Peterson, Carla L. *The Determined Reader: Gender and Culture in the Novel from Napoleon to Victoria*. New Brunswick, N.J.: Rutgers University Press, 1986.

Pocquet de Livonnière, Claude. *Règles du droit françois*. Paris, 1756.

Poovey, Mary. *The Proper Lady and the Woman Writer: Ideology and Style in the Works of Mary Wollstonecraft, Mary Shelley, and Jane Austen*. Chicago: University of Chicago Press, 1984.

———. *Uneven Developments: The Ideological Work of Gender in Mid-Victorian England*. Chicago: University of Chicago Press, 1988.

Preston, John. *The Created Self: The Reader's Role in Eighteenth-Century Fiction*. London: Heinemann, 1970.

Radford, Jean, ed. *The Progress of Romance: The Politics of Popular Fiction*. London: Routledge & Kegan Paul, 1986.

Reardon, B. P., ed. *Collected Ancient Greek Novels*. Berkeley and Los Angeles: University of California Press, 1989.

Reeve, Clara. 1785. *The Progress of Romance Through Times, Countries, and Manners*. 2 vols. Reprint. New York: Garland, 1970.

Reiss, Timothy J. *The Meaning of Literature*. Ithaca, N.Y.: Cornell University Press, 1992.

Rich, Adrienne. "Jane Eyre: The Temptations of a Motherless Woman." In *On Lies, Secrets, and Silence*, 89–106. New York: Norton, 1979.

Richardson, Samuel. *Clarissa; or, The History of a Young Lady*. 1747–48. Edited by Angus Ross. Harmondsworth, Middlesex: Penguin Books, 1985.

———. *Pamela; or, Virtue Rewarded*. 1740. Ed. Margaret Anne Doody. Harmondsworth, Middlesex: Penguin Books, 1980.

Richetti, John J. *Popular Fiction Before Richardson: Narrative Patterns, 1700–1739*. 1969. Oxford: Oxford University Press, 1992.

Richmond, Hugh M. *Puritans and Libertines: Anglo-French Literary Relations in the Reformation*. Berkeley and Los Angeles: University of California Press, 1981.

Roberts, Bette B. "Sophia Lee's *The Recess* (1785): The Ambivalence of Female Gothicism." *Massachusetts Studies in English* 6, no. 4 (1978): 68–82.

Robertson, Fiona. *Legitimate Histories: Scott, Gothic, and the Authorities of Fiction*. Oxford: Oxford University Press, 1994.

Robbins, Susan Pepper. "Jane Austen's Epistolary Fiction." In *Jane Austen's Beginnings: The Juvenilia and "Lady Susan,"* ed. J. David Grey, 215–24. Ann Arbor: University of Michigan Research Press, 1989.

Rogers, Katharine M. "Sensibility and Feminism: The Novels of Frances Brooke." *Genre* 11 (1978): 159–71.

Ross, Trevor. "Copyright and the Invention of Tradition." *Eighteenth-Century Studies* 26, no. 1 (Fall 1992), 1–28.

Rousseau, Jean-Jacques. *Emile, ou De l'Education*. Translated by Allan Bloom. New York: Basic Books, 1979.

———. *Julie, ou La Nouvelle Héloïse*. 1761. Edited by Michel Launay. Paris: Garnier, 1967.

Rousset, Jean. "Une Forme littéraire: Le Roman par lettres." In *Forme et signification: Essais sur les structures littéraires de Corneille à Claudel*, 65–108. Paris: Corti, 1962.

Rowe, Elizabeth. *Friendship in Death: In Twenty Letters from the Dead to the Living*. London, 1728.

Sahlins, Peter. *Boundaries: The Making of France and Spain in the Pyrenees*. Berkeley and Los Angeles: University of California Press, 1989.

Said, Edward W. "Jane Austen and Empire." In *Raymond Williams: Critical Perspectives*, ed. Terry Eagleton, 150–64. Boston: Northeastern University Press, 1989.

Schiebinger, Londa. *The Mind Has No Sex? Women in the Origins of Modern Science*. Cambridge, Mass.: Harvard University Press, 1989.

Schofield, Mary Anne. *Eliza Haywood*. Boston: Twayne, 1985.

———. "Romance Subversion: Eighteenth-Century Feminine Fiction." In *Sexuality, the Female Gaze, and the Arts*, ed. Ronald Dotterer and Susan Bowers. Selinsgrove, Pa.: Susquehanna University Press, 1992.

Schofield, Mary Anne, and Cecilia Macheski, eds. *Fetter'd or Free? British Women Novelists, 1670–1815*. Athens: Ohio University Press, 1987.

Schor, Naomi. *Breaking the Chain: Women, Theory, and French Realist Fiction*. New York: Columbia University Press, 1985.

———. "La Pérodie: Superposition dans 'Lorenzaccio.'" In *Discours et Pouvoir*, ed. Ross Chambers. Ann Arbor: Dept of Romance Languages, University of Michigan, 1982.

———. "Portrait of Gentleman: Representing Men in (French) Women's Writing." *Representations* 20 (Fall 1987): 113–33.

Sedgwick, Eve Kosofsky. *The Coherence of Gothic Conventions*. 1980. New York: Methuen, 1986.

———. "Jane Austen and the Masturbating Girl." *Critical Inquiry* 17 (Summer 1991): 818–37.

Séjourné, Philippe. *Aspects généraux du roman féminin en Angleterre, de 1740–1800*. Paris: Jean Gap, 1966.

Showalter, Elaine. *A Literature of Their Own: British Women Novelists from Brontë to Lessing*. Princeton, N.J.: Princeton University Press, 1977.

Showalter, English, Jr. *The Evolution of the French Novel, 1641–1782*. Princeton, N.J.: Princeton University Press, 1972.

Spacks, Patricia Meyer. *Desire and Truth: Functions of Plot in Eighteenth-Century English Novels*. Chicago: University of Chicago Press, 1990.

———. *The Female Imagination*. New York: Avon, 1975.

———. "Female Resources: Epistles, Plot, and Power." *Persuasions* 9 (1987): 88–98.

———. *Gossip*. Chicago: University of Chicago Press, 1986.

———. *Imagining a Self: Autobiography and Novel in Eighteenth-Century England*. Cambridge, Mass.: Harvard University Press, 1976.

Spencer, Jane. "'Of Use to Her Daughter': Maternal Authority and Early Women Novelists." In *Living by the Pen: Early British Women Writers*, ed. Dale Spender. New York: Teachers College Press, 1992.

———. *The Rise of the Woman Novelist: From Aphra Behn to Jane Austen*. Oxford: Blackwell, 1986.

Spender, Dale. *Mothers of the Novel: 100 Good Women Writers Before Jane Austen*. London: Pandora Press, 1986.

Spivak, Gayatri Chakravorty. "Displacement and the Discourse of Woman." In *Displacement: Derrida and After*, ed. Mark Krupnick. Bloomington: Indiana University Press, 1983.

Sprengnether, Madelon. *The Spectral Mother: Freud, Feminism, and Psychoanalysis*. Ithaca, N.Y.: Cornell University Press, 1990.

Spring, Eileen. *Law, Land, and Family: Aristocratic Inheritance in England, 1300 to 1800*. Chapel Hill: University of North Carolina Press, 1993.

Stanton, Domna. "The Fiction of Préciosité and the Fear of Women." *Yale French Studies* 62 (1981): 107–34.

Staves, Susan. *Married Women's Separate Property in England, 1660–1833*. Cambridge, Mass.: Harvard University Press, 1990.

Steiner, Wendy. *Pictures of Romance: Form Against Context in Painting and Literature*. Chicago: University of Chicago Press, 1988.

Stewart, Joan Hinde. *Gynographs: French Novels by Women of the Late Eighteenth Century*. Lincoln: University of Nebraska Press, 1993.

Stone, Harriet. "Exemplary Teaching in *La Princesse de Clèves*." *French Review* 62, no. 2 (Dec. 1988): 248–58.

Streeter, Harold Wade. *The Eighteenth-Century English Novel in French Translation: A Bibliographical Study*. New York: Publications of the Institute of French Studies, 1936.

Sullerot, Evelyne. *Histoire de la presse feminine en France, des origines à 1848*. Paris: A. Colin, 1966.

Sulloway, Alison G. *Jane Austen and the Province of Womanhood*. Philadelphia: University of Pennsylvania Press, 1989.

Tanner, Tony. *Jane Austen*. London: Macmillan, 1986.

Todd, Barbara J. "The Remarrying Widow: A Stereotype Reconsidered." In *Women in English Society, 1500–1800*, ed. Mary Prior. London: Methuen, 1985.

Todd, Janet. "Jane Austen: Politics and Sensibility." In *Feminist Criticism: Theory and Practice*, ed. Susan Sellers. London: Harvester Wheatsheaf, 1991.

———. *Sensibility: An Introduction*. London: Methuen, 1986.

———. *The Sign of Angellica: Women, Writing and Fiction, 1660–1800*. New York: Columbia University Press, 1989.

———. *Women's Friendship in Literature*. New York: Columbia University Press, 1980.

Todd, Janet, ed. *A Dictionary of British and American Women Writers, 1600–1800*. Totowa, N.J.: Allanheld, 1985.

———. *Jane Austen: New Perspectives*. New York: Holmes & Meier, 1983.

Todorov, Tzvetan. *Introduction à la littérature fantastique*. Paris: Seuil, 1970.

Tompkins, Jane. *Sensational Designs: The Cultural Work of American Fiction, 1790–1860*. New York: Oxford University Press, 1985.

Tompkins, Joyce M. S. *The Popular Novel in England, 1770–1800*. Lincoln: University of Nebraska Press, 1961.

Ulrich, Laurel Thatcher. *Good Wives: Image and Reality in the Lives of Women in Northern New England, 1650–1750*. 1980. New York: Random House, 1991.

Varma, Devendra P. Introduction to *The Recess; or, A Tale of Other Times*, by Sophia Lee. New York: Arno Press, 1972.

Versini, Laurent. *Le Roman épistolaire*. Paris: Presses universitaires de France, 1979.

Warhol, Robyn R. "Toward a Theory of the Engaging Narrator: Earnest

Interventions in Gaskell, Stowe, and Eliot." *PMLA* 101, no. 5 (Oct. 1986): 811–18.

Watson, Nicola. *Revolution and the Form of the British Novel, 1790–1825: Intercepted Letters, Interrupted Seductions*. Oxford: Oxford University Press, 1994.

Watt, Ian. *The Rise of the Novel: Studies in Defoe, Richardson, and Fielding*. Berkeley and Los Angeles: University of California Press, 1957.

Welsh, Alexander. *Strong Representations: Narrative and Circumstantial Evidence in England*. Baltimore: Johns Hopkins University Press, 1992.

Whitmore, Clara. *Woman's Work in English Fiction: From the Restoration to the Mid-Victorian Period*. New York: Putnam, 1910.

Williamson, Marilyn L. "Toward a Feminist Literary History." *Signs* 10, no. 1 (Autumn 1984): 136–47.

Wilt, Judith. *Ghosts of the Gothic: Austen, Eliot, & Lawrence.* Princeton, N.J.: Princeton University Press, 1980.

Wolstenholme, Susan. *Gothic (Re)Visions: Writing Women as Readers.* Albany: State University of New York Press, 1993.

Woodward, Carolyn. "Sarah Fielding's Self-Destructing Utopia: *The Adventures of David Simple*." In *Living by the Pen: Early British Women Writers*, ed. Dale Spender. New York: Teachers College Press, 1992.

Würzbach, Natascha, ed. *The Novel in Letters: Epistolary Fiction in the Early English Novel, 1678–1740*. Coral Gables, Fla.: University of Miami Press, 1969.

Index

In this index an "f" after a number indicates a separate reference on the next page, and an "ff" indicates separate references on the next two pages. A continuous discussion over two or more pages is indicated by a span of page numbers, e.g., "57–59." *Passim* is used for a cluster of references in close but not consecutive sequence.

avoiding domestic fiction as typically that produced by female authors
— 'mass of romance'
p + p spheres

30 exemplarity
maternal role supplanting providence in PC. the singularity of feudal self-presentation displacing exemplarity.

Dorothea von Mücke calls sympathy the anthropological deep value of the 18C. Virtue and the Veil of Illusion Stanford 1991. 104-5.

77 is there an even darker side to sympathy than this?

Library of Congress Cataloging-in-Publication Data

Alliston, April.
Virtue's faults: correspondences in eighteenth-century British and French women's fiction / April Alliston.
p. cm.
Includes bibliographical references and index.
ISBN 0-8047-2660-4 (cloth : alk. paper)
1. Epistolary fiction, English—History and criticism. 2. Women and literature—Great Britain—History—18th century. 3. English fiction—Women authors—History and criticism. 4. French fiction—Women authors—History and criticism. 5. English fiction—18th century—History and criticism. 6. French fiction—18th century—History and criticism. 7. Women and literature—France—History—18th century. 8. Epistolary fiction, French—History and criticism. 9. Literature, Comparative—French and English. 10. Literature, Comparative—English and French. 11. Letter writing in literature. 12. Letters in literature. I. Title.
PR858.E65A44 1996
823′.5099287—dc20 95-43736
CIP

This book is printed on acid-free, recycled paper.
Original printing 1996
Last figure below indicates year of this printing:
05 04 03 02 01 00 99 98 97 96